Sonia G

DEVELOPMENTAL THEORIES
THROUGH THE LIFE CYCLE

COLUMBIA UNIVERSITY PRESS   NEW YORK

Columbia University Press

Publishers Since 1893

New York   Chichester, West Sussex

Copyright © 2002 Columbia University Press

Library of Congress Cataloging-in-Publication Data

Developmental theories through the life cycle / Sonia
G. Austrian, editor.

    p.   cm.

  Includes bibliographical references and index.

  ISBN 0–231–11368–4 (alk. paper) —

  ISBN 0–231–11369–2 (pbk.)

  1. Developmental psychology. I. Austrian, Sonia G.

BF713 .D469 2002

155 — dc21   2001032449

Columbia University Press books are printed on
permanent and durable acid-free paper.

Printed in the United States of America

c 10 9 8 7 6 5 4 3 2 1

p 10 9 8 7 6 5 4 3 2

To Susan and Sarah Austrian
and Emily and Matthew Clarkson

With my love and appreciation for the pleasure
you have given me and my hope that your passages
through the life cycle will be smooth and happy

CONTENTS

ACKNOWLEDGMENTS

I would like to thank the students in my Human Behavior classes at the Columbia School of Social Work, who made me increasingly aware of the need to understand the goals and tasks of the different phases of the life cycle and reintroduced me to many of the important theorists.

I am extremely grateful to Dr. Patricia Kolb for her diligence and professionalism; it has been a pleasure to work with her. John Michel is a wonderful editor and an even better friend. Without his patience and sense of humor, this book never would have been completed. The library staff at the Weill Medical College of Cornell University has been very helpful, and Josephine LeDonne, once more, helped with a myriad of necessary tasks.

Finally, I will always be grateful to the late Carol H. Meyer for her support and encouragement.

CONTRIBUTORS

Sonia G. Austrian, MSW, DSW is Director of the Employee Assistance Program Consortium, serving the employees of five medical institutions. She is on the faculties of the Departments of Public Health and of Psychiatry at the Weill Medical College of Cornell University and is an Adjunct Professor at the Columbia University School of Social Work. Her field of practice has been health/mental health.

Nancy F. Cincotta, MSW is a preceptor in the Department of Social Work, Division of Pediatric Hematology/Oncology at the Mount Sinai Medical Center in New York City and a doctoral candidate at the Columbia School of Social Work. Her practice focuses on children and families facing chronic and life-threatening illness and death. She is a nationally recognized presenter, educator, and groups consultant.

Carolyn S. Hughes, MSW, Ph.D. is an Assistant Professor in the School of Social Work at the University of Alaska, Anchorage. Her expertise is in the areas of child abuse and family violence. Her research and teaching interests include life-span development, human diversity, and family violence.

Patricia J. Kolb, MSW, Ph.D. is an Assistant Professor in the Sociology and Social Work Department at Lehman College of the City University of New York. Her research and publications have focused on ethnic identity, intergenerational relationships, and nursing home placement processes and social services. She has conducted a national study of nursing home social services.

Randy H. Magen, MSW, Ph.D. is an Associate Professor in the School of Social Work at the University of Alaska, Anchorage. His publications concern group work and family violence. His current research involves examining connections between woman abuse and child maltreatment.

DEVELOPMENTAL THEORIES
THROUGH THE LIFE CYCLE

Sonia G. Austrian

one two three four five six

INTRODUCTION

The life cycle has until recently been metaphorical, not descriptive or conceptual, suggesting an underlying sequence of events that everyone goes through rather than clear external milestones of development, although every life is also unique. There is evidence of awareness of the life cycle, the ages of man, in the ancient writings of the Talmud, the Chinese sage Confucius, and the Greek lawyer and poet Solon (Levinson and Gooden 1985:2). Though they differ with respect to religious and cultural context, these writings are similar in identifying several major phases: a formative preadult period lasting until ages 15 to 20; an early adult phase lasting from about 20 to 40, during which the person establishes a marriage, family, and occupation; middle adulthood, from 40 to 60, when the person most fully realizes their intellectual and moral powers; and late adulthood, beginning at 60. The texts all see the phases in terms of men; they differ chiefly when considering old age. Solon sees this period as the time of decline, with 70 representing the "ebb-tide of Death." The Talmud and Confucius both see old age as a time of new growth and freedom as the person becomes a wise elder with new relationships to his origin, his ending, and the self (Levinson and Gooden 1985:3).

Among the phases identified in the Talmud are:

5: age of beginning to read scriptures
13: bar mitzvah, commandments; more responsibility

18–60:   marriage, occupation; period of full strength; ability to understand
         and provide counseling
   60:   person becomes an elder
   80:   "Gevurah"—person has special strength of age as he approaches the
         boundary between life and death
   90:   the person is bent under the weight of years

Confucius identifies the following phases:

   15:   the age of learning
   30:   planting feet on the ground
   40:   no longer suffering from perplexities
   50:   knowing the biddings of heaven
   60:   hearing the biddings of heaven with a docile ear
   70:   following the dictates of the heart while no longer overstepping the
         boundaries of right

Solon recognizes these ages of man:

  0–7:   unripe
 7–14:   approaching manhood
21–28:   ripening to greatest completeness of powers as worth can be clearly
         seen
28–35:   marriage and children
35–42:   mind broadens
42–56:   man is at his best
56–63:   losing ability for speech and wit
63–70:   time to depart on the ebb-tide of Death

It is interesting that these early views of the life cycle concentrate chiefly on
adulthood, which was somewhat neglected by modern theorists until the
1960s.

    In considering psychological development within the life cycle, it is im-
portant to note that physical and psychological development begin at conception. Drugs and alcohol; poor nutrition; and maternal diseases such as diabetes, cardiac problems, and anemia as well as maternal stress may cause
damage to the fetus. Genetic problems may be caused by chromosomal factors. Chromosomes can also be affected by exposure to radiation or certain
chemicals. At birth, oxygen deprivation may cause minimal brain damage,

retardation, or cerebral palsy. During the first three months following birth, the baby's organs continue to grow at a rapid pace, and a poor physical environment can adversely affect biological development. The greatest period of neurophysiological development occurs from the end of gestation through the early weeks of postnatal life, with rapid structural and developmental changes continuing until they slow down at approximately age three. Traits such as gender, body type, and intelligence depend at least partly on genetic endowment; however, the same genetic endowment can result in a range of outcomes, depending on environmental factors.

The passage from infancy to adolescence involves striking behavioral, emotional, and cognitive changes culminating in a fairly well-established personality. Each stage of development has its own special challenges, organizing properties, and unique meanings. While clearly there is continuity throughout the stages, opportunity, temperament, cognitive abilities, and special talents are influencing factors. There are different rates of psychosocial change at various periods of life; the individual may change quickly or slowly, or even at times seem to be staying in one place.

Although chronological age is often associated with stage of development, there is no established one-to-one relationship between age and stage, which may be as much culturally determined as biological. While there are commonly recognized chronological age tasks and crises, they do not always identify cognitive, emotional, and social changes. Structured social roles and statuses tend to be more related to chronological age. Psychologically there are expectations about how people at different ages should feel about themselves, regard the future, recognize their abilities, and acquire knowledge of how to behave. Throughout the life cycle, people need love, social contact and attachment, outlets for aggression, and opportunities to develop mastery and competence. Environmental influences such as child-rearing practices and cultural concerns may result in different patterns of expectations and development. Spitz (1965:5) defines development as "the emergence of forms, of functions and of behaviors which are outcomes of exchanges between the organism [body] on the one hand, the inner [mind] and outer [external influences] on the other."

Theories of normal development provide parameters to help make sense of personal lives, showing what is generally expected at different stages of the life cycle and anticipating potential crises. Early theorists were chiefly concerned with early development and with adolescence. "Latency," approximately ages five through twelve, was viewed as a time when little occurred developmentally. Since the 1960s, much more attention has been given to adult development and to aging, as the population is living and working longer. Developmental theories provide a baseline against which children and adults can be measured and background knowledge that does not say how mental health professionals might intervene, but rather can indicate if there is a need for intervention. Theories are concerned with cognitive, affective, biological, and interpersonal variables that result in what is viewed as normal behavior at different life stages. They suggest how people grow and develop.

The process of human development is influenced by three interacting forces: biopsychosocial endowment, special talents, and temperament. It is important for mental health professionals to understand normal development, as they are constantly called upon to make decisions affecting their clients and must be cognizant about what is socially and cultural acceptable behavior and what is not. Milestones in normal development involve mastering various biological, psychological, and social tasks at predictable periods throughout the life cycle.

The theories presented in this book reflect the culture and life experience of the theorists, who transformed observable data into theoretical constructs in order to understand, predict, and control development and behavior within an average expectable environment.

Concepts of normality are clearly influenced by value patterns of the larger cultural community, which are determined by philosophical, historical, and religious influences. Over the centuries, philosophers, historians, and writers, as well as mental health professionals, have reflected changing attitudes. Normality is, in part, a cultural construct based on social norms that change from one setting to another as well as over time. Clearly social, political, economic, and biological forces will affect all the phases of the life cycle. Developmental theorists thus have difficulty making predictions about human development, as it is not possible to anticipate the impact of these variables in the future and a shift in any one will affect the others. Cultures may vary significantly with respect to what is age-appropriate as an independent variable, especially for adolescence. Thus development can only be understood in the context of the society and culture in which the individual has been raised and lives.

The term *normal* was coined by the ancient Romans and comes from *normalis*, which can be defined as "made according to rule" and "conforming to the standard or the common type: regular, usual, natural" (Offer and Sabshin 1984:364). Earlier, in ancient Greece, concepts of good health were central to philosophical issues: "health" was synonymous with "happiness." Plato saw this as a hierarchical concept, only attainable by those who had climbed the ladder of knowledge—the philosopher-kings. Thus, he took a utopian perspective. Aristotle also viewed happiness as hierarchical, with three levels: (1) the common level, that of sensual pleasure; (2) the superior level, at which happiness was equated with honor or political life; and (3) the level of true happiness, at which people led a contemplative life (Offer and Sabshin 1984:366–67). Thus, although the concept was not named until later, there has always been concern about normality. Major considerations must be for whom, under what circumstances, and in what context *normal* is defined.

Psychoanalytic theory views normality, or health, as flexibility and harmony among the parts of the psychic apparatus. Beginning with Freud, attention was paid less to external causes of psychopathology and more to the internal childhood processes that predisposed a person toward mental illness. Development was viewed as sequential, determined by biological givens, the results of earlier stages, and the experiences occurring at a given stage. The oedipal stage was believed to be the last important transforming phase in child development (Michels 1984:295). Normality and pathology were seen as different at each level. In infancy, normal means having the biological capacity for healthy psychological development; as development proceeds, this quality interacts with experiences that lead to a narrower range of potential outcomes. Pathology results from an inability to integrate what has gone before; normality refers to an individual relatively free of symptoms, flexible in the face of stress, and capable of personal and social happiness and creativity (Michels 1984:299).

Psychoanalytic theory, in the earliest stages, was linear. While Erik Erikson was heavily influenced by it, he was responsible for introducing a more psychosocial perspective on development, which has clearly shaped the work of most subsequent theorists. It was Erikson who first demonstrated the importance of identifying and understanding the social and cultural variables affecting development, moving theory away from a psychoanalytic orientation.

This book will consider some of the major theories concerning different stages of the life cycle. There is no one theory that encompasses all aspects of human development; thus, all of the partial theories are age- or domain-specific. While there are differences in how the process of development is conceptualized, there are several universal needs: (1) survival of the infant; (2) separation and individuation; (3) capacity for relatedness; (4) gender identification; (5) capacity for intimacy; and (6) adaptation to sociocultural demands. The chapters follow the accepted stages of the life cycle. Infancy and toddlerhood have been combined, as these two stages tended to overlap theoretically more than others. The authors have chosen the theories they regard as most important for understanding a particular phase, while recognizing that there are many other theories that deserve consideration but would be beyond the scope of this book.

BIBLIOGRAPHY

Levinson, D. J. and W. E. Gooden. 1985. "The Life Cycle." In H. I. Kaplan and B. J. Sadock, eds., *Comprehensive Textbook of Psychiatry/IV*, 1:1–13. Baltimore: Williams and Wilkins.

Lewis, M. and F. R. Volkmar. 1990. *Clinical Aspects of Child and Adolescent Development*. Philadelphia: Lea and Febriger.

Michels, R. 1984. "Psychoanalytic Perspectives on Normality." In D. Offer and M. Sabshin, eds., *Normality and the Life Cycle*, 289–301. New York: Basic.

Offer, D. and M. Sabshin. 1984. *Normality and The Life Cycle*. New York: Basic.

Spitz, R. 1965. *The First Year of Life*. New York: International Universities Press.

SONIA G. AUSTRIAN

one **two** three four five six

INFANCY AND TODDLERHOOD

INTRODUCTION

Although it is during infancy, toddlerhood, and early childhood, from birth to age six, that the greatest physical and mental growth and development occur, the literature shows that very little scholarly attention was paid to these life stages until early in the twentieth century. No significant theories about mental development were created, and what information existed was based on limited secondary sources. For many centuries, infants and children were regard as incapable of complex thinking and feelings about their world. The child's mind was seen as unorganized and unformed, and childhood experiences were felt to have little effect on later life. As a result, there is a paucity of primary source material such as diaries, letters, or any other documentation of changes in children's behavior and thinking. In 1787, a Mr. Tiedeman did publish his observations of his son's sequential development from birth to age two and a half (Gemelli 1996:17), but this was unusual.

The work of Charles Darwin was instrumental in establishing the importance of talking to children and observing their behavior in order to understand mental development. In 1877 Darwin published a diary documenting his son's early development (Gemelli 1996:18), believing that adults could better understand their own origins through talking with and observing their children. Piaget was later to use this approach, as he developed his theories of cognitive development by initially observing his own children.

While Darwin looked at normal development, much of the early work, in the first half of the twentieth century, was done by psychoanalysts concerned with pathology, using retrospective data. Sigmund Freud's theories evolved from interviews and psychoanalytic treatment of adult patients. In 1900, in *The Interpretation of Dreams*, he elaborated his theory that childhood events affect adults in ways that the adult is not aware of. Heavily influenced by psychoanalysis, developmental theorists were primarily concerned with "what went wrong," primarily in the mother-child relationship.

Beginning in the 1930s, Anna Freud extended Sigmund Freud's work, interviewing children and parents and psychoanalyzing children and adolescents. The theories that emerged from her work, and that of Heinz Hartmann and Robert White, indicate that the child's mind is, in fact, endowed with innate mental structures, and new structures evolve with normal maturation. The Freuds and Erik Erikson recognized the importance of the environment in early development and began the move toward a more biopsychosocial framework.

Other researchers took different approaches to understanding children. Piaget made a major contribution to knowledge about how cognitive processes develop and mature. Alfred Binet, in 1905, developed his first scales to test the intellectual capabilities of children by comparing the norms of performance known as the *mental age* with the *chronological age*. If they matched, intelligence was scored as average (Gemelli 1996:19). Behavioral theorists such as John B. Watson and Harry Stark Sullivan believed that behavior could be affected through a system of rewards and punishments.

By the 1960s, researchers interested in child development focused on observation of children rather than retrospective material. With the growth of the community mental health and feminist movements, there was increased recognition of the biological, social, psychological, and cultural factors that affect development. While there might well be a "normal," protected way for children to mature, many children were identified as not living in an "average expectable environment," so for them adaptation and coping presented a much harder challenge. It has also been recognized that while child development is for the most part a continuous process, progressing through predictable phases, there are also periods of disorganization and disequilibrium, especially when the child is under stress. This progression alternates at times with regression, but ought not to be construed as pathology.

Development begins with conception. The average pregnancy lasts approximately nine months, divided into three trimesters. The first trimester is especially critical, as it is when the heart, digestive system, brain, and central nervous system develop. By the end of this trimester the eyes, nose, mouth, and beginnings of the development of the extremities can be observed by sonograms. During the second trimester there is continued physical growth, a regular heartbeat can be heard, and the fetus is able to move inside the womb. It is in the final trimester, between six and seven months, that the infant becomes viable and, if born early, will probably survive, especially with the availability of high-tech neonatal care.

Clearly, the biopsychosocial well-being of the parents will affect the embryo and fetus. Factors that could lead to problems include, from the father, unhealthy sperm and an Rh factor incompatible with the mother's. If the mother has poor nutrition, abuses alcohol or drugs, smokes excessively, has rubella during the first trimester, or is HIV-positive, potential problems include premature or still birth, retardation, or the baby being born addicted. There is also the possibility of genetic problems and problems due to environmental hazards. To avoid and detect such problems, genetic counseling and prenatal assessment tools such as ultrasound, amniocentesis, and blood tests are available. One and five minutes following birth, an Apgar test can be administered to assess heart rate, breathing, muscle tone, reflex response, and skin color. Each item is given a score of zero to two, with a total score of seven to ten viewed as normal. This is a very important test, for effective intervention is often possible as the problematic area(s) are identified (Apgar 1958).

A child in the first three years experiences a prolonged period of immaturity and vulnerability, longer than that of any other known species. There are many skills to be acquired, tried, modified, and mastered. Ideally, much of the time is spent in the care of nurturing, loving, protective adults who will provide the strong, predictable attachments and environments essential for human development. Historically this was meant to be accomplished through an intact, nuclear family; a strong, nurturing, predictable relationship with a mother; access to a supportive extended family and community; and a hopeful approach to the future. In the past three decades, much has changed. Mothers are in the home less, with 53 percent returning to work before their child is a year old; there is little evidence of fathers filling in when the mother is out of the home; grandparents, if in the area, may also be employed; and the government and business have not provided the support to accommodate these societal changes (Carnegie 1994:3).

SIGMUND FREUD

Sigmund Freud is recognized as the "father of psychoanalysis." He began his work in the late nineteenth century, and his theories dealt with both normal and abnormal adult behaviors, though they were derived from the study of what he believed was "abnormal." Much of his work with patients was an effort to understand the unconscious material that motivates actions. This he did by examining, with the patients, remembered dreams, daytime fantasies, verbal associations, and sometimes observable behavior. Freud believed in *psychic determinism*—that nothing occurs by chance but results from powerful unconscious conflicts; thus, early experiences control later ones.

Freud's major contribution to developmental theory was the recognition that the individual goes through defined developmental stages. While much of his work has been expanded or even repudiated, it was a significant beginning. Freud also introduced the importance of the environment, although in a much more limited way than did later theorists and mental health professionals trained in a biopsychosocial perspective. His focus was limited to conflicted relationships, particularly those of children with parents.

Freud was trained in Austria in the late nineteenth century as a neurologist. Initially concerned with the biological aspects of what appeared to be diseases of the nervous system, he felt that he must explore the psychological causes, the "workings of the mind." His initial interest was the phenomenon of *hysteria*, a diagnosis frequently given to women (Austrian 1995). His early work with patients, together with a neuropathologist, Jean-Martin Charcot, relied heavily on hypnosis. Though patients presented with physical symptoms, Charcot and Freud saw hysteria as a psychological disorder with symptoms that could be modified or even cured through hypnosis. Freud soon realized that not all patients could be hypnotized and that successful treatment depended to some extent on the doctor-patient relationship. His reliance on hypnosis decreased. In his further work with patients, Freud became aware that there existed some unconscious yet active resistance to recalling significant events that had been traumatic, which he called *unwillingness*. Freud then made the goal of therapy the examination and interpretation of this resistance. He also felt that a force he called *repression* was responsible for removing from awareness a memory that would otherwise be unacceptable to the patient's conscious ethical standards. From these discoveries, Freud evolved a new method of treatment called *free association*, in which he urged his patients to verbalize all their thoughts as they occurred during a session, omitting (or censoring) nothing, no matter how irrelevant or disconnected it might seem. This became the core of what is known as psychoanalysis.

Freud identified what he called *drives*, which are also referred to in the literature and by other analysts as *instincts*. The drives spur people to seek gratification and produce a state of psychic excitation in response to stimulation. He used the term *cathexis* to identify the amount of psychic energy directed or attached to the object of gratification, which is a mental representation of a person or a thing. Cathexis is a psychological, not a physical concept. Initially Freud focused on the sexual (erotic) drive, with its accompanying energy, libido, and felt that only sexual impulses and experiences were subject to repression. Later he also acknowledged aggressive (destructive) drives with their own energy. He came to see that in some thoughts and actions, both drives coexisted. Initially accepting a patient's "memories" as real, Freud went on to believe that childhood fantasies were just as important to the unconscious.

PSYCHOSEXUAL DEVELOPMENT (GENETIC MODEL)

Freud believed that a child is born highly vulnerable and that its survival the first few years depends entirely on its parents/caretakers, especially the mother. He identified *erotogenic zones*, areas of the body charged with psychosexual energy, which in the earliest years are areas involving mucous membranes, but as the individual matures can be any part of the body that provides a sense of satisfaction. Initially the erotogenic zones are oral (mouth) and anal (anus) and later they include the genital area. It is toward these that the child directs its emotional energy (cathexis).

Freud felt that children, after they are aware of external objects, have diffuse sexual feelings, with the parents being the initial objects of erotic feelings and their counterpart, jealous aggression. *Libido* is Freud's term for the biological force, or energy, of the sexual (or pleasure-seeking) drive, the root of bodily or sensual pleasure-seeking activities. Freud thought that libido could be connected to two pregenital phases, oral and anal, and two genital phases, latency and genital, with the phallic phase between. Adult sexuality—genital sexuality—results from a coming together of the earlier phases. Prior to this, the child may find satisfaction from more than one source, which Freud referred to as being "polymorphously perverse" (Freud 1905:191). Later Freud would recognize the aggressive drive (instincts), but he did not give the aggressive energy a specific name.

The *oral phase* is characterized by the infant first obtaining pleasure from sucking breast or bottle and later from a substitute, thumb sucking. Between birth and approximately eighteen months, the infant is primarily concerned with gratification of its feelings of hunger. It expects that the mother will provide breast or bottle. Sucking, with its stimulation of the mouth and lips, is experienced as pleasurable. Freud referred to satisfaction from the infant's own body as *autoerotic* (Freud 1905:181–82). This phase is nongenital and autoerotic and extends from birth to about 18 months. The child is initially totally self-centered. It gets pleasure from its own body, especially from the mouth, lips, and tongue, but toward the end of this period begins to learn that pleasure can come from an external source and begins to differentiate itself from the mother, recognizing first "part objects," such as the breast, and then the "whole" mother with some sense of continuity. Freud felt that the mother/caretaker in this phase lays the foundation for feelings of security, self-esteem, and basic trust as well as the ability to tolerate frustration.

The *anal phase*, extending from about eighteen to thirty-six months, is more active, as the child becomes more involved with the environment. The child no longer needs to rely on sucking and can chew food. The primary erogenous zone is the alimentary canal, particularly the anus. Feces and its odor are of interest to the child, and it experiences the retention or expulsion of feces as both pleasurable and unpleasurable. Freud believed that the central concern of this phase is self-mastery and that a core issue involves the mother using both manipulation and discipline in an effort to toilet train the child, resulting in approval or disapproval. During this period the child also develops some ambivalence toward the mother when her wishes differ from its own, but successful resolution also includes greater independence and autonomy.

The *phallic phase* extends from the end of the third year into the fifth year, and Freud believed that it leads to the most intense and fateful period in object relations that the child ever experiences. Object relationships at this point have a significant degree of stability and permanence. The child will experience pleasurable physical sensations from manipulation of the genital area, and will usually masturbate unless stopped due to parental/caregiver disapproval. It is also interested in the genitals of others, particularly the penis, and often there is exhibitionism. For the girl the clitoris is analogous to the penis, and as the boy fears castration, the girl fears genital injury. During the phallic phase the Oedipus/Electra complex emerges, a very intense experience the results of which Freud saw as crucial in development. Freud believed that illness, absence, or death of a parent or the birth or death of a sibling during this phase negatively influences the passage through it.

Between ages three and a half and six, the child goes through the oedipal, or phallic, phase, which because of the physiological differences is somewhat different for young boys and young girls. For both sexes the strongest relationship has been with the mother, the first love object. It is at this point that sibling rivalry, in addition to rivalry with the same-sex parent, may be an issue as the child wants the mother exclusively.

In the *Oedipus complex*, a boy becomes aware that the closeness and soothing he receives from his mother is shared also with his father. Freud believed the boy feels anger and jealousy and a wish to be rid of the father in order to have sole possession of the mother. The boy also feels guilt and anxiety about retaliation by the all-powerful father. Young boys fear castration as punishment for their feelings toward the parents, and if they have seen female genitals, they believe that it has happened for some people. In time the boy experiences anger at the "rejection" by the mother, accepts that he cannot take her away from the father, overcomes his anger, and strives for identification with the father.

The *Electra complex* is a term Freud initially rejected and later accepted to define a girl's experience in the phallic phase. As she matures she becomes aware that she does not have a penis. Freud felt that with this realization comes a sense of loss at not being able to have all the positives identified with being male, and thus a sense of inferiority. The girl then experiences devaluation of the mother and rage toward her for "depriving" her of a penis, which she "needs" in order to have her mother as her father does. This stage is more difficult for the girl than the boy, as it involves turning against the primary caretaker, the mother. The girl will turn her affections toward the father to give her the penis her mother did not give her, or a symbolic substitute, a baby. The girl then experiences "rejection" by the father. Freud felt that resolution is harder and slower for the girl than for the boy, as it involves a slow fading of penis envy and expectations of possessing the father, together with lessening of the devaluation of the mother and subsequent identification with her. Freud felt the girl continues to regard the mother, and herself, with no penis, as inferior.

Freud was aware that psychosexual development does not always follow this pattern. He felt that it was essential that each phase be successfully negotiated or there would be "unfinished business" that would be carried into the next phase and lead to pathology in later life. He believed that *fixation of li-*

bido, in which the libidinal cathexis to an object in an earlier period persists, can occur at any phase and stunt development. The individual continues to experience pleasure from a pregenital phase; this will ultimately affect adult character traits. A classic example is of a person whose toilet training was harsh and perhaps premature, becoming an adult who is rigid, "withholding," and perhaps compulsive about cleanliness. Freud also recognized that *regression* to a phase where a child attained satisfaction may occur in times of stress. For instance, a child who is anxious about school may once again find comfort in thumb sucking.

TOPOGRAPHICAL MODEL

Through his study of dreams, Freud recognized that they contain distorted or disguised wishes or needs that would not be acceptable to the conscious mind in their pure form. He also postulated that a censorship system selectively allows the person to remember some dreams while not permitting others to come into consciousness. From this evolved his topographical model.

Freud postulated that the mental apparatus is divided into three parts: unconscious, preconscious, and conscious. The *unconscious* contains memories, impulses, and wishes that are unacceptable to the conscious ego and cannot be brought into consciousness no matter how hard the individual may try. Freud was the first in his field to recognize the unconscious as vital to the understanding of human behavior, and he made it the cornerstone of his psychoanalytic theory. He regarded it as barred from consciousness by a force within the mind, namely repression. Unconscious material is not directly available, but it influences thoughts and actions and may emerge in dreams, fantasies, or in symptoms such as a phobia. The unconscious seeks gratification, has no sense of time, and is not concerned with reality. Freud felt that it is the most significant influence on mental and behavioral functioning.

The *preconscious* has a role in censoring dreams and interprets them into acceptable, logical forms. It operates in terms of the *reality principle*, which delays or prohibits gratification of impulses and wishes. Information, ideas, and wishes not necessarily in our conscious awareness are in our preconscious and with effort can be made conscious. Anything that is conscious resides in the preconscious before and after becoming conscious.

The *conscious* inhibits the discharge of impulses and wishes that are unacceptable to reality. It represents overt behavior, affects, and thinking. It orders time and perceptions and tests reality.

Structural Model

Freud's structural model is based on the assumption that the id comprises the entire psychic apparatus at birth and that the ego and superego, originally parts of the id, are differentiated as the individual matures. The individual's personality, made up of these three parts, is a psychodynamic system. The parts are involved with each other and also with the environment.

The *id* is the first part of the personality to develop and is present at birth. It is the seat of the instincts and the unacceptable thoughts, impulses, and fantasies, and contains a reservoir of psychic energy. It has as its goal immediate gratification of wishes and demands and the instinctual needs. It involves *primary process thinking*, which is not governed by logic, judgment, or time but by the *pleasure principle*, where the individual seeks only gratification and pleasure and avoids pain and discomfort, and comprises the psychic representations of the drives. It "demands" immediate gratification and has a disregard for reality. The id houses the instincts that produce a level of tension that demands activities to reduce it. What brings pleasure is "good," what brings unpleasure is "bad." The id remains entirely in the unconscious.

The *ego*, Freud thought, emerges out of the id in response to conscious external demands, as the infant becomes more aware of the environment between six and eight months. The ego's primary role is as a mediator between the demands of the id (internal) and those of reality (external). It also must mediate between the id wishes and the censure of the superego. When the ego is overwhelmed by the strength of the id impulses, the prohibitions of the superego, and the reality of the external world, it will experience anxiety based on fantasy or reality. Freud believed that the birth trauma is the strongest cause of anxiety. In its effort to respond, as the ego matures, it develops unconscious *ego defenses*, including repression and regression.

The ego is governed by the reality principle, which allows gratification only of the appropriate wishes and demands of the id. It deals with unacceptable id demands through the mechanism of repression. It functions primarily in the preconscious and the conscious, yet having emerged from the id, it has a part that remains unconscious and involved in repression. The ego controls motility and memory, and functions through *secondary process thinking*, whereby gratification is delayed, cathexis is more stable, rules of syntax and logic apply, and drive energy is channeled for more appropriate tasks. It recognizes the demands of reality and is characterized by more mature thinking. The ego is fairly well established by age three, though of course it continues to mature. Physical growth, experience, increased verbal ability, identification with affects and behavior of early objects, and sophistication of thought all contribute to ego maturation.

The *superego* is the last part of the mental apparatus to develop. Freud saw the superego as the "heir" of the Oedipus complex. As the child gives up the longed-for love object, the ego promotes identification with the parent of the same sex and repression of sexual longings for the parent of the opposite sex. Since the superego is connected to the id's wishes and the ego's sense of reality, it functions both consciously and unconsciously. It can function as both an ally and the master of the ego.

The superego begins to develop at about five years of age and is firmly established between ages nine and eleven. The child identifies with and internalizes the standards, morality, and prohibitions of the parent. The superego is affected by the *conscience* that alerts the person to what is unacceptable, and includes the *ego ideal*, which Freud felt represents what is acceptable according to parental expectations and morals. Freud believed that the stronger the oedipal strivings (id), the harsher the superego and that as females do not have to undergo castration anxiety, they have weaker superegos.

While Freud's major contribution to psychiatry was the development of psychoanalysis, he made a major contribution to the field of mental health, as he was the first theorist to think in developmental terms. He first identified stages of development, what he saw as a recognizable psychodynamic system that affected the formation of the personality, and recognized environmental influences, albeit composed primarily of the mother/caregiver relationship and to a lesser extent the father relationship. His model was linear, a medical model, and thus not congruent with an ecosystems perspective. His patient population and professional affiliations were rather limited, and thus he gave little attention to the impact of culture on human development and behavior. Again reflecting his times, Freud devalued women, seeing them as lesser than men and frustrated by not being male.

Psychoanalysts require special training in order to explore the unconscious; without this training, it may be dangerous to try to interpret dreams and fantasies. However, mental health professionals making biopsychosocial assessments are certainly influenced by analytic thinkers, as they are aware of the effect of the unconscious and preconscious on clients' thoughts, actions, and revelations in therapy.

While there has been much criticism of Freud's work, especially his rigidity and seeming sexism, he began the process of concern with personal development and motivated others to refine his theories or develop new ones. He was the first person to develop a clear picture of the very great importance of significant others in early development. He tended to neglect the direct influence of the father, focusing on the mother/caregiver, siblings, and playmates, and only later on the father (Brenner 1973:97). However, although the majority of his patients were women, he never really fully developed a theory of female development other than the Electra complex, which evolved from his Oedipus complex and was necessitated by the fact that the female has no penis. Freud believed that early relationships influence the course of a child's development to the extent that later ones do not, that a personality is quite well developed when the Oedipus/Electra complex is resolved and the superego established. He did not accept that later life stages will, or can, alter the personality.

NANCY CHODOROW

Nancy Chodorow, a psychoanalyst with a strong interest in family and especially in sexual inequality, has been a fervent critic of Sigmund Freud's work as applied to women. Influenced by the work of Ernest Jones, Karen Horney, and Melanie Klein, and very involved with the feminist movement, she published *The Reproduction of Mothering* in 1978. In 1994, in *Femininities, Masculinities, Sexualities: Freud and Beyond*, Dr. Chodorow continued to critique Freud's apparent lack of interest in and devaluing of women.

Dr. Chodorow has written that while most of Freud's patients were female, he was not interested in women, not very knowledgeable about them, and rarely wrote positively about them. She sees him as a product of his milieu, a patriarchal society, and feels that he made unfounded assumptions about how men and women *ought* to be, guided by his misogyny. Freud equated "maleness with humanness" (Chodorow 1978:143). He devalued women, believing that following the resolution of the oedipal conflict, women differ from men in that they have less of a sense of justice, are overwhelmed by jealousy and shame, and are vain and make no contribution to civilization. Further devaluing females, Freud believed that all children are initially masculine, with "femaleness" only an issue at puberty (Chodorow 1978:146). The clitoris he saw as masculine because it is sexually active and can be gratified without penetration. In contrast, femininity is vaginal and passive.

Chodorow regards as another major distortion Freud's belief that the desire to be a mother arises out of penis envy and that a baby is a symbolic substitute for a penis. Chodorow sees the desire to mother from a very different perspective that includes a different theory about the resolution of the oedipal conflict. She argues that Freud virtually ignored the strong maternal identification for girls as well as the infant's crucial attachment to the mother.

Finally, Chodorow asserts, Freud described female sexuality entirely through the eyes of men; and he saw women as inhibited (Chodorow 1994:4). Chodorow is very interested in gender development. The desire to mother exists for a girl at the very beginning of life, with the intense, seemingly exclusive, dependent bond with the mother. This bond, together with societal expectations, leads to what Chodorow calls the "reproduction of mothering." Like other theorists (to be discussed), Chodorow acknowledges that there is a process of separation and differentiation from the mother that the infant must go through, and that the quality of care affects the child's sense of self, capacity for object relations, and view of the mother and the environment. She believes that the mother-infant relationship has the qualities of exclusivity and mutuality. The child at an early age becomes aware of the father but sees him as more separate than the mother, while the father tends to view the young child as a potential grown-up. The infant's father will often actively play with it, while the mother will more often hold and cuddle it.

The early phases of mothering create conscious and unconscious attitudes and expectations in the developing child. Chodorow does not believe that the infant possesses any adaptive ego capacities and that therefore, the mother functions as the external ego to help alleviate anxiety and master the drives and the environment. Rather, she sees the mother's role at each stage as having to gauge how much separation the child can take and how to develop ego strengths, a difficult role where she must balance overprotection and what appears to be emotional deprivation.

Chodorow believes that gender identity is firmly established by the age of three for both sexes. It begins at birth and develops with increased language ability. Parents are unambiguous about gender identity from birth, and this must be internalized by the child, along with knowledge about gender differences, before an Oedipus complex is possible. Thus gender identity is a pre-oedipal phenomenon, and conflicts around this as well as sexual knowledge may affect the oedipal experience.

Gender identification, Chodorow believes, does not result, as Freud thought, from the resolution of the oedipal but is a product of conscious teaching about gender differences (Chodorow 1978:89). It is socially constructed and heavily value laden. She feels that the family structure provides different experiences for girls and for boys in oedipal object relations and how these are internalized. The length of the preoedipal phase differs for girls and boys, and there are gender differences in mother-child relationships, rooted in the process of mothering. Between mother and daughter there is greater fusion, with the mother experiencing some sense of narcissistic extension. Thus there is prolonged symbiosis with greater denial of separateness. Boys are viewed, even as infants, more as objects who are gender opposite, and the mother may be consciously or unconsciously seductive. Therefore, she may push the son out of the preoedipal phase into an oedipal relationship, as their early relationship has been sexualized while the mother-daughter one has not.

Chodorow's interpretation of the Oedipus complex is based on the fact that mothers are primary and fathers secondary, with respect to early caretaking and socialization. This results in different relational capacities for girls and boys based on varied modes of differentiation of the ego and its internalized object relations. The girl's Oedipus complex is not merely the transferring of love from mother to father coupled with the giving up of the mother, but rather a continuation of the internal and external importance of the relationship to the mother, with the addition of the important relationship to the father. Chodorow firmly believes that because of the differences in resolving the Oedipus complex, there is greater complexity in female development of self-definition and personality than male. Mothering by women in early years results in relational capacities in girls that are lacking in boys. Girls recognize that they are less separate than boys and have more permeable ego boundaries. Female internalized object relations structures are more complex and present ongoing issues that also affect superego development (Chodorow 1978:93).

Chodorow's research focus has included the differences in the development and nature of male and female heterosexual object relations. While Freud focused on the girl's cathexis to the father, Chodorow sees the capacity for heterosexual object relations, for both boys and girls, as evolving out of family structure and importance of both parents. Fathers do tend to consciously sex-type children more than mothers and may more overtly encourage female heterosexual behavior. The girl continues a significant relationship with the mother throughout the oedipal period, and the process becomes multilayered as this dependence and attachment to the mother continues with the addition of a triangulated, sexualized attachment to the father (Chodorow 1978:129). A girl oscillates between mother and father. A boy experiences a more complete oedipal phase, as his oscillation is not as pronounced and his heterosexuality is less "chancy"—he has had emotional satisfaction and involvement from the mother (woman) while the girl is less likely to have had an emotionally exclusive, or intense, relationship with the father (man). In addition, the girl does not hang on to the Oedipus complex as intensely as a boy does, as she has no fear of castration. Chodorow does not feel that gender personality for either sex in the oedipal period has to do only with conscious and intended identification; the ego is modified in internal object relations through different kinds of relationships that involve different ways of working through conflicts, developing defenses, and reacting affectively.

In her more recent work (1994, 1996), Chodorow has recognized that the world in which children are raised has changed a lot as more women are in the work force, families are having fewer children, and children go to school at earlier ages. She also recognizes the greater importance of the father and the potential advantages of equal parenting. Women, however, although not necessarily mothers, will probably always have the major role in child rearing; this is seen even in countries where nonfamilial childcare is common, such as Israel, the Soviet Union, and China.

ANNA FREUD, HEINZ HARTMANN, AND ROBERT WHITE

These three theorists are discussed in the same section because they influenced each other, but more important, they all made significant contributions to developing ego psychology's awareness of the importance of the environment, a factor that Sigmund Freud for the most part neglected. As a result of their work, psychoanalytic theory moved from elucidation of unconscious motivational conflict and a view of the mind as partitioned to emphasis on the whole person and its relationship to both inner and outer reality. The focus became the ego's autonomy and self-sufficiency. These theorists believed that people have to struggle to satisfy internal id instincts and also to find satisfaction from mastering life's external obstacles. The three reviewed here took leading roles in the extension of Freud's original theories.

ANNA FREUD

While the id and related physiological zones were central to S. Freud's theories, his daughter Anna's interest was primarily the ego, which she, too, initially believed emerged from the id, was inescapably bound to it, and was unavoidably regulated by the superego (Monte 1980:154). Later she began to accept the concept of innate, conflict-free ego functions. In 1936, Anna Freud published *The Ego and the Mechanisms of Defense*, which legitimized interest in this aspect of ego functioning and was a major step beyond S. Freud's structural theory. Anna Freud thought defenses that had been viewed as obstacles to reaching the unconscious were habitual emotional responses when the ego felt the need to respond to anxiety. In her initial writings about defenses, she felt that the chronology of the development of defenses was very difficult and uncertain (A. Freud 1966:53). However, she later came to believe that defenses do have a chronology and specific age-appropriate times when they should be used; too early or too prolonged use could be viewed as unhealthy (A. Freud 1965:177). Denial and projection are examples of defenses normally used by young children. Use of repression too early is potentially damaging.

Beginning with a paper she wrote in 1922, Anna Freud spent nearly sixty years developing techniques for the analysis of children and adolescents. As a result, Dr. Freud became interested in normal development and the environment's impact on it. During World War II, she observed many children who were orphaned, had survived concentration camps, or in other ways were affected by the war, and she became very aware of their resilience.

Although trained and analyzed by her father, who arrived at his theories through reconstruction of childhood events as he analyzed adults, Dr. Freud was more interested in directly exploring a child's life history through observation as the child lived it. Child analysis, she believed, is needed when development is impaired due to the possibility of threatened fixation at some phase; the goal must be healthy future functioning. The child's ego and superego are immature and subject to physical, psychological, and environmental threats. Full-blown "neurotic symptoms" are not usually observed in children. Clearly the methodology for child analysis differs substantially from that for adult analysis, particularly as the daydreams and fantasies of children are not retrospective but based on current experiences with external reality. In addition, the child analyst is much more involved with the patient, as a positive emotional attachment is essential. The analyst will, during treatment, become the child's ego ideal, sometimes a source of difficulties between parents and analyst.

From their observations, Dr. Freud and her colleagues developed a *metapsychological profile* procedure based on direct observation of the child and indirect observation of family interaction. This led to a major, and original, contribution, the Diagnostic Profile (A. Freud 1965), based on the concept of Developmental Lines, which emphasize developmental sequences of personality functioning, especially id-ego interactions, as well as the ego's capacity to adapt to personal, interpersonal, or situational environmental demands. The profile was a forerunner of the biopsychosocial assessment. Specific instructions were given about what behavioral and psychological data to gather, with very little left to intuition. The diagnostician then integrated the observations and supplementary history into a unified picture of the child's overall functioning and development that indicated appropriateness, consistencies, inconsistencies, and apparent deficits. Review of these data were done using psychoanalytic and ego developmental theories as conceptual guides for diagnosis and as predictors of effectiveness of therapy. The profile was arrived at by considering the child's developing id, ego, and superego; the conflicts among these inner agencies; attitudes; and age-appropriate developmental achievements. Attention also was given to parental personalities, actions, and expectations; family atmosphere; and the culture in which the child was raised. Dr. Freud felt that while different developmental lines were observed for different areas of maturation, there was close correspondence among the lines: as an infant reached one level in a sequence, it should reach corresponding maturity in another developmental sequence. However, she was aware that some children might develop irregularly, with earlier maturation in some areas than in others. She cautioned that this should not be viewed as pathology but rather as variation.

The following prototypes of the Developmental Lines move the totally dependent infant through different areas required in the transition from infant to adult.

From Dependency to Emotional Self-Reliance and Adult Object Relations (A. Freud 1965:65–66)

1. The biological unity of the infant and mother, with the mother included in the child's narcissistic milieu and matching this with narcissistic possessiveness of the infant. There is no recognition of separation of self from other. Dr. Freud did, however, acknowledge the subdivisions of this period made by Margaret Mahler.

2. The "part object," or need-fulfilling relationship, identified by the analyst Melanie Klein, based on the infant's needs and drive derivatives, where the infant requires the object to meet needs and withdraws again when they are satisfied. Thus the mother is partly externalized.

3. Object constancy; the child maintains an inner image of the object.

4. Ambivalent relationships in the preoedipal, anal-sadistic phase where

the child may be observed as clinging, with fantasies of dominating and controlling the love object.

5. The object-centered phallic-oedipal phase, with positive, possessive feelings toward the opposite-sex parent coupled with jealousy and rivalry with the same-sex parent.

6. The latency period, with the lessening libido transferred from family to peers, teachers, and activities.

7. A preadolescent phase, with a return to earlier attitudes and behaviors (see 2 and 4).

8. Adolescence, with establishment of genital supremacy and libido, which is directed toward opposite-sex objects outside of the family.

Developmental Lines Toward Body Independence (A. Freud 1965:68–71)

1. Infant is nursed by bottle or breast, and will eventually get pleasure from sucking fingers, blanket, or other inanimate objects. Nursing might be on demand or on a schedule.

2. Weaning, which may be initiated by infant or mother. In the latter case, if done abruptly, there may be problems in introducing new solids and tastes.

3. Even as the infant becomes more proficient in self-feeding, food and the mother are still very much intertwined in the infant's mind.

4. Meals become a battleground for mother and child, with food fads that Dr. Freud believed to be related to the newly acquired concept of disgust related to anal training and the infant craving for sweets, a substitute for oral sucking.

5. Food becomes less associated with the mother, but Dr. Freud believed that irrational attitudes toward eating were related to infantile sexual concepts such as the possibility of impregnation through the mouth and reaction formations against cannibalism and sadism. She interpreted a fear of getting fat at this stage as a fear of pregnancy.

6. In latency there is a decrease in sexualization of eating as the child enjoys eating and develops preferences.

Developmental Lines from Wetting and Soiling to Bladder and Bowel Control (A. Freud 1965:72–75)

1. Infant has complete freedom to wet and soil; is unaware of the mother's role in making it clean and comfortable.

2. This second phase is affected by physiological maturation and by psy-

chological maturation as the infant moves from the oral to the anal phase of development. Dr. Freud, like her father, felt that this is a period of great ambivalence, as bodily products are cathected with libido and thus "gifts." This period is also affected by the aggressive drive, resulting in rage, anger, and disappointment aimed at the object and observed as temper tantrums. Ambivalence and curiosity about the body also characterize this phase.

3. The child internally accepts the mother's and the environment's attitude toward bodily cleanliness and control of bladder and bowels. Anal wishes and traits are modified and transformed into such highly regarded qualities as tidiness, punctuality, and reliability. Dr. Freud cautioned that this preoedipal anal control is vulnerable and that environmental stress or object loss may result in "accidents."

4. Bladder and bowel control are finally secure. Concern for cleanliness no longer is related to libidinous feelings toward the object but becomes an autonomous ego and superego concern for control over anal drives.

Developmental Lines from Irresponsibility to Responsibility in Body Management (A. Freud 1965:75–77)

Dr. Freud felt that knowledge of these lines was sketchy and that how body management evolves depends greatly on the quality of mothering, with the spectrum ranging from a well-cared-for child who expects to be nurtured and protected to the child with poor or no mothering who then must be both mother and child.

1. In the first few months, the infant turns aggression outward as self-injury through biting and scratching. Infant begins to recognize causes of self-induced pain.

2. As the ego develops and becomes more oriented to the outside world and to the concept of cause and effect, and has a greater awareness of the reality principle, the child is more able to perceive potentially dangerous situations or wishes. The child, however, may remain highly vulnerable depending on the level of ego maturation; some may require greater protection than others.

3. Ultimately the child internalizes the importance of cleanliness and of following medical orders if ill, although it still expects the mother to protect and heal. Dr. Freud believed that fear, guilt, and castration anxiety could in some cases motivate the child to be concerned about body safety.

Developmental Lines from Egocentricity to Companionship
(A. Freud 1965:78–79)

1. The infant begins with a selfish, narcissistic view of the object world.
    Other children are either not perceived at all or viewed as disturbing the
    mother-infant relationship and thus as rivals.
2. Other children are treated as inanimate objects. They can be played with
    or rejected and no response is expected from them.
3. Children begin to want to involve others as "helpmates," with the task
    more important than the relationship. This is felt to be the minimum re-
    quirement for socialization and acceptance by older siblings or in a pre-
    school setting.
4. Children begin to have feelings for other children—love, hate, fear, ad-
    miration. There is awareness of the wishes and feelings of other children
    and a sense of equality. Friendships are now possible.

Developmental Lines from the Body to the Toy (A. Freud 1965:79–80)

1. The infant's first play is autoerotic, involving the mouth, fingers, body
    surface, and vision. If it also involves the mother's body, the infant per-
    ceives no clear distinction.
2. The infant's attention and object libido expand beyond the bodies of the
    mother and child to transitional objects (usually soft), such as a blanket,
    a diaper, a stuffed animal, or a pillow.
3. More inanimate objects become part of the infant's interests and are
    cathected with both libido and aggression (ambivalence); they may be
    alternately cuddled and discarded or maltreated.
4. Cuddly toys become less important, except at night when they appear to
    help the child go from an active to a passive, narcissistic stage. Dr. Freud
    felt that during the day, toys that become important gratify an instinct or
    are invested with displaced and sublimated drive energies. She believed
    the choice of toys follows an order:
    a. Toys for filling-emptying, fitting in, making messes serve as dis-
        placement from interest in body openings and functions
    b. Moveable toys are preferred as the child became more mobile
    c. Building materials are used for construction and destruction cor-
        responding to the ambivalence of the anal-sadistic phase of devel-
        opment
    d. Toys related to masculine and feminine attitudes are used for role

> play, to show to the oedipal object, and for staging the Oedipus com-
> plex while interacting in group play
>
> 5. In latency, achievement in sports, hobbies, and games becomes impor-
>   tant as the child has greater impulse control.

Anna Freud, like her father, saw the ego as very much in partnership with the id, but went beyond classical analytic thinking to a belief that the ego has some functioning independent of the id. Her theories of personality development were more fluid and went beyond classical theory as she introduced the importance of the environment and interpersonal relationships. Anna Freud did not view the child or the ego as a victim of the id or superego but as having a capacity for mastery.

HEINZ HARTMANN

Heinz Hartmann has been referred to as the "enthusiastic father" (Monte 1980:181) of ego psychology. The publication in 1939 of his book *Ego Psychology and the Problem of Adaptation* broadened psychoanalytic theory. He was interested in expanding classical theory to make it more relevant to normal and pathological personality development.

Hartmann, unlike the Freuds, believed that the id and ego develop simultaneously and function independently yet in synchrony. They evolve from an undifferentiated matrix with reciprocal influences on each other, emerging together as "products of differentiation" (Hartmann 1939:102). Each has its own biological roots and energy source. The ego thus exists not just to resolve conflict between the id and the external world but also to deploy an innate set of developing and maturing autonomous functions that help in adaptation to the world. These activities he referred to as emerging from the conflict-free sphere (Hartmann 1939:11). Hartmann believed that ego functions such as memory, learning, and some defenses are part of (and prerequisites for) the ego's relationship to the id.

Hartmann separated the ego's autonomy functions into two parts: those with primary autonomy—innate, conflict-free functions important for adjustment to the environment, including perception, memory, learning, reality testing, and motility; and those with secondary autonomy—functions that develop or lose their autonomy through conflict with the id but are modified through maturation and learning to aid in adaptation.

Hartmann believed that both libidinal and aggressive energy can be neutralized, moved from the instinctual to the noninstinctual, and that this occurs when an ego function is independent of the id and its available energies are focused on adaptation and mastery. For secondary autonomous functions to develop, the energy is neutralized, the conflict removed, and the ego function restored or added to those already aiding adaptation.

Adaptation to the environment, vital to development, Hartmann saw as a reciprocal and evolving, not a static, process. The person might make changes in the environment (alloplastic) or might need to make changes in the self (autoplastic). The changes must be accomplished within "an average expectable environment," provided by the core love object, the mother, and guided by the reality principle.

For the individual to adapt and to develop, Hartmann believed that the ego has four tasks, involving reconciliation of intersystemic and intrasystemic conflicts (1939:39):

1. maintaining a balance between the individual and its external realities
2. establishing harmony within the id among its competing instinctual drives
3. maintaining a balance among the three competing mental agencies: id, ego, and superego
4. maintaining a balance between its role in helping the id and its own independent role that goes beyond instinctual gratification

Hartmann devised a list of ego functions that he believed important to observe in assessing cognitive and interpersonal functioning (1950:114–15):

1. motility
2. perception of inner and outer reality
3. protective barrier against excessive internal and external stimulation
4. reality testing
5. thinking and intelligence
6. translating thinking into action
7. inhibition or delay of tension reduction
8. recognition of danger producing signal anxiety and defenses
9. anticipation of actions, goals, effects, and consequences
10. time perception
11. character formation
12. ability to synthesize, integrate, and thus adapt to reality

Hartmann's work strengthened S. Freud's relatively weak concept of the ego, making it autonomous and central to adaptation to the environment. This laid the foundation for the theory of adaptation. Hartmann also recognized the minimum environmental conditions, an "average expectable environment," necessary for adequate survival.

Robert White

Robert White's major contribution to developmental theory, which extended Hartmann's work, was to recognize that the ego has complete motivational independence from the id's energies and its own autonomous source of energy, and that the individual has an innate urge toward mastery and adaptation. He thus freed the ego from the id. Hartmann had suggested that the ego's energy results from neutralized sexual and aggressive (id) energies and that Freud had only considered the former as available to the ego. Thus, White believed that need satisfaction was not the basic motivation for human behavior, and psychoanalytic theory was too limited. He postulated that people were motivated by additional drives with goals of exploration, activity, and manipulation (1959:305). In addition, he felt that from birth, individuals possess the competence to deal with the environment, which he termed *effectance* (Monte 1980:190). The ego's independent energy is the *energy of effectance motivation*, and the infant experiences *feelings of efficacy*. The infant is constantly learning and developing the capacities to deal effectively with the environment and a sense of greater autonomy and mastery. By toddlerhood, the child has made great gains in achieving competence. Based on his theory of effectance motivation and mastery learning, White reconceptualized the psychosexual stages of development as proposed by Freud. It is important to note that White did not seek to replace Freud's model but to augment it by identifying an additional independent drive, effectance motivation.

THE ORAL STAGE. Freud believed that the hunger instinct underlies the pleasures and pains of the infant's first year and that the infant is passively dependent on the object perceived as part of the self. White thought this very limited and felt that the infant, concerned primarily with hunger, is also testing the ability to cope with the environment through playing with body parts, crawling, playing peek-a-boo, and learning how to elicit responses from others in the environment. The infant learns to make the world interesting and enjoyable as it strives toward mastery. Mastery of the object, he believed, starts with the infant in this stage, minimizing pain (neglect) and maximizing pleasure (love).

THE ANAL STAGE. Freud believed that at this developmental level the anus is the erogenous pleasure zone and that toilet training is a battleground for mother and toddler in the struggle over independence, with the infant submitting to the demands of the parents and of the culture. White saw this also as a limited view and focused on the negativism of the normal two-year-old. Children at this age want to do things for themselves even if they are thwarted by the tasks. White felt that the child is intentionally negative, choosing to walk away, attempting to assert his/her rights, and meaning to say no. Increased motility coupled with negativism increases the sense of autonomy.

White recognized that this can be a very trying time in toddler-mother relationships and that the mother's attitude, whether too strict or too permissive, will affect the toddler's quest for competence. He cautioned also that successful bowel training involves physiological as well as psychological readiness. Freud believed that out of the anal stage evolved the anal traits of orderliness, parsimony, and stubbornness. White's effectance model saw these traits, if not too extreme, as active, competent ways to adapt to and master the environment.

THE PHALLIC STAGE. Freud believed that this phase revolves around maturation of the genital organs and the development of the Oedipus complex. At the end of it, at about age five, the superego begins to emerge as part of identification with the parent of the same sex. Mobility, language, curiosity, and capacity for imagining oneself in adult roles are now fairly well developed.

White generally accepted Freud's oedipal formulation, but suggested that it was possible that the child might go through these growing steps toward greater competence without experiencing increased genital sensitivity and oedipal strivings. Development of mobility, language, and imagination add to the growing senses of competence, productivity, and mastery. He believed that children learn their sex roles as they develop and not as a result of conflict resolution. Identification and introjection of parental prohibitions does not cause superego formation; rather, it occurs in the ever-developing process of working out a compromise among instincts, need for parental approval, and parental frustration. The developing child chooses to be competent like the parent and thus have its love reciprocated.

In addition to reconceptualizing Freud's psychosexual stages, White applied his competence model to other areas of psychoanalytic theory. Freud believed that the ego was central to reality testing and to identifying and mediating the demands of the environment. Hartmann identified the ego's ability to anticipate and postpone gratification as an autonomous ego function, independent of the id's conflicts with reality. White felt that the infant learns to anticipate and to delay gratification by becoming more competent. With experience, the infant learns to expect that something "efficacious," though perhaps not based solely on its needs, can be done to alleviate "pain" (White 1963:187). Reality becomes clearer as the infant experiences what is feasible and what is impossible in the course of its development.

White stressed the importance of the child's acquiring a sense of competence that will then develop and increase its sense of self-esteem. This, he believed, is done by mastering a sequence of challenges. A growing sense of efficacy is present as the child develops new skills, integrates new experiences, and is independent of the id's wishes. White believed that a range of play activities and a stimulating environment help the ego, and thus the child, in its efforts to develop competence, for the child seeks out opportunities to be effective.

The works of these three theorists moved ideas about personality development from the view that it is determined by id-ego conflicts to the realization that while some of the progression from immaturity to maturity is the result of innate anatomical, physiological, and neurological processes, these in turn are very much affected by the environment and interpersonal relationships and are more fluid than rigidly structured. Developmental tasks are not controlled by affects and impulses but involve mastery of them. Ego growth, essential to achievement of developmental tasks leading to mastery, involves advancing from primary process to secondary process thinking and from governance by the pleasure principle to recognition of the reality principle. Children and adults were thus seen as active in determining their lives as they develop mastery and not just as victims of internal conflicts or unsupportive environments.

All three of these theorists felt that the quality of mothering is a major factor in normal development. All, but especially White, believed that the child can develop only in an interpersonal milieu. Together they made a major step in developing ego psychology as their work recognized conflict-free ego capacities, the contribution of the defenses, and the influence and importance of the environment in the process of adaptation and mastery necessary for growth and development.

MARGARET MAHLER

Margaret Mahler was a psychoanalyst whose work was based epistemologically on the drive/structural theory of Sigmund Freud. Her theoretical orientation could be referred to as "psychoanalytic ego psychology" (Goldstein 1995:3). Mahler was also influenced by the words of A. Freud, Hartmann, and White that focused on the functioning of the ego. She was known as a member of the American, as distinct from the British, object relations theory group, whose theoretical belief was that object relations are core to the development of *all* other ego functions. In addition, Mahler believed that in order to develop intrapsychic, consistent, internalized object relations, essential to its identity and its ability to form mature, satisfying relationships, the individual must attain the level of development where it can perceive itself and other as separate. Like S. Freud, Mahler based her thinking on the belief that an infant at its "biological birth" is in an immature state and absolutely and totally dependent on the mother. In addition, Mahler shared with Freud the belief that the capacity for object relations is the most reliable factor in assessing the mental health of the individual and predicting therapeutic success. However, Mahler, unlike Freud, believed that the roots of identity and enhanced ego strength occur earlier than the oedipal period. Her emphasis on the primacy of the mother-child relationship in the developmental process differed from Freud's more paternalistic theories. Mahler's model is linear, with each stage leading to consolidation of individual identity and establishment of stable relations with others. Each stage must be accomplished for healthy development; failure to accomplish a phase, she believed, was the precursor for later psychopathology. Mahler did recognize that derivatives of separation and individuation issues might surface at other times in the life span, but they should be resolved by the fourth year.

Mahler's work derived initially from her observations of highly disturbed children, identified as autistic, in inpatient settings. Later she observed "normal" mothers and children, ages four months to four years, individually and together, both at the Masters Children's Center, a preschool in New York City, and during periodic home visits. Mahler's hypotheses from her observations were grounded in psychoanalytic assumptions. She was, however, very concerned about what "went wrong" for severely disturbed children in the developmental process and focused on documenting the normal child's "psychological birth" (Mahler, Pine, and Bergman 1975:3) and development of object relations. Mahler and her associates concluded that the process of separation-individuation essential to becoming a healthy person with normal ego development occurs in six independent, sequential phases: two forerunners and four actual stages. Separation is viewed, for the child, as an intrapsychic process of accepting separation from the mother.

PHASE 1 (FORERUNNER): NORMAL AUTISM

Mahler in 1983 changed the name of this phase from the more pathological sounding "autism" to "awakening." This phase lasts from birth to one month and is organized by the physiological needs of eating and sleeping. She believed that there are no autonomous ego functions and no awareness of external objects, as the infant is undifferentiated. The infant's stimulus barrier is still very strong, much like in the fetal stage, and serves as protection from extremes of stimulation. The main goal and achievement of this phase is physiological stability outside of the mother, with a homeostatic balance of the physiological mechanisms. Toward the end of the first month, Mahler felt, the infant moves from a stage of *primary narcissism* to the beginnings of *secondary narcissism* where, while still feeling that it is omnipotent and that satisfaction is based on its own needs, the child has limited recognition of an "other" as a needs satisfier.

PHASE 2 (FORERUNNER): NORMAL SYMBIOSIS

The infant is in this stage from approximately one to five months of age. Mahler believed that during this phase there are cracks in the autistic shell and greater awareness of the mother, the needs-satisfying object. The term *symbiosis* is used in its metaphorical sense, not to denote what occurs between two individuals of different species. It describes a sense of oneness, a fusion, with an inability to perceive where the infant and the mother begin and end and thus an inability to differentiate between the need-satisfying behavior of the infant and the mother. Toward the end of this phase, the symbiosis lessens and the child is somewhat aware of "me" and "not me," yet still governed by secondary narcissism. The concept of "good" mother and "bad" mother begins to emerge. The good mother immediately meets the infant's needs, while the bad mother delays immediate gratification. At this stage the infant cannot integrate these two objects into one.

The infant begins gradually to be aware that some experiences are good (pleasure) and some are bad (unpleasure or pain). Some of the development during this phase depends on interaction with the mother, who serves as mediator between the infant and external stimuli, which in themselves have little or no meaning to the infant. Mahler stressed the role of good mothering throughout the six phases in assisting the process of individuation, with the infant's needs being absolute and the mother's relative. In this symbiotic phase, the quality of the mother's handling influences the formation of the inner core of self.

Following these two "forerunner" phases, Mahler believed that the infant and mother enter four phases of separation-individuation.

PHASE 3 (FIRST SUBPHASE): DIFFERENTIATION AND DEVELOPMENT OF THE BODY IMAGE

This phase lasts from approximately five to nine months, characterized by Mahler as the "hatching" phase marking the beginning of the infant's *psychological birth*, leading to becoming an alert, perceptually aware person (Mahler, Pine, and Bergman 1975:53). Mahler characterized the infant in the symbiotic phase as in a passive state of "lap-babyhood" (Mahler 1972a:334). Beginning at about six months, the infant becomes more active in interactions with the mother, pulling her hair, trying to feed her, touching parts of her face, and at the same time showing interest in inanimate objects that can be grasped or put in its mouth. The infant now has the capability to recognize the mother visually and tactilely. These explorations enhance awareness of boundaries and differentiation. At seven or eight months the infant is able to distinguish the mother from other people, and stranger anxiety may be observed as the infant appears somewhat anxious about while also fascinated by people other than the mother. A secure infant will probably experience more curiosity than anxiety.

Mahler saw separation as awareness of self as a discrete entity, and individuation as awareness of self as a functioning person, separate from the mother. The process starts in this phase with a greater sense of "me" versus "not me." The mother should be able now to shift from immediate gratification of the infant's needs to an appropriate period of waiting. The infant develops some autonomous ego functions, particularly impulse control, frustration tolerance, perception, cognition, memory, and reality testing. At the end of this phase, it begins to move toward active and separate functioning as certain sensorimotor patterns develop more rapidly.

PHASE 4 (SECOND SUBPHASE): PRACTICING

In this phase, from approximately ten to fourteen months, the infant builds on the achievements of the last phase. As noted, the infant can differentiate between its own and the mother's body, can identify its own mother from other people, and has stronger autonomous ego capacities. However, the mother remains the object of greatest interest.

A major achievement assisting in separation-individuation is greater locomotion, which marks the peak of "hatching," begun in phase 4. Crawling extends the area for exploration, but walking gives a new dimension to the environment as the infant can regard it from an upright position. The infant, proud of these accomplishments, will move away from the mother physically but quickly return to her as "home base" and a source of emotional refueling. The ability to move on its own marks the end of infancy and the beginning of childhood, initially the period known as toddlerhood. This is usually a happy period for a child who delights in new abilities and new experiences. According to Mahler, the infant acts as though "the world is his oyster" (Mahler 1972a:336). The external environment has broadened and is full of surprises, and the child continues to enhance its sense of mastery. The child enjoys this greater independence, yet still wants to know the mother is there to meet its needs. The child has yet to integrate good and bad and continues to split the mother, and the self, into all "good" or all "bad."

There are times when the mother and toddler must be separated, and how the child copes with this, Mahler felt, depends on the tone set by the mother. If the mother is anxious the toddler will be, and if the mother minimizes the experience the toddler will usually accept known substitutes. Some toddlers may appear to be "low-key" during the mother's absence and may even cry; however, Mahler believed that the toddler, rather than being as active as usual, might actually be concentrating on a mental image of the mother to minimize the loss. This is also a time when the child may find comfort in a transitional object such as a favorite blanket or toy.

PHASE 5 (THIRD SUBPHASE): RAPPROCHEMENT

During this phase, from approximately fourteen months to two years, the toddler's language and cognitive abilities increase. It continues to be increasingly aware of its separateness, yet paradoxically, it is more sensitive to the mother's absence. The toddler will appear to function in a contradictory fashion, sometimes being hypervigilant about the mother's activities and "shadowing" her, at other times suddenly darting away. This behavior suggests some ambivalence toward separation as the toddler alternates between trying to deny and prevent it and initiating it. Yet at the same time there is greater interest in other "love objects," particularly the father and other familiar adults.

Between eighteen months and two years, Mahler believed, the toddler undergoes a *rapprochement crisis* with an almost overwhelming fear of separation and a resurgence of separation anxiety, expressed through tantrums, whining, and clinging. The toddler continues to be very curious and obviously has cognitive growth; however, it may become less self-sufficient and want to share new skills and experiences with the mother. There is conflict between wanting independence and fearing that the mother, and her love, will be lost. Mahler attributed this to the toddler's inability to differentiate its wishes and desires from those of its mother: if the toddler wishes to leave the mother then the mother will wish to leave it, which is too threatening (Mahler, Pine, and Bergman 1975:96). Although the toddler has some capacity to form a mental image of an absent mother, it is not firmly established. For some, this period results in realization that the world is *not* his or her oyster, and that she or he must assume some responsibility for coping.

At about twenty months, toddlers become aware of bodily differences. Like Freud, though for children at an earlier age, Mahler felt that this is much harder for girls to accept than boys and that girls blame the mother and feel disappointed in her. Girls also go from symbiosis to identification with the mother, which makes it harder for them to establish ego boundaries than for boys, who are aided in establishing autonomy by physical differences from the mother and identification with the father. While Mahler saw this as similar to Freud's oedipal period, she felt this crisis occurs at a much earlier age for girls, while boys later encounter castration anxiety. Neither Freud nor Mahler acknowledged the impact of society on developing gender identity.

Finally, during the rapprochement phase, the developing ego begins the process of resolving the split between "good" and "bad" mother and synthesizing the two. It is very difficult to accept that the good mother and the bad mother can be the same person. Mahler also felt that the developing ego has traces of the symbiotic phase, when there was no differentiation of self and mother and thus if the mother could be "bad," then the child could also, which is impossible! With normal development and good mothering, the ability of the ego to synthesize and integrate matures, and mixed feelings and perceptions are unified.

PHASE 6 (FOURTH SUBPHASE): CONSOLIDATION OF INDIVIDUALITY

This final phase of Mahler's theory of separation-individuation covers the end of the second year through the third year of the toddler's life. It is clearly a continuation of the previous phase, with the mother finally established as a separate entity in the external world whose "good" and "bad" aspects have been consolidated. In psychoanalytic terms, the toddler has begun to have a sense of *object constancy*, which enables it to maintain a mental image of the mother when she is absent; thus the child no longer fears losing the mother or her love if it has received good, consistent care resulting in basic trust. The child has finally established a unified representation of the mother that is intrapsychically available in the absence of the love object. A mature sense of object constancy involves relating to the other as a whole person, not just a satisfier of needs, and recognizing and tolerating ambivalent feelings and accepting that the other has both strengths and limitations.

The toddler shows the beginnings of individuality, its unique identity. Verbal ability is the chief means of communication and the content of play becomes much more purposeful and imaginative, while at the same time reality testing increases. The toddler knows the names of other people and of things and begins to understand the concept of "yours" and "mine" as applied to possessions. The toddler is also much more able to amuse itself. It has some rudimentary sense of time, especially if there is a routine to the mother's presence and absences. Thus as the final phase ends, Mahler believed, the toddler has achieved a stable self-construct, a sense of "me" separate from the love object, the mother, and is well on the way to establishing its own uniqueness.

Mahler was clearly influenced by earlier developmental theorists whose work also had built on that of Sigmund Freud. She disagreed with S. Freud in believing that the roots of conflict resolution, identity formation, and ego strengths are established much earlier than the oedipal period. She also placed much more importance on the mother's role in successful development. Mahler agreed with A. Freud, Hartmann, and White about the importance of good mothering, the existence of autonomous ego functions, and the importance of developing the capacity for mastery.

Throughout Mahler's formulation, the role of the mother is prominent. The mother must be able to separate from the infant. If she is overprotective, has not resolved her own issues about separation-individuation, or has unconscious conflicts about her role, this may impede the infant's progress toward independence. If there appears to be a need for assessment of the mother, it should include information about how she has coped with separation and loss in the past as well as the role of this particular child in her life, for some women have greater problems when separating from either the first (or only) child or from the last child.

Daniel Stern's work, which will be discussed next, is often compared to Mahler's. While his conclusions are not as different as some believe (Applegate 1989), there is no question that he challenged and sought to revise traditional psychoanalytic developmental theories. Though the construction of Mahler's theories involved observation, they rested on preconceptions based on psychoanalytic theory. She felt that psychopathology results from regression to an earlier phase of development. Stern, basing his work on direct observation, believes that the process of developing senses of self does not necessitate completing the previous stage and that psychopathology can emerge at any time in the life span, often due to environmental stresses.

DANIEL STERN

Daniel Stern's seminal book, *The Interpersonal World of the Infant*, was published in 1985. Dr. Stern is a child psychiatrist whose contribution to developmental theory is based on what he refers to as the "observed infant," rather than the "clinical infant." The "observed infant" is just that, an infant whose behavior and interaction with the primary caregiver are observed and recorded. The "clinical infant" is created, or re-created, later in life, in therapy, by the client and the clinician through memories and transferential material, and influenced by the clinician's training and orientation. Stern's studies were based on observable behavior and his assumptions about the senses of self and the domains of relatedness garnered through observation reports. He feels that his observed infant represents normal development, and his theory is prospective rather than retrospective.

Stern's work derives epistemologically from that of Harry Stark Sullivan and Heinz Kohut. Sullivan's Interpersonal Theory abandons Freud's drive concept of motivation and sees capacity for relatedness as the basis for psychosocial development. He proposed *zones of relatedness* to replace Freud's erotogenic zones as sources of pleasure and saw personality as developing through characteristic and habitual interpersonal relations. His was a "people-world" (Monte 1980:379), with feelings tied together by self and other. Sullivan divided personality development into six periods, each with a different and more sophisticated quality of interpersonal relationships, beginning with infancy and ending with late adolescence. Infancy is defined as birth through the development of language, and although the infant is not believed to differentiate self from world, it is able to personify self and others. Sullivan felt that the infant recognizes a "good me" who has satisfying relationships with others, a "bad me" who experiences tension and anxiety in relationships with others, and "not me," which Sullivan thought was experienced only by a severely disturbed self. Parallel to "me" is the personification of "good mother" and "bad mother." Sullivan believed that in toddlerhood, the period from the acquisition of language to the beginning of school, the child undertakes "as if" performances by role playing the behavior and mannerisms of parents or acting "as if" he or she is a parent. These role plays will help the child establish its male or female role.

Heinz Kohut, a founder of self-psychology whose work was primarily with narcissistic patients, viewed the *nuclear self* as the basic component of the psychic structure. He challenged Freud's drive theory, believing that it was flawed in not recognizing important interpersonal interactions necessary for healthy development, especially in the area of self-esteem. Kohut's nuclear self is formed in infancy, and for healthy development it requires "good mothering." This nuclear self consists of the infant's basic ideals, ambitions, and self-esteem, and it is the mother who must provide the *empathic* environment to encourage the thrust toward independence and to make the child's sense of omnipotence more realistic. Kohut believed that a strong sense of self must exist prior to the oedipal conflict and that secure parenting at this phase promotes self-esteem and healthy development.

The self and its boundaries are the heart of Stern's theoretical speculation. He believes that the self is present from birth and not a derivative of the id and the ego. The sense of self and other influences all social experience, is the organizing perspective for all interpersonal events, and is the basic organizing aspect of development.

Stern's basic assumption is that senses of self exist prior to self-awareness and language. He differs from earlier developmental theorists in that he does not feel that each developmental stage must be successfully completed before the next is begun or that if the stage is not accomplished the unsolved issues willresult in fixation and pathology. He believes that rather than replacing each other, each sense of self remains fully functioning, maturing and coexisting with the other senses of self, as distinctive forms of experience between self and other.

Stern believes that some rudimentary senses of "self processes" exist prior to self-awareness and ability to verbalize: (1) a sense of agency, which involves determining one's actions and having a sense of control rather than being controlled externally; (2) a sense of physical cohesion, without which the person would feel fragmented and depersonalized; (3) a sense of continuity in time; (4) a sense of affectivity, without which there can be anhedonia and dissociative states; (5) a sense of subjective self that can achieve intersubjectivity; (6) a sense of creating organization; and (7) a sense of transmitting meaning (Stern 1985:6–7). Maturation permits these senses to emerge and to become more sophisticated.

Stern feels that the major issues of orality, autonomy, attachment, independence, and trust are lifelong, and that problems can emerge at any point and are not related to the lack of resolution of any developmental stage. Stern's formulation was influenced by but differed from those of Freud, Erikson, and Mahler, which were all based on a psychoanalytic approach. Stern focuses on development through interpersonal experiences rather than the effects of the drives. Like Mahler and the British school of Object Relations theory as represented by Melanie Klein, Stern emphasizes how the infant experiences self and other and regards that differentiation as crucial for development. Unlike Mahler's linear view of development, Stern's is nonlinear, transactional from birth, and rooted in reality rather than fantasies or delusions.

Stern studied infants from birth to about age three and felt that the central issue was the development of a sense of self. The senses of self and the capacity for relatedness become increasingly complex as the infant develops. Four senses of self can be identified: the sense of an emergent self, the sense of a core self, the sense of a subjective self, and the sense of a verbal self. He believes that a person continues to build on all of these senses of self throughout life. Stern is concerned with the infant's subjective life and experiences with relatedness. While the senses of self arise, for the most part, out of awareness, they grow as the person develops greater verbal skills and the capacity for self-reflection. The senses of self organize the ability to have social experiences, and how the child experiences itself in relation to others becomes the organizing principle for all interpersonal interactions throughout life.

Stern found that infant development occurs in spurts; the periods between two and three months, nine and twelve months, and fifteen and eighteen months are the periods of greatest change. Between them there is relative quiescence as the infant appears to integrate the new sense of self.

THE SENSES OF SELF

1. THE SENSE OF AN EMERGENT SELF (BIRTH TO TWO MONTHS). Stern differs from other theorists in not believing that an infant ever goes through an "undifferentiated" state or an "autistic" phase. He puts little emphasis on the "awareness of separation" in early development, as he believes that the infant, almost from birth, is aware of a separate "other." The infant is *physiologically* equipped to interact with others. Stern believes that it experiences a sense of emergent self and is born with self-organizing processes that allow it to eat, sleep, and suck with no confusion between self and other. The infant can also distinguish among some stimuli. As it experiences forming a relationship with an other, it enters the *domain of emergent relatedness.*

The infant, during this phase, starts a range of diverse experiences that Stern believes are directed toward social interaction. The interactions produce affects, perceptions, sensorimotor events, and memories (Stern 1985:28), and begin the process of establishing a sense of organization. All learning and all creative acts in the present and future are the products of organization, a process begun as part of the Domain of Emergent Relatedness. Toward the end of this phase, eating, sleeping, and fussing lessen and the infant begins to make eye contact with the other, smiles more intentionally, and coos when content. Stern refers to this as a state of *alert inactivity* (1985:39) in which the infant may appear quiet but is absorbing external events. The infant begins to appear quite different and involved in interpersonal activities.

2. THE SENSE OF A CORE SELF (TWO TO SIX MONTHS). During this period, Stern feels that the infant consolidates a sense of self as a separate, cohesive physical unit with boundaries. This is experiential integration, out of conscious awareness. He rejects the concept of a "symbiotic" phase, believing that the infant is aware of a distinct, coherent body with control over its actions and of its own affectivity, and has a sense of continuity and knowledge of being separate from the other. Sense of a self and an other is essential before a merger- or fusionlike experience can occur (Stern 1985:69–70).

The core self has four aspects: (1) a sense of *self-agency* involving control of actions, initiative, knowledge of the consequences of one's actions, and what Stern views as the most fundamental part of the core "self-experience," a sense of volition by which the infant can begin to know if an action is self-willed or other-willed; (2) a sense of *self-coherence* with boundaries and locus of integrated actions: the infant can begin to recognize what sights, sounds, and touches emanate from itself and what come from the other, although it may be somewhat confused when interacting with the other at close range rather than at a distance; the infant can recognize the form of the other even if there are some changes in distance or position, and can distinguish between *primary* other and additional people; (3) a sense of *self-affectivity* where the infant has its own patterned feelings related to certain actions and experiences; even at the beginning of this phase, the infant can experience joy, distress, interest, and anger; and (4) a sense of *self-history* and continuity with its past: motor memory is established early and memory for visual perceptions between five and seven months; Stern believes that affects change very little over time. He introduced the concept of an *evoked companion*, whose presence continues throughout life and involves memory of past experiences with another whether that person is present or not. This is the experience of being with, or in the presence of, a self-regulating other (Stern 1985:112). In early life, if the memory is good, it forms a basis for trust and security. When there is a loss, Stern feels, the evoked companion can be "present" through imagined interactions, daydreams, and memories.

These four senses provide the infant with the ability to integrate and to organize a core sense of self. Stern recognizes that the infant needs the internal capacities, opportunity, and integrative abilities, and the existence of a parallel, complimentary process, that must occur with a core other. Thus, along with the sense of a core self, a *sense of a core other* also develops, and an active awareness of an organized experience of self with other. This is a very social phase in which the infant smiles, vocalizes, is aware of familiar faces and voices, and can link gazes with the other. The goal is not autonomy or individuation, but rather the beginning of sharing subjective thoughts and feelings. Obviously much of the activities at this age involve an other. The infant needs this person to regulate many activities and experiences and to help it develop feelings of security and attachment. An affective spectrum can also only be built through the interaction with an other. However, Stern believes that while experiences of the self are dependent on the presence or absence of the other, they belong to the self and are not a product of fusion with the other. The infant at this stage experiences (though out of conscious awareness) itself as a unique, coherent, physical entity with an affective life and a history (Stern 1985:26), separate from the mother. At this point Stern saw the infant as operating within a *domain of core relatedness*.

At the end of the development of senses of core self and core other, the infant changes once again: it has greater physical coordination, can manipulate objects, and experiences a period of greater interest in inanimate objects than in people. The infant does, however, want to share experiences, events, affects, and even inanimate objects. Stern acknowledges the need throughout for "good mothering" that involves appropriate and consistent responsiveness to the infant, particularly its physical needs. The child needs a self-regulating other who will assist in controlling stimulation, arousal, tension, and excitation.

3. *The Sense of a Subjective Self (seven to fifteen months).*
Stern believes that early in this phase, the infant discovers that it and the other have minds. It also becomes aware (though not consciously) that the other may have feelings that are not congruent with its own. The infant can sense these feelings, can share the focus of attention, and can begin to attribute intentions and motives to others.

As the infant becomes aware of shared memories and experiences, it enters the *domain of intersubjective relatedness.* An empathic process begins to evolve, bridging the minds of the infant and the other, allowing psychic as well as physical intimacy. Interactivity is deliberately sought out in the form of joint attention to an activity, sharing of intentions, and sharing of affective states.

Stern refers to the sharing of affective states as "the most pervasive and clinically germane feature" of intersubjective relatedness (Stern 1985:138). *Interaffectivity* is defined as parental mirroring and empathic responsiveness. If successful, it enhances the infant's feelings of security and the ability to achieve attachment goals. As the process evolves, there is affect attunement where the focus of attention is not so much on behavior but on the feelings behind the behavior, and there is emotional resonance. Stern believes that the three features that can be matched between participants in the attunement process are intensity, which may be equal or may change over the period of the event; timing, which usually is matched; and shape, where the infant and the mother may be involved in the same activity or the activity may be slightly modified, such as when an infant moves an arm or leg in a pattern and the mother responds with the same pattern, but using her head. Attunement goes beyond imitation and involves sharing of feeling that make intersubjective merger and unity possible. Stern saw such "symbiotic" merger and undifferentiation as possible not at birth but with somewhat developed emotional and cognitive growth.

Attunement, the main feature of the sense of subjective self, recasts behavior through nonverbal metaphor and analogue and prepares the infant to move toward use of symbols in the form of language. As Kohut viewed the self as the basic component of the psychic structure, Stern sees the subjective sense of self as basic to development. With it exists an organized perspective about the self and its domain of relatedness to others.

4. *The Sense of a Verbal Self (after fifteen months).* By the time the infant enters this phase, it has acquired a lot of knowledge about its body, inanimate objects, and—of greatest importance—how social interactions

occur. In this final stage of Stern's theory, it usually is able to verbalize with varying degrees of sophistication, and also has a more conscious sense of self and other as having personal knowledge and experiences that can be objectified and communicated through symbols (language). The child has a greater capacity to be self-reflective and to encounter limitless possibilities for comprehending and producing language; thus it has enhanced possibilities for greater interpersonal experiences. The infant operates within the *domain of verbal relatedness.*

While the other domains continue to operate, they are more personal and immediate. The acquisition of language moves relatedness onto a more impersonal, abstract level. The infant is more able to communicate about people and things that are not present and participates in symbolic play. Stern feels that during this phase, the infant can objectify itself, core gender identity is established, the infant is capable of acts of empathy, and interpersonal interactions can have a past, present, and future. In addition, language, rather than facilitating individuation and separation, actually allows the infant to move to the next level of development where mental commonality with the other will be further solidified as they "speak the same language." Stern believes that the infant prior to language lives in a reality of its own inner experience, but with language comes the possibility of distortion, so the infant moves further beyond inner reality.

In 1990, Stern published *Diary of a Baby,* covering key developmental stages from birth to age four. He based his "diary" on his clinical observations and, like Piaget, partly on his observations of his own children. He acknowledges that the diary is made up of "part speculation, part imagination, part fact" (Stern 1990:5), based on his current knowledge of development. Earlier, he had felt that in development there were periods of greatest growth with somewhat dormant periods in between: two to three months, five to six months, nine to twelve months, and fifteen to eighteen months. In the *Diary* he discusses five successful "worlds of experience" that his infant, "Joey," goes through: (1) at six weeks, the world of feelings; (2) at four months, the immediate social world; (3) at twelve months, the world of mindscapes; (4) at twenty months, the world of words; and (5) at four years, the world of stories.

Stern believes that at six weeks, an infant is concerned not with how or why something happens, but only with the experience and the related feelings: thus the world of feelings. Hunger is the most powerful example of a feeling that starts slowly and then escalates, taking over the life of the six-week-old, whose concern is the feeling and not where it comes from. The experience of hunger also involves the other, for the infant reaches out for comfort while experiencing the feelings inwardly. While feeding is the infant's main concern here, Stern believes that at this stage the infant is beginning to form a mental model of the mother, a process that can later be extended to other significant people.

At four and a half months, the infant enters the immediate social world, in which he is involved in a "rich choreography"(Stern 1990:7) with the mother that includes interaction of feelings, sustained eye contact, responding to each other's smiles, and imitating sounds. Stern feels that the face, particularly the eyes, is of particular interest at this age, with beginning awareness of its importance throughout life in reading the feelings and behavior of others. Joey also experiences a sense of agency as he becomes aware that things are different because of what he does. If he turns his head or closes his eyes, things are different. He is increasingly aware that he and his mother are different and that the actions of each cause different effects. The infant is now aware of at least three separate people, himself, his mother, and his father, and in some cases, some additional significant others.

At twelve months the infant enters the world of mindscapes. Stern believes he is aware of having a mind with wishes, desires, feelings, thoughts, memories, and intentions. The infant is also aware that his mind can be in sync with that of the other, but that some things are shared—an intersubjective mindscape—and some remain internal. Motives, desires, intentions, and feelings from this stage on become part of the content of the child's mind. Stern observed that the infant, at this point, turns to the mother not for physical gratification as much as for emotional regulation and is now capable of exhibiting behaviors that show attachment when she is absent (he or she is miserable) or when she is present (he or she is elated). It is significant that Stern recognized that since many mothers now work, a child can form the same kind of attachment to the regular caregiver as to the mother. As the toddler masters walking, he or she will explore and move away from the mother, but the pull of attachment will bring him back periodically to "check in."

Stern believes that at twenty months, the infant makes the transition to child, entering the world of words as the capacity for language and symbolization emerges. Children are able to understand language before producing it and can mentally play out events in the past, present, and future. While this is an enormous developmental leap, it can also cause problems, as language can be misunderstood or parents can assume a greater capacity for understanding than is realistic.

Finally, at age four, the child enters the world of stories. The child is able to tell stories about events or experiences he has had, and also can use his imagination in creating stories, although these may seem to have been experienced as real. The story is also a social exchange, as there must be a teller and a listener. The autobiographical quality of many of the stories also represents the child's attempt to solidify an identity.

Stern views the infant as a very good "reality tester"; he feels that distortion in relationships as well as defenses really does not develop until the toddler has language, and with it greater use of symbols. Because pathology is not linked to a phase of development, when it does emerge, Stern believes it gives the clinician greater freedom for exploration of possible environmental causes. Stern recognizes that further research is needed to better synthesize the findings about the observed infant and the clinical infant.

ERIK ERIKSON

Erik Erikson was born in 1902 in Germany and raised by his mother and his physician stepfather. After graduation from the equivalent of high school, he traveled through Europe as an artist. Following his friend Peter Blos, he went to Vienna, where he met Anna Freud, taught in her Montessori school, and was analyzed by her. Fleeing the Nazis, Erikson came to Boston in 1933, where he worked initially with two anthropologists, Margaret Mead and Ruth Benedict, and then at Harvard Medical School. He later worked at the Mt. Zion Rehabilitation Clinic with military casualties and at the Yale Medical School and Institute of Human Relations. While in New Haven he was awarded a grant for a field trip to the Southwest, where he studied child rearing among the Sioux and later, the Yurok Indians on the Pacific coast, which contributed to his developing psychosocial perspective. Erikson spent many years at the University of California at Berkeley and then returned to Massachusetts, where he worked at The Austin Riggs Clinic and again at Harvard. He died at age 92 at his home on Cape Cod. Although he was referred to as "Professor Erikson" and supervised many psychologists and psychiatrists, Erikson never earned an academic degree beyond high school.

Erikson, interested in healthy developmental theory, took on the enormous task of looking at the entire life span and the developmental crises that must be dealt with in sequence for healthy development. He recognized inner and outer conflicts and felt that in negotiating these stages, the individual emerges from each with increased judgment, sense of self, and inner unity. Like Hartmann, he was concerned with adaptation to the environment beginning in infancy; considered together, their work establishes a theoretical framework in which the environment and instinctual drives interact and direct behavior. Erikson viewed development as resulting from a combination of biological, cultural, social, and psychological factors, merging within the ego. He postulated that at each different stage there is a psychosocial "crisis" that, when resolved, enhances ego mastery.

Although trained as a psychoanalyst, Erikson broadened his focus from instinctual dynamics to placing greater emphasis on psychosocial dynamics. He believed that Freud's work did not show appreciation of environmental, cultural, and interpersonal factors in personality development. While paying close attention to the id and the superego, Erikson felt that the responsibility for adjustment and development of a sense of self rested most strongly with the ego. He believed that the ego matures and develops in an epigenetic sequence involving psychosexual and psychosocial factors, with each stage depending on resolution of the prior stages. What emerges is partly genetically determined and partly determined by the external social environment. Erikson's first five stages build on Freud's psychosexual stages. He initially postulated a total of eight sequential stages involving ego crises, states of disequilibrium, and accompanying critical tasks, which enhanced competency and guided healthy life span development. In his last years, he formulated a ninth stage, a sense of one's own integrity versus a feeling of defeat or despair about one's life as physical deterioration occurs. Each stage has positive and negative factors, both of which are incorporated into the person's identity. Each stage must be gone through before the individual can successfully go on to the next stage. The successful resolution of each crisis, Erikson felt, further enhances the individual's sense of self and ego identity.

For each of the crises, Erikson proposed parallel *ritualizations*, repetitive, orienting, playful, and socializing mechanisms prescribed by the person's culture, and *ritualisms*, forms of estrangement from self and society (Monte 1980:244–45). Thus, he recognized positive and negative elements and hoped that the former would outweigh the latter. Erikson saw ritualizations as having seven important functions: social; determining destiny; indicating worthiness; interpreting; sanctification; providing moral structure; and affirming identity (Erikson 1977:82–83).

At the end of each stage, Erikson felt that a new psychological "virtue" (strength) is acquired. Each successive stage with its accompanying crisis is related to the basic demands of society; thus, the life cycle and society's institutions evolve together. Following are the three stages the child goes through from birth up to latency.

Acquiring a Sense of Trust Versus a Sense of Mistrust: Hope
(birth to eighteen months)

Throughout the first year, the infant's contact with the environment is mediated by the mother, whose role is to meet needs. This primarily involves satisfying hunger, and this stage corresponds to the psychoanalytic oral phase. If these needs are met lovingly, consistently, and efficiently, the infant will develop *basic trust*. This is seen initially in the infant's ability to be aware when the mother is out of sight and not react with anxiety or anger. The developing infant will explore the boundaries of trust and if it has been made to feel secure and loved, will be able to accept parental restrictions. The secure infant has a sense of mastery and will seek out new experiences and challenges. The virtue, or ego strength, accompanying basic trust is the capacity to *hope*, to believe in the attainability of wishes. With this strength, the child can take risks and not feel overwhelmed by frustration or failure. The ritualization of this period is *mutual recognition and affirmation* of the mother-child bond. The infant is now able to move to an awareness of "I."

If the infant has not had love, consistency, and a reliable environment, it will develop a sense of *basic mistrust*, which Erikson believed can result in serious psychopathology. The ritualism of this stage is *idolism*, a distortion of the mother-infant bond where an illusion of the mother's perfection exists that can result in later pathological narcissistic idealization of the self with unrealistic expectations and overdependence.

Acquiring a Sense of Autonomy Versus a Sense of Shame and Doubt: Will
(eighteen months to four years)

The child now has greater voluntary muscle control, which Erikson believed leads to a greater sense of self-control. This is first seen in the deliberate act of dropping objects from the high chair or out of the crib or playpen. Within a psychoanalytic framework, this period corresponds to the anal period and the battle of wills around toilet training. Erikson believed that this must be carefully handled by the mother in order to protect the sense of basic trust established in the first stage. A demanding parent will turn this process into a battle of wills when the child refuses to comply.

The crisis for this stage of ego development is the child's need for independence and autonomy in dealing with its own bodily functions. As the child develops greater self-control with parental support, it lays the foundation

for later security in making its own free choices. If the child is overcon-
trolled by the mother and is shamed into accomplishing toilet training, it
will begin to distrust and feel negative toward the parent who does not
support independence.

If this stage is successfully mastered, the infant's sense of ego identity, of "I,"
will be enhanced. The virtue, or ego strength, that results is *will*, the capacity for autonomy, enabling the child to exercise free choice, self-restraint,
and self-control. If this is a problematic phase, the child will experience
shame and doubt and may become self-conscious. Erikson saw this stage
as decisive for establishing a ratio of love and hate, cooperation and will-
fulness, and freedom of self-expression and its suppression (Erikson
1993:254).

The ritualization of this stage, which Erikson called *judicious*, is the ability
the child develops to differentiate, within its culture, good and bad. With
the newfound sense of autonomy there is a playful testing of limits with
adults and to some extent with peers. Erikson cautions that if this testing is
viewed essentially negatively, it may result in negative identity in adolescence, a self-fulfilling prophecy.

The ritualism is *legalism*, resulting in self-righteousness, or a lack of impulse
control resulting in a tendency toward exploitation of the law for one's
own gain.

Acquiring a Sense of Initiative Versus a Sense of Guilt: Purpose
(four to six years)

Erikson felt that, having acquired a sense of autonomy, the child is able to see
itself as a person but still needs to solidify its identity through identification with a parent. This stage corresponds to Freud's phallic phase culminating in the resolution of the Oedipus complex.

Although Erikson's work differs to some extent from classic psychoanalytic
theory, he did believe that girls experience genital trauma when they realize that they lack a penis, resulting in turning away from the mother, who
has failed them, toward the father. Unlike Freud, however, Erikson focused not on the trauma but rather on a unique, positive sense of competence. He recognized that there are similarities and differences in ego formation of men and women, and felt that in "giving up" the parent of the
opposite sex, the infant increases identification with the same-sex parent,
which assists in the evolution of the superego. With this identification, the
child begins to pursue idealistic goals and causes, seen more in the next

stage of development. In this stage, infantile sexuality and the incest taboo, the fear of castration, and the emerging superego all unite in moving the child toward its own identity while retaining parental standards and values.

The further development of language and locomotion enables the developing child to expand his imagination, including the ability to have frightening thoughts. The child has greater ability to initiate fantasies, actions, and ideas as well as to interact with other children and to plan. The crisis of the stage is complex, for it involves further awareness of what the child can or cannot do as it tries to balance its developing sense of initiative against the residue of oedipal guilt in the superego. Erikson believed that the child arrives at this balance through imaginative play. The virtue (ego strength) that emerges at this stage is *purpose*, the capacity to envision and pursue its own goals, based on internalized standards. If this stage is not resolved, the child will not feel the release from inner oedipal guilt.

The stage-specific ritualization is *authenticity*. The child in its play is able to relive and correct past and present experiences and to anticipate new ones. It is also able to experiment with different roles and identifications. The result is further solidification of "I," influenced by the child's growing awareness of what it may want to be and what realistically it can be.

The ritualism is *impersonation*, with the child moving among roles with no apparent commitment to any. Erikson felt that there is a greater danger of assuming a negative role than of taking no role.

PLAY

Erikson placed a lot of importance on play, the "work" of children, with its goal, development of greater mastery, defined as "a function of the ego, an attempt to synchronize the bodily and the social processes with the self" (Erikson 1993:211). Play initially is based on the infant's exploration of its own body and to a lesser extent on objects it can reach. This self-centered form of play, which orients it to its environment, Erikson called *autocosmic* play. The infant then moves into a world of surrounding toys, which Erikson termed the *microsphere* of play (Erikson 1993:220–21). By nursery school age, the child enters another phase of play, the *macrosphere*, where activities are shared and the child's imagination allows it to take whatever materials are available and "make" them into something else, such as using a chair as a horse. At this point, the child becomes more aware of what is and is not its own to do with as it wants. Erikson endowed each of these spheres, leading to mastery of reality through the toddler's experimentation and planning, with its own sense of reality and mastery.

Erikson has been criticized for placing too much emphasis on the biological differences between females and males and the expectation that each sex handles toys differently, with females moving toward domesticity and males toward outside work. However, his work made a very significant contribution to the theories of personality development: a more general acceptance of the concepts of identity, identity crisis, lifelong development, ego strength, and psychosocial development. He also brought to the fore the importance of recognizing differences between male and female development. While Erikson did not dismiss the concept of unconscious conflicts, he emphasized the interaction of the person and the environment in enhancing the ego's capacity for mastery.

Erikson wrote from a psychosocial perspective, recognizing the impact of inner and outer reality on the increasingly sophisticated developing ego. Like Freud, he believed that the healthy individual functions well in both love and work and placed great importance on the environment, starting with that provided by the parents. It must also be noted that while earlier theorists focused on the mother-child relationship, Erikson recognized the importance of both parents, siblings, peers, and teachers.

Erikson's work is very compatible with a biopsychosocial perspective. More than other developmental theorists, he recognized the importance of social, racial, class, gender, and cultural factors. He believed that personality development begins with three *social* needs: social attention; competence needed to master the environment; and structure and order in social affairs (Greene 1991:83). He also recognized that each stage may be "revisited" under stress in later life, while still emphasizing that resolution of each crisis results in a strength.

JEAN PIAGET

Jean Piaget was a Swiss biologist-psychologist-philosopher, born in 1896, who wrote extensively about intellectual development from birth through adolescence. His began with the naturalistic study of his own children. Although he had worked on developing standardized tests, he believed that they were too rigid and thus allowed data to be lost. His later work used a clinical methodology in which questions referred to objects or events with which the child was involved. Data were collected through observing manipulation of objects as well as language. In addition, Piaget set up a measure of thinking by which he proposed an opinion different from the child's and encouraged the child to support its own position.

Piaget had an early interest in epistemology, the study of knowledge (Ginsburg and Opper 1988:2). When he began his work on human development, there had been little research on intelligence; his initial goal was to understand what constituted it. He believed that the function of intelligence (cognitive structures) was to achieve equilibrium between the individual and the environment. As a child develops and becomes aware of increasingly complex aspects of the environment, it changes its way of dealing with environment changes in order to regain equilibrium. Piaget saw intelligence as a cognitive organization and adaptation to what the child perceives as its environment, a process that extends from the organization of the innate reflexes in infancy through the end of adolescence, with the level of achievement dependent on the individual's capabilities and maturation.

Piaget was interested in studying cognitive development, the succession of intellectual structures the child develops in order to interact with the environment. He was concerned with what the child does cognitively, the "how," rather than emotionally. Beginning with intense, detailed observation of his own three children, Piaget assembled an enormous set of empirical data based on observation, interviewing, and testing of children of all ages. His approach was very different from that of Freud, who gathered information from adult patients about their childhoods and rarely studied children themselves. Piaget believed that the thought processes and content of young children differ qualitatively from those of older children—at different ages, they use different methods of thinking. When the child begins to acquire knowledge its thinking is egocentric, a tendency that decreases with greater ability to differentiate objects. Like Freud, Piaget believed that children must go through a sequence of developmental stages of which none can be omitted, but unlike Freud, he concentrated on intellectual (cognitive) development rather than on emotions. He saw the acquisition of intelligence as a gradual series of mental processes resulting in a succession of intellectual stages.

While Piaget's ideas are very imaginative and novel and have heavily influenced theorists concerned with intellectual development, translations of his writings have led to criticism that he is very difficult to understand. Thus an effort will be made in this section to include definitions of some of his key concepts.

Piaget focused on the optimal level of intellectual functioning while, of course, acknowledging the impact of physical maturation and hereditary factors. He believed that all organisms inherit two basic, related "invariant functions" (Ginsburg and Opper 1988:17), *organization* and *adaptation*, related to intelligence and to *schemas* and *psychological structures*.

Schemas (also called schemes) are the cognitive structures, or patterns, that make repeatable behaviors possible. These behaviors enable the individual to adapt to and organize the environment, and they are constantly being modified throughout life. *Psychological structures* are organized, predictable patterns of behavior and thinking, which are basic to a child's actions at a given developmental stage. The structures change and are arrived at through experience as the individual matures, until what will be adult intelligence is achieved during adolescence. These are very similar to schemas, another subprocess, but are more complex.

Organization, or operations, involves the need for and ability of the developing individual to integrate schemas, as well as physical and psychological structures, into higher-order coherent systems or psychological structures. Schemas and structures can be manipulated by cognitive processes. *Adaptation* may differ from individual to individual or from one developmental stage to another, but is an innate tendency of all humans to adjust to the environment. The processes of adaptation and organization require two complementary, simultaneous, balanced processes, *accommodation* and *assimilation*.

Accommodation is the tendency of the individual to change perceptions and actions in response to new environmental demands. In Piaget's terms, preexisting as well as new schemas accommodate new environmental situations, modifying the cognitive system to fit the environment. *Assimilation* involves the individual's ability to deal with the environment using existing and developing schemas, incorporating existing or new external reality into preexisting schemas and structures. *Equilibrium* is the balance between assimilation and accommodation, which when achieved results in the individual moving to the next developmental stage.

As the individual matures, new structures must be developed, building on the old and enhancing interaction with the environment. Intellectual development, Piaget's main interest, happens in a series of stages that require different types of interaction with the environment and thus different psychological structures.

Sensorimotor is the first stage identified by Piaget. It is the period during which an infant begins the process of developing intelligence. Piaget divided this period into six stages covering birth to age two.

PHASE ONE: BIRTH TO ONE MONTH. The infant, Piaget believed, makes no distinction between self and nonself. However, it is active and initiates behavior, not passive or completely helpless. To the infant at this age, all experience is a global, fused mass, which Piaget described as having a sense of *global causality* (1954:250ff) with no differentiation between what self and nonself.

The infant is born with a sucking reflex (a psychological structure), and as it experiences pleasure from sucking, it will do so even between feedings. The sucking schema then extends beyond the nipple/bottle to fingers, blankets, and toys, and thus the infant's environment expands. In the early months of infancy the child's universe has no perceivable stability or permanence. Objects exist only when present, as sensory experiences, and the infant exhibits egocentricity—the object appears only as a result of his or her desires and wishes. Thus the infant lacks a sense of *object permanence.*

Piaget believed that at this stage, when language does not exist and learning is dominated by reflexes, *activity* is the main mode of learning and thus the origin of intelligence. By the end of this stage the infant has begun to follow the principle of organization and the innate sucking capacity has expanded its environment through experience.

PHASE TWO: ONE TO FOUR MONTHS. The infant's life continues to be centered on its body, and its habits and actions are still very simple. Piaget characterized its behavior as a *primary circular reaction*: the infant undertakes an action, centered on its body, which by chance leads to satisfaction. The infant will then continue to repeat this activity, by trial and error, until it becomes an organized schema.

Toward the end of this stage, the infant has developed the ability to recognize cues for activities that will satisfy needs. For example, the way it is held suggests feeding will take place and hunger will be satisfied. The infant has also developed greater visual capacity and is better able to differentiate between things and to experience some stimulation from new objects as well as heightened curiosity about them.

The infant begins to relate to others, although it is still very egocentric. It imitates actions or sounds made by others if it is already capable of performing them, but not if they are unfamiliar. Thus the infant repeats already established schemas. Coordination of sight and sound, so that the infant turns to see what produces a sound, is a very early move toward establishing awareness of external objects. The infant has some emerging habit patterns that acquire greater efficiency and skill, which Piaget termed *reproductive assimila-*

tion. However, the concept of "object" is very rudimentary: although the infant looks at objects, it has no reaction when they disappear from view.

PHASE THREE: FOUR TO TEN MONTHS. During this stage, the infant's world expands as it is able to manipulate objects and to crawl, or perhaps even walk. Piaget termed these new experiences *secondary circular reactions* because the infant is much more involved with the external environment. Events initially occurred by chance, but in this stage the infant acquires the capacity to reproduce what is interesting; its behavior thus is more intentional. It will expand usual patterns to new experiences if they do not differ too much from the familiar. This represents *generalized assimilation*. The desire to repeat an event of interest provides motivation and directs action for what is still a trial-and-error process. Piaget did not regard this as "intelligent behavior," as the infant's actions are reproductions of what has occurred rather than newly developed behaviors, though he did see this stage as the beginnings of thought.

The infant begins to experience some sense of organization and awareness that events and objects go together—the stage of *feelings of efficacy* (Piaget 1954:250). The infant maintains its egocentricity, as it feels that its desires dictate external responses: if it is hungry, the person with food will appear. It is aware that events occur but is not concerned with why.

There are some beginnings of object permanence; the infant in this phase will search for an object if it has caused its disappearance by dropping; however, it will not search if the disappearance was caused by another. The infant can now return to an object even if there has been an interruption in play or a refocusing of its attention. If the interval is brief, the infant will resume its activity, an important step toward establishing the concept of object constancy. The infant can also recognize an object if only a part is visible, while in earlier stages the object did not exist unless the whole was there.

PHASE FOUR: TEN TO TWELVE MONTHS. The infant enters a phase of *elementary externalization and objectification of causality*. At this point it can have some concept of what is self and what is not and some diminution of egocentricity, although the importance of events and objects remains primarily in terms of the self. Piaget referred to this view as "magico-phenomenalistic": "magical" because the infant sees physical causality governing events and "phenomenalistic" because of the subjectivity of the infant's concept of reality in that his wishes control his world (Piaget and Inhelder 1969:18).

Piaget felt that during this period there is "coordination of secondary schemas" (Ginsburg and Opper 1988:50). What had been trial and error (or accident) becomes more planned as the infant has a goal in mind. It will first try old schemas to remove obstacles to achieving the goal. If not successful, it will try to modify them and finally arrive at one that will remove the obstacles. Thus the infant employs a schema that is the means to overcome the obstacles, different from the schema used to achieve the goal, and is aware that the obstacles have some relation to the goal. Piaget saw this behavior as *intelligent* since it is intentional. During this phase, the infant becomes more aware of others, has some ability to anticipate actions, and can make some connections between events.

The infant has better hand-eye coordination and begins to be able to imitate the actions initiated by others; however, they must be familiar. The capacity for imitation, Piaget believed, is the forerunner of mental symbolism. At this phase imitation is the result of observed behavior, which in later stages will become internal. The infant is also able to move objects and will search for them if they disappear, thus showing a sense of object permanence. It can distinguish objects from each other (*recognitory assimilation*). Piaget believed that as the infant becomes increasingly aware of greater separation from the environment, *decentration*, a decrease in egocentrism, occurs.

PHASE FIVE: TWELVE TO EIGHTEEN MONTHS. *Tertiary circular reactions* defined this stage for Piaget. The toddler starts to walk and becomes more curious about objects and searches for novelty. Through a greater capacity to explore, it becomes aware of the differences between the properties of objects and learns through experience. It also has an expanded capacity to imitate and attempts to mimic new behaviors.

Piaget felt that the beginning of *logical thought* occurs during this period, which he characterized as *real objectification and spatialization of causes* (Monte 1980:353); the toddler becomes aware that the causes of events may be located outside itself, recognizing the existence of independent and realistically permanent objects. Egocentricity is no longer the sole mode of relating. Intelligent behavior is further developed as the child becomes more sophisticated in recognizing environmental demands and the need to accommodate them.

PHASE SIX: EIGHTEEN MONTHS TO TWO YEARS. Piaget saw this as a period of transition to the next phase of development, where mental symbols and words provide object permanence in the absence of the object. Symbolic thought allows the toddler to move from the limited world of the here and now. It has reached a major milestone, as it is able to retain a mental representation of an object in its absence.

The toddler at this stage has the beginnings of language, a new means of structuring reality, and is capable of *representative* activities, such as using an object to represent something known, e.g., a chair that stands for a car. Language, though very limited, enables the toddler to store information that links past, present, and future events. Interpersonal experiences increase in importance and are sought out, as the toddler's world has lost much of its egocentricity through significant interaction with objects and with the environment. Rapidly developing behavioral schemas range from the initial, hereditary automatic behavior to, at age two, interest in the environment and ability to manipulate objects, but only objects immediately present in the child's vision.

Preoperational is the term for Piaget's second stage of cognitive development, covering ages two to seven years. It begins at the point when the child is acquiring greater ability to retain symbols. Piaget referred to this as the *semiotic function* that enables the child to represent something absent by an object, a word, or a mental symbol. This goes beyond time and space. The semiotic function uses mental symbols, language, and symbolic play. Piaget called the ability to use symbols *preoperational intelligence.*

As in the sensorimotor stage, imitation is a factor, but it is internal and detectable. The symbol involves accommodation, as it helps meet the demands of the environment through internal initiation that modifies behavior. The child moves to a new level where it is able to evoke past objects and words. Mental symbols may be visual images, familiar sounds, or even bodily sensations; however, they are not as detailed as the actual object. The images, Piaget believed, may be conscious or unconscious, but affect behavior. The capacity to form mental images is essential to the development of mature object constancy.

Piaget also developed a set of terms to be used in this developmental stage. For the semiotic function, he used the terms *signifiers* and *signified*. *Signifiers* are the words, objects, visual images, or events (mental symbols) that represent something else to the individual. Some mental symbols may be personal and idiosyncratic and therefore not transmittable to another. When the signifier is a *sign*, such as a word or a picture, it can convey information to others. Other symbols may be concrete rather than mental, as when the child uses one object to represent another.

The *signified* is what the symbol or word stands for. It is not a real object but represents the child's intellectual construction of the real. It is knowledge of the object, not the object itself. It can be perceived as good or bad. For example, a child's experience riding a bicycle may make the term *bicycle* represent something positive or negative (Ginsburg and Opper 1988:76).

Piaget felt that the stage from ages two to four is a very vulnerable period, especially with respect to language. The child, who still has a limited vocabulary, must respond to commands it may not fully understand and is unable to verbalize its own feelings and needs. These difficulties result in feelings of inadequacy, frustration, and conflict with significant others (Ginsburg and Opper 1988:78). Through symbolic play, a cathartic process, the child may act out conflictual situations so that they are resolved in its favor. Play, of course, is the "work" of children, and as the child develops between two and four it is increasingly able to plan play and to distinguish between the make-believe and real worlds. Play moves from individual to parallel to playing with others. Self-esteem grows as the child attains greater language, physical, and social skills.

As language develops, words refer not only to actual events but also to absent or imagined objects and events. Piaget believed that language at this stage is initially egocentric, conveying facts and criticisms, not explaining anything to others, with little sense of causality, and based on the assumption that others will agree. While the child from ages four to seven may show a decline in egocentric language, its awareness of others' point of view is still limited. It may also fantasize that words will accomplish what actions have not been able to do. As children interact more with other children, they will repeat what the others say in what Piaget referred to as a *collective monologue*.

Between ages two and four the child develops the capacity to reason. Initially its reasoning ability is limited to memories of what occurred in previous similar situations, with distortions that may serve its needs. Piaget called the child's later reasoning *transduction* (1954:232), a process between deduction (going from general to particular) and induction (going from particular to general). Transduction goes from one particular to another without generalization. The child sees relationships between particulars even when none exist.

Piaget's major contribution to developmental theory was a highly creative, in-depth review of the cognitive development of the child. He was probably the most important researcher to explore the sensorimotor developmental period. His observations of his three children were generalized by later psychologists. He was essentially an independent investigator who, although aware of Freud's work, branched off into his own area of interest, cognitive development, not based on Freudian concepts. While he saw developmental stages as sequential and felt that each must be gone through, he believed that in some form each stage continues into those that follow. Old phases are not destroyed by new ones but are built into the perspective of the newer ones, with biological maturation and the child's own experiences influencing cognitive development.

LIMITATIONS AND NEED FOR RESEARCH

A clear limitation of the theories presented is that they are based on research with very homogeneous populations. The studies and conclusions come from observation and analysis of white, middle-class infants and toddlers, often raised in nuclear families. Although they referred to the importance of the culture in which a child is raised, none of the theorists discussed looked at this in depth or attempted comparisons with control groups. Therefore, while their contributions, beginning with Sigmund Freud's, are integral to understanding the stages a child goes through and the optimal conditions for successful growth and development, we must be aware of the context of the child's life. We must not jump to conclusions that either the parenting or the child is "abnormal" when within the culture, the behavior observed is "normal."

Unfortunately, the literature yields no in-depth studies of the development of minority children, nor even any significant comparative studies. What there is deals with specific behavioral or task-related problems. Researchers need to consider new variables when applying existing developmental theories to other than white, middle-class children and design studies with greater concern for culture and socioeconomic status.

Developmental theories proposed by mental health professionals, especially those concerning infants and toddlers, were created in Western society and reflect its expectations. Looking at other norms for development has been the domain of anthropologists and some cross-cultural psychologists, whose empirical studies often are based on comparisons of age-related performance of tasks. Little attention has been paid to the process of development that takes place within different cultures. Theories are culture exclusive rather than inclusive. Since the majority of children in the world grow up under vastly different conditions, expectations and beliefs surrounding them may well differ from those assumed to be "normal" by European and North American theories. There is a need for "culture-inclusive" theories that recognize that culture and personality are interlocked in a reciprocal relationship (Valsiner 1989:4).

While families must function as part of a larger community of social relations, economic roles, values, and institutions, they also have their own rituals, myths, beliefs, and behavioral expectations rooted in their culture, which clearly influence development. In the theories presented here, the concept of mothering has focused on the experience of white, middle-class nuclear families, which may not be the appropriate model for some communities of other classes or colors where mothers, working or not, have fewer choices. More research is needed on mothering when a child is raised in a lesbian or gay family, focusing on what areas of assimilation and adaptation, if any, may differ from the "norm." A study by MacPhee, Fritz, and Miller-Heyl (1996) of 300 lower-class mothers, American Indian, Hispanic, and Anglo, showed that maternal self-esteem, competence, and sense of self-efficacy were crucial for all in their child-rearing efforts. More studies are needed to identify the common and the different emotional needs and qualities mothers may have in order to function well under different conditions.

As the ecosystem perspective and the need for biopsychosocial assessment have become accepted guides for understanding individuals and families, development must be viewed contextually, with culture an essential factor. The environment in which a child develops is, in part, organized culturally, so investigators need to look at how infants and toddlers, as well as older children, assimilate and accommodate to familial cultural expectations and the rest of their environment. Many clients come from Third World countries, so it behooves practitioners to understand possible differences in developmental theories and parental expectations. A study by Harwood, Schoelmerich, Ventura-Cook, Schulze, and Wilson (1996) involved a comparison of middle- and lower-class Anglo and Puerto Rican mothers of toddlers (twelve to twenty-four months old). The researchers found that the most commonly studied variable in studies of sociocultural differences in child rearing is socioeconomic status. They believe that this and culture are both important in determining parental beliefs, but that these variables must be disentangled (2447). Looking at cultural differences with regard to long-term socialization goals and child behavior, they found that Puerto Rican mothers' greatest concern was proper demeanor, that the child be respectful, obedient, and accepted by the larger community. Self-maximization, the child being self-confident, independent, and able to develop his/her talents and abilities, was the major concern of Anglo mothers. However, for both groups, proper demeanor and

self-maximization outweighed self-control, lovingness, and decency as especially desirable toddler behavior. Clearly, judging from this study, in order for
children to gain these different attributes, there must be some difference in
mothering.

Garcia-Coll (1990) believed that extant literature on the development of
minority infants was plagued with theoretical and methodological problems
caused by confounding socioeconomic background and ethnicity—two
variables that, in fact, need to be isolated (270). In addition, the limited research lacked appropriate comparison groups; assessment tools were culturally biased; observers frequently were from different ethnic backgrounds; and
cross-sectional samples, often small, involved African American and Hispanic mothers, rarely Native Americans or Asians.

While most theoretical models emphasized the multifactorial nature of
early development, Garcia-Coll urged more research on what she identified
as the five major influences on developmental outcomes for minority infants,
which operate synergistically: cultural beliefs and caregiving practices; health
status and health care practices; family structure and characteristics; socioeconomic factors; and biological factors (1990:271).

Little attention has been paid to the many children for whom the early
years are very difficult. For poor children in the United States, rates of infant
mortality and low birth weight are too high and rates of immunization too
low. More children are born into poverty; many have substandard care and
are born into single, teenage-parent, isolated homes. Race, class, and gender
are not isolated variables but are interlocked with racism and sexism, which
clearly affect the distribution of economic resources. The United States is an
immensely unequal society in terms of wealth and thus the benefits and privileges that accompany higher incomes. While children from all ethnic groups
and family structures live in poverty, the rates are higher for African American and Hispanic children under three than for white children. Families with
children under three constitute the single largest group living in poverty in
the United States; more children under three live in poverty than do older
children, adults, or the elderly (Carnegie 1994:17). These children are neglected by our society when compared with children in most other industrialized
societies. There are few defined institutions to assist and advocate for these
children before they enter preschool, and parents have trouble advocating for
them. The children cannot speak up and the parents see themselves as having
very little clout. Often a woman raising a family in poverty will be depressed,
which clearly affects her ability to mother.

The risk factors for the 12 million American children under the age of three are enormous. Twenty-five percent live in poverty, 25 percent are in single-parent homes, 33 percent of those under age one are victims of physical abuse, and over 50 percent of mothers of children under three work out of the home (Carnegie 1994:xiii). It is well known that adverse prenatal and postnatal environmental conditions, including poor nutrition, environmental toxins, premature birth, chronic illness, and central nervous system injuries, can affect child development in ways that may compromise brain functioning, leading to cognitive, physical, and behavioral problems, some of which may be irreversible. A study by Pollitt (1994) showed that iron-deficiency anemia is a major public health problem. Twenty to 24 percent of poor African American and Hispanic children have this disease, which can result in poor performance in mental and motor tests (283). Impoverished minority children have less frequent contact with medical professionals than middle-class white children and often are sent to school with respiratory, ear, or gastrointestinal problems if their mothers lack medical information or have to go to work with no available child care. In addition, children living in poverty may suffer from malnutrition.

While children under three are of major concern because of the importance of a good foundation for physical and mental development, they may be less visible since they are too young for most well-supervised government programs such as Head Start. A new study released by the National Center for Children in Poverty has shown that children under six remain the poorest age cohort in the United States. The percentage of poor children with working parents has increased significantly since the last survey eight years ago. In 1993, 54 percent of poor children lived in families where at least one parent worked; the percentage in 1998 was 63 percent. While the changes in laws have removed many children from the welfare roles, poorly paying jobs mean that 17 percent of children living with a single mother who works are still living in poverty. Children living with unmarried mothers are five times more likely to be poor than those with married parents. The poverty rate for Hispanic children under six rose 54 percent between 1993 and 1998, compared with 30 percent for white children and 15 percent for African American children. This study supports the need for policy examination and change, as it concludes that the rate of children living in poverty would have been 23 percent higher without the earned-income tax credit (Lewin 1998:19).

For middle- and upper-class women the choice of staying home and fulfilling the role of mother used to be the norm. Since the mid-1970s, when a second income became desirable, if not necessary, and women, influenced by the feminist movement, elected to pursue careers for personal growth and identity, there was a significant decrease in women as primary caregivers. In 1997, 63 percent of married women with preschool-age children worked outside of the home, five times as many as in 1950 (Cherline 1998:39). Most of them see their main concern as locating good child care.

The government must be responsible for protecting all children, but especially those viewed as at risk. Prevention is essential but often not reimbursable. Health and nutritional education, as well as early intervention programs, would in the long term be cost-effective. Quality child care in the early years is essential, and programs similar to Head Start are needed for younger children.

Child care workers need to have training and some form of accountability. The quality of child care varies tremendously according to income. Only 5 percent of preschool-age children of working mothers are cared for in their home by a nanny or an au pair. Nannies receive salaries ranging from $250 to $800 per week plus benefits; an au pair, usually in the United States for a year on an exchange program, receives about $150 per week plus room and board. Twenty-five percent of all children of working mothers and 60 percent of those from poor families are cared for, often for a fee, by a nonparental relative. Twenty-nine percent of working mothers send their preschool children to day care centers and 15 percent of those children are in family day care, which for the most part is not regulated (Cherline 1998:41). A review of center-based infant and toddler care showed that while most states require centers to follow guidelines, 67 percent of the states received overall day care center ratings of poor to very poor, indicating that children are being cared for in environments that do not meet basic standards. No state received a good or optimal rating. The review also showed that state standards for child care training were unacceptable in almost all states. Thus, these children are spending most of their waking hours in environments that do not meet basic standards to assure safe and healthy early childhood development (Young, Masland, and Zigler 1997:535).

In addition to better child care facilities, parents need more flexible work schedules to allow more involvement by both parents, and maternal leave needs to be extended from twelve weeks to possibly six months; parenting education needs to be readily available; and education on human sexuality, pregnancy, and parenthood must begin as early as elementary school. A United Nations study found that the United States is one of the few countries in the world without a national paid maternity leave policy, whereas most

Western European countries have a child allowance regardless of income and employment status (Cherline 1998:41).

Thus, while it is important to understand the evolution of developmental theories, mental health professionals need to put them in perspective. More research is needed to examine the developmental stages and expectations for children from diverse backgrounds. Looking at the effects of different ways of interacting, beliefs, and expectations on the process of development should identify alternative or different "normal" developmental patterns and enable better understanding of what may now be viewed as deficits in order to provide needed accommodation and education.

Services for children are very fragmented and could be improved by a return to the ideals of the settlement house movement, which enabled parents and children to find out about and obtain resources. We have senior citizen centers; perhaps it is time to establish centers for those at the opposite end of the age spectrum. Resources and services for parents of children at risk need to be clustered and linked in order to be effective. To ensure healthy development, our society must provide easy access to medical care, housing that is not substandard, neighborhoods that are not segregated in ways that promote fear and potential for antisocial behavior, and employment that offers a living wage. Without these changes, many children will grow up in poor health, with their civil rights violated through prejudice and discrimination, and ultimately a poor self-image.

CONCLUSION

Infancy and toddlerhood are the most important phases of development, for it is during these early years that a child makes enormous strides, physically and emotionally. A good, loving, consistent, safe environment will make a major contribution to the foundation for successful mastering of later developmental stages.

Although challenged and modified by later theorists, Sigmund Freud was the groundbreaker in establishing that individuals pass through a succession of developmental stages. As seen in this chapter, later theorists extended and refined his thinking while continuing to accept that a sequence in development does exist. Although they differ on the later effects of not successfully negotiating a stage "on time," all clearly accept that the attainment of "normal" developmental milestones has a lasting effect. The theories presented provide a way to organize observations of early childhood behavior in order to plan intervention, if necessary, and to predict future behavior and adaptation.

As the theories have become more sophisticated, researchers have acknowledged that developmental guidelines help to show if a child is progressing and developing normally and have begun to recognize the importance of the child's environment. They are also increasingly aware that differences in physical maturation cause some variation in when and how tasks are mastered.

Neubauer and Neubauer (1990), in their book, *Nature's Thumbprint*, address the issue of "nature versus nurture." They recognize that the effects of our genetic make-up may be somewhat elusive, although our knowledge is rapidly expanding. This must be considered in assessing the development of an individual. Clearly there are some genetic diseases, such as sickle cell anemia, whose effects are well known; with greater knowledge, more subtle effects of genes will be identified. The Neubauers' study of identical twins reared separately showed the effects of heredity, as the timing and patterns of development and maturation were very similar even in different environments. Their observations, together with knowledge of different cultural beliefs and expectations, support the current thinking that both nature *and* nurture affect development.

In conclusion, knowledge of developmental norms is an essential part of assessment, especially of infants and toddlers. If a developmental assessment suggests deficits or other areas of concern that may need intervention, the mental health professional must look carefully and objectively at the child, the parents and their needs, and the environment in which the child is being raised. Early intervention programs can prevent and resolve problems that might in the future become more difficult to handle.

Although the current treatment restrictions of managed care may not allow for it, mental health professionals have a history of psychoanalytically oriented, or psychodynamic, exploration over an extended period of time that seeks to elicit history useful in understanding current problems. From the post–World War II era until the 1960s, taking history was a major part of the therapeutic process, with many sessions devoted only to it. Gradually, as short-term interventions have become more sought out and often mandated, history taking is more limited to what is felt to be relevant to the presenting problem. It is hoped that in the future a middle ground can be reached so that too little history will not result in overlooking important areas needing intervention. Developmental information, culturally based, often presents clues to what is problematic in later life.

BIBLIOGRAPHY

Andersen, M. L. and P. H. Collins. 1992. *Race, Class, and Gender: An Anthology*. Belmont, CA: Wadsworth.

Apgar, V. 1958. "The Apgar Scoring Chart." *Journal of the American Medical Association* 32:168.

Applegate, J. 1989. "Mahler and Stern: Irreconcilable Differences?" *Child and Adolescent Social Work* 6:163–73.

Austrian, S. G. 1995. *Mental Disorders, Medications, and Clinical Social Work*. New York: Columbia University Press.

Berzoff, J., L. M. Flanagan, and P. Hertz. 1996. *Inside Out and Outside In*. Northvale: Jason Aronson.

Brenner, C. 1973. *An Elementary Textbook of Psychoanalysis*. New York: Doubleday.

Call, J. D., E. Galenson, and R. L. Tyson, eds. 1983. *Frontiers of Infant Psychiatry*. 2 vols. New York: Basic.

Carnegie Corporation of New York. 1994. *Starting Points*. New York: Carnegie Corporation of New York.

Cherline, A. J. 1998. "By the Numbers." *New York Times Magazine* (April 5): 39–41.

Chodorow, N. J. 1978. *The Reproduction of Mothering*. Berkeley: University of California Press.

——. 1994. *Femininities, Masculinities, Sexualities: Freud and Beyond*, Lexington: University Press of Kentucky.

——. 1996. "Theoretical Gender and Clinical Gender." *Journal of the Americal Psychological Association* 44 (supplement): 215–38.

Crockenberg, S., K. Lyons-Ruth, and S. Dickstein. 1993. "The Family Context of Infant Mental Health II. Infant Development in Multiple Family Relationships." In C. H. Zeanah, ed., *Handbook of Infant Mental Health*, 38–55. New York: Guilford.

Elise, D. 1991. "An Analysis of Gender Differences in Separation-Individual." *The Psychoanalytic Study of the Child*, 46:51–67. New York: International Universities Press.

Erikson, E. H. 1959. "Identity and the Life Cycle." In *Psychological Issues*, I (I): 50–100. New York: International Universities Press.

——. 1977. *Toys and Reasons*. New York: Norton.

——. 1993. *Childhood and Society*, 2nd ed. New York: Norton.

Freud, A. 1963. "The Concept of Developmental Lines." *The Psychoanalytic Study of the Child*, 18:243–65. New York: International Universities Press.

——. 1965. *Normality and Pathology in Childhood*. New York: International Universities Press.

——. 1966. *The Ego and the Mechanisms of Defense*. Rev. ed. New York: International Universities Press.

——. 1989. "Child Analysis as the Study of Mental Growth (Normal and Abnormal)." In S. I. Greenspan and G. H. Pollock, eds., *The Course of Life. Vol. I*. Madison, WI: International Universities Press.

Freud, S. 1905. "Three Essays on the Theory of Sexuality." *The Standard Edition*, vol. 7. London: Hogarth, 1953.

——. 1923. "The Ego and the Id." *The Standard Edition*, vol. 19. London: Hogarth, 1961.

Freud, W. E. 1967. "Assessment of Early Infancy." *The Psychoanalytic Study of the Child*, 22:216–39. New York: International Universities Press.

——. 1971. "The Baby Profile Part II." *The Psychoanalytic Study of the Child* 26:172–95. New York: Quadrangle Books.

Friedman, S. L. and H. C. Haywood. 1994. *Developmental Follow-Up*. San Diego: Academic Press.

Garcia-Coll, C. T. 1990. "Developmental Outcome of Minority Infants: A Process-Oriented Look Into Our Beginnings." *Child Development* 61:270–89.

Garcia-Coll, C. T. and E. C. Meyer. 1993. "The Sociocultural Context of Infant Development." In C. H. Zeanah, ed., *Handbook of Infant Mental Health*, 56–69. New York: Guilford.

Gemelli, R. 1996. *Normal Child and Adolescent Development*. Washington, DC: American Psychiatric Press.

Ginsburg, H. P. and S. Opper. 1988. *Piaget's Theory of Intellectual Development*. Englewood Cliffs, NJ: Prentice Hall.

Goldstein, E. 1995. *Ego Psychology and Social Work Practice*. 2nd ed. New York: Free Press.

Greene, R. R. 1991. "Eriksonian Theory: A Developmental Approach to Ego Mastery." In R. R. Greene and P. H. Ephross, eds., *Human Behavior Theory and Social Work Practice*, 79–104. New York: Aldine DeGruyter.

Greene, R. R. and P. H. Ephross. 1991. *Human Behavior Theory and Social Work Practice*. New York: Aldine DeGruyter.

Greenspan, S. I. and G. H. Pollack, eds. 1989. *The Course of Life*. Madison, WI: International Universities Press.

Halpern, R. 1993. "Poverty and Infant Development." In C. H. Zeanah, ed., *Handbook of Infant Mental Health*, 73–86. New York: Guilford.

Hartmann, H. 1939. *Ego Psychology and the Problem of Adaptation*. New York: International Universities Press/

——. 1950. "Comments on the Psychoanalytic Theory of the Ego." In H. Hartmann, *Essays on Ego Psychology*. New York: International Universities Press, 1964.

———. 1952. "The Mutual Influences in the Development of the Ego and the Id." *The Psychoanalytic Study of the Child,* 7:9–30. New York: International Universities Press.

Harwood, R. L., A. Schoelmerich, E. Ventura-Cook, P. A. Schulze, and S. P. Wilson. 1996. "Culture and Class Influences on Anglo and Puerto Rican Mothers' Beliefs Regarding Long-Term Socialization Goals and Child Behavior." *Child Development* 67:2446–61.

Kagan, J., D. Arcus, N. Snidman, W. Y. Feeng, J. Hendler, and S. Greene. 1994. "Reactivity in Infants: A Cross-National Comparison." *Developmental Psychology* 30:342–45.

Kohut, H. 1971. *The Analysis of the Self.* New York: International University Press.

———. 1977. *The Restoration of the Self.* New York: International Universities Press.

Lamb, M. E. 1984. "Mothers, Fathers, and Child Care in a Changing World." In J. D. Call, E. Galenson, and R. L. Tyson, eds., *Frontiers of Infant Psychiatry,* 2:343–62. New York: Basic.

Lamb, M. E., A. Nash, D. M. Telt, and M. H. Bornstein. 1996. "Infancy." In M. Lewis, ed., *Child and Adolescent Psychiatry.* Baltimore: Williams and Wilkins.

Lewin, T. 1998. "Study Finds That Youngest U.S. Children Are Poorest." *The New York Times,* March 15, 19.

Lyons-Ruth, K. and C. H. Zeanah. 1993. "The Family Context of Infant Mental Health: I. Affective Development in the Primary Caregiving Relationship." In C. H. Zeanah, ed., *Handbook of Infant Mental Health,* 14–37. New York: Guilford.

MacPhee, D., J. Fritz, and J. Miller-Heyl. 1996. "Ethnic Variations in Personal Social Networks and Parenting." *Child Development* 67:3278–95.

Mahler, M. S. 1972a. "On the First Subphases of the Separation-Individuation Process." *International Journal of Psychoanalysis* 53:333–38.

———. 1972b. "Rapprochement Subphase of the Separation-Individuation Process." *Psychoanalytic Quarterly* XLI (4): 487–507.

———. 1979. *The Selected Papers of Margaret S. Mahler, M.D.* Vol. II. New York: Jason Aronson.

Mahler, M. S. and J. B. McDevitt. 1989. "The Separation-Individuation Process and Identity Formation." In S. I. Greenspan and G. H. Pollock, eds., *The Course of Life,* 2:19–36. Madison, WI: International Universities Press.

Mahler, M. S., F. Pine, and A. Bergmann. 1975. *The Psychological Birth of the Human Infant.* New York: Basic.

McDevitt, J. B. and M. S. Mahler. 1989. "Object Constancy, Individuality, and Internalization." In S. I. Greenspan and G. H. Pollock, eds., *The Course of Life,* 2:37–60. Madison, WI: International Universities Press.

Meyer, C. H. 1993. *Assessment.* New York: Columbia University Press.

Monte, C. F. 1980. *Beneath the Mask*. 2nd ed. New York: Holt, Rinehart and Winston.

Neubauer, P. B. and A. Neubauer. 1990. *Nature's Thumbprint*. Reading, MA: Addison-Wesley.

Piaget, J. 1952. *The Origin of Intelligence in Children*. 2nd ed. New York: International Universities Press.

——. 1954. *The Construction of Reality in the Child*. New York: Basic.

Piaget, J. and B. Inhelder. 1969. *The Psychology of the Child*. New York: Basic.

Pollitt, E. 1994. "Poverty and Child Development: Relevance of Research in Developing Countries to the United States." *Child Development* 65:283–95.

Rogoff, B. and P. Chavajay. 1995. "What's Become of Research on the Cultural Basis of Cognitive Development?" *American Psychologist* 50:859–77.

Sameroff, A. J. 1993. "Models of Development and Developmental Risk." In C. H. Zeanah, ed., *Handbook of Infant Mental Health*, 3–13. New York: Guilford.

Shapiro, T. and D. Stern. 1989. "Psychoanalytic Perspective on the First Year of Life: The Establishment of the Object in an Affective Field." In S. J. Greenspan and G. H. Pollock, eds., *The Course of Life*, I:271–92. Madison, WI: International Universities Press.

Shaw, D. S., K. Keenan, and J. L. Vondra. 1994. "Developmental Precursors of Externalizing Behavior: Ages 1 to 2." *Developmental Psychology* 30:3555–64.

Sherman, A. 1994. *Wasting America's Future. The Children's Defense Fund Report on the Costs of Child Poverty*. Boston: Beacon.

Stern, D. N. 1985. *The Interpersonal World of the Infant*. New York: Basic.

——. 1990. *Diary of a Baby*. New York: Basic.

Sullivan, H. S. 1953. *The Interpersonal Theory of Psychiatry*. New York: Norton.

Turner, P. J. and J. Gervai. 1995. "Multidimensional Study of Gender Typing in Preschool Children and Their Parents: Personality, Attitudes, Preferences, Behavior, and Cultural Differences." *Developmental Psychology* 31:759–64.

Valsiner, J. 1989. *Child Development in Cultural Context*. Toronto: Hogrefe and Huber.

Weinberg, L. 1991. "Infant Development and the Sense of Self: Stern vs. Mahler." *Clinical Social Work* 19:9–22.

White, R. W. 1959. "Motivation Reconsidered: The Concept of Competence." *Psychological Review* 66:297–333.

——. 1963. "Ego and Reality in Psychoanalytic Theory." *Psychological Issues* II (3).

Young, T. Y., K. W. Masland, and E. Zigler. 1997. "The Regulatory Status of Center-Based Infant and Toddler Child Care." *American Journal of Orthopsychiatry* 67:535–44.

Zeanah, C. H., ed. 1993. *Handbook of Infant Mental Health*. New York: Guilford.

NANCY F. CINCOTTA

one two **three** four five six

THE JOURNEY OF MIDDLE CHILDHOOD: WHO ARE "LATENCY"-AGE CHILDREN?

INTRODUCTION

Children from approximately age five through age twelve, or to the beginning of puberty, are considered to be in "middle childhood." This stage encompasses the years typically thought of and remembered as childhood, a time of carefree activities, with simultaneous overwhelming cognitive growth. The naiveté of infants and toddlers gives way to the inquisitive nature of children who seek, beyond the repetitive "why" question, to learn in more detail who, what, where, when, and how.

Although still deeply rooted within their families, children begin to think more autonomously, assert their independence, and form bonds with their peers and teachers that begin to influence their thinking, behavior, and dreams. While testing their newfound knowledge, strength, and capacities, they emerge as unique individuals. They are in the process of establishing themselves, a journey that can last a lifetime.

The infant, toddler, and preschool years are filled with rapid growth. Physical and emotional growth occur more gradually in middle childhood. As in other transitions, children make the shift from early to middle childhood with some variability. They separate from adult caretakers with differing degrees of ease and adapt to new environments, master skills, and take on new challenges in different ways.

Children in this age group are viewed in distinct ways, depending on the cultural or societal context. In some cultures, there is an expectation that children can endure work according to their physical strength. In tribal communities, they are expected to master tasks of survival such as hunting, confirming their maturity. In agricultural societies, they are often working in the fields as the youngest component of the labor force.

The Random House dictionary defines *latency* as: "1. [psychoanalytic] The stage of personality development, extending from about four or five years of age to the beginning of puberty, during which sexual urges lie dormant. 2. [pathologic] The interval between exposure to a carcinogen, toxin or disease causing organism and development of a consequent disease. 3. [physiologic] The interval between stimulus and reaction." (*Random House Unabridged Dictionary* 1993). It is a misnomer to characterize this stage in development as latent, by any definition; this diminishes the cognitive, social, and emotional advances of this period.

The years from age five through twelve are in fact middle years, between ages that have been well defined and categorized, but far from dormant. At a glance, the child's capability at age five bears limited resemblance to the child's capability at age twelve. This is a period in which the toddler-turned-preschooler develops the knowledge and skills that will serve as the foundation for subsequent cognitive, emotional, and social growth. Each child will establish individual strengths that will serve as the precursors to adult development and relationships and lead him or her into adolescence.

Children experience periods of imbalance during middle childhood. There are universal changes such as those in child care arrangements, with attendant challenges to attachment, and transitions to school, initially to kindergarten and later from elementary school into junior high school, as well as individual crises that may occur such as divorce, death, or illness. For some children these events can present difficulty, whereas for others they can serve as stimuli for growth.

Poverty influences middle childhood in many ways. Children may not be able to be carefree if they are compelled to take on more responsibility because parents or caregivers are overwhelmed by excessive work, insufficient pay, or unemployment. Children may be forced to be alone at earlier ages and for longer periods. School achievement or even attendance may not be a priority if the family system is so stressed that food and housing are dominant concerns. If children live in chaotic family environments during a stage in which they are learning "the rules," they may have difficulty integrating emotional and intellectual gains into their lives.

Children often are hurried through middle childhood, directly and indirectly, by exposure to sex and violence, particularly on television and in video games; by having to travel alone at younger ages; by unmonitored access to the Internet; and even by experiences with drugs and alcohol. A recent study of third and fourth graders (Robinson, Wilde, Navracruz, Haydel, and Varady 2001), based on the well-documented premise that exposure to violence in the media and children's aggressive behavior are related, sought to assess the effects of reducing television and video game use on "perceptions of a mean and scary world." The children in the intervention group (an eighteen-session, six-month curriculum) had statistically significant decreases in peer ratings of aggression, as well as observed differences and parental reports of changed behavior.

Children once dressed exclusively in play clothes that accommodated their higher levels of physical activity, propensity toward outdoor play, and use of expressive art materials. Today, they often wear expensive designer clothes and footwear, miniature adult apparel, including items that may be sexually provocative. Children have increasing independence, knowledge, and access to knowledge. They are being encouraged, and often pressured, to read at younger ages, although there is no clear correlation with future academic achievement or performance (Mills and Jackson 1990). There are more full-day than half-day kindergarten programs than ever before, and after-school programs for this age group are popular. For an estimated one million children in the United States, home schooling has become an alternative (Lines 1998).

David Elkind (1988, 1997) has warned against pushing children too fast in an age-inappropriate manner. Latency-age children bear much of the burden of a faster-paced society. Adults are spending more time at work than ever before; children are shuffled between activities in part due to their parents' schedules. Children's time outside of school has become more structured; they participate in extracurricular pursuits at earlier ages. Doing nothing, as in "those lazy, hazy days of summer," previously part of the culture of a child, is no longer promoted or valued. Some children no longer just go out to play, they have "play dates." They are infrequently left free to explore what they would do if there were nothing to do. There is no time for daydreaming. Television and computers have replaced quieter moments. Rarely do you hear a child say, "Turn off the television. I want to read now."

In this speeded-up society, adults are resigned to Elkind's concerns; there is no turning back for today's children. Parents may rationalize and say it is a good learning experience for an eight-year-old to be home alone. However, Pettit and colleagues (Pettit, Laird, Bates, and Dodge 1997) found that more hours of self-care during the early school-age years correlated with poorer behavioral adjustment and academic performance. Elkind's recommendation is that given the stress imposed on them, children should be taught skills to help them cope effectively with what is expected of them. For example, the "latchkey" child should be offered assistance such as phone numbers for reaching a parent, the police, and a neighbor, and instructions on what to do in case of fire.

Rituals and routines are important components in the structure of the middle childhood years. As children begin to organize and classify their knowledge, they come to depend on routines to help them consciously and unconsciously deal with new issues and experiences. Birthdays, secular and religious rituals, and common developmental milestones all help them to find their place in the world. They are seeking to be connected to the larger society through attachments in school, with their peers, with their teachers, in social activities, and in their families.

The entire course of middle childhood could be called "the collecting years," because children develop interests in accumulating cards, rocks, dolls, stuffed animals, and other items of worth to them. With collecting comes organizing and categorizing. This makes sense, given these children's newly acquired conceptual skills and their emerging sensitivity to how things are structured.

PHYSICAL DEVELOPMENT

Physical and emotional growth parallel each other; some children develop more quickly and some at a slower pace. Compared to infancy and the toddler years, physical growth is more gradual during middle childhood. In general, children appear thinner than they did as preschoolers. Their "baby belly" pares down to a more streamlined look. They grow approximately 2 to 2.5 inches per year and double in weight from 40 pounds to about 80 pounds, gaining approximately 4.5 to 6 pounds each year.

These biological changes enable a greater sense of capacity, strength, endurance, and ability. Children are able to master certain tasks, such as riding a bicycle, as they are strong enough to push their weight, tall enough to reach the pedals, and coordinated enough to maintain their balance. Ultimately their cognitive capabilities allow them to develop a sense of direction and safety, so they can use the bike to extend their freedom. This increased mobility results in enhanced autonomy and self-esteem.

Latency-age children are not dependent on caretakers for their toileting needs, although they may require help at times. Bedwetting is not an uncommon problem at this stage. Nighttime enuresis is known to cluster in families and is found in 15 percent of five-year-olds and 10 percent of six-year-olds, falling in prevalence by about 15 percent a year after that. Although at one time thought to be a psychological problem, enuresis is more often linked to immature bladder development or hormonal imbalance. Pharmacological and behavioral treatments have the best effects. The majority of cases of bedwetting in which there are no associated medical problems resolve spontaneously.

In the United States, there has been a disturbing and striking trend over the last fifteen years. The average weight for school-age children has increased, as time spent indoors watching television outweighs time spent in outdoor play and fast food has become a staple of the American diet (see table 1).

The end of middle childhood is usually accompanied by a growth spurt, marking the onset of puberty. Although there are heritable factors, pubertal changes appear to be influenced by environmental determinants as well. Development of breasts and growth of pubic hair is occurring earlier in American girls, especially in African Americans. In a 1997 study, Herman-Giddens and colleagues found that the mean ages for breast development in white and African American girls were 9.96 and 8.87 years, and for pubic hair development, 10.51 and 8.78 years, respectively. These milestones are being achieved approximately one year earlier than at the last turn of the century for white girls and two years earlier for African American girls (Herman-Giddens et al. 1997). The age of onset of menstruation has decreased steadily in industrialized countries over the last century, but has not shown the same recent changes as the other pubertal characteristics. Nonetheless, the average age of menarche in the United States is now 12.8 years, compared to approximately 14 years a century ago (Bullough 1981). Environmental factors implicated in the timing of sexual maturation include level of physical activity, nutrition, and stress.

American society is focused on appearance, particularly height and weight. Children are constantly bombarded by media representations of an ideal physique, which has become thinner and thinner over time. Eating disorders are increasingly common, with origins possibly in middle childhood.

TABLE 1. Overweight children and adolescents 6–17 years of age, according to sex, age, race, and Hispanic origin: United States, selected years 1963–65 through 1988–94

[Data are based on physical examinations of a sample of the civilian noninstitutionalized population]

AGE, SEX, RACE, AND HISPANIC ORIGIN[1]	1963–65 1966–70[2]	1971–74	1976–80[3]	1988–94[4]
6–11 years of age, age adjusted		Percent of population		
Both sexes	5.0	5.5	7.6	13.6
Boys	4.9	6.5	8.11	4.7
White	5.4	6.6	8.1	14.6
Black	1.7	5.6	8.6	15.1
White, non-Hispanic	—	—	7.4	13.1
Black, non-Hispanic	—	—	8.6	14.7
Mexican	—	—	14.5	18.8
Girls	5.2	4.4	7.1	12.6
White	5.1	4.4	6.5	11.7
Black	5.3	4.5	11.5	17.4
White, non-Hispanic	—	—	6.2	11.9
Black, non-Hispanic	—	—	11.6	17.7
Mexican	—	—	10.7	15.8
12–17 years of age, age adjusted				
Both sexes	5.0	6.2	5.6	11.4
Boys	5.0	5.3	5.3	12.4
White	5.2	5.5	5.3	13.1
Black	3.6	4.4	6.0	12.1
White, non-Hispanic	—	—	4.5	11.8
Black, non-Hispanic	—	—	6.1	12.5
Mexican	—	—	7.7	14.8
Girls[5]	5.0	7.2	6.0	10.5
White	4.8	6.6	5.4	10.0
Black	6.4	10.5	10.2	16.1
White, non-Hispanic	—	—	5.4	9.3
Black, non-Hispanic	—	—	10.5	16.0
Mexican	—	—	9.3	14.1
Totals by sex				
Boys				
6–8 years	5.1	6.3	8.1	15.4
9–11 years	4.8	6.7	8.1	14.0
12–14 years	5.2	5.4	5.4	11.5
15–17 years	4.8	5.2	5.1	13.1
Girls[5]				
6–8 years	5.1	4.1	7.1	14.6
9–11 years	5.2	4.7	7.1	10.8
12–14 years	5.0	8.6	7.8	13.9
15–17 years	4.9	6.0	4.5	7.5

TABLE 1. (continued)

— Data not available.

[1]The race groups, white and black, include persons of Hispanic and non-Hispanic origin. Conversely, persons of Hispanic origin may be of any race.
[2]Data for children 6–11 years of age are for 1963–65; data for adolescents 12–17 years of age are for 1966–70.
[3]Data for Mexicans are for 1982–84.
[4]Excludes one non-Hispanic white adolescent boy age 12–14 years with an outlier sample weight.
[5]Excludes pregnant women starting with 1971–74. Pregnancy status not available for 1963–65/1966–70.

NOTES: Overweight is defined as body mass index (BMI) at or above the sex- and age-specific 95th percentile BMI cutoff points calculated at 6-month age intervals for children 6–11 years of age from the 1963–65 National Health Examination Survey (NHES) and for adolescents 12–17 years of age from the 1966–70 NHES. Age is at time of examination at mobile examination center. Some data for 1988–94 have been revised and differ from the previous edition of Health, United States.

SOURCE: Centers for Disease Control and Prevention, National Center for Health Statistics, Division of Health Examination Statistics. Unpublished data. 284 Health, United States 1998 (Source document: http://www.cdc.gov/nchswww/sata/hus98.pdf)

There are also societal biases regarding height, so much so that synthetic growth hormone is sometimes used to allow undersized but otherwise normal children to attain average adult heights.

TOOTH LOSS AS A METAPHOR FOR EMOTIONAL GROWTH

The entire process of tooth loss occurs within the years of middle childhood. At approximately six years of age, children begin to lose their deciduous teeth (also known as baby or milk teeth), a process that culminates in the growth of adult teeth. This symbol of change has been of great significance throughout time and across cultures. According to Townend (1963), in primitive societies, methods of disposal of the first deciduous tooth included throwing it to the sun, into a fire, between the legs, or onto or over the roof of the house; offering it to a mouse, often at a hole near the hearth; burying it; hiding it away from animals; placing it in a tree or wall; and swallowing it (by the mother, child, or animal). The action is often accompanied by some sort of incantation. Wells (1991) points out that it is not the variety of customs that is so remarkable but the fact that different cultures feel so strongly about the loss of a tooth that they do something about it.

Tooth loss and regrowth can be viewed as a metaphor that weaves through middle childhood. The entire process, from the tooth loosening until it actually falls out, is most unusual. It is initially difficult to imagine part of the human body becoming so fragile that it ultimately disconnects itself. Children will very likely have parted with hair and certainly with nails by the time they lose their first tooth, but deliberately, as part of normal grooming and self care. Teeth are the only part of the anatomy designed to fall out naturally and then grow back. Once the tooth is out, the lure is not over. Loss of a tooth can be viewed as a rite of passage, as outlined by van Gennep (1960) in three stages: separation—tooth loss; transition—the gap left behind; incorporation—appearance of the replacement tooth. Wells (1991) refers to the loss of the tooth as symbolic of middle childhood: the separation from parents on school entry, the transition to school, and the incorporation into a community of peers.

A child's appearance with missing teeth, and then with teeth seemingly too big for the mouth, are constant reminders that the body and mind are in transition. Class pictures of six- and seven-year-olds are typified by missing front teeth. Very early in middle childhood, children begin to be vain and self-conscious about their teeth, eyeing them in the mirror, comparing theirs to others.' Unlike other changes that are either hidden, not yet occurring, or not open for discussion during these years, teeth and their loss are visible and apparent to the child and everyone else.

Regardless of when a tooth falls out or how or when it grows back, younger children often cannot wait until they lose their first tooth. But there is no control over the process. At an age when appearance begins to hold more importance, losing a tooth or waiting for a new tooth to come in can affect a child's self-image adversely. However, because this milestone is universal, its impact is minimized.

The trauma of tooth loss may be assuaged by its replacement with money or a gift given by the "tooth fairy." This is a uniquely American phenomenon. The tooth fairy, like other fairies, conjures up visions of all that is good. If you place the tooth under your pillow at night, you will be rewarded with money or a toy. In Europe the tooth is left for, and claimed by, a mouse that leaves behind nothing but the assurance that another tooth will replace it.

Inherent in this process is the embodiment of the future as new, stronger teeth emerge. Later in life, problems with teeth represent aging, the body's decline, in contrast to the direct association with growth during the latency period. Throughout life, teeth remain something that connects adults to their early development—in their loss, in their symbolism, and in the memories provoked each time they see a child from this age period with missing teeth.

Peer Relationships During Middle Childhood

A five-year-old notices his friend has fallen off his bicycle. The bike is broken. The friend sits with him, and soon both children are crying. When an adult comes over to see what's going on, the child immediately says, "I am here to help my friend." "Do you know how to fix his bike?" the parent asks. " No, I am helping him cry!"

The transition to kindergarten brings about significant shifts in the composition of children's peer networks. Prosocial behavior, such as cooperative play, has been noted to facilitate peer relationships and successful transitions to school (Ladd and Price 1987). As middle childhood progresses, children spend more and more time with peers, usually in same-sex gatherings (Maccoby 1990). Close friendships between boys and girls in middle childhood are uncommon and may be hidden in acquiescence to peer pressure. The character of play differs, boys tending to play in larger groups and in more structured games. It is estimated that between the ages of seven and eleven, 40 percent of a child's time is spent interacting with peers (Hartup 1983).

As opposed to adult-child relationships, peers interact roughly as equals and resolve conflicts through negotiation. Sullivan notes,

> If you look very closely at one of your children when he finally finds a chum—sometime between eight and a half and ten—you will discover something very different in the relationship—namely, that your child begins to develop a real sensitivity to what matters to another person. Preadolescence is marked by the coming of the integrating tendencies which, when they are completely developed, we call love, or, to say it another way, by the manifestation of the need for interpersonal intimacy. (Sullivan 1953:245–46)

Children's concepts of friendship develop throughout this period. The youngest children tend to focus on sharing and on proximity and familiarity, selecting friends who live in the same neighborhood and do the same activities. Older children are more concerned with removing inequalities among friends and cooperating, and are beginning to take into account internal qualities they admire in selecting friends. Preadolescents find equality in personalities and relationships and discuss friendship as it relates to empathy and sharing of intimate thoughts. In general, the process of friendship moves from an external focus to an emphasis on internal characteristics (Bigelow 1977; Youniss 1980).

It should not be surprising that peer relationships are influenced by the nature of relationships with parents and siblings. French and Underwood cite evidence that childhood peer interactions are influenced in part by the character of parent-child connection during infancy. Competent social relations may be fostered by parents' warmth, moderation of control, sensitivity, and democratic child-rearing practices (French and Underwood 1996).

Relationships in these earlier years are often activity focused. In one of a series of articles on "gender equity" in a lower school program, a teacher tells of a game called "Chase" that was often played during outdoor activity time. Typically what occurred during Chase was that the boys chased the girls. The teacher chose to have a class meeting, clearly wanting to change the stereotypical postures of aggressor and victim in the game. She explained that she felt that it was unfair for teams to be based on inherent physical characteristics, that a girl had to be chased just because she had been born a girl. The children were able to identify with having been treated unfairly. They reconfigured the game themselves and chose teams without regard to gender. However, after a winter indoors during which the children had formed (nonexclusionary) clubs, the game began anew, again along gender lines. The children explained that the members of the boys' "X-Men Club" were playing against members of the girls' "Polly Pocket Club"; the marketing tactics of the toy industry had confounded the teacher's earlier efforts. After another class meeting, the children's consciousness was raised and the game was again reorganized in a gender-balanced fashion. The children were quite content with being either the chaser or the "chasee" (Manhattan Country School 1998).

According to Ladd, problems with peer relations may be considered severe when they: (1) deviate substantially from age norms, as when a child has fewer playmates than most children his or her age; (2) appear chronic rather than acute, as when a child is rejected by classmates year after year; (3) appear overly frequent or intense, as when a child generalizes the use of aggressive behaviors to many situations or exhibits violent outbursts; and (4) have a major effect on the child's self-perceptions and emotional well-being, as when a child's lack of friends appears to precipitate low self-confidence or depression (Ladd 1988).

During middle childhood, participation in team sports and clubs becomes common. Scout troops, school clubs, church groups, and other organized gatherings provide opportunities for children to explore and expand skills, build relationships, take on greater responsibility, and further develop their sense of community. This is a time when teachers, scout masters, tutors, family members, and friends emerge as mentors and companions. It is also a time of interest in "superheroes" who must repeatedly confront good and evil.

SECRETS

The concept of the secret underscores the changes occurring in middle childhood. Before children can differentiate themselves from parents, the concept is a moot point. Younger children believe that others automatically know what they know, and assume that they know what others know. Thus there is no need for secrets. As children become able to differentiate themselves from their parents and have a separate reality, many emotional developments occur. They can define intentions as prerequisites for action and can conceal their intentions, a requirement for keeping a secret.

A cross-sectional study examining secrecy in middle childhood found that five- and six-year-olds would tell their mothers a friend's secret, such as minor and major wrongdoings or embarrassments, in most circumstances but would not tell an innocent secret such as a surprise for their mother's birthday. Ten- and twelve-year-old children, however, most often would not tell a parent a secret. The strength of the peer bond is such that it can overcome other moral imperatives (Watson and Valtin 1997).

MEMORY

Latency-age children have little if any memory of wearing diapers; however, they can readily recount sequences of events in their present lives and from the recent past. Autobiographical memory, enduring, chronologically sequenced memory of significant events from one's own life, begins in the later preschool years. Changes in memory function at this age reflect developmental change that results from the ability to use language as a cognitive tool. By four or five years of age, a child can use language as a system that enables reflection and manipulation of thought and action not in the immediate present (Nelson 1996). The years of middle childhood are remembered by adults in greater detail and in sequential fashion in actual memory, as opposed to reconstructed "snapshot" images of earlier life.

Children become aware of their ability to retain and forget experiences. For example, an eight-year-old boy who was trying to deal with the death of his mother became concerned that he was beginning to forget her. Meta-memory, reflections on one's own thinking, becomes possible as children become receptive to the comments of others and as their facility with language increases.

> [The] theoretical claim here is that language opens up possibilities for sharing and retaining memories in a culturally defined format for both personal and social functions. . . . According to this line of reasoning, the dramatic change from infantile amnesia to a life history in memory results from the child's emerging ability to use language in extended forms of discourse in exchanging "stories" with others and thus acquiring the narrative forms that characterize enduring memories. (Nelson 1996:155)

COGNITION

Middle childhood is a time when children are cognitively, emotionally, and socially prepared to learn in a group. As they evolve through this period, school achievement becomes more important. The gains children make in school will parallel the gains they make elsewhere.

As they approach age five, children start to move away from the protective watch of parents and other caregivers and begin to test and understand their freedom in thinking and action. Kindergarten, school for the four-and-a-half- to five-and-a-half-year-old, marks the beginning of a long educational journey. The first day of school is often the first major transition remembered by parents. Rarely does it occur without a parent or child shedding a tear, unlike earlier milestones, which are generally met without ambivalence.

At school the children are expected to function independently in an environment with a higher ratio of children to adults than they have previously known. Five is the age at which this experience becomes universalized, even mandatory, in American culture. Robert Fulghum claims that "All I really need to know I learned in kindergarten" (Fulghum 1988): for example, at lunchtime the children must fend for themselves, whether asserting themselves in a line to get food or actually eating. There is no adult ensuring that they have eaten; they have been delegated the responsibility. This is a major step on the road to independent survival.

Even though children develop skills at different times, starting school begins a process of synchronization of learning, bridging the knowledge gaps among peers. School becomes the arena for standardization, whether in terms of math scores or public health measures such as immunizations and vision screening. It is where children become identified as part of a cohort and are evaluated in relationship to one another for strengths and weaknesses. However, true learning is not about getting one right answer but rather about how to explore the answers.

By five years of age, most children have learned letters and are sounding out letter combinations and words as they begin to gain competence in reading. They comprehend so many that they believe they understand everything. They pursue the meanings of new words with a sense of urgency. Recognition of colors is routine, with an occasional unusual color emerging in conversation. Five- and six-year-old children have an appreciation of music, and more ability to remember melodies and lyrics of songs. Their world is a combination of fantasy and newfound logic. These children can easily count, many to 100, with great achievements in their conceptualization of numbers and memorization skills. They are learning to add, subtract, and compare small numbers and concepts, such as that if you have six people and nine pieces of watermelon, three people can have seconds.

By this stage in development, children have acquired the notion of gender constancy; they understand what gender they are and that it will not change throughout life. They have begun to form a sexual identity and to develop an understanding of their role in their family. Although the primary focus of the child's life remains the family, relationships with peers become more interactive and take on more significance. Empathy and helping skills begin very early. By age five, children will worry about the well-being of their peers and family members and will readily offer concrete support. When a classmate has "stitches," a common occurrence in the five-to-seven age group, children will eagerly inquire about the details and are able to express concern. When a child is absent from school, his classmates are interested in knowing why.

Five-year-olds like to play with dolls and puppets. They are natural animators. Constructions of blocks and connecting toys become more elaborate as children's imaginations and capabilities grow. Building and destroying things allows them to cultivate their creative energies. Five-year-olds retain an interest in play materials such as paint, clay, sand, and water from younger ages, while developing facility with others that require more fine motor skills, such as beads, origami, sewing, and Legos. The jokes and tricks of five- and six-year-olds, if not perfect, bear more resemblance to humor and magic than they did in the earlier years. Their added cognitive skills actually make this group funnier than their younger peers.

DEVELOPMENTAL CHANGES IN MIDDLE CHILDHOOD

FIVE TO SEVEN

In 1965, Sheldon H. White popularized the notion of the five-to-seven-year shift as the time when children can begin to take on responsibilities, do simple tasks, and in some cultures, become part of the labor force (White 1965). In Western and other cultures, from the Middle Ages on, the "age of reason" was felt to be seven years (White 1996).

Between five and seven years of age, children begin to learn more independently. This is facilitated by their capacity to pay attention, understand and respond to rules, and maintain self-control. Their ability to cooperate, share ideas, and be sensitive to the needs of others creates an environment in which they can learn. As children become more discerning in general, their palates seem to become a little less discriminating, making it easier for them to eat a variety of foods and therefore be away from home. By six years of age, most children are self-sufficient and largely independent in activities of daily living, allowing them to do more and to have more significant interactions with their peers. As they learn to tell time and to understand the seasons, their sense of time changes. However, it is not to be expected that six-year-olds will be able to sit for any length of time without an outlet for their seemingly boundless physical energy.

Middle childhood is a period of explosion of structured learning. Reading, writing, and arithmetic, the foundations for formalized learning, are established. Six- and seven-year-olds can understand relationships between numbers. Letters, sounds, and words come together, resulting in the ability to read.

Much study has been given to linguistic development, the mechanisms by which children learn and assimilate new vocabulary (Walley 1993). Early school-age children have a greater sense of more words and are closer to being able to understand words in context, a skill that develops over the next several years. Preschoolers learn two to four new words a day, four-year-olds know 2,500–3,000 words, and first graders know 7,000–10,000 (Anglin 1989;

Pease and Gleason 1985). Five- and six-year-olds demonstrate a beginning mastery of complex rules of grammar and syntax. They are eager to be read to and to try to read to others, or to share stories. Writing performance progresses on a continuum: the five-year-old writes or copies words needed for work or play, such as making a sign for a play activity; the six-year-old writes words, phrases, or sentences to convey meaning, such as making a shopping list; and the seven-year-old uses writing to convey meaning for different purposes, such as writing a story about a personal experience (Meisels 1996). At each age in these early years, as language and cognition increase, children's jokes become a more regular part of their routine, and riddles and puns emerge.

Younger children are often afraid of a variety of things, including the dark, ghosts, snakes, skeletons, basements, attics, slimy things, and monsters, and are subject to nightmares and night terrors. More realistic fears involving bodily harm and physical danger become more frequent as children get older (Bauer 1976). Of worries reported by 70 percent of a group of seven-year-olds, nearly half were event-related concerns such as a motor vehicle accident, while less then one fourth were imaginary or nighttime fears (Stevenson-Hinde and Shouldice 1995).

Six- and seven-year-olds may struggle at times, trying to find their place. They have begun to be able to reason, yet they are sometimes treated like the babies they just were. Alternatively, with their new competencies, they no longer have someone paying attention to their every word; this may periodically evoke statements such as, "You don't care about me," or "No one wants to talk to me." Six- and seven-year-olds are more sensitive to responses from others, particularly parents, and can say "You hurt my heart," or "My stomach sank when you said that." These children may struggle with separation from caregivers, and with issues of not getting their way. They like to be in control, yet rely on rules set by others to afford them the structure they need in order to thrive. They desire to know more, to be more grown up, but lack cognitive and emotional autonomy.

Early school-age children spend increasing amounts of time with peers and can more easily identify attributes they do and don't like in other children. This contact with peers may lead to a new appreciation that not everyone's life is the same. For example, a child whose father is ill and who has only known that reality may assume that all families have the same limitations imposed on them. When the child gets to school and connects with friends who have young, energetic fathers, the differences will become apparent. Children's inner representations of the world are now being influenced by multiple external factors. Issues of religion, economic status, work styles, family constellations, and family responsibilities are among the differences they begin to appreciate.

This is a time when children develop more refined motor skills, leading to greater physical aptitude and independence. Because they can adhere to the rules and meet the physical demands, team sports, such as baseball and soccer, or other activities like gymnastics become more important parts of their lives. They also enjoy fine motor activities, but may become frustrated by their lack of coordination.

Given the opportunity, children will play with what they choose. Girls may play with remote-control cars and Legos and boys may play with dolls and dress up, but societal stereotypes influence the process in latent and manifest ways, resulting in "engendered" children. If a child grows up in a community that values difference, the child will value difference. If a boy is given the message that playing with dolls or nurturing is bad, or if a girl is given the message that girls don't play with bugs, then they are deprived of opportunities for growth.

SEVEN TO NINE

Children seven to nine years old learn quickly, tire easily, and are anxious about new experiences, yet can be joyfully childlike in expression. They are more independent from family, but will eagerly stay close to home. They have great attachments to their primary caregiver, and are happy both on family adventures and playing with friends. Issues that arise in school with classmates and with teachers can enable these children to become more adept in communication with friends and family.

Intuition gives way to logic and game playing gains complexity. With reason comes a more sophisticated sense of the universe; children in this age group learn to understand time. Seven-year-olds' new facility in reading and writing expands the parameters of their worlds dramatically. Their abilities to categorize and to plan set them apart from younger children. They love to collect items such as trading cards, dolls, and rocks. These activities and hobbies display their newly developed abilities in organization and memorization.

Seven- to nine-year-olds can be paradoxical. They are not quite independent enough to be on their own but not dependent enough to need close watching. Unsupervised time increases, as they enjoy being alone and are entirely able to entertain themselves. Their capacity for emotional connection and intimacy with others expands, as does the amount of time they spend with peers. These are sensitive years, because these children are more able to evaluate themselves. Having just learned to be reflective, they have not yet perfected a strong emotional veneer in response to their own or others' appraisals of them.

An eight-year-old child's physical growth may slow, but everything else is happening rapidly. Children are moving, thinking, and acting quickly. They are much less introverted and have acclimated to the routine of school, enjoying their competence. Reading affords them volumes of emotional, intellectual, and practical realities, and allows for a richer fantasy life.

Societal perceptions of the learning needs of children have changed in recent decades. Children are becoming computer proficient before they have learned to read and write. Some elementary schools oppose the incorporation of computers into the curriculum before third grade, arguing that computer learning does not allow the child to integrate tactile and visual stimuli in the same way as do actual puzzles or expressive materials. Computer learning does not emphasize skills utilized when more is left to the imagination and when responses are not immediate; it does not allow the child to contemplate the next move, let alone alternative avenues of thought.

Nine-year-olds have a varying range of emotions and can exhibit behavior that is unpredictable. Not being shy, these children are "in your face" while showing sensitivity to their own needs as well as those of others. Their increased awareness allows them to reach new highs and lows of feelings, and their emotional range is quite striking. These children explore new territory emotionally and physically, and have more opinions and attitude. Their behavior may seem somewhat capricious, with mood swings. This volatility may have its roots in nine-year-olds' attempts to assimilate cognitive and emotional gains while trying to come to grips with a new host of feelings and sensitivities. Sometimes they have trouble maintaining this balance and may seem like they are erupting emotionally, but the storms pass. At this age, children begin to censor their thoughts and impulses and so begin a process of screening information from parents and others. They begin to have a more separate life as a result of actual emotional, intellectual, and practical experience.

Children in this age group are easily embarrassed. They are more aware of their potentialities and limitations than they were before. They can actually think differently and reflect upon what they are thinking. They are more critical of themselves, feeling that "I could have done better" and, as an extension, of their caregivers: "You should have known."

Children between seven and twelve years of age are inclined to be dramatic. They are the most likely to get on stage for school and social events. They are more outgoing, reflective, sensitive, curious, and critical. Although they are performers, they may not actually achieve peak performance levels. They need to take tasks to completion, verifying the rules of order and logic they have just learned. The nine-year-old is better able to master tasks than the seven-year-old, who was able to contemplate taking them on but might not have excelled in the process. This is a period of refining motor skills. Sports activities and interests expand to include jumping rope, skateboarding, and skating. Other unique skills emerge during this time, such as snapping fingers, whistling, wiggling the ears, and crossing the eyes.

Eight- and nine-year-olds may seem more grown up than they actually are. They possess increasingly sophisticated understanding of rules, structure, and systems. Children who appear to be able to discuss complex issues openly may still benefit from play (dramatic or fantasy driven) as a safer and perhaps more effective medium than words for self-expression.

By nine years of age, there is a clearer shift of emotional energy from family to friends. Children can be true, committed friends, and their friendships can become more intimate. The ease of same-sex relationships continues. However, media portrayals of strong sexual identification and other cultural changes have led children to earlier interest in individual relationships with those of the opposite sex, predominantly with neighbors and school friends. While much more serious about their relationships with peers, they still enjoy adult companionship and attention, particularly on their terms.

For children nine and older, this is a period of physical and emotional growth toward independence. They are establishing their own identity, but they have not yet truly come into their own. They may have issues with regard to self-worth and may have trouble accepting compliments and criticism graciously. They can be more anxious than younger children, seemingly less certain, and more cautious. These children have increasingly realistic evaluations of themselves, are able to assess and accept discipline as fair or unfair, and are more accepting of rules, if they are logical. They have many and more varied interests. Collections are still important but are more complex.

Verbal and mathematical skills increase, language becomes much more sophisticated, and abstractions are better understood. Life and death are more realistically contemplated. The previously carefree child is beginning to have worries that parallel those of adults. Nine-year-olds are more discriminating and understand the boundaries between adult and child. They are more logical and reasonable, but may struggle with knowing what their place is, what they are allowed to do, and how to manage the range of emotions they are experiencing.

Adults have preconceived notions about how children should behave at this age. One does not often hear a five-year-old described as "mature" or a seven-year-old as "young for his age," but one often hears of a nine-year-old being immature or notably responsible. Some children have baby-sitters through their early teen years, whereas others start baby-sitting by age nine.

TEN TO TWELVE (PREADOLESCENT)

As they approach age ten, children remain connected to childhood in activities and emotions though being pulled toward adolescence. The unique attributes of this age group may be frequently overshadowed by the impending upheaval. The "preteen" years show the cumulative effects of childhood. Preadolescents have learned decision-making skills and know their own minds.

Ten- to twelve-year-olds are able to develop interpersonal intimacy, have evolved in their cognitive and emotional ability, and have internalized a sense of morality and caring. They develop a capacity for assessing others and for self-reflection. They can seem very capable. With each passing year they have more freedom and more responsibilities; many of them are baby-sitting, delivering newspapers, or working at other part-time jobs. They are making choices about their lives and are thinking about the future, anticipating changes. These children are seeking to understand life more completely and when affected by a crisis, they will still seek parental guidance and reasoning.

The preceding decade of learning allows the preteenager, who remains a little awkward, to emerge into the person he will be. Linguistically speaking, fifth-graders have command of between 39,000 and 46,000 words (Anglin 1989). Younger children have greater linguistic capabilities, felt to be related to greater plasticity in brain structures associated with language acquisition. Placed in a new environment, they will easily adopt a new language and retain a native comprehension of it; after age twelve, this is less likely.

The academic transition to junior high or middle school, which occurs during this period, has been identified as a stressful life event for children, sometimes associated with depression, academic failure, and use of addictive substances. Preparation for junior high school, including building skills for responding to peer pressure and for decision making, has been recognized as a way to deal with the stress and to minimize subsequent deviant behavior (smoking, drinking, and using drugs) as a means of adjusting (Epstein, Griffin, and Botvin 2000; Gilchrist, Schinke, Snow, Schilling, and Senechal 1988; Snow, Gilchrist, Schilling, Schinke, and Kelso 1986).

Preadolescents want to spend more time with their peers, although they still go along on family vacations and enjoy family time. They are more aware of their sexuality and are beginning to be interested in more intense individual relationships. Sexual preferences are said to be determined by adolescence, suggesting that at this age, children explore and question their initial feelings about sexuality. In keeping with this, appearance is a major issue. At this time, a perceived drop in self-esteem can affect a child's outlook on life. Twelve-year-olds enter adolescence grounded in reality, which serves them well when they experience the volatility of the teen years.

MIDDLE CHILDHOOD IN PERSPECTIVE

Childhood is a time of infectious laughter and unconditional joy and excitement, but also a time of animated annoyance, stomping out of the room, and running away from conversations. These peak levels of emotion are characteristic of children in middle childhood. Their lives are delightful, but at times hard to make sense of. As they get older, they are more able to contain their emotions and to cope with day-to-day issues.

Quantifying the gains that children make during this period is difficult. Imagine a child entering middle childhood clinging to parents and teddy bears, unable to read, and then exiting this stage ready for high school. In cognitive, social, emotional, and moral dimensions, there is a quantum leap in development during these brief seven years. These have been called "the collecting years," not exclusively because of the objects that children acquire but also because of the friendships they form, the memories they build, and the cognitive gains they make. Children learn to be realistic, responsible, self-evaluating, compassionate individuals during this period, skills that are invaluable for their eventual growth into adulthood.

SIGMUND FREUD

The concept of latency was introduced by Sigmund Freud in 1905 in *Three Essays on the Theory of Sexuality*. In 1926 he further defined it as "characterized by the dissolution of the oedipal complex, the creation or consolidation of the superego and the erection of ethical and aesthetic barriers in the ego" (S. Freud 1926:114).

Freud believed that following the resolution of the Oedipus complex and the emergence of the superego, the child's libidinal and aggressive impulses are sublimated, become latent, and are rechanneled into nonsexual outlets such as play and school. However, the latency child is still in conflict—struggling against the pressure of masturbation with accompanying oedipal and preoedipal fantasies. The libidinal impulses became obscured through a process of learned shame, disgust, and morality. Freud felt that a psychological event, resolution of the oedipal conflict, signaled the beginning of latency while a maturational event, puberty, marked the end. With the development of the superego and further maturation of ego functions comes greater ability to control instinctual impulses. Latency marks a halt in the progression of infantile sexuality.

This is a relatively calm period in psychosexual development between the conflict of the preoedipal and oedipal periods and the turmoil of adolescence. The superego matures as values, ideals, and sublimations emerge; it becomes stronger, internalized, and integrated within the rest of the personality structure. The child refines social skills and acquires new roles and abilities. There is an increase in relationships with peers and adults outside of the family and greater awareness of the rules of both community and family.

Children in this phase move from seeing their families as the authority and source of beliefs and wishing to be like them to feeling disillusioned with their parents and overvaluing other adults and families. The *family romance* may result, in which children fantasize that their *real* parents are "noble," not ordinary like those they imagine adopted and raised them. Freud believed that children replace a parent with a "superior" one because they long for earlier days when they viewed that parent as the noblest and strongest (S. Freud 1908:45). There may also be a conscious fantasy of having a twin to escape feelings of loneliness as children move away from their families. The world expands greatly during the latency period as the child gets ready for adolescence, when strong sexual impulses will reemerge and separation and individuation again is a task.

ANNA FREUD

While Sigmund Freud constructed his view of development from the recollections of his adult patients, Anna Freud devoted almost sixty years to the analysis of children and adolescents and developed her theories from direct observation. In 1965 she made a significant original contribution by presenting her formulation of interdependent *developmental lines*, each with its own history and vicissitudes. These lines represent the sequence of child maturation from complete dependency to relative independence, from irrationality to rationality, and from passivity to active relations with the environment. The common theme is gradual mastery of oneself and of life's demands as the ego's capacities to adapt increase.

Anna Freud defined latency as:

> The postoedipal lessening of drive urgency and the transfer of libido from the parental figures to contemporaries, community groups, teachers, leaders, impersonal ideals, and aim-induced, sublimated interest, with fantasy manifestations giving evidence of disillusionment with and denigration of parents. (1963:248)

Freud believed that with a decline in the strength of the instinct, there is a "truce" in the defensive war waged by the ego. The ego then becomes stronger, less helpless and submissive in its relationship to the outside world, and the child replaces complete dependence on the parents with identifications, introjecting the wishes, requirements, and ideals of parents and teachers. In latency the ego has acquired the superego as an ally in the struggle to master the instincts (A. Freud 1966:144–51). The child is able to direct energies and attention toward the external world and away from inner experiences and anxieties. Thus her or his focus moves toward environmental solutions and external changes rather than introspection and insight into inner conflicts. Anna Freud felt, as had her father, that in the process of moving away from the family, all children must denigrate their parents, often believing in the family romance that their "real" parents are better and kinder than the family who "adopted" them. A second common conscious fantasy in latency is that of possessing a twin. This, too, originates in disappointment by the parents in the oedipal situation, resulting in the search for a partner who will give the child all the love, attention, and companionship desired and will provide an escape from the loneliness and solitude the child experiences when the desire to possess a parent has met with failure. It is a compensatory relationship (Burlington 1952:1, 81).

Freud believed that children cannot be fully integrated into school until this period, when libido has been transferred from family to community. There is a move from "play" to "work," as the child is able to:

1. control, inhibit, or modify impulses to use materials aggressively or defensively in order to use them positively and constructively to build, plan, learn, and share;

2. carry out preconceived plans with minimal regard for the lack of pleasurable yield and intervening frustration and maximum regard for pleasure in the ultimate outcome; and

3. achieve not only the transition from primitive and instinctual to sublimated pleasure accompanied by a high degree of neutralization of the energy employed, but also the transition from the pleasure principle to the reality principle needed for success in work. (1965:82)

Latency-age children attach more importance to avoiding anxiety and displeasure than to direct or indirect impulse gratification. Freud postulated that there is a decline in children's intelligence at the beginning of latency, because earlier their intellectual achievements were connected to inquiries about sex and when this becomes taboo, a general prohibition and inhibition is extended to other areas of thought. At the end of latency, the child's intellectual capabilities appear to be restored. In addition, Freud felt that latency children not only do not dare to indulge in abstract thought but have no need to do so, and that the intellectual work performed by the ego is therefore solid, reliable, and connected to action (A. Freud 1966:164–65).

Thus in latency the child moves from egocentricity to companionship, play to work, irresponsibility to responsibility, and further develops the ego functions of exploration and construction. Proficiency in playing games is now possible and desired and results from the ability to form companionships. Hobbies also emerge in latency and may continue throughout the life cycle (A. Freud 1965:83–84).

ERIK ERIKSON

Erikson termed the normal crisis occurring from ages six through twelve "Industry vs. Inferiority." The central theme of this developmental stage, which coincides with the child's first major school experience, is "I am what I learn" (Erikson 1959:82). The child leaves the safety of the family for a wider society and seeks recognition through producing good "work" outside of the home. Erikson summarized the desired resolution of the crisis:

While all children at times need to be left alone in solitary play or, later, in the company of books and radio, motion pictures and television, and while all children need their hours and days of make-believe in games, they all, sooner or later, become dissatisfied and disgruntled without a sense of being able to make things and make them well and even perfectly: it is this that I have called a *sense of industry*. (1968:123)

This is a time when children are still invested in play activities but also want to be successful in mastering academic skills. As they develop competencies, even in play, they achieve a sense of industry or productivity. If children fear that they will never succeed at the required tasks, they may develop a *sense of inadequacy* and *inferiority*. This is an age of cooperation, of shared endeavors in both planning and implementation. A child will feel inferior if consistently confronted by what he or she cannot do or if he or she perceives that performance is not up to his or her own or others' standards. A sense of inertia may overtake the child. Successful resolution of the crisis between industry and inferiority leads to the development of the virtue, or ego strength, of *competence*, "the free exercise of dexterity and intelligence in the completion of tasks unimpaired by infantile inferiority" (Erikson 1964:124). The ritualization is *formality*, the proper form of making, doing, cooperating, and competing. The ritualism is *formalism*, forgetting the purpose and meaning of performance in favor of technique and proficiency (Erikson 1977:106). Finally, there is the common danger that throughout the long years of school a child will never acquire enjoyment of work and pride in doing at least one thing really well. Erikson believed that "this is socially a most decisive stage [and forms] the lasting basis for co-operative participation in productive life" (1968:125–26).

As children play together and peer relationships mature, mastery and problem solving expand from the individual to the group. Erikson felt that children at this stage are defined by their attempts at mastery of new tasks. The basic adult attitude toward work is established during middle childhood (Erikson 1963). Children acquire personal evaluation standards and a sense of their contribution to a greater society. Most become motivated to achieve success, some with greater and some with lower expectations. Erikson believed that

children at this age *do* like to be mildly but firmly coerced into the adventure of finding out that one can learn to accomplish things which one would never have thought of by oneself, things which owe their attractiveness to the very fact that they are not the product of play and fantasy but the product of reality, practicality, and logic; things which thus provide a token sense of participation in the real world of adults. (1959:84)

Through the mastery of skills, a child develops a sense of competence and acquires new responsibilities. The more a child achieves success at "work," the more intrinsically motivating the work is—success begets success. Adults significant to the child encourage him or her to develop skills and achieve mastery through praise, interest, encouragement, and sometimes rewards. The winning of a medal, the completion of a project to bring home from school or camp, or any private or public acknowledgment all afford the child a sense of accomplishment. Components associated with the mastery or completion of a task include curiosity about an activity, the willingness to learn, and the ability to stay focused on the project until completion. Industry encompasses an eagerness to develop skills and to contribute to society in a meaningful way.

A sense of inferiority comes from both the child and the people and organizations in its world. If a child cannot master a skill for any reason, she or he may feel inferior. All children at one time or another feel inadequate based on physical, emotional, social, cultural, educational, or experiential circumstances, even those who are positive and capable and take on challenges willingly. No one readily masters all skills. Comparisons between individuals and the ways those significant to the child respond to failures of any kind may generate feelings of inferiority. School, as the child's workplace, represents the larger community, and failure there can have implications in other areas of development. Successful resolution of the industry vs. inferiority crisis will ready the latency-age child to move into adolescence, prepared to deal with its crisis of identity.

Erikson was interested in play, which he viewed as the "work of childhood." He designed an experiment involving 300 boys and girls ages ten to twelve, who were asked to construct "imaginary moving pictures" with toy figures and blocks. He detected early in the experiment common elements of design and topography that distinguished the constructions of boys from those of girls. He concluded that the organization of the play space paralleled the morphology of the child's genital equipment, with the boys building protrusive, extensive, intrusive, and upward projections and the girls preoccupied with interiors and enclosed space (Erikson 1950:98–106). Erikson believed that how children manipulate toys spatially reflects the organization of their egos psychologically. The symbolism of play shows how children interpret emotions. Play and artwork are major means of expression for the younger children in middle childhood, and use of metaphor may be the most appropriate avenue for addressing difficult issues.

Jean Piaget

At the start of middle childhood, age seven, Piaget observed a change in the child's cognitive development from *preoperational* to *concrete operational*, each phase with its own distinctive patterns of thought. In the preoperational period, cognitive activity is characterized as *centration*—the child is only able to concentrate on one dimension of a situation. With maturation, the child's cognitive ability is characterized by *decentration*, the ability to focus simultaneously on several dimensions of a problem (Ginsburg and Opper 1988:154). Concrete operations is the most extensively studied of Piaget's stages; however, it also the stage for which there are the greatest gaps in the list of English translations (Inhelder and Piaget 1958:xiii).

Piaget's work began by considering children's use of language via a naturalistic method. In studying two groups of children, twenty of ages six to seven and thirty of ages seven to eight, Piaget found that the younger children used primarily egocentric speech while those older than seven became increasingly proficient at verbal communication. He believed that young children need not communicate clearly, as they are primarily with adults who make major efforts to understand their thoughts and desires, while older children spend more time with peers, who are not as attuned to their individual "language." Older children will challenge each other verbally to listen to the opinions of others, and thus force each other to move from egocentrism and develop better modes of communication.

Thought Content. Piaget was interested in children's beliefs about dreams, meteorology, steam engines, and many other familiar areas of concern. The belief of preoperational children is *animism*, in which objects such as the Sun and Moon are regarded as alive in the same sense as people are. The next stage of belief is *artificialism*, where the child believes that the object is the result of an outside agent, such as God. The final stage is *participation*, in which the child perceives some vague connection between people and things that does not involve creation.

In middle childhood, the child ceases to believe in animism, artificialism, and participation. Her or his explanations for events may be crude and based on what is learned in school (Ginsburg and Opper 1988:94–95). Concrete thought is essentially attached to empirical reality (Inhelder and Piaget 1958:250).

MORAL DEVELOPMENT. Piaget sought to determine how children develop moral judgment by observing boys playing marbles. He believed that rules of games and how they are implemented reflect the children's own thinking and not that of their parents. Piaget felt that the essential aspect of morality is the tendency to accept and follow a system of rules that regulate interpersonal behavior. He chose marbles believing that the rules of the game are developed by the children, so the game is almost exclusively theirs. These rules have usually been made by external sources. Prior to age seven, there is an egocentric quality to the game as children play by their individual rules with little concern for competition and winning, really playing alongside each other rather than together.

Piaget called the next phase, which lasts from age seven to ten or eleven, *incipient cooperation*. Initially the child has only some mastery of the rules that can result in conflicts; however, there is the beginning of cooperation and awareness of the point of view of others. Between six and eight, the child moves from an authoritarian view of the rules as defined by parents or older children to a more democratic approach of mutual respect and reciprocity. By age eleven the stage of *genuine cooperation* begins: the child has a thorough sense of the rules that have been developed in cooperation with the other players. Changes in rules are permitted as long as they are perceived as fair.

As the child develops, he or she gains greater freedom from parental supervision, rules, and opinions. Spending more time with peers, children assume greater responsibility for their own lives, see themselves as equal to others, and begin to form their own moral codes. They may be faced with beliefs contrary to those taught earlier and come to accept that rules may be fallible. The relationship to adults changes from one of deference to one of greater equality.

Piaget also studied the development of judgments about explicitly moral situations by telling children stories posing a moral dilemma that they were asked to resolve. In one story an act was performed that unintentionally resulted in considerable damage, while in the other a negligible amount of damage was caused by a deliberately improper act. Up to the age of ten, Piaget found two kinds of answers: a *subjective* view that the perpetrator's guilt is determined by the nature of his motives rather than the degree of damage;

and *moral realism*, in which guilt is determined not by intention but by quantity of damage. As children mature, the subjective response becomes more prevalent (Ginsburg and Opper 1988:101–105).

CLASSIFICATION. To study classification, the ability to group objects according to common characteristics, Piaget changed his research emphasis from verbal observation, with a heavy reliance on language and imagination, to a clinical method, where questions were related to concrete objects or events and the children answered by manipulating objects rather than relying solely on language. The concepts of counterarguments or countersuggestions were also introduced.

Piaget identified three stages in the development of the child's ability to classify objects. The first two stages, between ages two and seven, are preoperational; the third stage, seven to eleven, is called concrete operations. By the age of seven, children are able to construct hierarchical classifications and comprehend *inclusion*, placing new objects in systematic relationships with objects already classified (Inhelder and Piaget 1958:248). The children can decenter, as they can think simultaneously in terms of the whole and its parts. However, Piaget observed that this does not apply to hypothetical objects; classification is concrete, only possible with real objects. Further research indicated that concrete operational children are able to understand and manipulate *ordinal* relations, but only on a concrete level. Piaget named the gap between hypothetical and concrete reasoning *vertical decalage*.

CONSERVATION. In a famous series of experiments, Piaget examined children's ability to understand conservation, the physical reality that despite changes in its shape, the quantity of matter does not change. In an experiment designed to demonstrate conservation of liquids, two identical flasks are filled with water to a predetermined height. These are presented to the child, who is asked if they contain the same amount of liquid. The child generally responds that they do. The water from one is poured into a taller, narrower container. The child is asked if the amount of liquid is still the same. Children at the preoperational level will respond in one of two ways. They may indicate that there is more in the taller container, concentrating on one dimension only and failing to appreciate that the volume must be conserved. Other preoperational children may become confused and indicate that one flask has more because it is taller, only to reconsider that the shorter one has more, because it is wider, and then become confused. To Piaget this indicated a step toward conservation in that the children are considering more than one aspect of the situation simultaneously, yet cannot reconcile them (Piaget 1952, 1979, 1983).

It is not until approximately seven years of age, the beginning of the stage of concrete operations, that a child reliably answers that the amounts are equal and don't change just because one has been poured into a differently shaped container. Children are able to decenter, that is, to consider both the height and the width of the longer flask. Their explanations include *inversion* or *negation*, the return to the starting point by canceling an operation already performed; *identity*, the fact that despite a change in container, the amount of liquid has not changed; and *compensation* or *reciprocity*, in which a change in one dimension of the container is compensated for by a change in another dimension so that the product of two reciprocal operations is not a null operation but an equivalence (Inhelder and Piaget 1958:272–73). To Piaget this signified children's ability to think more systematically and to consider alternate forms and states of objects and people.

The concrete operational child is characterized by decentration, the ability to consider several factors or dimensions of a problem before arriving at a conclusion. The two major cognitive accomplishments of this stage are classification, the ability to form categories, and conservation, the ability to conceptualize sameness where there are apparent differences. The child is able to be flexible, to focus simultaneously on several dimensions of a problem, and is attuned to change and reciprocity. He or she is sensitive to transformations and able to reverse the direction of thought: thinking is dynamic, not static (Ginsburg and Opper 1988:155). Having learned to think logically on a concrete level, the child is ready to move into Piaget's final period of intellectual development, that of *formal operations*.

LAWRENCE KOHLBERG

Lawrence Kohlberg's research on stages of moral development, which he labeled "cognitive development," was heavily influenced by Piaget's work. Kohlberg was an undergraduate at the University of Chicago in 1948; he earned his bachelor's degree in his first year and remained in Chicago to pursue graduate work in psychology, focusing on Piaget's concepts of moral development. He taught at Chicago until 1968, then moved to Harvard, where he remained until his death in 1987.

Kohlberg initially formulated his stage theory of moral development after analyzing the responses of a sample of seventy-two upper-middle to lower-class boys, ages ten, thirteen, and sixteen, to hypothetical moral dilemmas. The prototype story presented to the children was "Heinz Steals the Dog."

> In Europe, a woman was near death from a special kind of cancer. There was one drug that doctors thought might save her. It was a form of radium that a druggist in the same town had recently discovered. The drug was expensive to make, but the druggist was charging ten times what the drug cost him to make. He paid $299 for the radium and charged $2,000 for a small dose of the drug. The sick woman's husband, Heinz, went to everyone he knew to borrow the money for the drug, but he could only get together about $1,000, which is half of what it cost. He told the druggist that his wife was dying and asked him to sell it cheaper or let him pay later. But the druggist said "No, I discovered the drug and I'm going to make money from it." So Heinz got desperate and broke into the man's store to steal the drug for his wife. Should the husband have done that? (1963:19)

Kohlberg later used the same format with a sample of sixteen-year-old delinquent boys and a sample of fifty thirteen-year-old boys and girls. The goal was not to discover the answer to the story's final question, but rather to learn how the children arrived at it, the thought and reasoning behind their judgment. Analysis of these data resulted in the identification of six developmental types of moral thought grouped into three moral levels, each with two subtypes, defined as:

Level I: Premoral Level (ages four to ten)
    Type 1. Punishment and obedience orientation
    Type 2. Naïve instrumental hedonism

Level II. Morality of Conventional Role Conformity (ages ten to thirteen)
    Type 3: Good boy morality of maintaining good relations, approval
      of others
    Type 4: Authority maintaining morality

Level III. Morality of Self-Accepted Moral Principles (ages thirteen to sixteen)
    Type 5: Morality of contract, of individual rights, and of democratically accepted law
    Type 6: Morality of individual principles of conscience (1963:13–14)

In addition, Kohlberg identified five ego strengths that correlate with moral conduct: intelligence; tendency to anticipate future events and to choose the greater remote outcome over the lesser immediate outcome; capacity to maintain stable, focused attention; capacity to control unsocialized fantasies; and self-esteem or satisfaction with the self and the environment (Kohlberg 1964:390–91).

Refining his work, Kohlberg postulated three levels of moral development, each with two substages that roughly correspond to Piaget's stages of cognitive development: preoperational, concrete operational, and formal operations. These newer defined levels reflect a perspective based more on socialization:

Level 1: Preconventional Morality (ages four to ten)
    Stage 1: Egocentrism
    Stage 2: Concrete individuation

Level 2: Conventional Morality (ages ten to thirteen)
    Stage 3: Mutual interpersonal expectations
    Stage 4: The societal point of view

Level 3: Postconventional Morality (begins at adolescence)
    Stage 5: The social contract and individual rights
    Stage 6: Decisions based on conscience and logic

It is during the middle school years that children progress from Kohlberg's *preconventional* morality level to *conventional* morality. In stage 1 of the preconventional level (level 1), moral behaviors are determined externally, in *heteronomous reality*, and governed by children's awareness that rewards or punishments might result from their thoughts and actions. It is a highly egocentric period based on the child's needs and desire to avoid negative consequences. She or he does not really understand or uphold conventional or societal rules and expectations. However, in stage 2, *instrumental morality*, there is indication of thought involving exchange and reciprocity (Kohlberg 1964:172) as the child becomes somewhat more aware that others have opinions and is more concerned with fairness. Children are focused on the pragmatic results of an action, and rules are primarily followed if they benefit the child or a loved one.

In level 2, *conventional morality*, the opinions of others become important and behavior conforms more to societal expectations. In stage 3 (age ten to eleven), judgment is based on pleasing others and winning approval, a social-relational moral perspective. It is exemplified by the "Golden Rule" and acknowledges that mutual relationships and shared feelings are more important than self-interest. Children at this stage tend to stereotype moral behavior in terms of being a "good" friend, sibling, or child, in the context of the family, school, and local community.

In stage 4 of conventional morality, the child's judgment is based on whether a behavior upholds or violates the laws of society as a whole. The perspective is no longer egocentric but rather that of a "good citizen"; moral behavior is defined by actions consistent with social conventions, norms, rules, and values. Rules are obeyed, except in extreme cases when they conflict with other defined obligations, and the rules of society are seen as necessary for maintaining the social order (Kohlberg 1976:34).

Kohlberg believed that most people do not go beyond level 2, stage 3 or 4. He believed that his research supported his formulation of levels 1 and 2; however, level 3 was more philosophical in content and not empirically based.

CAROL GILLIGAN AND LYN BROWN

Carol Gilligan's research has been primarily with adolescent and adult women. However, between 1986 and 1990, she collaborated with Lyn Brown in a study of girls ages seven to sixteen who attended a private day school, the Laurel School, in Cleveland, Ohio. Their goal was to better understand women's psychological development (Brown and Gilligan 1992:9). In *A Different Voice* (1993), Gilligan's seminal work, she observed that people speak in at least two moral and relationship voices, "justice" and "care." Brown's work (1989) sought to examine the development of the "care voice" in maturing young girls, which is concerned with loving and being loved, listening and being listened to, and responding and being responded to. Eighty percent of the girls came from middle- or upper middle-class families and 14 percent were of color. The study sample was composed of twenty-five second graders (seven to eight years old), twenty fifth graders (ten to eleven years old), twenty seventh graders (twelve to thirteen years old) and thirty-four tenth graders (fifteen to sixteen years old). The girls were asked to describe experiences of relational and moral conflict and choice in their lives in open-ended clinical interviews. Data were interpreted to illustrate how their experiences related to perception and knowledge about relationships; their concerns about caring for themselves; inclusion and exclusion; differences and perspectives; not hurting others; experiences of interdependence, connection, and concern for the welfare of others; attachment and detachment; connection and disconnection; pleasure; loss; and isolation (Brown 1991:54–55). The goal was to explore the differences in perspective about relationships and how the caring voice sounds as girls mature.

Differences across age groups emerged. Psychologically, as the girls matured they became less dependent on authority, less egocentric, more differentiated, more autonomous, more aware of the complexity of perspectives in relationships, and better adapted to social and cultural conventions. However, developmentally there was a loss of voice, a struggle for authorization, increased confusion, and some defensiveness, as well as evidence that the girls replaced authentic with idealized relationships. Data show loss, struggle, and an inability to act in the face of conflict (Brown 1991:56).

Data about the second graders, which focused on how the girls characterized themselves and the way they spoke about relationships, show:

1. ability to articulate their thoughts and feelings about relationships directly with confidence and authority
2. willingness to tell others about bad or hurt feelings as well as those of love and loyalty
3. awareness of differences between people that could result in disagreement and hurt
4. knowledge that they may not always feel "nice" and can hurt others as well as be hurt, but wish not to hurt others
5. relationships that are genuine or authentic
6. knowledge of what others want them to be and do and thus the ability to anticipate reactions
7. capacity for careful attention and concern for others, wanting to be nice and fair
8. a clear sense of both the pleasure and the pain of relationships
9. a belief that what they have to say is important and should be listened to (Brown 1989, 1991; Brown and Gilligan 1992)

These young girls seemed capable of expressing healthy anger as a natural part of relationships, which gave them an air of authority and authenticity accompanied by a desire to speak and to be listened to. The descriptions of good and bad relationships given by both second and fifth graders were open and rich. Data about the fifth graders, again focused on how they characterized themselves and the way they spoke about relationships, show:

1. awareness of the painful aspects of cliques, common to this age group, and their vulnerability
2. concern about the risks to relationships of saying things carelessly or without qualification
3. recognition of mean, hurtful, and exclusionary behavior of others, yet reluctance to speak of their own feelings openly
4. felt pressure to be "nice" and "perfect" with no bad thoughts or feelings to win adult approval
5. knowledge about the complexity of relationships, yet desire for a simplified, idealized model of how they "should" be, what to say, and how to speak
6. closer attention to how adult women navigate the relational world
7. fascination with differences in how other people think and feel and with different views of reality
8. strong feelings about being listened to and being effective in relationships (Brown 1989, 1991; Brown and Gilligan 1992)

Data about the seventh and tenth graders show the beginnings of a shift, as the girls tended to describe relationships in terms not connected to their own experiences and to describe relationship conflicts idealistically. They valued helping, and not hurting, others. The seventh graders showed awareness of a struggle between selfishness and selflessness (Brown 1991:59). They wanted to be nice and caring yet felt this involved negating part of themselves that might be viewed as selfish. This conflict made them worry about loss of self-regard and independent thinking (Brown 1989:140). It is a struggle for authority. However, many still had a strong sense of self, an ability to know and voice their feelings and thoughts and to give authority to their experiences (Taylor et al. 1995:23).

The researchers noted that in addition to a shift from an authentic to an idealized view of relationships, there was a move from assertive and confident authorization of feelings and thoughts in the younger girls to confusion, self-doubt, and ambivalence in the adolescent girls (Brown 1991:61). Second graders would talk until they felt they were being heard or found creative ways to make others hear them. Fifth graders also indicated that they felt entitled to be heard, as they were making worthwhile contributions. Seventh graders had become aware that speaking up can be disruptive and began to question whether they were, in fact, entitled to speak or wonder aloud about how things are. Speaking about themselves and their feelings and thoughts could be dangerous. They were more sensitive to the power of adults and peers and external expectations. They showed awareness that something about themselves and relationships can be lost and must be protected. The older adolescents showed a real struggle with interpretation and voice, issues of self-authorization. They discounted their knowledge of relationships as lacking authority or value and often chose silence in threatening situations. They had lost the self-assurance of the younger girls.

These data supported Gilligan's conclusions that adolescent girls experience a "crisis of connection" as they try to bring their earlier knowledge of caring and relationships to a culture that devalues this knowledge and experience. Brown added that "what at face value appears to be a quintessentially adolescent struggle for identity and a voice that is effective and understandable is . . . a struggle to recover and to hold on to or authorize a complicated view of relationships based on observation and experience" (1991:64). Children at this stage struggle to regain knowledge about themselves and relationships that they had earlier and that in the passage from childhood to adolescence has been idealized, stereotyped, lost, or buried. They take a risk in valuing their relationship knowledge in a culture that rewards individuation and separation. To be other than selfless is to be "bad." Brown felt the process begins when fifth graders have a desire to be "perfect," with no bad thoughts or feelings. Seventh graders are aware that something about themselves is being lost, that they must protect their real feelings in a judgmental world by moving them "underground."

Girls moving from middle childhood to adolescence struggle with the observations they make and the messages they receive about relationships and about goodness and success. Brown felt that the strengths seen in the second and fifth graders had been lost by the seventh and tenth graders. As the girls matured, they became less dependent on external authorities, less egocentric, better able to distinguish their own feelings from those of others, and more aware of the diversity of human experience, yet they also showed a loss of voice, a struggle to authenticate their own experiences and respond to their own feelings and thoughts (Brown and Gilligan 1992:6). Development from a care perspective includes recognition of and belief in one's contribution to relationships, a sense of ownership of values and beliefs, and the confidence to express thoughts and feelings (Brown 1989:201). Brown urged parents, teachers, and therapists to listen to the girls and to help the older ones reclaim and authorize earlier knowledge in order to resist oppressive conventions and stereotypes and to avoid pressure to be "nice" (Brown 1991:68).

SUSAN HARTER

Susan Harter is a professor of psychology and head of the developmental psychology program at the University of Denver. In contrast to Carol Gilligan and Lyn Brown's work, Harter found that some adolescent boys and girls have a "drop in voice," lowered self-esteem rather than complete loss of voice. She demonstrated that this is not an issue of gender but rather is associated with concern about "false self behavior." She maintains that adolescents with low levels of perceived social support adopt false personas in an effort to win support from peers and family. The false self represents an "altered voice," not saying what they think; this is what Gilligan had previously identified as loss of voice in girls.

Susan Harter has emerged as a rigorous, prolific researcher. Over the past two decades her work has been devoted to understanding child and adolescent development, recognizing that cognitive, emotional, and social relationships are not separate in children's minds and thus needed to be researched together. She is focused on understanding children and adolescents' constructions of themselves through examination of self-concept, self-esteem, scholastic motivation, role relationships, anger, depression, suicide, and perceived competence. She has observed children's limitations when the emotion of a situation exceeds the parameters of their thought, as in the case of multidimensional thought in a unidimensional mind. An astute clinician, Harter has shown how cognitive and emotional development parallel each other.

COGNITIVE AND EMOTIONAL DEVELOPMENT. Harter and Buddin sought to understand how children develop the ability to experience multidimensional emotional thought. They proposed a four-level sequence of understanding simultaneous emotions throughout middle childhood (Harter and Buddin 1987):

Level 0. The youngest children (mean age 5.2) simply deny that two feelings can simultaneously coexist. The child denies that he or she can have two feelings at the same time because he or she cannot simultaneously relate, integrate, or coordinate two representations that refer to different emotions, no matter how similar they appear to be. Thus, the child cannot relate "happy" to "glad" or "sad" to "mad" simultaneously.

Level 1. Children mean age 7.3 show the first appreciation for the simultaneous experience of two emotions, but this understanding is restricted to combinations in which emotions of the *same* valence are directed toward a *single* target ("If your brother hit you, would you be both mad and sad?"; "I was happy and glad that I got a new puppy for Christmas"). Children at this level report that two feelings cannot be directed toward different targets simultaneously, and opposite-valence feelings cannot co-occur.

At level 1 the child is beginning to develop representational sets for feelings of the same valence, constructing separate emotion categories, one positive and one negative. Feelings within each category are becoming somewhat differentiated from each other (e.g., happy versus glad within the positive representational set, mad versus sad within the negative set). However, the emotions within a given set are not yet sufficiently differentiated to allow the child to direct them toward different targets simultaneously. The child cannot yet simultaneously control variations within a given emotional set or variations in targets in order to relate the two variations to each other. This is the first cognitive limitation of level 1. The second limitation is that the child cannot yet integrate the sets of positive and negative emotions, which are viewed as conceptually distinct and therefore incompatible. Thus, emotions of opposite valence cannot be experienced as simultaneous.

Level 2. At this level (mean age 8.7), children can bring two *same*-valence feelings to bear on different targets simultaneously ("I'd be mad if she broke my toy and sad that she went home"; "I was excited I went to Mexico and glad to see my grandparents"). However, they deny the simultaneity of opposite-valence feelings: "I couldn't feel happy and scared at the same time; I would have to be two people at once!"

At level 2, the child overcomes the first cognitive limitation of level 1 by developing *representational mappings* that permit her to control and relate variations within a same-valence emotional set to variations within a set of targets. Thus, the child can map one emotion onto one target ("mad that she broke my toy") and attach the second, same-valence emotion to a different target ("sad that she went home"). However, the child has not yet overcome the second cognitive limitation of the previous level and still cannot integrate the sets of positive emotions. This limitation precludes acknowledging positive and negative emotions simultaneously.

Level 3. The child (mean age 10.1) demonstrates a major conceptual advance in that he or she can now appreciate simultaneous *opposite*-valence feelings. However, these emotions can only be brought to bear on different targets. Thus, the negative emotion is directed toward the negative event ("I was mad at my brother for hitting me") and the positive emotion is directed toward a different, positive aspect of the situation ("but at the same time, I was really happy that my father gave me permission to hit him back"). In other cases the two targets are even more discrete, for example, "I was sitting in school feeling worried about all of the responsibilities of a new pet, but I was happy that I had gotten straight As on my report card."

At level 3, the child advances to *representational systems* and can now integrate the sets of positive and negative emotions and acknowledge them simultaneously. However, the child cannot yet bring two opposite-valence feelings to bear on a single target. Rather, he or she enacts a shift of focus, directing the positive feelings to a positive target or event and then cognitively shifting the focus of the negative feeling to a negative event. The concept that the very same target can simultaneously have both positive and negative aspects is not yet cognitively accessible (Fischer 1980).

Level 4. At this level, children (mean age 11.3) become able to describe how opposite-valence feelings can be provoked by the *same* target, for example, "I was happy that I got a present but mad that it wasn't exactly what I wanted"; "If a stranger offered you candy, you'd be eager for the candy but also doubtful if it was OK"; "I was happy I was joining the new club but also a little worried because I didn't know anyone in it."

At this level the child overcomes the limitations of the previous period and can acknowledge that the same target can provoke both a positive and a negative emotion. The cognitive advance appears to be the child's newfound capacity to differentiate one target into positive and negative aspects and then coordinate these aspects with the corresponding positive and negative emotions simultaneously.

Each of the levels in this analysis involves developmental change with regard to the number and type of representations that the child can simultaneously control, coordinate, or integrate. The levels place increasingly greater cognitive demands on the child, resulting in a systematic, age-related progression in children's understanding of their emotions. However, direct observation revealed that children experience simultaneous emotions but are evidently not aware of it (Harter and Buddin 1987). This information is critical in informing our understanding of how children think about themselves. Discovering a profile of emotional development is so complicated that it is often easier to utilize very concrete testing questions to identify related concepts. Actually interviewing children and asking direct questions regarding emotion and their perceptions of it opens another window into the development of the thinking process. Understanding that a child perceives that you think exactly as he does and that you like what he likes influences your reaction when he changes television stations at age four, as opposed to six years later, when he clearly understands that you have separate thought processes.

DEVELOPMENT OF THE SELF. Harter studies the development of the self in relationships, how children and adolescents see themselves, and how their self-perceptions and actions are influenced by their relationships with others (Harter 1999:ix), a cognitive *and* social process. Shame and pride are the most appropriate prototypes of self-representation, as they are cognitive-emotional as well as social constructions. The ability to reflect on accomplishments or transgressions and feel personal pride or shame is very dependent on socialization experiences and does not emerge before middle or late childhood (Harter 1999:89). Harter's empirical research showed that children ages five to six use the terms *ashamed* and *proud* for the first time, but only in reference to parental reactions, with no acknowledgment of their own feelings. Children ages six to seven show beginnings of awareness that shame and pride can be directed by the self toward the self, and are beginning to incorporate others' observations into their own perceptions. Children ages seven to eight appear to have internalized standards for pride and shame and can spontaneously identify these feelings in the absence of parental observations. In order to go through the above sequence, children must experience external affective reactions before they are able to internalize them (Harter 1999:106–107).

Harter sees middle childhood as a time when children are able to differentiate their abilities, compare their performances to those of others, and more realistically evaluate their competencies. The danger is possibly perceiving themselves as incompetent and inadequate. Children who are praised and supported will have pride in their accomplishments, while those who are criticized may develop feelings of shame. If they receive unconditional support for who they are and for their attributes as individuals, they will experience their selves as authentic (Harter 1999:14). If there is a discrepancy between the children's behavior or performance and parental expectations, they will feel guilt and shame.

From ages five to seven, children continue to have very positive self-representations and to overestimate their virtuosity. However, it is during this period that they begin to link opposites, especially with respect to good and bad, although they still have difficulty recognizing that a person can possess both favorable and unfavorable attributes or integrate positive and negative emotions. The all-or-nothing perspective can lead to self-attributes that are all felt to be positive if the child has felt supported, or all negative if unsupported.

The self-attributes of children ages eight to eleven become increasingly interpersonal as relations with others, particularly peers, become more salient in developing the self. They define themselves as "nice," "helpful," "mean," "smart," "dumb," with trait labels representing cognitive, hierarchically constructed concepts in which behavior is subsumed under a higher-order generalization (Harter 1999:48–49). From this ability to form higher-order concepts comes the ability to form a representation of overall self-worth. Harter does not believe that the child is capable of a sense of global self-worth until middle childhood, when areas of success as well as areas of limitations can be identified and accepted. For this age group, these areas involve scholastic and athletic competence, physical appearance, and peer acceptance. The child has moved from all or nothing to being able to integrate positive and negative concepts of the self into a more balanced presentation of abilities. Emotionally, the child gradually becomes better at recognizing and accepting that the same target can elicit positive and negative emotions simultaneously.

Support from others is also a major determinant of self-esteem, especially for younger children (Harter 1987). Harter and co-workers examined levels of perceived social support from parents, teachers, classmates, and close friends. They found that for older children and adolescents, perceived approval from classmates and parents was the best predictor of self-esteem. Another factor is whether support is perceived as conditional, that is, if it is received contingent upon meeting someone else's expectations. Even when controlling for level of perceived support, conditionality correlates negatively with self-esteem. The conclusion is that if support is conditional it impairs self-esteem, because it does not connote approval of the self as self but suggests alternative behaviors that will please external sources.

Nurturance, support, and approval will help develop positive self-esteem, while rejecting, punitive, or neglectful responses will result in a poorer self-image.

BOYS AND GIRLS

In 1992, the American Association of University Women (AAUW) published a report, *How Schools Shortchange Girls*, the results of an examination of gender bias in American schools by the Wellesley College Center for Research on Women. Covering twenty years of published research on girls in preschool through the twelfth grade, this controversial document concluded that girls received significantly less attention than boys from teachers, and that this was especially true of African American girls. It cited work by Myra and David Sadker that found that teachers unknowingly discriminated against girls by calling on boys more often, asking them more challenging questions, and actually finishing work for girls while telling boys they were able to do it themselves. The report also contended that schools were providing inadequate education on sexuality in the face of then-skyrocketing rates of teenage pregnancy and that the contributions of women—referred to as the "evaded curriculum"—were marginalized in textbooks and classroom discussions. Perhaps most notably, the report decried the unequal representation of girls in higher-level math and science courses and their poorer performance on standardized tests in those subjects. Contributing factors were culture-based sex role socializations and perceptions of inferior occupational status accorded to women (AAUW 1992).

A 1998 follow-up report, *Gender Gaps: Where Schools Still Fail Our Children*, an analysis of approximately 1,000 research documents on gender issues in primary and secondary education published between 1990 and 1998, revealed progress in the schools. For students in middle childhood, it found that white girls outperformed boys in reading and writing, while white boys did better in history, geography, math, and science. However, by eighth grade the girls did better in math and reading, although the gap between the sexes was less than for minority boys and girls. Fourth-grade Hispanic girls outscored Hispanic boys in reading and history, and by eighth grade outscored them in math and reading. African American girls in fourth and in eighth grade outscored African American boys in science, reading, and history. The report also stressed the effect of successful female athletes in challenging stereotypes about body image, physical beauty, leadership, and competitive skills. Girls felt less pressure to appear deferential, modest, and immaculately groomed.

New concerns have been voiced regarding the effects on developing boys of enforcing cultural stereotypes. Parents expect their sons to act tough, to be strong and protective; peer standards dictate that boys don't cry. At the same time, boys are criticized for being insensitive. Dan Kindlon, a psychologist affiliated with Harvard Medical School and the Harvard School of Public Health, and Michael Thompson, a psychologist with extensive experience in a variety of schools and in private practice, assert in their book, *Raising Cain*, that society has "systematically steered [boys] away from their emotional lives toward silence, solitude and distrust" (Kindlon and Thompson 1999:xv). There is a tendency to assume that boys are self-reliant, confident, and potentially successful, and thus not emotional and needy. Boys have feelings, but often are treated as if they do not. An additional problem in middle childhood is that teachers in elementary school are, for the most part, females who may have difficulty with boys' high activity level and lower impulse control. Curriculum emphasizes reading, writing, and verbal ability, skills that develop more slowly in boys than in girls (Kindlon and Thompson 1999:23), thus putting boys at a disadvantage and possibly resulting in fears that they will never measure up and little sense of joy from learning. Physical size is also of concern for boys this age; bigger boys tend to get more respect while those who are smaller may be made to feel inadequate. Prestige and popularity are also often associated with excellence in sports, creating a "caste system" (Kindlon and Thompson 1999:85). Most boys will experience cruelty from peers, teachers, or family members and will respond with stoicism. It is difficult for them to express their feelings and they appear to take pride in not doing so. They want to be seen as strong and brave, yet inside they struggle with being young, having high expectations, wanting to please parents and teachers, and lack of self-knowledge. Saying how bad they feel would be a sign of weakness. Stoicism thus results in emotional isolation from family and friends that for many boys is better than appearing weak.

Kindlon and Thompson made the following recommendations for nurturing boys in order to enable them to develop strong emotional lives and to become empathic human beings (1999:241–58):

1. Give boys permission to have an internal life, approval for the full range of human emotions, and help in developing an emotional vocabulary so that they may better understand themselves and communicate more effectively with others.

2. Recognize and accept the high activity level of boys and give them safe places to express it.

3. Talk to boys in their language—in a way that honors their pride and their masculinity. Be direct with them; use them as consultants and problem solvers.

4. Teach boys that emotional courage is courage and that courage and empathy are the sources of real strength in life.

5. Use discipline to build character and conscience, not enemies.

6. Model a manhood of emotional attachment.
7. Teach boys that there are many ways to be a man.

Boys need help to not accept stereotypical views of how they should be, to see that they are entitled to a full range of human experiences and that vulnerability is not limited to girls, but is part of being human and acceptable for all.

Concerns about gender stereotypes, societal constraints on development, and "problems of engendering" have resulted in highly publicized research efforts and conclusions drawn from practice. Providing support and a nurturing environment to developing children regardless of race or gender gives them a voice and nurtures society as a whole.

CHALLENGES: TRIALS AND TRIBULATIONS OF MIDDLE CHILDHOOD

Children in middle childhood are often gleeful. They are not burdened by adult concerns and their carefree nature allows them to enjoy each moment to the fullest. Therefore, they are often more resilient than older children when faced with a crisis. However, this should not suggest that an individual child may not experience significant anxiety or other difficulties.

Charles Schaefer lists warning signs of serious psychological difficulties:

1. prolonged, constant anxiety, apprehension, or fear that is not proportionate to reality
2. signs of depression, such as growing apathy and withdrawal from people
3. an abrupt change in a child's mood or behavior so that he just does not seem to be himself anymore; for example, a very considerate and reliable child suddenly acts irresponsibly, self-preoccupied, and hostile to others
4. sleep disturbances, such as sleeping too much, not being able to sleep enough, restless or nightmarish sleep, not being able to get to sleep, or waking up early
5. appetite disturbances, including loss of appetite, gain of weight due to excessive eating, or eating bizarre substances such as dirt or garbage
6. disturbances in sexual functioning, such as promiscuity, exposing oneself, or excessive masturbation (Schaefer and Millman 1994:x)

LEARNING DISABILITIES. Learning disabilities, attention deficits, and hyperactivity are most often diagnosed after children enter school and show performance problems as they are faced with academic demands, standardized tests, and the need to function in a community of peers. Public Law 101–476, the Individuals with Disabilities Education Act, defines a learning disability as a "disorder in one or more of the basic psychological processes involved in understanding or in using spoken or written language, which may manifest itself in an imperfect ability to listen, think, speak, write, spell, or to do mathematical calculation." Learning disabilities are found in 4 percent of all school-age children and a significant number of children in special education classes (Chalfant 1989). Symptoms, which affect more boys than girls, include impulsivity, lack of attentiveness in class, difficulty retaining written information, poor fine motor skills, and apparent problems in receptive and expressive language.

It is in middle childhood that children develop the ability to compare their performance to that of their peers. With this come potential problems in the self-constructs of learning-disabled children.

SUICIDE. Although there are no good sources of data on suicidal ideation among preadolescents, it is probably underestimated, as adults may have difficulty conceiving of young children as capable of such thoughts (Jackson, Hess, and van Dalen 1995). Possible motives for suicidal behavior in children suggested by Rosenthal and Rosenthal (1984) are self-punishment, avoidance, merger with a lost significant object, and repair of an intolerable situation. Depression, aggression, general psychopathology, and ego defense mechanisms of denial and projection have all been correlated with persistent suicidal ideation in children, as has a preoccupation with death (Pfeffer 1989; Pfeffer, Lipkins, Plutchik, and Mizruchi 1988). It is imperative to consider the motive as well as the act in understanding and preventing suicide (Cohen 1993).

Methods of suicide considered or attempted by preadolescents include, in order of decreasing frequency, jumping from a height, poisoning, hanging, stabbing, drowning, running into traffic, and setting oneself on fire. The suicide rate in the United States for children under fifteen years of age was recently found to be twice as high as that of twenty-five other industrialized nations combined (0.55 compared with 0.27 per 100,000). When firearm-related suicides were tabulated, the difference was eleven times greater (0.32 compared with 0.03 per 100,000). The only country with a higher childhood firearm-related suicide rate than the United States was Northern Ireland (Division of Violence Prevention 1997). Both homicide and suicide in childhood have been associated with poor funding of social programs, economic stress related to participation of women in the labor force, divorce, ethnic strife, and social acceptability of violence (Briggs and Cutright 1994; Gartner 1991).

CHILD ABUSE. In 1997, child protective services agencies investigated more than two million reports alleging maltreatment of more than three million children. The national rate of children reported abused was 39.1 per 1,000 in the population (U.S. Dept. of Health and Human Services 1999).

The most common physical indications of child abuse include unexplained, poorly explained, or unusual injuries, such as cigarette or other suspicious burns, bruises, welts, lacerations, abrasions (including but not limited to belt marks), head injuries, internal injuries, fractures, or a combination of these. Child abuse should also be considered when evaluating children who are overly compliant, remarkably passive or aggressive, or exhibiting attention-seeking behavior. Presenting symptoms might include changes in sleep patterns, changes in school behavior and academic performance, overt depression, withdrawal, and acting out.

Almost from birth, children are at risk for sexual abuse, but the risks increase steadily from age three to adolescence. Some of the common signs of sexual abuse are vaginal discharge, injuries to or inflammation of the genitalia, signs of other physical abuse, and depression.

CHANGE AND LOSS. Some children have a difficult time with change, which is an inherent part of their lives. They enter a new grade every year. Their daily lives, friends, and activities are frequently changing. Though it is difficult to understand, positive change can provoke a negative response, particularly in middle childhood, when children thrive on routines.

Changes in family or personal environments that occur during normal development, can be stressors. A new sibling automatically changes the child's position in the family. No longer having the complete physical and emotional attention of his or her parents may represent a loss to the child, even with a new sibling relationship. Actual loss of a family member, a pet, or friends; moving to a new community; or changes in the household constellation secondary to changes in parental employment or marital situation can create emotional distress.

In a longitudinal study of middle-class divorced families, Wallerstein found that the children had ongoing feelings of sadness, neediness, and fantasies of more nurturing, protective environments, which they perceived as characteristic of intact families. Many saw the divorce as an impediment to close relationships with their fathers. Adolescents whose parents had divorced when they were younger presented anxiety about relationships, commitment, betrayal, and abandonment in present and future relationships (Wallerstein and Corbin 1991).

Elkind discusses the impact of divorce on everyone in the family, especially the children. As with many of life's stressful events, the adults involved have their own difficult time dealing with the situation. As a result, they may not fully recognize the emotional needs of their children. Children often feel rejected and feel a sense of loss of both parents and of the former family situation. Divorce is a family issue, not the child's alone, and the child should not be identified as the problem or the patient in this circumstance (Elkind 1988).

Children are particularly sensitive to a parent's illness or death. If a parent, grandparent, or sibling suffers a major illness, children will be exposed directly or indirectly to family members' worries and emotional reactions. They commonly develop concerns focused on the symptoms of the illness or treatment, for example, bleeding, or hair loss due to chemotherapy. In the absence of developmentally sensitive explanations, children will create their own interpretations. Their fantasies are often worse than reality and need clarification. They may fear that their parent will die, even if the illness is not a terminal one, and experience guilt or a sense of responsibility and anxiety over the health of the well parent (Christ et al. 1993).

Death anxiety naturally surfaces at junctures in life when cognitive development or perceptions of individuals' places in the life cycle make death more apparent. It initially emerges in the latency period and is characteristic of preadolescence (Toews, Martin, and Prosen 1985:134), a time when children finally come to understand the irreversibility, universality, and inevitability of death (Hostler 1978). During this stage of development, children often experience diffuse anxiety over a period of time and refer to concerns about their own death and the deaths of others without the anxiety reaching pathological proportions.

In the face of death of a parent, children will be sad and tearful and will grieve, but they will also continue to be connected to playful activities that make them happy. This is sometimes confusing to adults and may give the false impression that children are incapable of grief, rather than the reality that they grieve differently. Children are narcissistic, which helps them to be resilient. Part of their emotional journey is worrying about who will take care of them. Thus it is part of the adult grieving process to assure children that they will always be taken care of, and then to ensure that this is true. Mourning parents must be able to step outside of their own grief to recognize the needs of their children. A nurturing environment even at times of great duress, separation, stress, or loss can serve to facilitate emotional growth.

PARENTS OF LATENCY-AGE CHILDREN

Middle childhood can be a confusing time for parents. From age five to twelve, children's activities and needs may change, but their underlying reliance on caring adults to nurture them remains the same. As they grow emotionally and become more independent, children want to perform certain tasks alone. This need for autonomy may create the false impression that the parent is no longer needed, but in fact the parent's role as nurturer, provider, mentor, and companion remains critical. Latency-age children need parents to share in their activities and achievements. Additionally, they need them to be present, emotionally and physically, and are sophisticated enough to know if a parent is distracted or uninterested.

Parenting itself gets harder during middle childhood. Children require logical answers, explanations, and clarifications. It is an interesting time, as the parent-child dyad is interacting differently. There are shifts in all relationships when the child first enters school. A new homeostasis is created with new demands on the household members. Seemingly overnight, parenting now involves a dynamic between families. If a child in one family is not allowed to use a word, for example, *stupid*, and another child uses it, the child may become confused about what the rules are. Parents must become clearer in their own convictions and in what they are willing to concede.

As children in this age group gain physical strength and intellectual competence, adults delight in teaching and delegating tasks to them. A challenge for parents who strategically employ reason, with room for negotiation in their child-rearing practices, is to understand when to be controlling and when to nurture freedom of thought and action. Parents often struggle with how much independence to afford their children, how much time to be home with them, how much responsibility to give them, how to create opportunities for them, and how to help them become self-reliant. By the time this developmental period ends, children are moving toward independence, autonomous relationships, and much more freedom in decision making.

CONCLUSION: MOVING ON

The evolution of children through middle childhood is not limited to cognitive and physical development but includes biological, environmental, societal, cultural, familial, and individual factors. There are problems that plague

---

children around the world, such as poverty, famine, child labor, and war, and events idiosyncratic to the life of a particular child that prevent him or her from thriving. To understand what factors are emotionally protective for children, we must look toward earlier and later development. Issues that emerge in adolescence have underpinnings in middle childhood. To effectively address societal problems of adolescence such as substance abuse, teenage pregnancy, and suicide, risk assessment, prevention, and education must begin early and should be available to all children, not just cohorts at risk.

Middle childhood is the age from which experiences are first remembered and can be recalled in detail. Major transitions during middle childhood—moving from school to school or from neighborhood to neighborhood, or change in family constellation—will likely remain vivid in the child's mind. Memories are powerful tools because of the actual experiences from which they are created and how they are reconstructed. One's sense of self is in large part a compilation of autobiographical memories.

Erikson thought it appropriate for the child to exit middle childhood feeling competent, as though he or she could do anything. Competence, and the emotional recognition of it, fosters security and growth through each successive stage of development.

Does middle childhood truly prepare a child for adolescence? Feeling comfortable with oneself and developing strength, aptitude, interpersonal skills, and cognitive skills all serve to enhance self-esteem, which enables children to make mature, responsible decisions. With a strong foundation in communicating and learning, the ability to establish relationships and negotiate with others, a framework for utilizing sound reasoning, and the capacity for abstract thought, children move more easily into adolescence. The skills they have mastered during the "latency" years see them securely into the next phase of development, on the road to adulthood.

BIBLIOGRAPHY

American Association of University Women Educational Foundation. 1992. *How Schools Shortchange Girls: A Study of Major Findings on Girls in Education.* Washington, D.C.: American Association of University Women.

——. 1998. *Gender Gaps: Where Schools Still Fail Our Children.* Washington. D.C.: American Association of University Women.

Anglin, J. M. 1989. "Vocabulary Growth and the Knowing-Learning Distinction." *Reading Canada* 7:142–46.

Bauer, D. H. 1976. "An Exploratory Study of Developmental Changes in Children's Fears." *Journal of Child Psychology and Psychiatry* 17:69–74.

Bigelow, B. 1977. "Children's Friendship Expectations: A Cognitive-Developmental Study." *Child Development* 48:246–53.

Briggs, C. and P. Cutright. 1994. "Structural and Cultural Determinants of Child Homicide: A Cross-National Analysis." *Violence and Victims* 9:3–16.

Brown, L. M. 1989. *Narratives of Relationship: The Development of a Care Voice in Girls 7 to 16.* Ph.D. diss., Harvard University.

——. 1991. "A Problem of Vision: The Development of Voice and Relationship Knowledge in Girls Ages Seven to Sixteen." *Women's Studies Quarterly* 19 (1): 52–71.

Brown, L. M. and C. Gilligan. 1992. *Meeting at the Crossroads.* New York: Ballantine.

Bruner, J. S., A. Jolly, and K. Sylvia. 1976. *Play—Its Role in Development and Evolution.* New York: Basic.

Bullough, V. 1981. "Age of Menarche: A Misunderstanding." *Science* 213:365–66.

Burlington, Dorothy. 1952. *Twins.* London: Imago.

Chalfant, J. C. 1989. "Learning Disabilities: Policy Issues and Promising Approaches." *American Psychologist* 44:392–98.

Christ, G., K. Siegel, B. Freund, D. Langosch, S. Hendersen, D. Sperber, and L. Weinstein. 1993. "Impact of Parental Terminal Cancer on Latency-Age Children." *American Journal of Orthopsychiatry* 63 (3): 417–25.

Cohen, Y. 1993. "Suicidal Acts Among Latency-Age Children as an Expression of Internal Object-Relations." *British Journal of Psychotherapy* 9:405–13.

Division of Violence Prevention, National Cdenter for Injury Prevention and Control, Centers for Disease Control. 1997. "Rates of Homicide, Suicide, and Firearm-Related Death Among Children—26 Industrialized Countries." *Morbidity Mortality Weekly Report* 46 (5): 101–105.

Elkind, D. 1988. *The Hurried Child.* Rev. ed. Reading, MA: Addison-Wesley.

——. 1997. *All Grown Up and No Place to Go: Teenagers in Crisis.* Rev. ed. Reading, MA: Perseus Books.

Epstein, J. A., K. W. Griffin, and G. J. Botvin. 2000. "Role of General and Specific Competence Skills in Protecting Inner-City Adolescents from Alcohol Use." *Journal of Studies on Alcohol* 61 (3): 379–86.

Erikson, E. H. 1959. "Identity and the Life Cycle." *Psychological Issues* Monograph 1 (1). New York: International Universities Press.

——. 1963 [1950]. *Childhood and Society.* New York: Norton.

——. 1964. *Insight and Responsibility.* New York: Norton.

——. 1968. *Identity, Youth, and Crisis.* New York: Norton.

——. 1977. *Toys and Reason.* New York: Norton.

Fischer, K. W. 1980. "A Theory of Cognitive Development: The Control and Construction of Hierarchies of Skills." *Psychological Review* 87:477–531.

French, D. C. and M. K. Underwood. 1996. "Peer Relations During Middle Childhood." In N. Vanzetti and S. Duck, eds., *A Lifetime of Relationships*, 155–80. Pacific Grove, CA: Brooks/Cole.

Freud, A. 1963. "The Concept of Developmental Lines." *Psychoanalytic Study of the Child*, 18:245–65. New York: International Universities Press.

———. 1965. *Normality and Pathology in Childhood*. New York: International Universities Press.

———. 1966. *The Ego and the Mechanisms of Defense*. New York: International Universities Press.

Freud, S. 1905. *Three Essays on the Theory of Sexuality*. Standard Edition, 7:125–245. London: Hogarth Press, 1953.

———. 1908. *Family Romances*. New York: Collier, 1963.

———. 1926. *Inhibitions, Symptoms and Anxiety*. Standard Edition 20:77–175. London: Hogarth Press, 1959.

Fulghum, R. 1988. *All I Really Need to Know I Learned in Kindergarten*. New York: Villard.

Gartner, R. 1991. "Family Structure, Welfare Spending, and Child Homicide in Developed Democracies." *Journal of Marriage and the Family* 53:231–40.

Gilchrist, L. D., S. P. Schinke, W. H. Snow, R. F. Schilling, and V. Senechal. 1988. "The Transition to Junior High School: Opportunities for Primary Prevention." *Journal of Primary Prevention* 8:99–108.

Gilligan, C. 1993. *In a Different Voice*. Cambridge: Harvard University Press.

Ginsburg, H. P. and S. Opper. 1988. *Piaget's Theory of Intellectual Development*. Englewood Cliffs, NJ: Prentice Hall.

Halpern, E., and L. Palic. 1984. "Developmental Changes in Death Anxiety in Childhood." *Journal of Applied Developmental Psychology* 5:163–72.

Harter, S. 1986. "Processes Underlying the Construction, Maintenance, and Enhancement of the Self-Concept in Children." In J. Suls and A. G. Greenwald, eds., *Psychological Perspectives on the Self*, 3:136–82. Hillsdale, NJ: Lawrence Erlbaum.

———. 1987. "The Determinants and Mediational Role of Global Self-Worth in Children." In N. Eisenberg, ed., *Contemporary Issues in Developmental Psychology*, 219–42. New York: Wiley.

———. 1999. *The Construction of the Self*. New York: Guilford.

Harter, S. and B. Buddin. 1987. "Children's Understanding of the Simultaneity of Two Emotions: A Five-Stage Developmental Acquisition Sequence." *Developmental Psychology* 23 (3): 388–99.

Harter, S., P. Waters, and N. R. Whitesell. 1997. "Lack of Voice as a Manifestation of False Self Behavior: The School Setting as a Stage Upon Which the Drama of Authenticity Is Enacted." *Educational Psychologist* 32:153–73.

Hartup, W. W. 1983. "Peer Relations." In P. H. Mussen, ed., *Handbook of Child Psychology, vol. 4: Socialization, Social Development, and Personality*, 103–96. New York: Wiley.

Herman-Giddens, M. E., E. J. Slora, R. C. Wasserman, C. J. Bourdony, M. V. Bhapkar, G. G. Koch, and C. M. Hasemeier. 1997. "Secondary Sexual Characteristics and Menses in Young Girls Seen in Office Practice: A Study from the Pediatric Research in Office Settings Network." *Pediatrics* 99 (4): 505–12.

Hostler, S. L. 1978. "The Development of the Child's Concept of Death." In O. J. Sahler, ed., *The Child and Death*, 1–28. St. Louis: C. V. Mosby.

Inhelder, B. and J. Piaget. 1958. *The Growth of Logical Thinking*. New York: Basic.

Jackson, H., P. M. Hess, and A. van Dalen. 1995. "Preadolescent Suicide: How to Ask and How to Respond." *Families in Society* 76 (5): 267–79.

Jacobs, J. E. 1983. "Learning Problems, Self-Esteem, and Delinquency." In J. E. Mack and S. L. Ablon, eds., *The Development and Sustenance of Self-Esteem in Childhood*, 209–22. New York: International Universities Press.

Johnson, J. E. and T. D. Yawkey. 1988. "Play and Integration." In T. D. Yawkey and J. E. Johnson, eds., *Integrative Processes and Socialization: Early to Middle Childhood*, 97–107. Hillsdale, NJ: Lawrence Erlbaum Associates.

Kindlon, D. and M. Thompson. 1999. *Raising Cain: Protecting the Emotional Life of Boys*. New York: Ballantine.

Kohlberg, L. 1963. "The Development of Children's Orientations Towards a Moral Order: I. Sequence in the Development of Moral Thought." *Vita Humana* 6:11–33.

——. 1964. "Development of Moral Character and Moral Ideology." In M. L. Hoffman and L. W. Hoffman, eds., *Review of Child Development Research*, 1:383–431. New York: Russell Sage Foundation.

——. 1971. "Stage and Sequence: The Cognitive-Developmental Approach to Socialization." In D. A. Goslin, ed., *Handbook of Socialization Theory*. Chicago: Rand McNally.

——. 1976. "Moral Stages and Moralization: The Cognitive Developmental Approach." In J. Lickona, ed., *Moral Development Behavior: Theory, Research, and Social Issues*, 31–53. New York: Holt, Rinehart, and Winston.

Ladd, G. W. 1988. "Friendship Patterns and Peer Status During Early and Middle Childhood." *Journal of Developmental and Behavioral Pediatrics* 9:229–38.

Ladd, G. W. and J. M. Price. 1987. "Predicting Children's Social and School Adjustment Following the Transition from Preschool to Kindergarten." *Child Development* 58:1168–89.

120

Lewis, M., ed. 1996. *Child and Adolescent Psychiatry*. Baltimore: Williams and Wilkins.

Lines, P. 1998. *Homeschoolers: Estimating Numbers and Growth*. National Institute on Student Achievement, Curriculum, and Assessment, Office of Education Research and Improvement, U.S. Department of Education.

Maccoby, E. E. 1990. "Gender and Relationships: A Developmental Perspective." *American Psychologist* 45:513–20.

Manhattan Country School Newsletter. 1995. *Gender Equity Project: The Chasers and the Chased*. 1998. http://www.mcs.pvt.k12.ny.us/sampler/v2index.html.

——. 1998. *Gender Gaps: Where Schools Still Fail Our Children*. Washington: American Association of University Women Educational Foundation.

Meisels, S. J. 1996. "Performance in Context: Assessing Children's Achievement at the Outset of School." In A. J. Sameroff and M. M. Haith, eds., *The Five- to Seven-Year Shift*, 407–31. Chicago: University of Chicago Press.

Miller, P. H. 1989. *Theories of Developmental Psychology*. New York: Freeman.

Mills, J. R. and N. E. Jackson. 1990. "Predictive Significance of Early Giftedness: The Case of Precocious Reading." *Journal of Educational Psychology* 82 (3): 410–19.

Nelson, K. 1996. "Memory Development from 4 to 7 Years." In A. J. Sameroff and M. M. Haith, eds., *The Five- to Seven-Year Shift*, 141–59. Chicago: University of Chicago Press.

Newman, C. J. 1977. "Children of Disaster: Clinical Observations at Buffalo Creek." *Annual Progress in Child Psychiatry and Child Development* 149–61.

Nickerson, E. T. and K. S. O'Laughlin. 1983. "The Therapeutic Use of Games." In C. E. Schaefer and K. J. O'Connor, eds., *Handbook of Play Therapy*, 174–88. New York: Wiley.

Pease, D. and J. B. Gleason. 1985. "Gaining Meaning: Semantic Development." In J. B. Gleason, ed., *The Development of Language*. Columbus, OH: Merrill.

Pettit, G. S., R. D. Laird, J. E. Bates, and K. A. Dodge. 1997. "Patterns of After-School Care in Middle Childhood: Risk Factors and Developmental Outcomes." *Merrill-Palmer Quarterly* 43 (3): 515–38.

Pfeffer, C. R. 1989. "Preoccupation with Death in 'Normal' Children: The Relationship to Suicidal Behavior." *Omega Journal of Death and Dying* 20 (3): 205–12.

Pfeffer, C. R., R. Lipkins, R. Plutchik, and M. Mizruchi. 1988. "Normal Children at Risk for Suicidal Behavior: A Two-Year Follow-up Study." *Journal of the American Academy of Child and Adolescent Psychiatry* 27 (1): 34–41.

Piaget, J. 1952. *The Origins of Intelligence in Children*. New York: International Universities Press.

——. 1979. *The Child's Conception of the World*. New York: Harcourt Brace.

———. 1983. "Piaget's Theory." In P. H. Mussen, ed., *Handbook of Child Psychology*, 1:103–28. New York: Wiley.

Random House Unabridged Dictionary. 1993. New York: Random House.

Robinson, T. N., M. L. Wilde, L. C. Navracruz, K. F. Haydel, and A. Varady. 2001. "Effects of Reducing Children's Television and Video Game Use on Aggressive Behavior." *Archives of Pediatric and Adolescent Medicine* 155:17–23.

Rosenthal, P. and S. Rosenthal. 1984. "Suicidal Behavior by Preschool Children." *American Journal of Psychiatry* 141:520–25.

Schaefer, C. E. and H. L. Millman. 1994. *How to Help Children with Common Problems.* Northvale, NJ: Jason Aronson.

Snow, W. H., L. Gilchrist, R. F. Schilling, S. P. Schinke, and C. Kelso. 1986. "Preparing Students for Junior High School." *Journal of Early Adolescence* 6:127–37.

Stevenson-Hinde, J. and A. Shouldice. 1995. "4.5 to 7 years: Fearful Behavior, Fears, and Worries." *Journal of Child Psychology and Psychiatry* 36:1027–38.

Stolorow, R. D. 1974. "A Note on Death Anxiety as a Developmental Achievement." *American Journal of Psychoanalysis* 34 (4): 351–53.

Sullivan, H. S. 1953. *The Iinterpersonal Theory of Psychiatry.* New York: Norton.

Taylor, J. M., C. Gilligan, and A. M. Sullivan. 1995. *Between Voices and Silence.* Cambridge: Harvard University Press.

Terr, L. C. 1984. "Chowchilla Revisited: The Effects of Psychic Trauma Four Years After a School-Bus Kidnapping." *Annual Progress in Child Psychiatry and Child Development* 300–17.

Toews, J., R. Martin, and H. Prosen. 1985. "Death Anxiety: The Prelude to Adolescence." *Adolescent Psychiatry* 12:134–44.

Townend, B. 1963. "The Non-Therapeutic Extraction of Teeth and Its Relation to the Ritual Disposal of Shed Deciduous Teeth." *British Dental Journal* 115:312–15, 354–71, 394–96.

U.S. Department of Health and Human Services. 1999. *Child Maltreatment 1997: Reports from the States to the National Child Abuse and Neglect Data System.* Washington, D.C.: Department of Health and Human Services.

van Gennep, A. 1960. *The Rites of Passage.* Trans. M. B. Vizedom and G. L. Caffee. Chicago: University of Chicago Press.

Walker, L. J. 1989. "A Longitudinal Study of Moral Reasoning." *Child Development* 60:157–66.

Wallerstein, J. and S. Corbin. 1991. "The Child and the Vicissitudes of Divorce." In M. Lewis, ed., *Child and Adolescent Psychiatry*, 1108–18. Baltimore: Williams and Wilkins.

Walley, A. C. 1993. "The Role of Vocabulary Development in Children's Spoken

Word Recognition and Segmentation Ability." *Developmental Review* 13:286–350.

Watson, A. J. and R. Valtin. 1997. "Secrecy in Middle Childhood." *International Journal of Behavioral Development* 21 (3): 431–52.

Watterson, B. 1987. *Calvin and Hobbes.* Kansas City: Andrews and McMeel.

Wells, R. 1991. "The Tooth Fairy in North American Folklore and Popular Culture." In P. Narváez, ed., *The Good People: New Fairylore Essays,* 426–53. Lexington: University Press of Kentucky.

White, S. H. 1965. "Evidence for a Hierarchical Arrangement of Learning Processes." In L. P. Lipsitt and C. C. Spiker, eds., *Advances in Child Development and Behavior,* 187–220. New York: Academic Press.

White, S. H. 1996. "The Child's Entry Into the 'Age of Reason.'" In A. J. Sameroff and M. M. Haith, eds., *The Five- to Seven-Year Shift,* 17–30. Chicago: University of Chicago Press.

Youniss, J. 1980. *Parents and Peers in Social Development: A Sullivan-Piaget Perspective.* Chicago: University of Chicago Press.

SONIA G. AUSTRIAN

one two three **four** five six

ADOLESCENCE

INTRODUCTION

Robert Coles, a well-known Harvard University psychiatrist, notes that no other aspect of the life cycle has commanded as much attention from novelists, social scientists, and journalists as adolescence. He postulates that this may be because adolescents, their habits, interests, and developing sexuality, "have a hold on us that is tied to our own memories." Coles further believes that the power of attachment adults feel toward their adolescents is because they are "reminders, legatees, and long-standing witnesses to our lives" (Coles 1998:135–36).

The *Shorter Oxford English Dictionary* defines *adolescence* as "the process or condition of growing up; the period between childhood and maturity" (Onions 1947:25). The word is derived from the Latin verb *adolescere*, which means "to come to maturity" (Marchant and Charles 1945:14). The word first appeared in the English language in 1482 and referred to the period between childhood and adulthood, ranging from ages fourteen to twenty-five for males and twelve to twenty-one for females (Blos 1979:406). It must be distinguished from *puberty*, the specific time when a person matures sexually and becomes physically capable of reproduction.

Adolescence can easily be described as "the best of times, the worst of times," and for many passing through this stage of development it may be both. Adolescence never occurs in a social vacuum; passage through this phase is critically affected by the structure of the society in which the individual is raised. Many cultures have rites of passage when the child enters adolescence or adulthood that mark a socially defined status or role change, such as marriage and parenthood. In Western culture, adolescence usually is a gradual transition from childhood to adulthood. In the United States, the age at which a person may move from being an adolescent to being an adult may vary, not only due to parental and cultural expectations but also because of state laws determining the age at which one may work, obtain a driver's license, marry, be treated as an adult offender, or be eligible to go to war.

During adolescence, the individual goes through many biopsychosocial changes. The rate of physical growth and development is second only to that which occurs in infancy, and adolescents come in all sizes and shapes. Tasks include moving from dependence on families or caregivers to independence, facing major decisions about the future, and trying to establish an individual identity. For some, these tasks are made easier by a supportive environment, while for others the environment may be unsupportive or even destructive. Decisions encountered include whether or not to commence sexual activity as well as what is sexual identity; whether or not to use alcohol and drugs; and how to integrate relationships and work goals. There are nearly 60 million teenagers in the United States (Powers 1998:G1). Many of the problems and pressures they face today are greater than those of the past decade or two (Offer, Schonert-Reichl, and Boxer 1996:278). Higher divorce rates, family mobility, increased numbers of teenage unwed mothers, competition for schools and jobs, and easier access to alcohol and drugs make adolescents more vulnerable. Their opportunities to choose clearly are influenced by socioeconomic and cultural factors, as well as experiences in the earlier stages of development.

Adolescence is often referred to in the literature as made up of three overlapping stages. In young adolescence (ages twelve to fourteen), when puberty is a major factor, youths often are concerned with bodily appearance and what may be considered "normal." Conformity may be a defense against rejection and disapproval, and peers have great influence over dress, leisuretime activities, and even manner of speech. Children at this stage usually have friends of the same sex and a particular need for acceptance of their own bodies, emotions, and skills. Adolescents, more often girls, tend to have a lowering of self-esteem. In both young and middle adolescence, friendships can be very intense and based on self-disclosure and empathy, not seen as much in earlier stages. Their friends enable adolescents to begin to distance emotionally from parents as they seek a sense of autonomy and identity. However, studies have shown that when seeking help, 89 percent consulted friends and 81 percent consulted family members. Those who sought help from parents had a better self-image than those who did not (Schonert-Reichl, Offer, and Howard 1995:174).

In middle adolescence (ages fourteen to sixteen), many teenagerss form heterosexual relationships, which may involve decisions about sexual behavior as well as alcohol and drug use. During this period, they are very much in search of an identity, a difficult task, and can experience periods of elation, but also irritability, moodiness, and depression. Peers remain important and often are very influential in interpersonal and social skills development. A struggle may emerge between conformity and other value systems. Relationships with parents alternate between dependency and independence, with a driver's license representing a rite of passage. Social, athletic, or academic success produces marked growth in self-esteem.

The older adolescent (sixteen to nineteen) must confront approaching adulthood and must consider the consequences of decisions and of behavior. This is a time to solidify personal and vocational skills and roles, as well as value systems, sexual identity, and occupational identity. The older adolescent also grapples with his or her formulation of the meaning of life.

Some of the researchers discussed here have also made major contributions to theories about the earlier developmental stages, and some have focused specifically on adolescence. While adolescence generally has been thought of as the period from ages thirteen to eighteen, it is now often considered to start as young as ten or eleven and may continue into the twenties (McGrath 1998:29). The task of establishing independence often is not completed by eighteen, as people continue to depend on their families during their higher education, young adults may return home for economic reasons following graduation from post–high school programs, and adolescent single mothers may need to remain in their family home while trying to pursue education or employment and raise a child. Thus, the end of adolescence as graduation from high school and leaving home for a job, marriage, or higher education may no longer be the norm; our contemporary society has been "accused" of prolonging adolescence.

As in the earlier chapter on infancy and toddlerhood, most of the theories discussed here evolved from observation of white middle-class subjects, often males. The more recent studies have focused on, or at least included, females and more diverse populations.

SIGMUND FREUD

Sigmund Freud believed that adolescent and adult development is determined in the first five or six years of life. Therefore, he was not really very interested in what happened after the resolution of the oedipal conflict; he did, however, address puberty to a limited extent. Freud believed that following the resolution of the Oedipus complex, there is a latency period when the sexual impulses are suppressed and the child finds nonsexual outlets. At puberty, the person has the capacity for orgasm and is biologically able to procreate, due to hormonal and anatomical developments; libido resurfaces, localized in the genital area. Adult, primarily genital sexuality emerges if the adolescent has successfully mastered the previous stages of psychosexual development. Freud referred to this as *the genital period*. There is a resurgence of the sexual instincts that are directed toward genital primacy, and the appropriate love object is a heterosexual partner, although Freud did recognize that everyone has same- and opposite-sex aspects of their psychological make-up. With the onset of puberty, physical and psychological changes occur that give infantile sexual life its final, "normal" shape. Until adolescence, sexual life is autoerotic, but with adolescence the formerly cathected erotogenic zones are subordinated to the primacy of the genital zone. Freud believed that the earlier developmental periods finally culminate in the establishment of *genital primacy*, which, while having the altruistic purpose of reproduction, is also experienced as pleasurable. Both boys and girls in the early stages of puberty experience a resurgence of oedipal fantasies, which must be overcome and repudiated. This may be followed by a period of sexual fantasies before real relationships can begin. A related process is the adolescent's effort to detach from parental influence and authority, which may be viewed as oppositional but is necessary for civilization to progress from the older to the new generation. Freud believed this process to be much easier for boys than for girls and stated that some girls are not able to detach, persist in childish love attachments, and will become "cold wives and remain sexually anaesthetic" (Freud 1905:227). If detachment does not occur, boys may fall in love with older women and girls, with older men.

Freud believed that with adolescence there are three possible sources of sexual stimulation: external, through direct manipulation and stimulation of the genitals and other erotogenic zones; internal, from hormonal discharges within the body; and external memories and internal impulses from pregenital periods (Freud 1905:208). Stimulation with the resulting sexual tension is the first step toward adult intercourse and the goal of procreation. Sexual intimacy, true affection, and reproduction are the developmental tasks. Freud believed that everyone has same- and opposite-sex aspects of their psychology, but that with maturity a heterosexual identity is the norm. Thus the resolution of the genital period can only be achieved through "object finding" of a heterosexual partner.

Freud was somewhat aware that the process of forming an identity is also a task of adolescence; he recognized that the adolescent will often identify with some highly cathected person in the environment who may be known or a historic or fictional character (Brenner 1974:119). These identifications, Freud believed, help to mold the superego in a way acceptable to the moral standards and ideals of the culture.

In *Three Essays on the Theory of Sexuality*, written in 1905, Freud once again showed little knowledge of women. He felt that in adolescence the sexual development of boys and girls differs greatly and that what happens for boys is more straightforward and understandable. He saw puberty as the period when there is a sharp distinction between boys' and girls' characters, and this contrast has a decisive influence on the rest of their lives. Puberty, he felt, brings up a strong resurgence of libido in boys and of repression in girls. Freud believed that girls have a greater inclination to view sexuality in terms of shame and disgust, leading to repression and a tendency to passivity in sexual relations. The repression, which could result in neurosis, may increase as the erotogenic zone moves from the clitoris to the vagina. Girls, at puberty, must acknowledge and accept their fear of castration (Freud 1931:229) with an accompanying awareness of a wound to their narcissism, leading to a sense of inferiority (Freud 1925:253).

Boys at puberty establish primacy of the genital zones as they experience growth of external genitalia, and have only to discharge "sexual products" (Freud 1905:207) with the goal of reproduction. This, Freud believed, is not of concern to girls or "castrated" boys. He felt that the genitalia are very complex apparatuses ready in adolescence to be "put into operation" (Freud 1905:208). Boys experience erection and girls experience lubrication of the vagina. Boys, he believed, experience stronger libidinous feelings and therefore overvalue sexuality. Freud felt that puberty is simpler for boys than for girls, as the penis remains a constant erotogenic zone from childhood.

Freud believed that the major task of adolescence is moving object choice from same-sex friends to opposite-sex relationships. This is achieved because of the attraction between the different sexual characteristics and the resurgence of earlier (oedipal) hostility toward the same-sex parent, along with attraction to the parent of the opposite sex. Freud appears, in his writings, to have been homophobic; he cautioned against boys being educated by male teachers or having "men servants," which might lead to sexual "inversion."

ANNA FREUD

Anna Freud's primary interest was in working with children and, to a lesser extent, with adolescents. As an analyst, she believed that the wealth of material about childhood gave credence to theorists' conclusions, but that adolescence "is a neglected period, a stepchild where analytic thinking is concerned" (Freud 1958:255). She believed that at puberty, the instinctual processes are of primary importance, resulting in character changes with accompanying disturbance of psychic equilibrium. It is a turbulent period, as the adolescent experiences new internal demands caused by sexual maturation and the associated intensified sexual drive. Adolescent upset is inevitable, as the internal balance of latency is precarious and does not allow for the quantitative and qualitative changes of puberty. What appears to be adolescent upheaval is actually internal adjustments (Freud 1958:264).

Dr. Freud described adolescents as egoistic, seeing themselves as the center of the universe and thus the sole object of interest, yet at the same time capable of self-sacrifice and devotion (Freud 1966:137). They can be passionate about people or ideas and then suddenly behave in a contradictory fashion. While appearing selfish and materialistic, they can also be idealistic. Moods range from cheerful optimism to blackest pessimism; energy levels range from enthusiasm to apathy. A desire for excessive independence alternates with clinging behavior (not unlike the earlier separation-individuation period). Freud referred to the debate over the importance of biological changes versus the importance of psychic maturity, concluding that both the physical and the psychic phenomena of puberty are important for adolescent development and the beginning of the capacity for mature sexual functioning, the capacity for love, and the formation of character as a whole (Freud 1966:139).

Anna Freud differed from her father's traditional psychoanalytic view that sexuality begins in the first year of life and puberty is of limited importance. She believed instead that there are two starting points in the development of sexual life, one in the first year, as discussed in an earlier chapter, and the second at puberty. Puberty, she felt, includes a recapitulation of the earlier infantile sexual period and a second recapitulation at the climacteric (Freud 1966:139). A major difference from the earlier period is that physical sexual maturity is attained and genitalia assume importance over the pregenital instincts.

At puberty there is a shift in the relationship of the id and the ego, resulting in disequilibrium and increased conflict. The id, whose impulses are strengthened by the physiological changes, vigorously wishes to pursue sexual wishes in the presence of a weaker ego. There is an influx of libido and the psychic balance that existed between id and ego during latency is upset, with the intrapsychic conflicts resurfacing. Aggressive impulses also intensify, and behavior may reflect a regression to oral and anal levels. Oedipal issues reemerge through fantasies and daydreams, and once again males are concerned about castration and females experience penis envy. At the same time, the superego, influenced by the people the adolescent identifies with, will also come into conflict with the ego as it attempts to deal with the id impulses. Thus changes occur in all three parts of the psychic structure.

During puberty and with the advent of bodily sexual maturity, Dr. Freud believed, the ego is focused on preserving the character formed during latency and in retaining supremacy over the id. At issue is not the gratification or frustration of instinctual wishes but the nature of the psychic structure established in childhood and latency. If victorious, the character formed in these earlier periods will be established, but the id impulses will be confined to the narrow limits of childhood and defense mechanisms and symptoms will be needed to hold them in check, resulting in a more rigid ego. However, if the id conquers the ego, the previously established character vanishes and adult life focuses on uninhibited instinctual gratification (Freud 1966:150). How this is resolved depends on the strength of the impulses, the ego's capacity to tolerate the instinct depending on the preestablished character, and finally, the qualitative factor of the nature and efficacy of the defense mechanisms available to the individual.

Dr. Freud recognized in her analysis of adolescents that for some, the increase of libido with its accompanying conscious and unconscious wishes and fantasies results in redoubled efforts to master instincts. As a result, some turn to the defenses of sublimation, asceticism, and intellectualization, which create distance between impulses and ideas. With sublimation, sexual impulses and energy are transformed into socially acceptable activities such as sports, the arts, and intellectual endeavors. In an ascetic phase, the adolescent fears the quantity, rather than the quality, of the instincts and will appear to mistrust enjoyment, bowing to prohibitions. In the extreme this will lead to renouncing any impulses associated with sexuality, avoiding peers, wearing asexual clothing, possibly developing phobias or even anorexia, and finding no means of substitute gratification (Freud 1966:153–58). It is usually a transitory phenomenon.

Dr. Freud believed that during adolescence there is an increase in intellectual interests and in intelligence. In latency and prepuberty there is initially a concern with concrete objects; this evolves into concern with abstractions and with friendships, which involves thinking about and discussing things, formulating "arguments." Rather than asceticism, the defense used is intellectualization—adolescents think and speculate about, and discuss, the instinctual side of life. They may develop a "philosophy of life" and may turn to worldly concerns as a distraction from thinking about instinctual pressures. Friendships and loyalty replace concerns about passionate object relations. Thus, instinctual processes are translated into intellectual processes and intellectualization functions as the defense against the pressure of the impulses. Linking instinctual processes to ideational content makes them available to consciousness and thus controllable.

Anna Freud recognized the important role of object relations in the life of adolescents, as they begin to detach libido from parents and cathect new objects. While some may withdraw (asceticism) and others turn from experiencing love objects (intellectualization), many will experiment with new attachments, including intense friendshipsand falling in love with others their own age, or attachment to an older person who may become a parental substitute (a "crush"). As the adolescent experiments, these relationships are often passionate, all consuming, and exclusive, yet frequently are of short duration with inconsistent feelings. Often these relationships exist only for the present; though the object may be forgotten and abandoned, Dr. Freud believed that what remains is a detailed memory of the form of the relationship. The adolescent then moves on to reproduce this with a new object. She recognized also the tendency of many adolescents to become as much like the chosen object as possible with changes in clothing, hairstyle, speech, handwriting, and even proclamation of new philosophical and political ideas. Clearly these early relationships are more fixations than true object relationships and have a high degree of identification as the adolescents establish themselves.

In conclusion, adolescents may take several routes to the goal of establishing healthy, normal object relationships, including asceticism, intellectualization, and identification. If these defenses do not become rigid and are transitory, the adolescent eventually will be able to give them up and form a solid relationship. While more of her focus was on the pathological manifestations of adolescence, Dr. Freud could identify two aspects that could be considered "normal": adolescence is an interruption of peaceful growth, and upholding a steady equilibrium between the id and the ego during adolescence would be abnormal (Freud 1958:275). The battle between the id and the ego has as its goal restoration of internal peace and harmony. This process might make the adolescent behave in an inconsistent and unpredictable manner: impulses may be fought or accepted or warded off successfully, or may overwhelm the adolescent; parents may be both loved and hated; rebellion and dependence will both be observed; and imitation of and identification with others as part of establishing identity and basic character may go from idealistic and generous to calculating and self-centered. Dr. Freud stressed that these behaviors might seem abnormal in other phases of life, but for adolescents they are part of the task of assuming an adult personality. Parents often need guidance at this stage more than their children do.

ROBERT WHITE

As noted in the chapter on infancy and toddlerhood, White (1975) expanded Sigmund Freud's formulations. He did not feel that the resolution of the oedipal conflict or the formation of the superego takes place in one relatively brief phase of development or through one unified process of conflict resolution. Instead, the male child learns his sexual identity and role, his special place in the family, and the permitted avenues of affection and aggressive competition through a gradual process, beginning much earlier than proposed by S. Freud. The superego forms not through identification and introjection but rather through a slow and somewhat complex learning process that results in a compromise among the pressures of instinctual urges, parental frustration and prohibitions, and the concurrent need for parental support.

According to White's competence model, the male child identifies with the father, whose competence he admires, and thus he desires a reciprocal love relationship with this esteemed person. Boys, White believed, identify slightly with their mothers but chiefly with their fathers, since both are male, a sex role he believed is learned quite early.

Finally, White defined what he saw as the resolution of the genital phase: a sense of identity with consolidation of feelings of past competence; studying and preparing for vocational choices; and embarking on relationships for social and sexual satisfaction. Thus he emphasized the ability to consolidate feelings of competence, mastery, and self-confidence during this phase, with the goal of achieving an identity.

White believed that the natural developmental process leads to a consistent and stable identity in late adolescence. With new circumstances and interpersonal relationships, the adolescent gains awareness of his or her ability to influence the world and feels greater confidence in personal growth. Self-perception becomes more organized and stable. In late adolescence, as ties to the family lessen, adolescents become more able to realistically assess interpersonal relationships. An increase in the repertoire of coping skills gives them greater ease, flexibility, and enjoyment in nonfamilial object relationships. Occupational choices also lead to a more stable sense of self. The adolescent is ready to move into adulthood.

ERIK ERIKSON

As discussed in chapter 2, Erikson postulated a total of eight sequential stages involving ego crises, states of disequilibrium, and accompanying critical tasks, which enhance and guide the individual's sense of self and ego identity. Each stage must be gone through and has both negative and positive factors that are incorporated into the person's identity. Each crisis also involves ritualizations and ritualisms. At the end of each stage, a new psychological "virtue" (strength) is acquired. Erikson believed that with the successful completion of the fourth stage, industry versus inferiority, childhood ends. The next stage, acquiring a sense of identity versus a sense of role confusion (ages thirteen to twenty-two), marks the beginning of adolescence.

In the course of resolving earlier crises, children acquire a sense of continuity; in spite of the fact that they are changing, there is a fundamental sameness. Erikson believed, however, that in adolescence, because of the rapidity of physical growth and of genital maturity, the earlier crises are resurrected and this sameness or continuity is questioned (Erikson 1950:261). Adolescence thus becomes a period of role experimentation leading to final choices after all identifications from earlier periods are integrated. The early bodily identity and the subsequent social identities merge in adolescence, which is the bridge between childhood and adulthood. Erikson saw adolescence as a psychosocial moratorium (Erikson 1950:262–63) during which the person may explore a range of options without making an immediate commitment. It is also a period between the morality learned in childhood and the ethics to be developed in adulthood. The adolescent is concerned about how she or he appears to others as compared to her or his self-image. Erikson stressed the importance of individual endowments, culture, and opportunities for different social roles in forming an identity (Erikson 1950:261). Peer involvement is intense during this phase of development, as peers provide role models and social feedback. "Falling in love" and "crushes" are common occurrences, more related to developing an identity than to meeting sexual needs (Erikson 1950:262). Adolescents spend time in the company of their peers or on the telephone with them, as they are the focus of interpersonal interaction.

Erikson referred to adolescence as a period of identity crisis; while the positive resolution is a sense of identity, the negative one is role confusion. The positive outcome is "being at one with oneself" and having a sense of belonging to a community that itself has a past, present, and future. Erikson recognized that an adolescent might opt for a "negative identity," choosing to identify with all that has been presented as undesirable or dangerous, becoming what is termed a troubled or disturbed adolescent. He felt that these adolescents choose to be "nobody," "someone bad," or even dead, rather than "not quite someone" due to chronic role diffusion (Erikson 1959:131–32). When this stage is completed successfully, adolescents have a sense of identity and the virtue, or ego strength, of *fidelity*, a strong sense of duty and loyalty to themselves and their culture, with an established core identity, a sense of self.

The ritualization of this period is commitment to an ideology coupled with a rite of passage involving identification with a peer group different from parents or teachers. The ritualism is *totalism*, in which adolescents commit themselves to an idea, a group, or a cause that defines them rather than achieving an individual sense of identity.

As is true of most of the theorists, Erikson based his stages mainly on study of male children. He did, however, recognize a difference in adolescent development between males and females, thinking that a girl holds her identity in abeyance as she prepares to attract a husband by whose name she will be known and by whose status she will be defined (1968). Thus a girl's identity depends on her relationships and not on separation, while a boy's identity and separation precede intimacy.

In summary, successful passage through this developmental stage should result in a sense of ego identity with a firmer sense of continuity, which will enable the individual to enter adulthood with the capacity to make appropriate personal and professional choices.

JEAN PIAGET

By the time a person reaches adolescence, Piaget believed, he or she has passed through three stages of cognitive development: sensorimotor, which he described as having six stages covering birth to age two; preoperational, from ages two to seven; and concrete operational, from seven to eleven. The final phase of intellectual development, he believed, begins at age twelve and is consolidated during adolescence; it is called formal operations. Piaget did not feel that all children are able to begin this phase as early as twelve; age of commencement may vary from one culture to another, but the phase is reached by fifteen (Piaget 1972:1). Further, he believed that adolescents vary in the ways that they apply formal operations, based on their aptitudes, interests, and areas of professional specialization. As in his work on the earlier stages of development, Piaget observed chiefly children from privileged backgrounds, but he did acknowledge that reaching this final stage of cognitive development might depend on environment, heredity, degree of stimulation, and appropriate neurological and physical development. He warned that under disadvantageous conditions, the cognitive level of formal operations might never be reached. As before, Piaget was not interested in the "right answer" as he studied the adolescents' work on scientific projects, but rather in how their cognitive process, the change in reasoning about observed data, differed from that of younger children.

The stage of formal operations is characterized by the ability to reason in terms of verbally stated hypotheses. Piaget divides this stage into two subphases: ages twelve to fifteen, a preparatory stage called emergent operational thought, when the adolescent tries the new approach but is still unable to arrive at systemic and rigorous assumptions based on hypothetical thinking; and the final stage, when the adolescent is more confident about his reasoning ability, can more spontaneously provide proofs, and can reflect on the results of working with hypotheses. Piaget saw the formal reasoning process as the capacity for reasoning in terms of verbally stated hypotheses, followed by the ability to deduce the consequences that the hypotheses imply and finally to attribute a decisive value to the logical form of the deductions (Piaget 1972:3). The adolescent, through dialogue and hypothetical reasoning, can consider others' opinions and experiences and decide to agree or disagree.

This is a clear advance over the earlier stage, when reasoning is determined in terms of concrete objects and their manipulation. The adolescent can now move from the real to the *possible*: he or she has the ability to link all possibilities and then draw logical conclusions. No longer is a problem based only on empirical results; the adolescent is more flexible and able to imagine what *might* occur. Many interpretations of data may then be feasible. Thus the adolescent forms a hypothetical analysis and then seeks out the empirical data to confirm or refute the hypothesis. Adolescent thought may thus be called "hypothetico-deductive" (Ginsburg and Opper 1988:201). Involvement in abstract and theoretical matters is possible. Adolescents will become interested in a range of concerns that may actually be beyond their experience and may lead to greater participation in society and the ideologies of significant adults. Often the result is a desire to change the social system. Clearly, a stimulating, accepting environment that encourages discussion, criticism, support, and the exchange of information enhances the possibility of forming and completing cognitive structures. Adolescent thought has now reached an advanced state of equilibrium in which cognitive structures can effectively adapt to a great variety of problems.

Two new related structures emerge during this period: combinational systems and propositional logic. In performing scientific experiments, the adolescent can carry out combinatorial analysis and permutation systems leading to combining propositions. Propositional logic involves the capacity for abstract thinking and the ability to combine in one operation the negation and the reciprocal, not possible in earlier stages (Piaget 1972:5). Negation and reciprocity are forms of reversibility that in the stage of concrete operations involve reversing operations on concrete objects; in formal operations, they involve reversing hypothetical propositions (Ginsburg and Opper 1988:197). Thus, formal operational thinking involves introspection, capacity for abstract thinking, logical thinking, and hypothetical reasoning.

Mental operations at this stage reach a high degree of equilibrium that is more flexible and effective. Structures are sufficiently stable to assimilate a range of new situations; by the end of adolescence, structures are almost fully formed and will undergo little modification. Thus the adolescent has reached the final stage of cognitive development, which will remain, with some refinement with maturity. The adolescent has moved from the world of objects alone to the world of ideas. Piaget felt that not all people are able to reach the final phase, and that thinking for many develops only to the first phase of formal operations.

PETER BLOS

Peter Blos is a psychologist and psychoanalyst who specializes in working with adolescents. His major contribution was to identify five *phases of adolescence*—he feels that the term *adolescence* is too broad and that different tasks need to be accomplished at different stages. Like most of the theorists writing about the stages of childhood, Blos appears to be more comfortable describing the course of adolescence for boys, although he does, at times, contrast it with that for girls. He acknowledges that his theories are based on adolescents "from the Western world" (Blos 1962:viii) and on clinical inferences derived from intensive case studies.

Blos sees sexual maturation, puberty, as representing the physiological changes that occur following latency. These changes result in new drive and ego organization, with adolescence representing the psychological aspects, the process of adaptation to pubescence. Thus, adolescence is characterized by physical changes that affect behavior. Instinctual drives intensify and there is some regression to infantile aims and objects of instinct gratification (Blos 1962:16). These are always disturbances within the balance of the psychic structure—oscillating progressions, regressions, and periods of standstill. Blos believes that only with successful passage through the stage of latency is the ego equipped to cope with the difficult adolescent tasks of differentiating and integrating. In latency, the ego must accomplish certain tasks in order to successfully cope with adolescence and entry into adulthood: an increase in cathexis of object and self representations (inner objects) with resultant automatization of certain ego functions; an increase in resistance of ego functions to regression (secondary autonomy) with an expansion of the nonconflictual sphere of the ego; formation of a self-critical ego that complements the superego, so that self-esteem has greater independence from the environment; an increase in verbal expression isolated from motor activity; and greater mastery of the environment through use of secondary process thinking to reduce tension, accompanied by the reality principle stabilizing capacity for postponement and anticipation in the pursuit of pleasure (Blos 1962:173–74). Latency involves mastery of the environment as childhood involves mastery of the body, and a task of adolescence is mastery of the emotions; all of these tasks include an orderly sequence of ego functions. Adolescence is also a period of sexual inhibition, with considerable ego and superego control over instinctual life.

Like S. Freud, Blos sees adolescence as the terminal stage in the course of psychosexual development, known as the genital phase, in which there is gradual sublimation of the erogenous zones to genital primacy. Blos recognizes that there is a wide range in the time of onset, duration, and point of termination of pubescence. Chronological age is not the chief determinant. Girls tend to begin their pubertal development and to achieve full growth earlier than boys. This variance can make extreme demands on adolescents' physical and mental adaptation. Psychosexual differences also occur, as Blos believes that girls do not resolve the Oedipal complex until adolescence, when physical differences between girls and boys are more obvious. The girl finally must undergo the massive repression of oedipal wishes that the boy experienced at the beginning of latency and thus consolidate development of the superego. Blos believes that the visibility of male genitalia also gives boys a clearer body image (Blos 1962:33).

Influenced by Freud and Erikson, Blos believes that the individual must go through all developmental phases, although he concentrated on only the adolescent stage. He identified five phases within it, culminating in the establishment of a sense of identity: preadolescence, early adolescence, adolescence proper, late adolescence, and postadolescence. Blos believes that adolescence involves a later and final stage of separation and individuation, similar to Mahler's rapprochement subphase. It is the critical time of sharpening boundaries and clarifying the self as distinct from others, culminating in a sense of identity and responsibility for one's own actions. For this reason he termed adolescence "the second individuation phase." The second individuation process begins in puberty with an increase in the libidinal drives and continues throughout all the phases of adolescence, until the person can find an external and nonfamilial love object.

Psychic regression and progression alternate; adolescence is the one phase of development where regression is necessary for completion of the stage-appropriate task. Adolescent development is contingent on, and determined by, individual tolerance for the anxiety, conflict, and guilt that may accompany regression and its use in psychic restructuring (Blos 1979:27–29). Regression will, in time, enable resolution of spheres of independence necessary for the formation of adult object relations and ego autonomy. Therefore, it must be viewed as an adaptive function upon which progress is predicated (Blos 1979:102). The task of psychic restructuring through drive and ego regression represents the most formidable psychic work of adolescence (Blos 1979:152).

PREADOLESCENCE

During this period there is a quantitative increase in instinctual pressure, both libidinal and aggressive. Almost any experience can be sexually stimulating, and instinctual gratification is confronted by a disapproving superego. The ego responds to this, as it has in the past, with defenses such as repression, reaction formation, displacement, and what Blos refers to as "socialization of guilt" (Blos 1962:59). There is growing involvement with peers, especially same-sex friends.

At this point, there is a turning toward the father, which Blos terms the "negative oedipal complex" (Blos 1979:136, 1991:12), that serves the purpose of helping to distance from the mother. The father is idealized and offers comfort and protection from the anxiety caused by the pre-oedipal "archaic" mother, resulting in a stronger ego. This is evident in greater social competence and physical prowess (Blos 1979:125).

Boys tend to show hostility toward girls, avoid them, or, if in their presence, show off and exaggerate in an effort to alleviate tension caused by the resurgence of the instincts and of castration anxiety. The mother is once again seen as active and powerful, and the boys' turning to same-sex friends, gangs, and the "homosexual stage of preadolescence" is viewed as a defense. Boys' fantasies, in this phase, are more often communicated as egosyntonic thoughts of grandiosity and smuttiness (Blos 1962:62).

Girls tend to deny their femininity and may strive to be tomboys due to the unresolved conflict of penis envy, or may appear to be very aggressive. Because they maintain an intense relationship with their mothers following the oedipal phase, they experience a prolonged and sometimes painful separation from the mother, which may result in overt conflict and an abrupt turn from the early homosexual stage of preadolescence toward heterosexuality, with the girl as the aggressor or seducer (Blos 1979:110).

Separation from primary love objects is the major task of the preadolescent period. Thus, there is a quantitative increase in the drives, accompanied by regression and attempts at separation. In the next phases there is a change in the drive quality, and regression lessens. Genitality is of greater importance and a new drive component emerges, *forepleasure* (Blos 1962:71, 1979:136).

EARLY ADOLESCENCE

Blos believes that during early adolescence and adolescence proper, a wider and richer emotional life develops, with the goal of growing up and answering the question, "Who am I?" (Blos 1962:71). Object relations become a central issue that will continue into the next phase. In early adolescence, close, idealized friendships emerge, usually with same-sex friends. This phase ends with a turn toward heterosexual relationships, leading to a final renunciation of early love objects by the end of adolescence proper and the finding of a new nonfamilial object.

Friendships often have a narcissistic quality, as often the friend is idealized, admired, and loved because he has traits the person would like to have and feels he or she can acquire by proxy. The friend thus represents the *ego ideal*. Boys experience this person as exemplifying perfection, similar to their identification with the father at the time of development of the superego at the end of the oedipal phase (Blos 1962:77–78). Thus, the first step in the consolidation of the ego ideal as a psychic institution takes place at the end of early adolescence (Blos 1979:138).

There may be transient homosexual activity and fantasies, which may result in an abrupt ending of friendships. With this shift in allegiance from family to nonfamily, Blos believes that during this phase the superego and ego are weakened. The superego, which emerged through the internalization of the parent, loses its power as the tie to the parent is lessened, and narcissistic and homosexual libido becomes bound in the formation of the ego ideal. The superego may appear adversarial and therefore not able to support the ego, which may appear weak, isolated, and inadequate. Thus, in early adolescence the libidinal model is "I love what I would like to be," which Blos regards as *narcissistic completeness*, seen in the homosexual phase of early adolescence. At the conclusion of this phase, the ego ideal transforms homosexual object libido into ego libido leading to heterosexual polarity and the establishment of the ego ideal as an "ego institution."

As noted above, Blos thinks himself more knowledgeable about the adolescent process in boys than in girls, noting that it is played out differently. Friendships are also of great importance to girls, and loss of a friend can be experienced as devastating. Idealization often is expressed as a crush involving a passive eroticized attachment to either a male or a female. The object chosen usually is only somewhat similar to a parent and often is strikingly dissimilar (Blos 1962:82).

Bisexuality is not uncommon in girls at this phase, and Blos feels it is related to narcissism, also observed in the idealized relationships entered into by boys. Girls, he believed, often experience their lives by proxy. He feels that during early adolescence "the illusory penis is maintained in order to protect the girl against narcissistic depletion" (Blos 1962:86) and that this bisexuality continues until the girl is able to turn libido from narcissistic attachment to her bisexual body image toward a heterosexual choice during the phase of adolescence proper. While crushes, fantasies, athletics, and intellectual activities may protect her from precocious heterosexual activity, Blos believes that the emotional availability of the mother or a maternal substitute is the main safeguard for passage through this phase.

ADOLESCENCE PROPER (OR MIDDLE ADOLESCENCE)

The adolescent entering this phase appears to sublimate love for the idealized parents and has greater interest in self-discovery, with intellectualization and asceticism as the primary defenses. He or she may become interested in global matters and has opinions on philosophical, political, and social problems that may be at variance with those of the parent. Blos's analysis of American adolescents identified a defense called *uniformism* that he felt resulted from a tendency to accept a code of behavior that permits the adolescent to divorce feeling from action in the ego's struggle against the drives and infantile object ties. Motivation comes from being equal to others and adhering to the "group norm." Protection against anxiety comes through a shared code of behavior and through "sameness." The sense of belonging to a group or gang meets social needs and protects against feelings of emptiness and loneliness as the adolescent disengages and may undergo a process similar to mourning. Uniformism also encompasses the defenses of identification, denial, and isolation and is a counterphobic device (Blos 1962:117–18). Parallel to this is "experimentation," a trial of ideas, behaviors, appearance, and choices before ego interests become more channeled and specific.

Fantasy life and creativity are at a peak. In this phase, girls, more than boys, will keep diaries or journals in which they write daydreams, secrets, and emotions they feel they cannot share with other people, even confidantes. However, the main task is finding a heterosexual object, as the adolescent is now ready to abandon narcissistic and bisexual object choices, but it is a gradual process.

Adolescence proper involves the final disengagement from primary love objects that constitutes a revival of the Oedipus complex and its final resolution. Involved are both object-lost and object-found, as the libido moves from familiar to new objects. Blos sees the experience of the final resolution of the Oedipus complex as quite different for girls and for boys. For the girl, the mother becomes the object of hostility accompanied by a feeling that she knows the father better than the mother does and an awareness of her negative feelings toward the mother. This affective negativism is a means of resisting regression. Blos, like Freud, believes that the resolution of the oedipal crisis is never accomplished with the same degree of severity and rigidity for a girl as for a boy and that the girl has less-repressed oedipal strivings (Blos 1962:106–108). The decline of the Oedipus complex is a slow process, which in some cases is not complete until late adolescence. Heterosexual object love will also bring to an end the bisexuality of the earlier phases.

Early choices may be infatuations or idealizations with the love object cathected with narcissistic libido, prior to the ability to experience real tender love. Often this early love object bears a similarity to the parent of the opposite sex and thus represents a transitional relationship. In the process of withdrawing object cathexis from familial to nonfamilial choices, the adolescent often appears quite narcissistic, with overvaluation of the self, self-absorption, oversensitivity to perceived slights, and distorted reality testing with respect to self-evaluation. This stage can be viewed as a delaying action to avoid definitely giving up early love objects but also can be seen as part of the process of disengagement. The previously overvalued parent is being devalued and the narcissistic, arrogant, rebellious behavior represents a withdrawal from the previously internalized parent. Eventually this behavior will decrease to a level where the ego maintains an adequate and appropriate supply of narcissism to support healthy self-esteem.

Homosexual experiences do occur during this phase. Blos believed that two preconditions for girls result in this choice: penis envy, for which the girls overcompensate by holding males in contempt, and an early maternal fixation resulting in a dependent, slavishly obedient child. In boys he found three preconditions: fear of the vagina as a devouring, castrating organ; identification with the mother, which may occur if the mother is inconsistent and frustrating while the father is either maternal or rejecting; and inhibitions or restrictions that equate all females with mothers and stem from the prohibitions of the Oedipus complex (Blos 1962:105). Decisive progress in emotional development lies in the progress toward heterosexuality. This can only be achieved after the pregenital drives are regulated to a subordinate role in favor of genital sexuality or orgasmic potency (Blos 1962:123). A higher order of thinking during this period is signified by a beginning awareness of the relevancy of one's actions in the present and the future. Thinking evolves to a point where the adolescent can reflect and consider possibilities.

In summary, Blos views this as a very complex and difficult phase with many components:

1. drive organization toward a clear and irreversible heterosexual position with a decrease in narcissism and libido turned outward toward a non-incestuous object of the opposite sex
2. reactivation of oedipal fixations, positive and negative, culminating in disengagement from the oedipal parent
3. more firm, though not complete, establishment of femininity and masculinity
4. ego initiation of defensive measures, restitutive processes, and adaptive accommodations with individual variations
5. cognitive processes that are more objective, analytical, and reality based
6. an idiosyncratic conflict and drive constellation delineated
7. internal strife, conflicts, and disequilibrating forces more focused

The adolescent now moves to the phase of late adolescence, when "Who am I?" becomes "This is me" (Blos 1962:127–28).

LATE ADOLESCENCE

Late adolescence, Blos believes, is a period of consolidation when the adolescent attains a sense of purposeful action, social integration, predictability, emotional consistency, and a stabilized sense of self-esteem, as well as increased ability to compromise and to delay gratification.

The phase of consolidation is characterized by five achievements: (1) a highly idiosyncratic and stable arrangement of ego functions and interests; (2) the extension of the conflict-free sphere of the ego (secondary autonomy); (3) identity constancy characterized by irreversible sexual identity; (4) relatively constant cathexis of object and self representations; and (5) stabilization of the mental apparatus that automatically safeguards the integrity of the psychic organism (Blos 1962:129). The ego is unified and shapes character and personality formation. Drive and ego fixations also play a part but are only two of the many contributing aspects. Superego and ego ideal influence the direction character formation will take, while the form itself is influenced by social institutions, traditions, value systems, and other aspects of the environment. Clearly, physical and mental endowments also strongly affect the process. Increased capacity for abstract thought further enables the consolidation of personality.

Thus, late adolescence is a decisive turning point in development that Blos, like Erikson, sees as a time of crisis. He believes that *trauma* is a universal phenomenon of childhood and that mastering it is a lifelong task. How the individual copes with it depends on ego strength and stability of the defenses. Blos sees the "primal damage" (trauma) as being replaced by symbolic representations and substitutes related to the physical and mental development of the child (Blos 1962:132). As adolescence comes to an end, the original threat is turned outward and its resolution is achieved within a highly specific system of interaction with the environment. The adolescent will then experience behavior and actions as meaningful, self-evident, and gratifying, and with some sense of urgency. Infantile conflicts become egosyntonic, with mastery enhancing self-esteem.

Blos believes that there are some aspects of the oedipal conflict that are not completely resolved in adolescence proper but are ultimately removed in late adolescence. The result is developed idiosyncratic ego interests and preferential cathexes with stable and dependable self-representations. Blos paraphrased Freud's statement that the superego is the heir of the Oedipus complex: "the heir of adolescence is the self" (1962:136).

POSTADOLESCENCE

As noted above, at this time there is a fixed hierarchy of ego functions, interests, attitudes, and defense patterns called *character* (Blos 1962:71). However, although much has been accomplished on the path to adulthood by the end of late adolescence, Blos believes there is an intermediate stage between adolescence and adulthood, *postadolescence*, necessary prior to attaining psychological maturity. During this stage, the various parts of the personality are integrated into a functional whole.

In spite of the accomplishment of earlier tasks such as conflicts about bisexuality (early adolescence), disengagement from early object ties (adolescence proper), and consolidation of social roles and identifications (late adolescence), Blos feels the task of "harmonizing the component parts of the personality" remains (Blos 1962:149). This is finally achieved when the individual makes occupational choices and goes through the process of courtship, marriage, and having children.

In late adolescence life tasks become clearer, but it is in postadolescence that the individual finalizes experimentation with choices and actions in order to arrive at the pathways to accomplishing the life tasks. Experimentation and thought about life goals during postadolescence should culminate in permanent relationships, roles, and vocational choices. The ego, no longer as burdened by instinctual conflicts, can now be useful in accomplishing these endeavors. The role of the superego is taken over to some extent by an emphasis on personal dignity and self-esteem, with the ego ideal replacing the idealized parent of earlier years. There is no longer such a great need to battle parents when a love object is selected; young people, and their parents, often are surprised to note that the "child" has taken on positive parental characteristics, values, and cultural traditions against which he or she once rebelled. Thus a reasonable rapprochement between the postadolescent and parental ego interests and attitudes can be achieved.

Blos is very concerned about the significance of the ego ideal (1962:184–86). He sees it as a differentiated part of the ego, cathected with narcissistic and homosexual libido, playing a role similar to that of the superego—but more personal, and less tyrannical and primitively cruel—yet remaining an aspect of the superego system (Blos 1979:326). The ego ideal begins to develop early in life, with its roots in "primary narcissism" (Blos 1974:47). In adolescence it develops further with the irreversible surrender of the negative (homosexual) oedipal position, and thus functions to promote and stabilize sexual identity. The ego ideal is rooted in the identification with the same-sex parent following the early resolution of the oedipal conflict, and in quantitative and qualitative changes during the course of development and ego maturation (Blos 1972:95). It gradually takes on some superego functions, most dramatically in adolescence, when the ego-superego relationship is radically revised. Early object ties are loosened and aspects of the superego are positively and negatively modified and integrated into the ego ideal, giving it additional content and direction.

The demands of the ego ideal are less irrational than those of the superego and thus are more egosyntonic. The superego, established at the phallic-oedipal phase, may be thought of as an agent of prohibition; the ego ideal, which reaches its definite structure in late adolescence, is an agent of aspiration. Self-esteem is very dependent on the ego ideal, for any discrepancies between it and self-representation can lower self-esteem. The ego ideal aims for perfection that, in fact, can never be attained; this is related to narcissism reverberating in ego ideal formation (Blos 1972:95). The ego ideal is the most uncompromising influence on the conduct of the mature person, and its position remains unequivocal (Blos 1979:369).

When the transitional phase of postadolescence comes to an end, Blos believes, higher orders of differentiation in psychic structure and personality organization have been achieved. Self and object representations have firmer boundaries (Blos 1979:118) and self-esteem is more stable. There is a stable arrangement of ego interests that, together with sexual identity, forms the core sense of identity. The plasticity and fluidity of adolescence diminishes through the phases, resulting in an integrated, constant, adaptive, irreversible structure. The adolescent is now ready to move into adulthood. The self, emerging through the developmental stages, now has reached relative stability with a firmer sense of reality and more realistic self-evaluation that increases the ability to think and to act appropriately. There is recognition of an intellectual, emotional, social, and sexual self, an effectively organized entity.

A new way of dealing with life is established. Behavior, attitudes, interests, and relationships appear to be more predictable, stable, and irreversible, which can be thought of as character. Blos identified four essential developmental preconditions for character formation and attainment of adulthood:

1. the *second individuation phase*, which involves regression and leads to replacement of love for parents by love of self or its ego ideal (potential perfection) and a consolidation of personality (Blos 1979:179–81)

2. *trauma*, essentially primal trauma, which is universally experienced and leaves a permanent residue. By late adolescence this residual trauma no longer results in "signal anxiety" but becomes an integral part of the ego with egosyntonic patterned responses, identified as character. Character is the conqueror of residual trauma and aids in furthering the individual's dependence on the environment. (Blos 1979:181–85)

3. *ego continuity* must be established by the adolescent. A child perceives things as he or she is told; thus, a task of adolescence is to restore the integrity of the senses. This involves disengaging, on an ego level, from the adult "caretaking" environment that formerly guarded the immature ego. Ego maturity gives a subjective sense of wholeness and inviolability. (Blos 1979:185–86)

4. *sexual identity*, which differs from gender identity established at an early age

Before physical sexual maturity occurs at puberty, the boundaries of sexual identity remain fluid. Character formation presupposes that the phase of bisexuality is past and that heterosexual identification as male or female has occurred (Blos 1979:186). Once these preconditions have been met, character is established and the adolescent process is ended; the highest form of psychic structure and function has been attained and internalized.

In summary, Blos made an important and influential contribution in identifying different phases of adolescence based on psychosexual development. He is heavily influenced by S. Freud, A. Freud, and Erikson. Blos recognizes the importance of the environment, which can be beneficial or noxious to the process of development, but his view of adolescence presupposes the opportunity for choices not always available. His work suffers from limited consideration of adolescent development in girls and his rejection of bisexuality and homosexuality as normal possibilities. Blos struggles with the question of when and how adolescence ends, noting that physiological changes signify entry but there are no reliable indicators of the end. He believes that attaining the four preconditions for character formation is as close as one can get to defining the end of adolescence and the entry into adulthood.

LAWRENCE KOHLBERG

Lawrence Kohlberg was a psychologist and a professor at the Harvard University School of Education. He had been a colleague of Erik Erikson and Carol Gilligan. Kohlberg's research began as part of his dissertation at the University of Chicago in 1958 with data collected from a cross-sectional sample of seventy-two Chicago males ages ten, thirteen, and sixteen, plus a group of twelve delinquent boys (Kohlberg 1984:xxix). He continued to base his theories on research with boys until 1969, when he began a longitudinal study of both males and females on a kibbutz. Kohlberg labeled his research approach *cognitive-developmental.*

In proposing his own sequential model of moral development, Kohlberg was very much influenced by the sequential model of cognitive development designed by Piaget and by the work of John Dewey. He was very concerned with moral judgment, which he defined as "the child's use and interpretation of rules in conflict situations" and the reasons for moral action (Kohlberg 1964:394), rather than merely the correct knowledge of rules and conventional beliefs. He saw this as judgments about good and right action. Kohlberg's theory of moral reasoning emphasizes justice. Kohlberg believed that judgment does not appear to become "moral" until early adolescence, while moral conduct appears earlier (Kohlberg 1964:408). Moral conduct is more specific to a situation, unstable over time, and influenced by social group and peer group norms, while moral judgment functions in the same direction regardless of social group.

Kohlberg postulated three levels of moral development, each composed of two stages. Like Piaget and Erikson, Kohlberg felt that an individual must pass through each of the stages in sequence. He believed that moral stages are related to cognitive development and to moral behavior and thus must be based on moral reasoning alone (Kohlberg 1984:172). He identified for his scoring system eleven universal values and issues that need to be considered in dealing with moral dilemmas:

1. law and rules
2. conscience
3. personal roles of affection
4. authority
5. civil rights
6. contract, trust, and justice in exchange
7. punishment and justice
8. the value of life
9. truth
10. sex and sexual love
11. property rights and values (Kohlberg 1976:43)

Like most theorists, he conducted his research mainly with male subjects. His method was to present dilemmas to children and adults and ask for the "right" solution. His goal was to discover not the solution, but how people arrived at it, the thoughts and reasoning behind their judgment. Kohlberg believed that morality is related to decision-making abilities and five ego functions: intelligence; ability to anticipate future events and to choose a greater, rather than lesser, future reward; ability to maintain stable, focused attention; capacity to control unsocialized fantasies; and self-esteem or satisfaction with self and the environment (Kohlberg 1964:390–91).

Kohlberg's first level, *preconventional* (or premoral), controls moral reasoning between about ages four and ten (Kohlberg 1984:172). Moral behavior is determined externally and governed by the child's awareness that reward or punishment might result from his thoughts and actions. The child obviously will try to avoid negative consequences. This is a highly egocentric stage, based on the child's needs, although in stage 2 there is some organization toward exchange and reciprocity (Kohlberg 1984:44). At this level the child does not really understand and uphold conventional or societal rules and expectations.

The second level, *conventional* (or role conformity), is experienced from latency into adolescence (Kohlberg 1964:402) and involves pleasing others and winning approval by conforming to and upholding the rules, expectations, and conventions of society just because they are society's rules, expectations, and conventions (Kohlberg 1976:33). While some standards are being internalized, the child still depends on others to define them. Thus he or she is no longer as egocentric but more concerned with maintaining norms, rules, and values sustained by relationships, groups, and society.

The third level, *postconventional* (self-accepted moral principles) is the final one, from ages thirteen to sixteen (Kohlberg 1964:402), and thus is the one discussed in this chapter. At this point moral judgments become internalized and less egocentric. The two stages at this level are stage 5: morality of contract, of individual rights, and of democratically accepted law; and stage 6: morality of individual principle and conscience. Behavior becomes based on principles rather than laws and takes into consideration the needs of others. The person understands and basically accepts the rules of society, based on formulating and accepting the general moral principles that underlie the rules (Kohlberg 1976:33). Judgment is made by principle rather than convention and adheres to the individual's reasons *why* something is right or wrong. Kohlberg believed that at this level true morality is achieved.

Kohlberg felt that some people never reach the final stage, just as Piaget questioned whether all could reach his final stage of formal operational intelligence. In two studies, Kohlberg found that only 10 percent of middle-class urban American males reached level T3 and that in a more privileged sample, Berkeley students, only 32 percent were at that level (Kohlberg 1966). Kohlberg questioned in later writings whether stages 5 and 6 should be defined as developmental end points in morality, as stage 4 appears to be the dominant stage for most adults (Kohlberg 1984:55–57). It must be noted, however, that while Kohlberg acquired empirical data to support his hypotheses about levels 1 and 2, there is less supporting level 3, since this level (especially stage 6) is based on metaethical and philosophical reflection on moral reasoning and lacks universality. It is a stage based on theoretical and philosophical speculation (Kohlberg 1984:215).

Stage 5, morality of contract, of individual rights, and of democratically accepted law, is the first in level 3, and it is at this point that the adolescent begins to define morality in terms of individual rights, dignity, equality, and mutual obligations (reciprocity). The adolescent is concerned for the well-being of others and of the community; he or she recognizes that laws are necessary, but is aware that they may need to, and can be, changed. He or she needs respect from the community. This is a contractual legalistic orientation with duty defined in terms of contract and avoidance of violation of the rights of others.

Stage 6, morality of individual principle and conscience, recognizes universal principles of justice that may go beyond existing laws, peer pressures, and social conventions. There is an orientation toward mutual respect and trust. Kohlberg's earlier writing discusses this stage more than his later work, because he believed that very few adolescents or adults ever reach this point. While the moral principles constructed are universal, the stage is not; he felt it exists primarily in democratic Western countries. The principles at this stage are abstract, and moral judgments are based on the highest principles concerning life, equality, and dignity. Morality is defined by ethical principles of justice, reciprocity, and respect for the rights of the individual, which are more important than the law. Kohlberg's empirical studies made him question the actual, rather than theoretical, existence of stage 6 and whether it should be dropped from his formulation. The empirical studies did, he believed, support the existence of stages and his belief that a person remains at a stage and then moves on to the next, with a period between involving mixed stages.

Kohlberg did some cross-cultural and some cross-class studies and believed that the stages of moral development are universal. In addition to subjects from the United States, his research included adolescents in Turkey, Canada, and Great Britain. He concluded that children in the United States reach higher levels than those in less developed countries and that middle- and upper-class children develop moral judgment faster and on a more advanced level than lower-class children. Kohlberg believed that the differences are cognitive and developmental, with lower-class children having a narrower picture of social order that limits their moral development (Kohlberg 1966 and 1984). The most conspicuous differences among social groups are developmental, paralleling age, rather than differences in cultural values or beliefs; middle-class children are more mature in their moral judgment and have more of a sense of potential participation in the social order (Kohlberg 1964:406).

For Kohlberg the most essential structure of morality is a *justice* structure based on the relationships of liberty, equality, reciprocity, and contracts between people (Kohlberg 1976:40–41). He saw moral conflicts as ones of perspectives or interest and the principles of justice as the basis for resolving these conflicts, for giving each party its voice. He defined the core of justice as "the distribution of rights and duties regulated by concepts of equality and reciprocity" (Kohlberg 1976:40). Thus he arrived at what is considered to be the justice orientation to morality. As noted above, his work with females was very limited and his writings support his view as the masculine orientation. It is the work of Carol Gilligan that led to greater awareness that women and men do not necessarily think and react in the same way.

CAROL GILLIGAN

Carol Gilligan is a psychologist and a professor at the Harvard School of Education. She has been a colleague of Erik Erikson and Lawrence Kohlberg, and was influenced by their work and that of Piaget. Dr. Gilligan recognized the problem that developmental theory, beginning with S. Freud, has been based on the life stages of boys and men, and she has made a significant contribution by demonstrating that the developmental paths for males and females are very different. She has focused primarily on adolescent and adult women. Prior to her work, women were repeatedly excluded from much theory-building developmental research, with the result that they appeared not to fit into existing models. The reasons were not questioned by theorists who viewed this as problematic for women. Unlike Freud and Kohlberg, Gilligan does not see gender differences as positive or negative, but rather as complementary. She believes that the development tasks for both adolescent girls and boys involve questions of identity and morality: What is true? What is of value? Who am I? Where do I call home? There is much overlap in Gilligan's writings about adolescent and adult women; this section will try to separate out the aspects most applicable to adolescence.

Gilligan's seminal book, *In a Different Voice*, first published in 1982, brought her to national attention and led to the formation of the Harvard Project on Women's Psychology and the Development of Girls. Dr. Gilligan and her associates have been concerned with women's "voices" as they differ from those of men in a patriarchal world as well as the connections between the political order and the psychology of the lives of women and men (Gilligan 1993:xii).

Gilligan defines and contrasts two aspects of the adolescent experience: psychological dissociation and political resistance. Psychological dissociation results in the adolescent losing a conscious awareness of knowledge and feelings that she feels may be dangerous. Political resistance is viewed as healthy and courageous, as girls take action against social and cultural conventions that encourage them to disconnect from self and others and thus not experience their feelings, knowledge, and desires. Political resistance can be *covert* when a girl chooses consciously to go "underground" and appears to comply with conventions for self-protection, but there is danger of accepting even harmful social behaviors. When it is *overt*, the girl will speak or act out against false relationships or conventions that require self-sacrifice or silence. This may involve rejection of racial, ethnic, class, and social stereotypes, which may make others feel threatened, yet will enhance a sense of independence. Thus a major problem is how to stay connected with both oneself and society. It is a story of risk and loss but also of strength and resilience (Taylor et al. 1995:26).

Gilligan's work also focuses on the different views of morality and identity held by males and females, which she and her colleagues have studied with a range of populations. An important contribution is her strong awareness of the impact of culture and socioeconomic status on women's thinking and on how realistic their goals and aspirations are. Dr. Gilligan's research populations covered a broader base than those of earlier theorists. The bulk of the research was done through face-to-face interviews.

Gilligan views adolescence as a naturally occurring time of transition between childhood and adulthood, and a time of epistemological crisis when issues of interpretation are foremost (Gilligan 1988:viii). A major area for interpretation is the phenomenon of separation. Past theorists, focusing on males, have put a premium on separation, individuation, and autonomy, with self-sufficiency as a hallmark of maturity, yet this conflicts with the realities of life—that long-term commitment and relationships with others are essential. Thus the goal for male adolescents is not in sync with the way adult life is structured; this can present a dilemma for adolescent girls trying to establish an identity, if they follow the criteria for boys.

In studying girls entering adolescence, Dr. Gilligan found that they are faced with a very difficult psychological dilemma: they fear that if they say what they are feeling and thinking as they did during latency, no one will want to be with them, but if they keep silent they will be alone. What further confuses them is an awareness of belonging to a society heavily influenced by powerful men; what then becomes necessary is a dissociation, a split between their experience and what is generally regarded by society as reality.

Gilligan believes that women begin in midadolescence to lose their voice: to not acknowledge what they know; to have difficulty listening to themselves; to experience a disconnection between mind and body, thoughts and feelings; and to learn to use their voice to cover up rather than to convey their inner world, with no clear sense of self. They question whether what they have seen really exists and whether what they have experienced is true; this results in personal doubt that compromises their ability to act on their own perceptions and to take responsibility for what they do. In addition to a fear of not being heard, adolescent women also are stopped in their actions by a fear of hurting others. As the adolescent matures and has greater capacity for reflective thinking, she will experience a crisis in identity and moral belief as she tries to find her own voice amid those of others and a way to represent her experience of relationships and her own sense of self, to remain both connected and separate. This is not an easy time, for the adolescent girl struggles with doing the right thing for others while also doing the right thing for herself and is very vulnerable to adverse judgments. Resolution comes with awareness of the importance of relationships, a sense of connectedness, and acceptance of the facts that the self and others are interdependent and that she is sustained by the ability to care in relationships. For girls it is often difficult to focus on the importance of self, as this challenges the conventional model of women as self-sacrificing; thus there is a conflict between selfishness, perceived as the exclusion of others, and selflessness, seen as the exclusion of self. Through the experience of engagement with others and involvement in dialogues with peers and with older women, adolescent girls are able to arrive at a solution acceptable to themselves and others. With resolution of these conflicts, an earlier sense of separation or dissociation is replaced by an adult sense of attachment and care, with the realization that connection (attachment) can be maintained in association with independence.

Identity is defined for girls in the context of relationships, with accompanying standards of responsibility and care. Boys do not define themselves through activity in relationships, but rather through separation and successful achievement. Intimacy becomes important only in late adolescence as boys are preparing for adult love and work. An empirical study by Lyons to test Gilligan's hypotheses on gender-related moral judgments indicated that a girl's self-definition is as *connected*, while a boy's is as *separate/objective* (Lyons 1988:40). Gilligan, whose work stresses the importance of women being heard and learning from listening to each other, believes that the adolescent girl's identity is formed through gaining a voice and that the self becomes known to the adolescent through experiences with different voices and viewpoints (Gilligan 1988:153). She stresses the importance of mother-daughter communication but also notes that girls may be more comfortable and freer expressing themselves with other women, such as a teacher, a relative, or an older family friend. Using her voice may make the adolescent feel vulnerable if she perceives a difference between her own perspectives and more commonly held points of view. Development and maturity come with an understanding of the truth about others coupled with greater security in revealing the true self.

Exploring the issue of the development of moral judgment, Gilligan felt that what she observed with adolescent girls differed greatly from the results of Kohlberg's research with boys, although both believe the essence of moral decisions to be the exercise of choice and the willingness to accept responsibility for that choice. Moral judgment always involves the relationship of self and others, but it can be organized in different ways, depending on how "relationship" is conceptualized. In adolescence, when a sense of connectedness is a major concern, the person who has branched out from the limited attachments of childhood must learn to distinguish between true and fantasized or exploitive relationships in order to avoid disappointment.

Gilligan believes that there are two modes of judgment, one associated with men and the public world of social power and the other associated with women and the privacy of domestic interchange (Gilligan 1993:67–69). The latter is concerned with feelings of empathy and compassion and real dilemmas, while the former is concerned with hypothetical dilemmas. Girls construct moral problems in terms of connection, care, and responsibility in relationships, while boys' thinking rests more on right and rules, a justice approach that draws attention to inequality and oppression. The morality of rights, or justice (boys), is based on mutual respect, a sense of fairness and reciprocity that involves balancing the scales, the claims of other and self. The morality of responsibility (girls) is based on equity, responsiveness, recognition of difference in need, and an understanding that leads to care and compassion, which draws attention to problems of detachment, hurt, or abandonment. For girls the issue in relationships is not *whether* to act, but *how* to act in order to be helpful, minimize hurt while protecting each person's welfare, and maintain the relationship. The moral conflict is how to be responsible for oneself in a way that is not in conflict with responsibility to others. Girls interviewed saw most moral dilemmas as centered on loyalty in relationships with friends, while boys saw moral dilemmas as those involving resisting peer pressure. For girls the dilemmas continue over time or repeated instances of the same problem, while boys view dilemmas as one-time occurrences and, having dealt with them, leave the situation, while girls tend to stay with the problem and the people involved.

Gilligan believes that depending on the circumstances, both girls and boys may use either mode of moral thinking; however, the method most used is gender determined. There is a dichotomy between the two moral orientations because detachment is viewed as the mark of mature moral judgment in the justice perspective (boys) while it is the moral problem in the care perspective, as it represents the failure to meet others' needs. Attention to individuals' needs and circumstances, the mark of mature moral judgment in the care perspective, is the moral problem in the justice perspective, as it implies a failure to treat others as equals (Gilligan and Attanucci 1988:82–83).

As adolescents develop, their thinking becomes more reflective and self-conscious. Their moral judgment orientation becomes entwined with their self-definition and feelings of personal integrity. Gilligan recognizes that how adolescents think also has a cultural base, with norms, values, and roles affecting judgment of what is the "right" way to feel, think, and act.

Gilligan and her colleagues did several studies of the psychological development of girls in private schools. One was at the Emma Willard school, primarily a boarding school, from 1981 to 1984; it is written up in *Making Connections* (Gilligan, Lyons, and Hanmer 1990). The researchers felt that ages eleven to sixteen are especially critical and that the crisis of this period involves relationship, a crisis of connection rather than of separation. Adolescence, Gilligan found, is the watershed of girls' development, a time when they are at risk of drowning or disappearing. They face the dilemma of whether to respond to others and abandon oneself or respond to oneself and abandon others. To respond to herself, the girl must resist the conventional view of women as good and selfless, while in responding to others she must resist the values of self-sufficiency and independence. The crisis of connection involves basic questions about the nature of relationship and definitions of reality (Gilligan 1990:25).

Twenty-three adolescent girls were interviewed annually for three years. While issues of separation and connection were foremost, as the girls matured they did not feel that they had to make a choice, but rather that these are compatible aspects of development that coexist and can assist each other. Independence was seen as improving the ability to meet one's own needs in a way that allows for appreciating others as people rather than instruments to meet needs. Not being as concerned about others meeting their needs, the girls felt they were better able to look outside of themselves and attend to the needs of others. Thus, the individual separates in order to enhance connectedness. Although initially fairness and listening are usually not associated, the adolescents at Emma Willard, as they matured, appeared to see them as intimately related concepts, fairness as a profoundly interpersonal process and listening as a moral phenomenon. Fairness involves the privacy of close relationships and is based on inner standards. Listening involves concern with school and world affairs, but is also regarded as an important factor in personal relationships (Bernstein and Gilligan 1990:147). It must be noted that the girls at Emma Willard, for the most part, came from privileged backgrounds that may have given them an environment safer than that experienced by less fortunate girls.

Another study of private school adolescent girls took place at the Laurel School, a day school. While the researchers found that an inner sense of con-

nection with others is a central organizing feature of teenage girls' development, they felt that the early adolescent years are a time of disconnection,
with a struggle between speaking or not speaking, knowing and not knowing, and feeling and not feeling (Brown and Gilligan 1992:4). This conflict affects the girls' feelings about themselves, relationships with others, and ability to have an impact on their world. They experience a loss of voice and a
struggle to take their own experiences seriously. With this come confusion,
defensiveness, and difficulty acting in the face of conflict. They also experience a division between what has been their experience and what broader society considers to be reality. In interviews, the subjects appeared somewhat
reluctant to portray themselves, their school, and their families as less than
ideal (Taylor 1995:193).

As the Laurel School subjects got older, the study showed that they were
less dependent on external authorities, less egocentric, and less locked into
their own experiences. They became more autonomous as they were able to
distinguish their thoughts and feelings from others' and to rely on, and take
responsibility for, themselves. In addition, they showed greater awareness of
the diversity of social and cultural experiences, as well as the political problems inherent in a patriarchal society. Generally they believed that people
were interested in them, who they were and what they had to say, but had
some concern about revealing what they felt were "unacceptable" parts of
themselves.

Although most of the theories on moral development have been generat-
ed from research on white, middle- and upper-class boys and girls, Gilligan
and her colleagues did some projects involving inner-city youths. Gilligan
believes that since moral concepts are learned through life experience and
observations, where one grows up must be an influence. She regards the
omission of inner-city populations in theory building as similar to the omission of girls, resulting in the loss of important perspectives. In looking at
both male and female adolescents in three lower-income Boston neighborhoods, the expectation was that they had intensely experienced more injustice, lack of attention, carelessness, and difficult choices than children in
more protective environments. The study focused on how they listened to
and represented their experiences of moral conflict, moral decision making,
unfairness, and not being heard (Bardige et al. 1988:160).

Gilligan's research shows that inner-city adolescent girls, similar to more
advantaged adolescents, have a more developed moral sense of care than of
justice. It had been anticipated that the social inequities that diminished
chances for equality and economic parity would result in feelings of indiffer-

ence and despair and that the inner-city girls would have different perspectives based on their perceived (and real) experiences of injustice, indifference, and failure of others to care. Almost all of the respondents identified situations in which they felt something had happened to them that was unfair and someone did not listen. The same gender differences were observed with this population as with youths from more affluent backgrounds; boys saw their moral dilemmas as involving friends, peer pressure, and sometimes pressure to do something they did not believe was right out of fear of losing friends or "losing face." Girls' dilemmas also involved friends but centered on loyalties, being pulled between two people or groups, both making claims on their time and commitment, while still trying to be individuals. The major difference between this population and the students in private schools was that the inner-city adolescents had a greater fear of making "wrong decisions" (Bardige et al. 1988:172).

In the late 1980s, Gilligan and colleagues conducted a study of twenty-six girls believed to be at risk for dropping out of high school and early motherhood. The group was made up of eight African American or Caribbean, four Latina, eight Portuguese, and six Irish or Italian American girls. All were from poor or working-class families. They were interviewed annually for three years with the focus on their feelings and thoughts about themselves, relationships, their lives, the future, experiences at school, and decisions about sexuality.

The participants differed from those interviewed in the private school studies in that they felt they *could* speak, because no one really cared what they said, although they were aware that having "a big mouth" could land them in trouble with parents and peers and at school. They viewed relationships as problematic, fearing betrayal or neglect, and experienced a sense of isolation and few safety nets. Interviewers found them to be quite open in acknowledging anger, betrayal, sexual desire, unfairness, and wanting power, which the middle- and upper-class girls, tending to feel social pressure or obligation, made them cover over or deny (Taylor, Gilligan, and Sullivan 1995:193).

Attitudes toward sexuality, relationships, and work are affected by race, class, and sexual orientation. The interviewers found that this sample was especially free in talking with interviewers who appeared to have had somewhat similar experiences. For example, black adolescents felt more comfortable with a black interviewer. The Latina and Portuguese girls felt somewhat caught between two worlds, as the culture at home focused on maintaining loyalty to family and adhering to cultural and familial restrictions on sexual activity while their peers from other cultures were much more open about their sexuality and more apt be sexually active. However, by tenth grade, some appeared depressed or silent as they attempted to resolve conflicts between the expectations of their culture of origin, the dominant culture, and their own feelings (Taylor et al. 1995:40). The black adolescents appeared not to have trouble with displays of anger and assertiveness that were regarded in the white culture as not "feminine." However, they were raised to assume the traditional female role of nurturer and caretaker but also encouraged to be strong and self-sufficient, and to expect to work out of the home.

The greatest difference among the four groups in this sample was in their relationship with their mothers. The white girls expressed feelings of closeness to their mothers, but felt they did not talk about anything of importance. The Latina and Portuguese girls felt that they could not talk to their mothers about boys, while the black girls felt comfortable talking with their mothers about most things, including sex. Thus for most, an open mother-daughter relationship was viewed with skepticism.

An interesting finding in this study was that for racial and cultural groups in which extended families are the norm, the girls formed important relationships with other women besides their mothers. Although the maternal relationship was important, the girls felt that emerging sexual interests, wanting time to be with friends outside of the home, and a desire for more freedom placed a strain on the relationship, as these needs came into conflict with their mothers' beliefs, values, and concern for safety (Taylor et al. 1995:118). Fear of gossip and rumors often kept them from talking with peers and further encouraged finding older friends whom they saw as dependable and a source of support. These women validated the girls' experiences and feelings and fostered self-respect and confidence by making the girls feel listened to. These relationships often complemented the relationship with the mother by providing a resource for unmet needs.

Questions about the future resulted in wishes similar to those of the girls interviewed at private schools: college, a well-paying job, a nice place to live, and eventually a family. While similar to the middle- and upper-class girls interviewed in that they described a wish for a life quite different from their mother's, these girls expressed the fear that spouses and children would consume their lives and not allow them to pursue their own goals, as had been true for their mothers. There was clearly a strong preference for a job or career before a serious relationship for the twenty girls who remained in the study.

This study showed that poor, minority adolescent girls have motivation and desire for achievement, have a future as well as a present orientation, do not automatically expect a future on public assistance, have an internal locus of control, and are not prey to negative influences of peers, thus contradicting damaging stereotypes. Although these girls responded much like the adolescents interviewed in the other Gilligan studies, the reality is that their opportunities will be much more limited. Thus, there was no need for greater aspiration, but rather for more opportunities and more connections to help prepare for the future.

Gilligan's major contribution to developmental theories is that her empirical studies proved that theories about boys do not necessarily apply to girls. For the most part, developmental theories have been derived from men's experience and competence, which served as a baseline, often to the detriment of women. For many, "thinking" was the province of men while "emotions" belonged to women. By *listening* to moral dilemmas, Gilligan established that women organize their morality around concerns with responsibility and care. She also identified two moral voices, *justice* with men and *care* with women. She believes, however, that men and women, given different circumstances, might use the moral orientation of the opposite sex. In a summary of six studies of groups of male and female adolescents including four longitudinal studies, Gilligan reported that 90 percent of the respondents revealed both orientations, but 65 percent relied more heavily on one. Ninety-two percent of the women used the care orientation with 62 percent preferring it. Sixty-two percent of the men included the care orientation with 7 percent preferring it. One hundred percent of men used the justice orientation and 93 percent preferred it, while 77 percent of women included it with 38 percent preferring it (Muuss 1988:227).

Finally, Gilligan's work established a gender difference with respect to identity. For boys it is linked to separation and autonomy and for girls, to connectedness and relatedness. While Gilligan's work begins with adolescence, she continues to follow women in adulthood in terms of moral judgment and of identity, paramount issues in adolescence. Gilligan's work in progress focuses on boys' development.

KOHLBERG AND GILLIGAN

In 1971, Gilligan and Kohlberg collaborated on a paper, "The Adolescent as a Philosopher," in which they set out to define adolescence at that time in America. They believed that the long-held theme in discussing adolescence, the "discovery of the self," is secondary to the view of this period as "a marginal role between being a child and being grown-up" (Kohlberg and Gilligan 1971:1052). The adolescent's need for independence and for fantasies about the future are part of the desire to be an adult, while the accompanying conflicts and instabilities represent the conflict between that desire and a role and personality not yet developed to this level. They believed that in the late 1960s and early 1970s social order was not as stable and as clear as it had been in the past, resulting in a deeper level of questioning about truth, goodness, and reality. While adolescents have always questioned adults' views and values, during this period the counterculture became so active that it added to the confusion as adults also questioned former conventional values and beliefs. Kohlberg and Gilligan both felt that culture offers alternative ideologies, but their validity rests on how successfully they embody principles of justice.

As the adolescent becomes more aware of subjective feelings and moods, she or he is also aware of ambivalence and conflicts of feelings. Gilligan and her colleagues relate this to arriving at Piaget's final level of cognitive development, formal operations. When this article was written, Gilligan appeared to accept Kohlberg's six-stage theory without identifying its greater applicability to males and, at this early phase of her career, clearly showed the influence of Piaget and Erikson.

More recently, Gilligan's primary criticism of Kohlberg's work has been that his formulations are based on the study of males and that he arrived at what she feels is an unsupported conclusion that women, who he believes are less mature, never are able to reach as high a level of moral judgment as men. She also has raised questions about the validity of his scoring of responses to the dilemmas he presented in his empirical research, from which he derived some of his conclusions about moral maturity. She feels that his scoring method does not deal with dilemmas of special relationships and obligations (Kohlberg, Levine, and Hewer 1983:24) and thus misrepresents the caring orientation in stage 3 reasoning (Kohlberg, Levine, and Hewer 1983:120).

Kohlberg did not agree with Gilligan that there are two separate moralities, justice and generalized fairness, and a separate opposing morality of care (Kohlberg 1984:229). He postulated that there are certain dilemmas where care is indicated to *supplement* the obligations of justice, and so the ethic of care is not in conflict with the justice ethic. He believed that the problem resulted from differing definitions of the word *moral*; his own stressed impartiality, universality, and the willingness to agree with others on "what is right." He saw Gilligan's definition as not including these attributes, but rather focusing on concern for the welfare of another, a feeling of responsibility or obligation, and an effort to engage in communication or dialogue. He did not see the two senses of the word *moral* as existing on the same level of generality and validity and proposed a spectrum of moral dilemmas and orientations, with personal moral dilemmas and special obligation at one end and the standard hypothetical justice dilemma and justice orientation at the other (Kohlberg 1984:232).

WILLIAM POLLACK

William Pollack, a psychologist, is the director of the Center for Men at McLean Hospital and associated with the Harvard Medical School Department of Psychiatry. His work was strongly influenced by Carol Gilligan's research on the voices of adolescent girls and women. Pollack focused on identifying the voices of boys who he believed desperately wanted to talk about their lives, things that hurt them, disconnection with parents, concerns about girls and sex, violence in school and on the streets, and their fears that they might not be as masculine as their peers. They were silenced by the "Boy Code," rules that favor male stoicism and make boys ashamed of showing weakness or vulnerability. Pollack concluded that boys in the United States are emotionally alone and experience isolation, depression, loneliness, and despair (2000:xix).

Pollack's study involved interviewing boys ages ten to twenty, from different socioeconomic backgrounds and different parts of the United States. The boys were given the choice of providing an oral or a written story in order to capture and identify their unique voice. The goal was to help the boys to be heard when they shared their real voices, to recognize impediments to this process, and to help those involved with the boys to find a new way to listen to them and provide them with a "safe" forum in which they could speak honestly and openly. Adults need to get behind the "mask of masculinity" (Pollack 2000:xxiv), the projection of bravado and stoicism, to reach boys' loving feelings as well as their sadness, loneliness, and vulnerability. Pollack made five suggestions to facilitate the process:

1. create a safe space: the *shame-free zone*, in which the boy feels loved and cared for and protected from embarrassment, humiliation, or bullying; there must be confidentiality and a sense of intimacy, connectedness, and empathy

2. allow *time* during which the boy can decide when he is *ready* to share, and during which the listener must be patient

3. provide multiple avenues for expression, including *action talk*; some boys are comfortable talkers, others express themselves better in writing, but many express themselves more easily through action or a combination of action and talk

4. provide *genuine listening* without judgment or interruption: listeners should show interest verbally and nonverbally and be encouraging and nonjudgmental; sharing a relevant anecdote about one's own life can strengthen the bond

5. give *recognition* and *affection*, as the boy is seeking affirmation, affection, and love, yet fears revealing these needs; encourage expression of a wide range of emotions, letting the boy know that "real boys and men" *do* cry (2000:xxv–xxxiv)

Pollack found that boys have a desire for connection, a longing to be able to be themselves, and a desire for change. The Boy Code, they feel, imposes an impossible test of masculinity, requiring them to appear tough and in control and to keep their true feelings secret. They feel pressure to have sex prematurely, to reject sharing feelings, to be overtly overly concerned with fitness, to abuse drugs and alcohol, to appear "cool," and to participate in bullying and even violence. There is an underlying sense of alienation and despair.

Pollack was struck by how frequently the tragedy at Columbine High School was brought up by the boys he interviewed. Adult concern about who might be violent and when the next tragedy would occur made the boys increasingly anxious and afraid. They feared being victimized, being falsely accused, but also feared that their own anger, sadness, and pain, all pushed underground by the Boy Code, might cause them to lash out, hurting themselves or others (Pollack 2000:5). The boys also spoke of fear of bullying, including physical assault. A study by the Centers for Disease Control found that 81 percent of the students surveyed admitted to bullying classmates to some degree, and a study by the National Association of School Psychologists showed that 160,000 children a day miss school because of fear of bullying (Pollack 2000:198). The boys interviewed who had attended Columbine High were severely traumatized and believed that the killers had been affected by never finding a place among their peers, which resulted in a buildup of anger.

The Boy Code severely limits what boys can say and do, thus limiting their options as they develop emotionally. They need to be encouraged to express their whole range of emotions and pursue their own dreams and destiny, without the primary emphasis being on what society defines as success. Homophobia must also be recognized as a prejudice that causes suffering for some boys trying to establish their identity.

Pollack concluded that boys want to be part of a society in which they can be themselves without the constant pressure to prove their masculinity. They want to be sure that they will be "safe," not fearful or anxious, if they show their emotions and speak in their own voice. The Boy Code needs to be dismantled, but this can only occur with the support and understanding of families and teachers who make the rules in the adolescents' environment. Boys can be greatly helped by mentors, who need not be men but must be people who will listen, be available, and be nonjudgmental. It will not be easy to overthrow the Boy Code and replace it with societal acceptance of boys who can speak of their desires and their vulnerabilities without fear or shame.

DANIEL OFFER

Daniel Offer, a psychiatrist, did not agree with the more psychoanalytically oriented theorists, such as A. Freud, Erikson, and Blos, that adolescence must be a time of turmoil based on identity crisis and that if it is not, there is a problem. He questioned the assumptions of the "turmoil theory" that adolescence has to involve significant disruption in personality organization characterized by mood fluctuation, unpredictable behavior, and rebellion against parents in order for the adolescent to be able to separate and form an identity, and sought to disprove it empirically. He saw adolescence as a transitional stage, a critical period in psychological development, in which the adolescent gradually adjusts to growth and development necessary prior to entering adulthood. He identified several key issues facing adolescents: emerging sexuality; separation from family; the quest toward forming a new nuclear family; increased motility; and striving for vocational identity and autonomy (Offer and Sabshin 1984:90).

While recognizing that empirical studies of a developmental stage might be problematic over time due to intervening social, economic, and cultural variables, Offer felt that such studies yield information that can be generalized to some extent. He did find a difference between adolescents questioned in the early 1960s and those at the end of his studies, with the latter more worried about the future, less hopeful about their ability to function as adults, less secure about their body image, and feeling greater pressure to be sexually active (Offer and Sabshin 1984:92). Offer's studies involved 20,000 adolescents believed to be normal (not disturbed or delinquent), covered two decades beginning in 1962, involved both males and females, and included not only subjects from white, middle-class families in the Chicago area (the majority) but also adolescents in Australia, Canada, Ireland, and Israel (these data were compared with data obtained about adolescents in the United States). Offer and Sabshin identified four perspectives on what constitutes normality: *health*, the medical approach, with no apparent pathology; *utopia*, a harmonious and optimal blending of the diverse elements of the mental apparatus with consideration of how an "ideal" person would behave; *average*, based on a bell-shaped curve with adequate functioning within the social, cultural, and familial settings; and *transactional systems*, an integration of biopsychosocial variables at specific stages in personal and historical time (Offer and Offer 1975:4–5; Offer and Sabshin 1984:433).

Dr. Offer believed that adolescents have an increased ability to think abstractly and logically and more social experience, and therefore have a more coherent and well-articulated sense of self than in earlier periods. He chose to obtain data on the sense of self through a questionnaire he developed, the Offer Self-Image Questionnaire (OSIQ), a self-descriptive personality test to rate the adjustment of adolescents ages thirteen to nineteen. Because level of development may vary according to content area, the questionnaire involved eleven scales covering impulse control; mood; body image; social relations; morals; sexual attitudes and behaviors; family relations; mastery of the external world; vocational and educational goals; psychopathology; and superior adjustment (coping) (Offer and Sabshin 1984:90). Data obtained from the questionnaire indicated that the vast majority of adolescents:

1. are happy, strong, and self-confident
2. do not feel inferior to others, including their peers
3. do not see themselves as being treated adversely
4. feel relaxed under usual circumstances
5. feel prepared for most things, are optimistic, and enjoy challenges
6. believe that they have control over their own lives
7. are work oriented, want to support themselves rather than depend on others, and feel they will succeed
8. enjoy group social experiences and like to help their peers
9. are not afraid of their sexuality and feel a friend of the opposite sex is important

10. do not perceive any major problems between themselves and their parents and feel that they are considered when family decisions are made (Offer and Sabshin 1984:91–94)

Although the majority of adolescents saw themselves as without any major problems, a significant minority were not very secure about their coping abilities and 20 percent indicated that they felt "empty" and saw life as presenting problems without apparent solutions (Offer and Sabshin 1984:96).

Data showed some differences between male and female adolescents. Males present a more positive body image and feel more positive about their impulse control and sexual attitudes than females. Females exhibit stronger moral attitudes and beliefs than males, with less evidence of antisocial acting out. Females also appear to value family and interpersonal relationships more than males and see themselves as having a better self-image, although the data show no real difference between male and female respondents. As noted above, some of the adolescents saw themselves as having problems coping. Young adolescent girls (thirteen to fifteen) have more psychiatric symptoms and problems coping than do older adolescent girls (sixteen to eighteen) or any cohort of adolescent boys. Older adolescent girls have more symptoms than older adolescent boys, but these are not significant when compared with younger adolescent girls. The symptoms seem to make these younger girls more prone to depression or phobias. Girls have more problems with their aggression and tend to turn it inward, becoming more introspective. They find the high school years more taxing than do boys (Offer and Sabshin 1984:96–97).

A major cross-cultural sample was made up of middle-class male and female adolescents, ages fourteen to eighteen, living in Australia, Canada, Ireland, and Israel. These data showed adolescents in the four other countries have more conservative attitudes toward their sexuality than adolescents in the United States. Although the majority of those in the United States feel positive about their relationships with their parents, even more adolescents in the four other countries feel this way, which Offer attributes to the increase in divorce rates causing adolescents in the United States to depend more on their peers than those in the other samples. It was found that Israeli adolescents cope better with the external world than adolescents in Canada and the United States, are more action-oriented, and appear to enjoy solving difficult problems. Irish and Australian adolescents were found to cope less well than the other three groups (Offer and Sabshin 1984:96–97).

The sample for what Offer called the modal adolescent project focused on ages fourteen to eighteen modal or typical adolescents, with the goals of assessing relative strengths and weaknesses; kinds of psychological problems; methods of coping; and reasons for failure if they were not successful (Offer 1969:3–4). *Normal*, for the purpose of this study, was defined as "average." The OSIQ was developed for this project, and the sample consisted of boys attending two suburban high schools (N = 73). The boys were first seen in their first year of high school when they completed the OSIQ, and followed directly or indirectly until they were twenty-two. Parents of these students were interviewed in order to get their evaluation of their child's adjustment. Students were also interviewed, six times over their three years in high school and twice following graduation, in semistructured clinical interviews. Psychological testing was done once in high school and once following graduation. Two teacher rating scales were also administered. In the final year, subjects were mailed a self-rating adjustment scale.

Data from the modal adolescent project showed that adolescence is a period of growth that does not usually involve serious disruption between generations or between the adolescent and his former identity (Offer 1969:192). What rebellion was observed was chiefly in early adolescence, ages twelve to fourteen, with both parents and adolescents finding everyday relationships more difficult (Offer 1969:185).

A major contribution of the modal adolescent project was the identification of three psychological growth patterns, even within this relatively homogeneous sample of white, middle-class adolescent males. The patterns were identified through scores on a variety of tests and measures, which included child-rearing practices; genetic background; experiential and traumatic factors; cultural, social, and familial surroundings; coping mechanisms; ideals; peer relationships; fantasy life; and basic personality structure (Offer and Sabshin 1984:416–17). The patterns were continuous growth (23 percent); surgent growth (35 percent); and tumultuous growth (21 percent) (Offer and Offer 1975:40–48; Offer and Sabshin 1984:417–22).

Continuous growth involves smoothness of purpose and self-assurance in the progression toward adult life, with parents supporting the need for independence. These adolescents have a trusting, affectionate relationship with parents and a capacity for good object relationships, with heterosexual ones becoming increasingly important in later years. Most important is that they are content with themselves and their place in life.

Surgent growth involves developmental spurts rather than a steady progression, with more concentrated energy spent mastering developmental tasks. These adolescents appear at times to be adjusting well, integrating their experiences, and moving ahead, while at other times they appear "stuck" and unable to move forward. They are not as free of problems and traumas; their backgrounds show more separations, deaths, and severe familial illnesses. Their defenses are not as strong, and thus they have more problems coping with unanticipated sources of anxiety, although they experience relatively few behavioral or emotional crises. They are less action oriented than the first group and more prone to depression, and disappointment in themselves and others. They experience more conflict with parents, wavering self-esteem, and later establishment of meaningful relationships with the opposite sex. They are less introspective than those in the continuous or tumultuous growth samples.

Tumultuous growth may look like adolescence described in psychiatric or psychological literature, yet youths in this pattern are able to test reality and to act accordingly. They experience much inner turmoil with overt behavioral problems at home and at school. They exhibit many self-doubts, have escalating conflict with parents, and need help mobilizing defenses and strengthening their weakened egos. Separation is a difficult and painful process; more experience anxiety and depression here than in the other groups. Many are seen as highly sensitive and introspective. Relationships with girls begin earlier, but with a more dependent quality. Though less happy with and more critical of their environment than the other two groups, this cohort functions as well academically and vocationally.

Finally, Offer administered the OSIQ anonymously to a group of sixty-two mental health professionals who had had experience with inpatient or outpatient adolescents. The instructions were "to complete the OSIQ with the same responses you believe would be given by a mentally healthy/well-adjusted adolescent of your same sex" (Offer, Ostrow, and Howard 1981:150). The most striking finding was the inability of the mental health professionals to predict how *normal* adolescents would describe themselves. They saw them as having more problems than what normal adolescents described. The mental health professionals predicted poorer self-images with problems in moods, social relationships, family relationships, and educational and vocational goals. This study strongly supports the need for more empirical research on normal adolescents, for most research has been done with disturbed or delinquent adolescents; thus, what mental health professionals believe is true about this stage of development is gleaned from study of the abnormal. Problems in adolescence should not be viewed as the norm if proper diagnoses and interventions are to be made.

RECENT EMPIRICAL STUDIES

A review of the literature shows few empirical studies involving normal adolescents. Most research has been done with adolescents suffering from mental disorders or classified as delinquent. A further limitation is that most subjects are middle-class, primarily urban, white adolescents, more often male.
The geographical location from which the population is selected also may
skew the results and limit how much they can be generalized. Some of the areas researched have involved ethnic identity, peer relationships, sexuality, homosexuality, relationships with families, and self-esteem.

Ethnic Identity

In a heterogeneous country such as the United States, ethnicity should be,
but often is not, a variable considered in evaluating expectations of adolescent behavior, values, and goals. A study of 12,386 adolescents in Colorado
looked at the effects of ethnic identity, ethnicity, and gender on well-being
(Martinez and Dukes 1997). The study involved white, black, Hispanic, Asian,
Native American, and mixed identity adolescents in junior high and high
school. Data showed that ethnic identity is a qualifier of the relationship between the independent variables of ethnicity and gender and the dependent
variables of global self-esteem, academic self-confidence, and purpose in life.
The greater the ethnic identity, the higher the ratings of self-esteem, academic self-confidence, and purpose in life.

This study yielded some important data and argues that multiculturalism
in schools can increase ethnic identity. The most salient results were: (1)
white adolescents had the lowest ethnic identity, but scored high on measures
of well-being, presumably due to their privileged position in our society; (2)
Native American adolescents scored low on ethnic identity and on well-being, possibly due to limited opportunities and discrimination; (3) Asians and
adolescents of mixed identity had intermediate levels of ethnic identity; and
(4) blacks and Hispanics had the highest levels of ethnic identity, possibly because they must deal with discrimination from an early age. The authors
concluded that ethnic identity is positively related to self-esteem, self-confidence, and purpose in life and lessens the impact of negative stereotypes and
social denigration.

Additional data from this study related to the effect of gender. Only on the
measurements of self-esteem was there a significant difference between male

and female respondents, with males scoring higher than females. While the female respondents scored higher on purpose in life and self-confidence, the differences were not statistically significant. Among the different ethnic groups, there were some additional interesting findings: black and Asian females showed higher levels of ethnic identity and self-esteem than males; white males had higher levels of ethnic identity than females; and there was less gender difference in responses from Hispanic and Native American adolescents than in responses from the other groups.

PEERS

Intimate friendships are known to be of major importance to adolescents, more than at any earlier developmental stage. A study of 48 high school juniors (24 female and 24 male) involved videotaping face-to-face interactions between subjects and their best same-sex and opposite-sex friends (McBride and Field 1997). Ethnic distribution was 35 percent Hispanic, 33 percent white, 18 percent African American, and 14 percent other, from families of middle to upper-middle socioeconomic strata.

Results of this study showed that females were more comfortable and playful with same-sex friends and saw these friends as more likable, compared with male-male or opposite-sex interactions. Females were found to spend more time discussing relationships, while males spend time roughhousing and in other physical activities. A limitation was a lack of data on how the friendships had evolved.

A study was made of 3,297 adolescents from three schools, one where the majority of students were African American, one where they were white, and one where although the majority were white, there was a large population of African American students. The study was designed to look at the structure of adolescent peer networks in grades 6 through 12 (Urberg et al. 1995). Each participant was asked to name 10 friends, and participants were matched to identified friends. The results showed that female students were more integrated into school social networks than males; girls made and received more choices about friends and had more mutual choices; and girls were more likely than boys to have a "best friend" and to belong to a clique. There was greater diversity in friendships identified by boys; with increasing grade level, there was greater selectivity in naming friends; and African American adolescents were less connected to school networks than white adolescents. Finally, adolescent peer networks are complex, and no one factor can give a clear picture of connection to social networks.

Social goals and beliefs involved in adolescent peer relationships were studied using a sample of 266 (127 male and 139 female) ninth graders, 96 percent white and middle-class (Jarvinen and Nicholls 1996). The findings included six goals—intimacy, nurturance, dominance, leadership, popularity, and avoidance—and six beliefs about what constitutes success in peer relationships: being sincere, having status, being responsible, pretending to care, entertaining others, and being tough. The study showed the importance of communal goals and beliefs, with girls scoring higher and enjoying more satisfactory social relationships than boys. With respect to academic success, it was found that those in the lower tracks placed less value on leadership and popularity among peers and did not feel it was necessary to share feelings with peers to be socially successful; they were found to have less satisfaction in social relations.

SEXUALITY

Adolescents are always faced with decisions about sexual activity. A longitudinal study was made of adjustment patterns of boys and girls experiencing early, middle, and late sexual intercourse (Bingham and Crockett 1996). The sample was made up of 414 white, middle- to lower-class, rural adolescents (216 female and 198 male), tested annually over a four-year period. Neither self-esteem nor level of affect were found to be longitudinally associated with timing of first sexual intercourse; there was a consistent association between positive psychosocial development and the postponement of first sexual intercourse; and adolescents who initiated sexual intercourse the latest had the poorest, rather than best quality, peer relationships but had the most positive family relationships, the greatest commitment to education, and the lowest level of problem behaviors. These conclusions suggest that adolescents who have sexual intercourse early have more problem behavior and poorer quality family relationships; timing is not the cause but the effect of these factors.

A study was made using data from two focus groups comprised of 8 African American and 4 Caucasian girls, 15 and 16 years old (Rosenthal, Lewis, and Cohen 1996). All but one had had consensual intercourse and 10 had had an STD or a pregnancy. The participants felt that they had experienced multiple pressures to engage in sex at an early age (mean 13.7), including the need to please their partner out of fear of losing the relationship; fear of the physical power of the partner; use of drugs and alcohol; curiosity and desire; the need to be accepted by peers who were sexually active; and romanticized notions about sex and boyfriends. The researchers felt that the girls were confused about their sexual feelings and activities and that the best way to avoid intercourse was to be in the presence of others, friends or family. Sex education programs for males as well as females were urged.

Homosexuality

There has been a dearth of professional literature about homosexuality, especially in adolescence (Fontaine and Hammond 1996). Thus there is very little empirical knowledge or data to assist adolescents who are exploring and clarifying their sexual orientation.

Since Stonewall in 1969 there has, however, been more open recognition of a cohort of adolescents who identify themselves as gay or lesbian and wish to be distinguished from adolescents who may experience homosexual desires or transient homosexual contacts. These adolescents come from every ethnic, religious, and socioeconomic background. Many have grown up alienated from social institutions and norms and often from parents who never had a same-sex orientation. They usually have gone through a period of "hiding," with accompanying feelings of isolation and diminished self-esteem. Finally "coming out" indicates self-acceptance and the desire to share this information about themselves. Researchers believe, also, that as cultural barriers against declaring homosexuality have lessened, the age of self-definition has dropped (Offer, Schonert-Reichl, and Boxer 1996:283).

Empirical studies of homosexual adolescents are difficult, as most are based on school populations and the schools or parents often refuse to permit participation. Lesbian, gay, and bisexual adolescents' experiences and feelings about physical, cognitive, psychological, and social tasks are similar to those of other adolescents; however, they experience more rejection, abuse, and even violence. In addition, while all adolescents cope with identity formulation and consolidation, the gay, lesbian, or bisexual faces more challenges when consolidating sexual identity. It is estimated that more adolescents question their sexual identity than actually define themselves as gay, lesbian, or bisexual. Studies have shown that support groups are most helpful for this group. In some, usually urban, communities, high schools have opened to accommodate gay and lesbian students, and it is hoped that this will result in samples that can be empirically studied.

An interesting study of eighty-three volunteering bisexual males, ages seventeen to twenty-three (Savin-Williams 1995), focused on the timing of pubertal maturation as it relates to self-esteem. The data showed that the development of this sample was similar to that of their heterosexual peers.

Pubertal development was associated with an increase in homoerotic sexual feelings and behavior, with early maturation for gay or bisexual males resulting in early onset of orgasms, frequent orgasms, and an early beginning of homosexual activities; timing of pubertal onset did not, however, affect number of lifetime sexual encounters with either male or female partners, onset of heterosexual encounters, frequency of orgasms in older adolescents, sexual orientation, or level of self-esteem. The mean level of self-esteem for homosexual male late adolescents did not differ significantly from a comparable group of heterosexual male late adolescents. The latter finding is significant, as the population was "normal" adolescents and the results differed from those obtained through studies of gays, lesbian, and bisexual adolescents in clinical settings.

FAMILIES

O'Koon (1997) studied 167 mostly Caucasian (88 percent) adolescents, 72 male and 95 female, with a mean age of 17 to consider the effects on self-image of attachment to peers and families. The Offer Self-Image Questionnaire and the Inventory of Parent and Peer Attachment were the instruments used.

The study showed that feeling secure with parental and peer relationships had a strong effect on positive self-image and seemed to ease adolescents' feelings of distress and overexcitability; females had significantly stronger attachments to peers than did males; and although neither males nor females had low scores in these areas, males scored higher in emotional tone, body image, social relationships, mastery of the external world. and psychopathology. Males showed stronger self-images and females showed stronger levels of attachment to peers; for both sexes, attachment to parents is important for general well-being, and a sense of security with parents and peers seems to be closely related to self-image. The authors caution that this study represents a very homogeneous group of middle- and upper middle-class adolescents.

A study by Fletcher et al. (1995) of 4,431 adolescents, 14 to 18, 43 percent male and 57 percent female, related parental practices and adolescent academic achievement, psychosocial competence, behavioral problems, and internalized distress. Subjects were selected to provide a sample representing different socioeconomic backgrounds, ethnicities, family structures, and communities. Ninety-one percent of the participants knew parents of at least some of their friends. Questions involved their opinion of the parenting practices of their own parents and those of close friends. The study revealed that adolescents' adjustment is linked not only to the authoritativeness of their own parents but also to that of the parents of their close friends. Adolescents who described their parents as authoritative earned higher grades, spent more time on homework, felt more competent, and had lower levels of delinquency and substance use. Boys with friends whose parents were seen as authoritative reported lower levels of peer conformity and lower levels of school misconduct. Girls who viewed friends' parents as authoritative showed better psychosocial functioning. A conclusion was that authoritative parenting is associated with competence and that competent adolescents tend to be attracted to and influenced by each other.

Another study examined the relationship between kinship support, family management, and adolescent adjustment in a sample of 155 (58 male and 97 female) African American adolescents, 14 to 19 years old, with 38 percent living in working-class two-parent households and 49 percent in one-parent, usually mother-headed, households (Taylor 1996). Findings showed that kinship support positively affects the family climate and parental practices, and the more that adolescents perceived their families as having a supportive kin system, the more they perceive their homes as organized and their parents as involved in their schooling. In turn, greater parental involvement lessens adolescent involvement in problem behavior and increases self-reliance and school performance, and when kinship support is not reliable, there is more psychological distress. Limitations of the study are that it was based on self-reports of the adolescents' adjustment and that kinship support and family structures were unrelated.

Separation, or disengagement, from family is a task of adolescence. As noted above, some theorists see this as a tumultuous process, while others feel that closeness and warmth continues in adolescents' relationships with their parents. A cross-sectional, longitudinal study was conducted with 220 (97 male and 123 female) middle- and working-class adolescents, studied first while in the fifth to eighth grades and then four years later, in grades nine through twelve (Larson et al. 1996). Findings showed that the amount of time spent with family decreased from 35 percent of waking hours to 14 percent, indicating disengagement, but due to other opportunities and pulls, not to family conflict; continued connection is stable with respect to time spent in one-to-one talking and alone with parents; family conversation about interpersonal matters increases with age, especially for girls; with age, adolescents see themselves as leading interactions; and although there is a decrease in favorable affect in the children and the family in early adolescence, this increases with age.

SELF-ESTEEM

One hundred and seventy-four adolescents were surveyed annually over a four-year period to measure changes in self-esteem and locus of control as well as gender differences (Chubb, Fertman, and Ross 1997). Fifty-seven percent were female and 43 percent male; 95 percent were white. The researchers sought to determine whether adolescence is a time of upheaval, when the variables of self-esteem and locus of control can be expected to change, or, if less stressful, whether these variables become more stable.

The results showed that self-esteem did not change significantly during high school, but that male self-esteem was statistically significantly higher than female self-esteem throughout the four years of high school. For the total sample, there was clear evidence that the loci of control became less external each year. The biggest drop for girls was between ninth and tenth grade, while for boys it was usually between tenth and eleventh grade; the researchers postulated that this may be due to the later onset of puberty for males. Overall there were no significant gender differences in locus of control for the duration of the study. This study represents a fairly small, homogeneous sample.

CONCLUSION

While mental health professionals often refer to "adolescent turmoil" as part of normal development, studies by Offer and colleagues revealed that approximately 80 percent of adolescents do not experience turmoil or psychological disturbance (Offer, Schonert-Reichl, and Boxer 1996:279). Adolescents today face more difficult problems and pressures than when Offer did his major work; they are confronted with higher parental divorce rates, an increase in unwed teen mothers, greater competition for jobs, and, for many, less involvement with an extended family. Clearly the opportunities and the obstacles adolescents face can change with the socioeconomic and political climate in which they are living.

A nationwide poll of 1,048 teenagers 13 to 17 conducted by *The New York Times* and *CBS* (Goodstein and Connelly 1998:A20) showed that while teenagers often are identified as beeper carriers who take shooting lessons as often as others take music lessons, listen to loud music, use drugs and alcohol, and mutilate their bodies with tattoos or piercing, they are also as wholesome and devoid of cynicism as were previous generations of adolescents. In fact, of those interviewed, only 18 percent had a beeper, less than 20 percent had a firearm, only 6 percent of the girls and 3 percent of the boys had body piercings, and 5 percent had a tattoo. The poll found that the majority did not drink or smoke, and fewer than 25 percent had had sex. They recognized drugs and violence as two of the biggest problems their cohort encounters. Unlike stereotypes, 51 percent of the adolescents felt that they got along with their parents very well and 46 percent "fairly well"; however, 55 percent did say they were not always able to talk about concerns with their parents, with 80 percent saying they "won't understand" and 20 percent saying the parents were "too busy." Girls had a lower self-image than boys; 54 percent of the boys said they felt positive about themselves, compared to only 39 percent of the girls. Both sexes said that what they would most like to change about themselves was their looks or body. These adolescents, polled in December 1997, politically were more liberal than their parents with respect to discrimination against blacks, generally more open-minded, and more trusting of government; like their parents, most approved of how President Clinton was doing his job.

Garrity, writing in *The Nation* (2001), found that appearance is the main problem encountered by female adolescents, followed by a loss of voice and the narrowing of desires and expectations. The increase in teenage girls' Web sites, she found, gives these adolescents a chance to express thoughts and feelings with physical privacy they do not have when dealing with school cliques or with societal and parental expectations. They feel free to relate in loud, defiant voices their ideas and thoughts and even to pretend to be someone else.

Adolescents, however, are a very diverse population, for in addition to the model suggested by the poll, there are others who follow rock and movie stars; who regularly smoke marijuana or have serious drug and alcohol problems; who are single mothers; and who are delinquents and truants, as well as some who fit several of these descriptions. However, studies in recent years by leading researchers have concluded that adolescents today are not in turmoil and are no more at risk for impulsive or rebellious actions than were their parents; nor are they, as a group, deeply disturbed or resistant to parental values (Males 1998:G8). Thus, though adolescence is not an easy stage of life and many decisions are made that will affect future stages, most youths are able to enter adulthood comfortable with their newfound identity.

BIBLIOGRAPHY

Adelson, J., ed. 1980. *Handbook of Adolescent Psychology*. New York: Wiley.

Arnett, J. J. and S. Taber. 1994. "Adolescence Terminable and Interminable: When Does Adolescence End?" *Journal of Youth and Adolescence* 23 (5): 517–37.

Bardige, B., J. V. Ward, C. Gilligan, J. M. Taylor, and G. Cohen. 1988. "Moral Concerns and Considerations of Urban Youth." In C. Gilligan, J. V. Ward, and J. M. Taylor, eds., *Mapping the Moral Domain*, 159–73. Cambridge: Harvard University Press.

Belenky, M. F., B. M. Clinchy, N. R. Goldberger, and J. M. Tarule. 1986. *Women's Ways of Knowing*. New York: Basic.

Bernstein, E. and C. Gilligan. 1990. "Unfairness and Not Listening." In C. Gilligan, N. P. Lyons, and T. J. Hammer, eds., *Making Connections*, 147–61. Cambridge: Harvard University Press.

Bingham, C. R. and L. J. Crockett. 1996. "Longitudinal Adjustment Patterns of Boys and Girls Experiencing Early, Middle, and Late Sexual Intercourse." *Developmental Psychology* 32 (4): 647–58.

Blos, P. 1962. *On Adolescence*. New York: Free Press.

——. 1967. "The Second Individuation Process of Adolescence." *The Psychoanalytic Study of the Child*, 22:162–87. New York: International Universities Press.

——. 1972. "The Function of the Ego Ideal in Adolescence." *The Psychoanalytic Study of the Child*, 27:93–97. New York: Quadrangle.

——. 1974. "The Genealogy of the Ego Ideal." *The Psychoanalytic Study of the Child*, 29:43–88. New Haven: Yale University Press.

——. 1979. *The Adolescent Passage*. New York: International Press.

——. 1991. "The Role of the Early Father in Male Adolescent Development." In S. I. Greenspan and G. H. Pollack, eds., *The Course of Life*, 4:1–16. Madison: International Universities Press.

Brenner, C. 1974. *An Elementary Textbook of Psychoanalysis*. New York: Anchor.

Brown, L. M. 1998. *Raising Their Voices*. Cambridge: Harvard University Press.

Brown, L. M. and C. Gilligan. 1992. *Meeting at the Crossroads*. New York: Ballantine.

Boxer, A. M. and B. J. Cohler. 1989. "The Life Course of Gay and Lesbian Youth: An Immodest Proposal for the Study of Lives." *Journal of Homosexuality* 17 (1–21): 315–55.

Chubb, N. H., C. I. Fertman, and J. L. Ross. 1997. "Adolescent Self-Esteem and Locus of Control: A Longitudinal Study of Gender and Age Differences." *Adolescence* 32 (125): 113–29.

Coles, R. 1998. *The Moral Intelligence of Children*. New York: Plume.

Deisher, R. W. 1989. "Adolescent Homosexuality: Preface." *Journal of Homosexuality* 17 (1–2): xiii–xv.

Erikson, E. H. 1950. *Childhood and Society*. 2nd ed. New York: Norton, 1963.

——. 1959. "Identity and the Life Cycle." *Psychological Issues*, I (I): 50–100. New York: International Universities Press.

——. 1968. *Identity: Youth and Crisis*. New York: Norton.

Esman, A. H. 1995. "Adolescence and Society." In R. C. Marohn and S. C. Feinstein, eds., *Adolescent Psychiatry*. Chicago: University of Chicago Press.

Fletcher, A. C., N. E. Darling, L. Steinberg, and S. M. Dornbusch. 1995. "The Company They Keep: Relation of Adolescents' Adjustment and Behavior to Their Friends' Perceptions of Authoritative Parenting in the Social Network." *Development Psychology* 31 (2): 300–10.

Fontaine, J. H. and N. L. Hammond. 1996. "Counseling Issues with Gay and Lesbian Adolescents." *Adolescence* 31 (124): 817–30.

Freud, A. 1958. "Adolescence." *The Psychoanalytic Study of the Child*, 13:255–78. New York: International Universities Press.

——. 1966. *The Ego and the Mechanisms of Defense*. Rev. ed. New York: International Universities Press.

Freud, S. 1905. "The Transformations of Puberty." In the *Standard Edition of the Complete Works of Sigmund Freud*, vol. 7. London: Hogarth Press, 1953.

——. 1925. "Some Psychological Consequences of the Anatomical Distinction Between the Sexes." In *The Standard Edition of the Complete Psychological Works of Sigmund Freud*, vol. 29. London: Hogarth Press, 1961.

——. 1931. "Female Sexuality." In *The Standard Edition of the Complete Psychological Works of Sigmund Freud*, vol. 21. London: Hogarth Press, 1961.

Garrity, B. 2001. "Some Cyberspace of Her Own." *The Nation*, March 19, 25–32.

Gerstel, C. J., A. J. Feraios, and G. Herdt. 1989. "Widening Circles: An Ethnographic Profile of a Youth Group." *Journal of Homosexuality* 17 (1–2): 75–92.

Gilligan, C. 1988. "Exit-Voice Dilemmas in Adolescent Development." In C. Gilligan, J. V. Ward, and J. M. Taylor, eds., *Mapping the Moral Domain*, 141–58. Cambridge: Harvard University Press.

——. 1990. "Teaching Shakespeare's Sister: Notes from the Underground of Female Adolescence." In C. Gilligan, N. P. Lyons, and T. J. Hammer, eds. *Making Connections*, 6–29. Cambridge: Harvard University Press.

——. 1993. *In a Different Voice*. Cambridge: Harvard University Press.

——. 1998. "Pain of Growing Up, in Girl's Voice or Boy's." *The New York Times*, April 24, B2.

Gilligan, C. and J. Attanucci. 1988. "Two Moral Orientations." In C. Gilligan, J. V. Ward, and J. M. Taylor, eds., *Mapping the Moral Domain*, 73–86. Cambridge: Harvard University Press.

Gilligan, C., N. P. Lyons, and T. J. Hanmer, eds. 1990. *Making Connections*. Cambridge: Harvard University Press.

Gilligan, C., J. V. Ward, and J. M. Taylor, eds. 1988. *Mapping the Moral Domain*. Cambridge: Harvard University Press.

Ginsburg, H. P. and S. Opper. 1988. *Piaget's Theory of Intellectual Development*. Englewood Cliffs, NJ: Prentice Hall.

Goodstein, L. and M. Connelly. 1998. "Teen-Age Poll Finds a Turn to the Traditional." *The New York Times*, April 30, A20.

Greenspan, S. I. and G. H. Pollock, eds. 1991. *The Course of Life*, vol. 4. Madison: International Universities Press.

Holstein, C. B. 1976. "Irreversible, Stepwise Sequence in the Development of Moral Judgment: A Longitudinal Study of Males and Females." *Child Development* 47:51–61.

Inhelder, B. and J. Piaget. 1958. *The Growth of Logical Thinking*. New York: Basic.

Jarvinen, D. W. and J. G. Nicholls. 1996. "Adolescents' Social Goals, Beliefs About the Causes of Social Success and Satisfaction in Peer Relations." *Developmental Psychology* 32 (3): 435–41.

Johnson, D. K. 1988. "Adolescents' Solutions to Dilemmas in Fables: Two Moral Orientations—Two Problem Solving Strategies." In C. Gilligan, J. V. Ward, and J. M. Taylor, eds., *Mapping the Moral Domain*, 49–86. Cambridge: Harvard University Press.

Kagan, J. 1971a. "A Conception of Early Adolescence." *Daedalus* (Fall): 997–1012.

——. 1971b. "The Three Faces of Continuity in Human Development." In D. A. Goslin, ed., *Handbook of Socialization Theory*, 983–1002. Chicago: Rand McNally.

Kagan, J. and R. Coles, eds. 1972. *Twelve to Sixteen: Early Adolescence*. New York: Norton.

Kasser T., R. M. Ryan, M. Zax, and A. J. Sameroff. 1995. "The Relations of Maternal and Social Environments to Late Adolescents' Materialistic and Prosocial Values." *Developmental Psychology* 31 (6): 907–14.

Kohlberg, L. 1963. "The Development of Children's Orientations Toward a Moral Order." *Vita Humana* 6:11–33.

——. 1964. "Development of Moral Character and Moral Ideology." In M. L. Hoffman and L. W. Hoffman, eds., *Review of Child Development Research* 1:383–431. New York: Russell Sage Foundation.

——. 1966. "Moral Education in the Schools, a Developmental View." *School Review* 74:1–30.

——. 1971. "Stage and Sequence: The Cognitive-Developmental Approach to Socialization." In D. A. Goslin, ed., *Handbook of Socialization Theory*, 347–480. Chicago: Rand McNally.

——. 1976. "Moral Stages and Moralization." In E. Likona, ed., *Moral Development and Behavior*, 31–53. New York: Holt, Rinehart and Winston.

———. 1984. *The Psychology of Moral Development*. New York: Harper and Row.

Kohlberg, L. and C. Gilligan. 1971. "The Adolescent as a Philosopher: The Discovery of the Self in a Postconventional World." *Daedalus* (Fall): 1051–86.

Kolhlberg, L. and R. Kramer. 1969. "Continuities and Discontinuities in Childhood and Adult Moral Development." *Human Development* 12:93–120.

Kohlberg, L., C. Levine, and A. Hewer. 1983. *Moral Stages: A Current Formulation and a Response to Critics*. Basel: S. Karger.

Larson, R. W., M. H. Richards, G. Moneta, G. Holmbeck, and E. Duckett. 1996. *Developmental Psychology* 32 (4): 744–54.

Lewis, M. 1996. *Child and Adolescent Psychiatry*. 2nd ed. Baltimore: Williams and Wilkins.

Lyons, N. P. 1988. "Two Perspectives: On Self, Relationships, and Morality." In C. Gilligan, J. V. Ward, and J. M. Taylor, eds., *Mapping the Moral Domain*, 21–48. Cambridge: Harvard University Press.

Males, M. A. 1998. "Five Myths, and Why Adults Believe They Are True." *The New York Times*, April 29, G9.

Marchant, J. R. V. and J. F. Charles. 1945. *Cassell's Latin Dictionary*. New York: Funk and Wagnalls.

Martinez, R. O. and R. L. Dukes. 1997. "The Effects of Ethnic Identity, Ethnicity, and Gender on Adolescent Well-Being." *Journal of Youth and Adolescence* 26 (5): 503–16.

McBride, C. K. and T. Field. 1997. "Adolescent Same-Sex and Opposite-Sex Best Friend Interactions." *Adolescence* 32 (127): 515–22.

McGrath, Charles. 1998. "Being Thirteen." *New York Times Magazine*, May 17, 29–30.

Monte, C. F. 1980. *Beneath the Mask*. 2nd ed. New York: Holt, Rinehart and Winston.

Murphy, J. M. and C. Gilligan. 1980. "Moral Development in Late Adolescence and Adulthood: A Critique and Reconstruction of Kohlberg's Theory." *Human Development* 23:77–104.

Muuss, R. E. 1988. *Theories of Adolescence*. 5th ed. New York: McGraw-Hill.

Muuss, R. E. and H. D. Porton. 1998. *Adolescent Behavior*. Boston: McGraw-Hill College.

Offer, D. 1969. *The Psychological World of the Teen-Ager*. New York: Basic.

———. 1987. "In Defense of Adolescents." *Journal of the American Medical Association* 257 (24): 3407–08.

———. 1991. "Adolescent Development: A Normative Perspective." In S. I. Greenspan and G. H. Pollock, eds., *The Course of Life*, 4:181–89.

Offer, D. and J. B. Offer. 1975. *From Teenage to Young Manhood*. New York: Basic.

Offer, D., E. Ostrow, and K. I. Howard. 1977. "The Self-Image of Adolescents: A Study of Four Cultures." *Journal of Youth and Adolescence* 6 (3): 265–79.

——. 1981. "The Mental Health Professional's Concept of the Normal Adolescent." *Archives of General Psychiatry* 38:149–52.

——. 1982. "Family Perceptions of Adolescent Self-Image." *Journal of Youth and Adolescence* 11 (4): 281–91.

Offer, D. and M. Sabshin. 1984. *Normality and the Life Cycle.* New York: Basic.

Offer, D., K. A. Schonert-Reichl, and A. M. Boxer. 1996. "Normal Adolescent Development: Empirical Research Findings." In M. Lewis, ed., *Child and Adolescent Psychiatry*, 2nd ed., 278–90. Baltimore: Williams and Wilkins.

O'Koon, J. 1997. "Attachment to Parents and Peers in Late Adolescence and Their Relationship with Self-Image." *Adolescence* 32 (126): 471–82.

Onions, C. T. 1947. *The Shorter Oxford English Dictionary* 3rd rev. ed. Oxford: Clarendon Press.

Paulson, S. E. and C. L. Sputa. 1996. "Patterns of Parenting During Adolescence: Perceptions of Adolescents and Parents." *Adolescence* 31 (122): 369–81.

Piaget, J. 1972. "Intellectual Evolution from Adolescence to Adulthood." *Human Development* 15:1–12.

Pollack, W. B. 1998. *Real Boys: Rescuing Our Sons from the Myths of Boyhood.* New York: Owl Books.

——. 2000. *Real Boys' Voices.* New York: Random House.

Powers, A. 1998. "Who Are These People, Anyway?" *The New York Times*, April 29, G1.

Rosenthal, S. L., L. M. Lewis, and S. S. Cohen. 1996. "Issues Related to the Sexual Decision-Making of Inner-City Adolescent Girls." *Adolescence* 31 (123): 731–39.

Rosenzweig, M. R. and L. W. Porter, eds. 1988. *Annual Review of Psychology*, vol. 39. Palo Alto: Annual Reviews.

Savin-Williams, R. C. 1995. "An Exploratory Study of Pubertal Maturation Timing and Self-Esteem Among Gay and Bisexual Male Youths." *Development Psychology* 31 (1): 56–64.

Schonert-Reichl, K. A., D. Offer, and K. I. Howard. 1995. "Seeking Help from Informal and Formal Resources During Adolescence: Sociodemographic and Psychological Correlates." *Adolescent Psychiatry* 20: 165–78.

Talwar, R. and J. V. Lerner. 1991. "Theories of Adolescent Development." In R. M. Lerner, A. C. Petersen, and J. Brooks-Gunn, eds., *Encyclopedia of Adolescence.* New York: Garland.

Taylor, J. M., C. Gilligan, and A. M. Sullivan. 1995. *Between Voice and Silence.* Cambridge: Harvard University Press.

Taylor, R. D. 1996. "Adolescents' Perceptions of Kinship Support and Family Management Practices: Association with Adolescent Adjustment in African American Families." *Developmental Psychology* 32 (4): 687–95.

Urberg, K. A., S. M. Degirmencioglu, J. M. Tolson, and K. Halliday-Scher. 1995. "The Structure of Adolescent Peer Networks." *Developmental Psychology* 31 (4): 540–47.

White, R. W. 1963. "Ego and Reality in Psychoanalytic Theory." *Psychological Issues* II (3). New York: International Universities Press.

——. 1975. *Lives in Progress.* 3rd ed. New York: Holt, Rinehart and Winston.

RANDY H. MAGEN,
SONIA G. AUSTRIAN,
AND CAROLYN S. HUGHES

one two three four **five** six

ADULTHOOD

INTRODUCTION

Adulthood is the period in the life cycle that has received the least scholarly attention, although it is the longest period in the life cycle, spanning the years from adolescence to old age. It has received more coverage in "pop" psychology, especially the concept of a "midlife crisis." While theorists have long been interested in childhood and adolescence, interest in gerontology only became apparent in the 1950s, due to increased government funding for programs and services for the elderly rather than greater involvement on the part of social science professionals. It wasn't until the 1960s, with the influence of Erik Erikson, that adulthood became an era to be studied.

Adulthood is less structured than earlier periods in the life cycle and involves decisions about many aspects of the individual's life. There may be conflicts between earlier structured goals and family values and identity, and individual goals and personal identity. In the early years of this phase, the person is at the peak of physical and intellectual capacities and may experiment with roles and identity before arriving at goals and expectations for the remainder of adulthood. In the later stage of adulthood, many people experience some degree of physical and cognitive decline, while others continue to perform very well. While all human development has biological, psychological, cultural, and social determinants that influence functioning more than chronological age, this is particularly true of adulthood.

Currently the largest cohort in the United States is moving through the middle years. They represent the best educated and most affluent cohort. From 1960 to 1985, those aged 45 to 65 increased by 24 percent. Between 1990 and 2050, the number of people in middle age will rise from 47 to 80 million, a 72 percent increase. The median age will increase from 33 in 1990 to 42 in 2050 as baby boomers move through middle age (Willis and Reid 1999:xv). With parents living longer and the "boomers" having children later, many find themselves in the "sandwich" generation, caring for parents and for children while also attending to careers reaching their peak.

In the twenties, the young adult focuses on self-actualization in love and work. Decisions to be dealt with include further education/training, career choices, sexual orientation, selecting a mate/companion, and whether to have children.

The thirties begin with evaluation of the twenties; some feel disappointment, anger, and guilt, while others view those years as vibrant, rich, and successful. Goals and tasks become more refined. There is greater pressure to form a lasting intimate relationship and to decide whether or not to have children. Being part of a community takes on greater importance, although the individual does not feel the need to depend on others and on institutions as in earlier periods. The adult may face a dilemma, wanting to think and speak in his or her own voice while also seeking affiliation and confirmation.

The forties are seen by some as "the last chance." There is less dependence on others and on institutions as the individual reaches a degree of seniority in the work world. The adult may experience some decline in physical functioning and is aware of being between the "young" and the "old," with responsibilities to both. With increasing awareness of the passage of time, there is existential questioning of self, values, and life itself, a sense of "quiet desperation," especially if reality and expectations are not in sync. For some, this provokes major changes in work and/or partner.

In the fifties, the adult usually feels mellower and less negative. She or he spends time in reflection and becomes less self-critical and not as subject to external demands. There is increased compassion for others and concern for the upcoming generations.

As noted in the previous chapters, most of the early theories evolved from observation of white, middle-class, male subjects. The more recent studies have focused on, or at least included, women and more diverse populations.

CARL G. JUNG

Carl Jung, a Swiss psychoanalyst, is recognized as one of the first theorists to look at adult development. Initially greatly influenced by Sigmund Freud, Jung extended the concept of stage theory to adults. His theory of adult development evolved from his analysis of patients and from his studies of mythologies, religious systems, dreams, and different cultural customs. Unlike Freud, Jung felt that personality development has not progressed very far by the end of adolescence, only as far as necessary for the person to begin living as an adult and assuming adult responsibilities. Levinson was later to refer to Jung as "the father of the modern study of adult development" (Levinson et al. 1978:4).

In 1907 Freud picked Jung as his successor to continue and complete his work. This was not to be, as Jung would later break with Freud. Initially both agreed that what they had found in exploring the unconscious were repressed, unacceptable infantile sexual and aggressive strivings. As Jung continued his explorations, he had great difficulty with Freud's concept of libido as a generalized and universal pleasure drive rooted in developing sexuality. Jung saw libido in broader terms, as a more neutral form of general psychic energy, a creative life force that underlies myths, religious dogma, and neurosis. Developing the "principle of equivalence," Jung felt that when conscious psychic energy is repressed, an unconscious substitute or symbolic alternate idea takes its place in consciousness (Monte 1980:271–72). His concept of the unconscious was also broader than Freud's; he viewed it as prospective as well as retrospective. Jung accepted Freud's concept of a personal unconscious, but added a *collective unconscious* transcending personal experiences, a concept that over the years has evoked controversy. The collective unconscious, Jung felt, is responsible for the spontaneous production of myths, visions, religious ideas, and dreams common to different cultures and different periods in history (Storr 1991:33). Jung also differed from Freud in believing that personality development is a process that continues into adulthood.

THE ARCHETYPES

Jung was aware of the importance of the external world. He defined *archetypes* as the primordial images and ideas common to all from the beginning of life, including possibilities of action, predispositions to responses to the external world, and potentialities for shaping experiences. These archetypes are prototypes or molds of emotional reactions that organize and shape the individual's interaction with the external, and the internal unconscious, worlds. Jung believed that the archetypes represent repetitions of reactions to events that have been established over thousands of generations of human development, are transmitted to future generations, and thus are part of the collective unconscious. They represent typical human experiences with immense emotional significance. The archetypes evolve in the individual psyche from undifferentiated images into increasingly complex internal figures. They are the organizing factors that shape, and are shaped by, our experiences throughout life. Jung did not place a theoretical limit on the number of archetypes, but he felt some are more important than others.

Very interested in mythology, Jung devoted much of his work to identifying specific archetypes in myths, dreams, fantasies, and art. In terms of personality, Jung felt that in addition to the positive aspect, there exists an inferior, undesirable aspect that we prefer not to recognize, called "shadow." Aware that the internal world is made up of opposites, Jung, analyzing his own personality, arrived at the conclusion that no man is exclusively masculine but also has feminine traits, which he tries to repress. He called the internalized, fundamentally unconscious, inherited, collective feminine image *anima*, and felt that this determines a man's relationship to women and his understanding of male-female relationships, giving him less one-sided and male interactions with and perceptions of others. The anima is based on real experiences with women as well as an archetype, the experiences of men with women throughout history. It produces in men sudden, unexpected changes in temperament or character; the man may appear to be moody, sentimental, and childish. The anima has an erotic, emotional character (Jung 1982:50; Storr 1991:47).

Similarly, women have an internal, inherited masculine image, which Jung termed the *animus*. He believed that, like the anima, the animus is not a single personification but rather a plurality of male figures embodying a woman's ancestral experience of men. The animus produces opinions in women that appear to be solid convictions and has a rationalizing character (Jung 1982:50), although the woman may appear to be argumentative, irritable, and opinionated (Storr 1991:47). To be complete, men and women need to recognize the male and female components of their personality (Jung 1917:207–209), but Jung cautioned against men identifying too strongly with the anima or women identifying too much with the animus. In summary, the anima and animus are personifications of parts of the personality that are opposed to the conscious ego and possess attributes of the opposite sex (Storr

1991:47). Jung believed that a person should not allow emotions to be in control or to take over the function of the ego, for then he or she will not be in the right relationship with the inner world.

Persona is another theoretical concept of Jung's. This is what the individual presents to others, based on societal expectations, the "public" self. The persona is an individual creation, as opposed to the archetype with its historical roots, and is an ideal image. It is a complicated system of relationships between the individual consciousness and society, similar to a mask designed to make a definite impression on others while concealing the true nature of the individual. Establishing a collectively suitable persona involves concessions to the external world so that the ego identifies with the persona; however, Jung cautioned that people may begin to believe they are who they pretend to be. In order to individuate and be self-aware, it is essential to distinguish between who one is and how one appears to others. The persona is the personality with which one identifies (Jung 1982:81–84). It is sometimes seen in contrast to the shadow, for identification with the social role allows one to remain unaware of antisocial impulses and inner feelings.

Introversion/Extroversion Typography

Jung initially postulated two different personality types. *Introverts* have a hesitant, reflective, retiring, somewhat defensive nature. Many are interested in the external world mainly when it affects their inner world. They are underinvolved with objects, insist on separateness, and run the risk of emotional isolation. *Extroverts* are outgoing, candid, quick to form relationships, and confident. They are more interested in the internal world when the external has disappointed them and may well be perceived as moody and egocentric. They can get overly involved with objects and may risk losing their individual identity. Jung believed there are specific functions necessary to mediate involvement with the external world and with the inner world of the personal and collective unconscious. He called the functions directed outward *ectopsychic* and those directed inward toward the ego *endopsychic*. His writing deals primarily with the ectopsychic functions emphasized in constructing his introversion/extroversion typology. The four ectopsychic functions are:

1. *sensation*—external facts arrived at through the senses and concerned with orientation to reality—tells that a thing exists, that it "is"
2. *thinking*—linking up ideas through concepts—tells what the thing is

3. *feeling*—tells whether something is acceptable or unacceptable; it is subjective and determines the thing's worth

4. *intuition*—made up of feelings about the origin and prospects of a thing—awareness of time, past and future of a thing—a psychological function that mediates perceptions in an unconscious manner and is more interested in possibilities than in the present (Jung 1968:11–14; Storr 1991:70–73)

Jung further classified these functions as *rational* or *irrational* depending on the degree of judgment and reasoning involved. He viewed sensation and intuition as irrational and thinking and feeling as rational. Thinking is opposed to feeling and sensation to intuition (Storr 1991:70). The types judged as irrational involve actions based not on reasoned judgment but on the absolute intensity of perception. Theoretically, a perfectly adapted person would be one in whom none of the functions predominates at the expense of its opposite. Jung then suggested how these functions operate in his two personality types, introvert and extrovert.

The introvert struggles to keep the ego independent of external influence. The *thinking* introvert is theoretical, intellectual, and impractical, and relates more to the inner than the outer world, ignoring practicalities. Introverted thinking is subjectively oriented and influenced by ideas. There is little involvement with the peripheral world and dependence on intimates. The *feeling* introvert appears to have no concern for the feelings or opinions of others and may project an air of superiority. Although inner emotions may be intense, emotional expression is minimal. The person may appear silent, childish, and indifferent. The *sensation* introvert's main concern is with a personal, subjective reaction to objective sensory events, which are evaluated as good or evil depending on how they affect the individual. Reality is sometimes misinterpreted, separating this introvert from the external world. He or she is often described as passive, calm, and artistic. The *intuitive* introvert appears aloof and unconcerned about concrete reality and external events, focusing on the inner world. Perceptions satisfy the self but may separate the person from others, so that she or he is seen as unique, a dreamer, a mystic (Jung 1933:471–511; Monte 1980:297–98).

The extrovert is powerfully influenced by social surroundings (the external world), to the detriment of subjective experience, and is greatly influenced by the experiences and values of others. The *thinking* extrovert does not go beyond external ideas and objects and is oriented to the object and objective data. "Oughts" and "musts" dominate the approach to values, resulting in the appearance of being dogmatic, objective, rigid, and cold. The *feeling* extrovert seeks harmony with the external world, makes friends easily, and appears to be intense, effervescent, and sociable. The orientation is to objective data, the object. Women often fall into this category. The *sensation* extrovert seeks new sensory experiences, conditioned by the object. These extroverts, usually men, often become connoisseurs of such things as wine or art and are usually good company. Introspection and self-concern are suppressed. The individual is concerned for the welfare of others and is described as realistic, sensual, and jolly. The *intuitive* extrovert has difficulty sustaining interest in something once the novelty wears off and looks for new possibilities. Little conscious, reflective thought is given to decisions, although most are good. Concern for others is limited; however, this type of extrovert inspires confidence and enthusiasm and is described as visionary, changeable, and creative (Jung 1933:428–71; Monte 1980:295–97).

Jung stressed that these types are not seen in pure form. He also felt that changes are possible as conditions in a person's life change. Jung valued extroversion and introversion equally, believing that a person needs to relate to both his inner (subjective) world and to connect with the outer (objective) world.

DIFFERENTIATION AND INDIVIDUATION

Jung was very concerned with individual development. Individuation, the process whereby a person develops unique traits, is the central concept of his theories and his major contribution. Within each personality he saw a range of conflicting themes. In addition to anima/animus and introversion/extroversion, he identified ego/shadow and personal unconscious/collective unconscious, and came to believe that the goal of personality development is to equally develop all parts of the psyche by accepting both the rational and the irrational. Failure to integrate the opposing tendencies can result in a sense of being torn apart. Jung termed the emergence and balancing of these unconscious, opposing tendencies *enantiodromia.*

Differentiation involves the development of differences, the separation of the parts from the whole. Jung believed that the functions of thinking, feeling, sensation, and intuition must be separated in order to avoid ambivalence. Differentiation accomplishes this and occurs as the irrelevant is isolated and excluded.

Individuation, Jung believed, does not occur until the later years. When the goal of reconciling opposites has been achieved and all elements are equally emphasized, the person has a fully differentiated, individuated personality that Jung called the *self*. Individuation is necessary and results from the development of the psychological individual as a differentiated being from the general collective psychology. Thus, Jung believed, there is a *process of differentiation* that has the goal of developing the individual personality. Individuation is more or less in opposition to the collective norm, as it means separation and differentiation from the general and construction of the particular. Jung saw individuation as an extension of the sphere of consciousness (Jung 1933:561–63).

Jung felt that the process of individuation does not occur until age forty, which he called "the noon of life," the meridian between the first and second halves of life. It is a time devoted to the "illumination of the self," which will continue through the remaining years. Prior to age forty, Jung felt personality development cannot progress further than breaking away from parents and doing what is needed to assume responsibilities for family, work, and community. People are hampered by inner conflicts and repressed desires and attributes. Jung believed that after forty, they are able to move closer to the opposite polarity, men becoming more concerned with relationships and women with the external world. With integration of opposites, there is greater acceptance of the self. Life after forty is focused more on individuation, understanding of the self and of one's relationship with the world.

Jung's break with Freudian theory and his belief in ambiguities, the mysterious, and the spiritual evoked much skepticism and criticism from psychologist and psychiatrists. In addition, many find Jung's work difficult to grasp (Storr 1991:100). However, he was among the first to look at adult development, and his thoughts on the male/female polarities as well as on individuation as a product of maturity were to heavily influence the work of Daniel Levinson.

ERIK ERIKSON

As discussed in previous chapters, Erikson postulated a total of eight sequential stages involving ego crises, states of disequilibrium, and critical tasks that enhance and guide the individual's sense of self and ego identity. As the person enters young adulthood, he or she reaches the sixth stage, which involves acquiring a sense of intimacy versus a sense of isolation, giving up, to some extent, one's newly established identity in order to fuse with others. In later adulthood the person will go through the seventh stage, acquiring a sense of generativity versus a sense of stagnation, extending him- or herself to others, particularly future generations.

ACQUIRING A SENSE OF INTIMACY VERSUS A SENSE OF ISOLATION

If the previous stages have been successfully completed, the young adult is ready to commit to affiliations and partnerships, even if they require compromises and sacrifices, without fear of ego loss. In this stage, the adult must be able to simultaneously be involved in intimate sexual fulfillment (love) while maintaining independence needed for productivity (work).

Erikson's concept of initial intimacy ranges from intense friendships to early sexual experimentation. He characterized later intimacy as healthy genital sexuality involving the following components:

1. mutuality of orgasm
2. having a loved partner
3. having a partner of the opposite sex
4. having a partner with whom one shares mutual trust
5. having a partner who is willing to regulate cycles of work, procreation, and recreation
6. having successfully completed all previous developmental stages (Erikson 1950:263–66)

Isolation is a fear of remaining separate and unrecognized, resulting in regression to an earlier phase of conflict with the "other," possibly resulting in borderline pathology (Erikson 1982:71). The virtue, ego strength, of this stage is *love* when the conflict between intimacy and isolation is resolved. The danger is that if the adult is not ready for intimacy, she or he will retreat into *distantiation*, a readiness to isolate. The ritualization is *affiliative*, establishing identity complementary to the person with whom one experiences intimacy. The ritualism is *elitism*, a sense of shared narcissism leading to exclusion of others from group membership (Erikson 1950:263–66, 1977:110).

ACQUIRING A SENSE OF GENERATIVITY VERSUS A SENSE OF STAGNATION

This seventh stage of ego development occurs in late adulthood, prior to the final stage, when Erikson saw the person as "old." It is primarily concerned with establishing and guiding the next generation. Erikson believed that a mature man needs to be needed and if he has successfully completed the previous stage, he will be concerned with the next generation, often, but not necessarily, his offspring. *Generativity* refers to establishing and guiding the next generation. It encompasses procreativity, productivity, and creativity (Erikson 1982:67). It involves the task of expanding ego interests and a sense of contributing to the future. Self interests are minimized in order to give greater consideration to generations to come (Erikson 1968:138) and to the transmission of values. If the person cannot find worth in guiding and aiding the next generations, he or she will regress to an obsessive need for pseudo-intimacy with an accompanying sense of stagnation, boredom, and personal impoverishment (Erikson 1950:267). Erikson saw this as *rejectivity*, the unwillingness to include specific groups or others perceived as a threat to "one's own kind" (Erikson 1982:68–69).

The virtue, ego strength, achieved is *care*, the right to be needed as well as the privilege of needing the young. It involves a commitment to take care of the people and ideas one has learned to care about (Erikson 1982:67). The ritualization is *generationa*lity, the feeling of knowing what one is doing in the roles of parent and teacher. The ritualism is *authoritism*, seizing authority and becoming oppressively insensitive (Erikson 1977:111).

ROBERT PECK

Robert Peck, a psychoanalyst, focused on the middle and old age life stages, believing that they involve different kinds of psychological learning and adjustments than occur earlier. Studying primarily men, Peck felt that there is greater variability in the chronological age at which crises are encountered than earlier in life, due to individual circumstances. Peck identified four stages of middle age in a format similar to Erikson's (Peck 1968:88–90).

1. VALUING WISDOM VERSUS VALUING PHYSICAL POWERS

Peck believed that after the late twenties, the individual experiences a decrease in physical strength, stamina, and attractiveness. There is, however, an increase in *wisdom*, which he defined as the ability to make the most effective choices among alternatives presented by intellectual perception and imagination and affected by emotional stability. He felt that life experience provides a wide range of emotional relationships going beyond those within one's family of origin or cultural subgroup.

Peck felt that men reach a critical transition point between their late thirties and late forties. If a man has put a premium on physical powers, as these decline he may become increasingly depressed, bitter, and unhappy and less effective in work and social roles. Those who go through this period more successfully change their values and see their "heads" as their chief resource and way to evaluate themselves, rather than their "hands." Thus in the first stage of physical decline, the successful adjustment is moving from physique-based values to intellect-based values in order to determine self-definition and behavior.

2. Socializing Versus Sexualizing in Human Relationships

Peck felt that the sexual climacteric is related to general physical decline. Success at this stage means valuing people more as individual personalities and companions than as sex objects. A couple's understanding of each other is deeper than earlier in life, when it was more egocentric.

3. Cathectic Flexibility Versus Cathectic Impoverishment

Although an ability to shift emotional investment from one person or activity to another is present throughout life, Peck felt that it is more crucial in middle age. At this stage, parents die, children leave home, and the circle of friends and relatives is diminished by death. However, this is also a time when many have the widest circle of acquaintances in the community and at work, within a wide age range. Thus the person who successfully completes this stage has emotional experience with a greater variety of people, roles, and relationships than were possible earlier. Those who are less successful have an impoverished emotional life, as they are unable to reinvest in new people, pursuits, or life settings.

4. Mental Flexibility Versus Mental Rigidity

Peck believed that a major issue throughout life is whether oneself or one's events and experiences will dictate one's life. People whose development is successful are flexible and use experiences as "provisional guides," while others use experience to establish a set of inflexible rules and are closed to new ideas. This can become a crucial issue in middle age, when Peck felt people are at their peak status and have worked out a set of "answers" to life.

Peck concluded that because life patterns in adulthood vary so much, chronological age is not the way to study middle age and aging. Some people over sixty-five may act, think, and feel more like people in middle age, while others at sixty-five may appear very old. He urged researchers to look at samples in terms of stage criteria rather than chronological age.

BERNICE L. NEUGARTEN

Bernice Neugarten was a psychologist who chaired the Committee on Human Development at the University of Chicago. Her work, on middle age and primarily on aging, was done in the 1950s and 1960s and was particularly important because she focused on women as much as on men, while earlier theorists had concentrated almost exclusively on men. Neugarten focused on age-status systems, noting that certain biological and social events are used to signify the transition from one age status to another, within a cultural context. A *social age clock* is the means by which society and culture dictate when in our life cycle we should do what, thus creating age norms. Age-status systems are based on chronological age but can vary in detail and formality. As society in the United States has evolved over time, there have been changes in social definitions of age groups, age norms, and relations between age groups (Neugarten and Moore 1968:5).

THE FAMILY

The family is an example of an age-status system in which social age is marked by social and biological events in the life cycle. At each stage the person takes on new roles, and status is adjusted in relation to extended family members. Neugarten worked in a period when people married and had children earlier and widowhood tended to occur later than in earlier generations. Thus the family cycle for parents and children was accelerated while the period of husband and wife alone, which Neugarten called the "gerontic" family, was extended (Neugarten and Moore 1968:7). A study of adults aged forty to seventy showed a high correlation between social class and age at successive points in the family cycle; the higher the class, the later events such as leaving the parental home, marriage, and births of first and last children occurred.

Neugarten, studying age-sex roles and personality in middle age, used the projective Thematic Apperception Test (TAT), feeling that responses would be relatively uncensored and more closely related to the subjects' personal values and experiences. The sample consisted of eighteen middle-class men and twenty-two middle-class women, ages forty to fifty-four; twenty-one working-class men and twelve working-class women, ages forty to fifty-four; fourteen middle-class men and thirteen middle-class women, ages fifty-five to seventy; and fifteen working-class men and thirteen working-class women, ages fifty-five to seventy. Four women had never married, and eight of the men and six of the women were childless. Data, when analyzed, showed that as women age they become more tolerant of their own aggressiveness and egocentric impulses, while men became more tolerant of their nurturing and affiliative impulses (Neugarten and Gutman 1968:71).

PSYCHOLOGICAL ISSUES OF MIDDLE AGE

Neugarten and her colleagues interviewed at length one hundred randomly selected, successful, highly introspective and verbal men and women, ages forty-five to fifty-five, in order to identify the salient characteristics of middle adulthood. It became evident that middle age is perceived as a distinctive period in the life cycle when people evaluate their positions within different life contexts such as body, career, and family, factors that may not be in sync, rather than chronological age. Middle-aged people tend to see themselves as bridges between generations within families as well as within the workplace and the community. The study found that women tend to define age status in terms of events in the family life cycle, such as children leaving home or awareness that the woman may be childless. Men see a closer relationship between lifeline and careerline, with middle age as a time to take stock of where they are with respect to their expectations. Men, more than women, are concerned about their health, and both men and women show more concern about the man's health. Men in this period feel increased job pressure or job boredom, while women have a greater sense of freedom, a better self-concept, and a chance to pursue latent talents and interests.

Both sexes studied felt that they viewed time differently in middle age. Prior to this phase, they had measured life in terms of "time since birth," and they now thought in terms of "life left to live," although few expressed a wish to be young again. Life was seen as finite. Both sexes saw middle age as a time of maximum capacity and ability to handle a complex environment and a highly differentiated self. Most felt that they had improved judgment and a better grasp of reality. Neugarten did not support the idea of a midlife crisis, but felt that men and women undergo a normal, gradual change in their perception of time.

Neugarten et al. identified the "executive processes of personality" in middle age as self-awareness, manipulation and control of the environment, mastery, competence, selectivity, and a wide range of cognitive strategies. Introspection was a major characteristic, observed as stock-taking, more self-examination, and the ability to structure and restructure experience. There was a greater sense of control over impulses (Neugarten 1968:98).

Comparing the upper middle-class sample of men to working-class men, Neugarten found that the latter saw life as paced more rapidly, with divisions in the lifeline at twenty-five, thirty-five, and fifty; middle age began at forty and old age at sixty. The upper middle-class sample viewed the period up to age thirty as a time for exploration and adjustment to adult roles; the working-class sample saw this as a time not for exploration but for giving up youth and taking on responsibilities (Neugarten 1968:144–45).

As a prelude to the above study, Neugarten interviewed one hundred educated women, forty-five to fifty-five, about their attitudes toward and experiences with menopause. This core group was then compared to three other samples, twenty-one to thirty, thirty-one to forty-four, and fifty-six to sixty-five. As would be expected, the greatest differences were seen between the two younger groups and the two older, women who have and have not experienced menopause. The majority of middle-aged women felt that menopause had not caused major discontinuity in life, that difficulties with it were not inevitable, and that they had had relative control over symptoms. There was uncertainty about the effects of menopause on sexuality, especially among those who had not completed menopause. Only four of the respondents felt that the most negative aspect was the inability to have more children. Many of the respondents stated that they would find the postmenopausal phase of life a happier and healthier time (Neugarten et al. 1968:195–200). They were pleased to no longer have the "annoyance" of menstruation and the responsibility of caring for small children.

Much of Neugarten's work was devoted to studying the elderly. This will be discussed in the next chapter.

DANIEL LEVINSON: THE SEASONS OF A MAN'S LIFE

Daniel Levinson was a psychologist on the staff of the department of psychiatry of Yale University. He believed that a developmental approach should be taken to the study of adulthood as had been done for the study of childhood. Middle age had become a "taboo" topic, for this period in the life cycle seemed to activate anxieties about old age, decline, and death. Thus, middle age as an interim phase was defined in negative terms. Youth, with its vitality, sense of mastery, and growth was over, and what was ahead was old age, characterized by vulnerability, withering, and the brink of nothingness (Levinson et al. 1978:x). Levinson felt that a problem was that there was no language to describe this period in the life cycle due to lack of any cultural definition and limited knowledge of how lives evolved within it (Levinson and Gooden 1985:2). His work made a significant contribution: although he started studying men following earlier theorists, he went on to study women with the goal of determining whether it would be possible to create a gender-free model of adult development while also creating a gender-specific conception of the development of women.

According to Levinson, the tasks of establishing adult development as a major field of study are describing the individual life course as it evolves; forming a conception of the life cycle and the place of adulthood within it; and determining how development proceeds in adulthood. Although Levinson identified stages of adult development, he saw a process of *individuation*, involving a person's relationship to himself and the external world, permeating all phases from birth to death (Levinson et al. 1978:195). With each phase the person develops stronger boundaries between the self and the world, as well as a stronger sense of who he is, what he wants, what the world is like, and what is expected of him. Greater individuation results in the person becoming more independent and self-generating, with the increased confidence and understanding needed to have intense attachments in the world and to feel part of it.

DEFINITIONS OF TERMS

Levinson believed that the terms *life cycle*, *life span*, and *life course* were often incorrectly used synonymously and offered the following definitions:

> *Life cycle* suggests that the life course has a particular course that follows a *basic sequence* from birth to death, with some cultural influences

and individual variations. An underlying order is the *temporal sequence* from birth to death. "Seasons" of the life cycle are relatively stable periods or stages that may be qualitatively different and have aspects in common with, or different from, those that precede or follow. Seasons are neither stationary nor static, as change goes on within and there is a need for transition from one to another. No season is more important than another. Metaphorically there is a connection between the seasons of the year and the seasons of the life cycle. Interest in the life cycle goes back to the "ages of man" referred to in the Talmud as well as in the works of Confucius and Solon.

Life span is simply the interval between birth and death.

Life course is the temporal "flow" of life, including events, relationships, achievements, and failures. It is a descriptive term, not a high-level abstraction, and refers to the *character* of a life from birth to death. *Course* implies stability and change, continuity and discontinuity, orderly progression, as well as stasis and chaotic fluctuation. (Levinson et al. 1978:6; Levinson and Gooden 1985:1)

Levinson also defined the term *era*, as:

a time of life with its own distinctive and unifying qualities that give it its "character." It is broader and more inclusive than a developmental stage and serves as a framework. The life cycle is made up of a sequence of eras. Each has its own biopsychosocial character and makes its own distinctive contribution to the whole. There are major changes in a person's life from one era to the next and lesser, but crucial, changes within eras. Eras overlap, and a cross-era transition terminates one and begins the next. Every era and developmental period begins and ends at a well-defined average age, plus or minus two years. (Levinson et al. 1978:18–19; Levinson and Gooden 1985:4)

ORIGINAL SAMPLE AND METHODOLOGY

Levinson was forty-six years old when he began his study, the goal of which was to create a developmental perspective on adulthood. His major emphasis was on men in the "midlife decade," from thirty-five to forty-five years of age. He had just passed through this period and felt he had crucially changed; he acknowledged that his choice of sample was made in part to understand his own adult development. Levinson limited his initial work to this cohort but would go on to cover all of adulthood as well as women. The first study was funded for four years by a National Institute of Mental Health grant and was multidisciplinary, involving psychiatrists, psychologists, and sociologists. His thinking was heavily influenced by that of Jung and Erikson.

Four subgroups of ten men were chosen from four occupational groups: hourly workers in industry, business executives, university biologists, and novelists. Levinson believed that work is the base for a person's life in society within a cultural, class, and social matrix and psychologically represents the fulfillment or negation of aspects of the self. The sample came from a variety of socioeconomic backgrounds, though it was tilted toward the higher end. Twelve percent were black and 88 percent were white. Fifty percent were Protestant and the remainder primarily Catholic or Jewish. Seventy percent had at least graduated from college, while 15 percent had not completed high school. Thirty-two men were in their first marriage, five were divorced and remarried, and three were divorced and not remarried. Eighty percent had children. Sources of information about the men came from wives, analysis of workplaces, and visits to their homes and offices in order to understand their external circumstances.

What Levinson called "biographical interviewing," combining aspects of a research interview, a clinical interview, and conversation between friends, was the core methodology. The interviews were generally held at weekly intervals and lasted one to two hours. Each man was interviewed for a total of ten to twenty hours over a two- to three-month span, and in most cases, again two years later. Parts of the Thematic Apperception Test (TAT) were used. The interviewing was geared to cover the entire life sequence up to the present, including information about family of origin, relationships, education, occupational choice, work history, leisure activities, interests, losses, perceived good and bad times, and turning points. A problem encountered early was that theories existed about childhood and adolescence that *might* explain what occurred in midlife, but there was a serious lack of useful theories concerning development from adolescence to age thirty-five. Levinson and his colleagues recognized that their work needed to go beyond the initial age range to theorizing about the whole period from the end of adolescence to the late forties. Thus the study focus expanded to include the late teens to late forties.

INDIVIDUAL LIFE STRUCTURES

In order to study "the character of a man's life and its evolution over a span of years," Levinson developed the concept of an *individual life structure*, the underlying pattern or design of a person's life at a given time (Levinson et al. 1978:42). Life structures evolve in a relatively orderly sequence during adulthood. Once they are determined, Levinson felt, it is possible to identify changes in personality, career, relationships, and other components of life over a standard sequence of developmental periods. Levinson emphasized the individuality of the life structure. He did not formulate his theory on stages of ego or any other specific aspect of development. Rather, he emphasized that everyone lives through developmental periods in unique ways. All encounter developmental tasks, but individual life conditions affect coping and mastery. The concept of life structures thus involves consideration of both the self and the environment. Adult development for Levinson meant *the evolution of the life structures*. Every transition involves terminating existing life structures and initiating new ones. Levinson looked at life structures from three dimensions:

1. the individual's *sociocultural world*, which involves class, religion, ethnicity, family, political system, and occupational structure; changes in any of these areas will modify the individual's life
2. what parts of the individual's *self* are conscious and what are unconscious; some formed prior to adulthood will continue to influence the individual into adulthood; the self is not a separate entity, but rather an element of the life structure that is drawn on or ignored in daily life
3. degree of *participation in the external world*, which involves the transactions between the self and the world represented by people, relationships, resources, and constraints (Levinson et al. 1978:420)

Levinson believed that life structures are influenced by the *choices* a person makes in all aspects of life. The primary components involve relationships with others in the external world. Choices are complex and related to both the self and the world, and the meaning and function of each choice must be considered within the individual life structure. Components that he believed most central are occupation, marriage-family, friendship and peer relationships, ethnicity, and religion. Levinson felt that at any given time, only one or two components occupy a central place in a structure, having greatest significance for the self and the evolving life course. The life structure forms a boundary between personality and social structures (Levinson and Gooden 1985:6).

The Life Cycle

Levinson believed that there are three closely interrelated tasks involved in the life cycle phase of adult development:

1. building and modifying the life structure
   a. in stable phases, the task is building a structure and enhancing life within it
   b. in a transitional period, the task is terminating the existing structure, exploring possibilities, and making new choices for a new structure
2. working on single components of the life structure
   a. forming and modifying a "dream"
   b. forming and modifying an occupation
   c. establishing love relationships leading to marriage and family
   d. forming mentoring relationships
   e. forming mutual friendships
3. becoming more individuated through reintegrating polarities

Levinson theorized that the life cycle is made up of the following overlapping periods:

1. early adult transition, ages seventeen to twenty-two
2. early adulthood, seventeen to forty-five
   a. entering the adult world (first adult life structure), twenty-two to twenty-eight
   b. age thirty transition (changing the first life structure), twenty-eight to thirty-three
   c. settling down (second adult life structure), thirty-three to forty
3. the midlife transition, forty to forty-five
4. middle adulthood, forty-five to sixty-five
   c. building a new life structure (first structure), forty-five to fifty
   d. age fifty transition, fifty to fifty-five
   e. culmination (second structure), fifty-five to sixty
   f. late adulthood transition, sixty to sixty-five

He recognized that these are the *average* ages for beginning and completing eras, with variation no more than five or six years. Eras are age-linked, and there are transitional periods, known as "zones of overlap," between them lasting three to six years and leading to choices that modify or change life structures. The tasks of the transitional periods are termination, individuation, and initiation. The period from ages seventeen to twenty-two is the *early life transition*, and the period from ages forty to forty-five is the *midlife transition*. Each *stable* period has specific tasks that differentiate it from other stable periods. The primary task is to build a life structure that involves making choices and pursuing goals and values (Levinson et al. 1978:49). The following paragraphs describe the eras of early and middle adulthood and the transitional periods.

EARLY ADULT TRANSITION (THE NOVICE PHASE). This is the period at which the era of childhood ends and adulthood begins. It links adolescence and early adulthood and involves five tasks:

1. moving out of the adolescent world while questioning it and one's place in it—a process involving separations, endings, and transformations
2. exploring possibilities in the adult world, testing living choices, and consolidating an initial adult identity
3. forming a dream with a place in the life structure
4. forming mentor relationships lasting on average two to three years
5. choosing an occupation and forming love relationships leading to marriage and family

EARLY ADULTHOOD. Levinson regarded this as the "most dramatic of all eras" (1978:21). Between twenty and forty, a man is at his peak of biological and intellectual functioning. However, this is a period of great contradiction and stress. As the young man struggles to define his place in society, he may be burdened by residues of childhood conflicts. He finds satisfaction, although accompanied by stress, through marriage, children, occupation, and lifestyle, contributing to himself and to society and going from "novice" adult to a more senior position. The early financial, social, and emotional burdens decrease as he approaches forty, but new ones, including care of elderly relatives, may replace them. In sum, the era is filled with internal energy, capability, and potential, and external pressure. Personal goals and societal expectations are interrelated and can be reinforcing or contradictory. Levinson further divided this period into three phases, each with its own tasks:

Entering the adult world extends from twenty-two to twenty-eight. Tasks are:

1. create a structure that will be a link between the "valued self" and adult society
2. make initial choices regarding occupation, relationships, marriage and family, values, and lifestyle
3. establish a balance between keeping options open, maximizing alternatives and avoiding commitments, and creating a stable life structure and becoming more responsible

Levinson, like Erikson, recognized that how a phase is negotiated will have lasting effects. With respect to task 3, if the desire to keep options open predominates, life may be transient and rootless; if the desire for a stable life predominates, the danger is premature commitment without sufficient exploration of alternatives.

The age thirty transition extends roughly from twenty-eight to thirty-three. It may produce uneasiness, an awareness that something is wrong or missing, and recognition that a change is needed. Tasks are working out the flaws and limitations of the previous phase and creating a more satisfying and serious structure for completing early adulthood; and by the end, making important new choices or reaffirming old ones. For some this is a smooth transition, but the majority of the men studied experienced a moderate or severe *developmental crisis*. The person may find the present structure "intolerable," yet face problems in establishing a new one. If the choices made in this phase are congruent with dreams, talents, and realistic possibilities, they will provide the basis for a relatively satisfactory life structure. If not, the person will suffer in the next period. Orientation is toward the future.

Settling down extends from thirty-three to forty and represents the culmination of early adulthood. The goal is to establish the central components of the structure such as work, relationships, family, leisure, and community activities while realizing earlier goals and aspirations. Initial tasks are:

1. establishing a *niche* in society by anchoring one's life, developing occupational competence, and becoming a valued member of society
2. "making it" through efforts to build a better life, to advance on a timetable
3. becoming a "full-fledged adult" in one's own world with a "personal enterprise" involving a direction to strive for with a goal of affirmation and advancement

Levinson believed that at the end of this phase, ages thirty-six to forty, there is a distinct period called *becoming one's own man,* when the person becomes a senior member of his group and can speak strongly and with authority. There are added burdens along with new rewards, and the man must give up more of the internal "little boy."

THE MIDDLE LIFE TRANSITION occurs from about age forty to forty-five. The concept of a midlife crisis during this transition became the most controversial part of Levinson's work; however, the term is frequently used in the vernacular. He believed that no single event marks the end of early adulthood, but rather there are three interweaving elements:

1. *changes in biological and psychological functioning*
    Although physical and mental functioning are somewhat diminished after forty, the man still leads a full and active life. The pressure of the drives is somewhat lessened, and he develops a greater capacity for intimacy, integrating the more "feminine" aspects of the self. He becomes more caring and compassionate. Many men undergo a midlife change in style of living and work. When positive, new roles have great personal and social value, but if negative, changes may be to save face with minimal contributions to self and society, a tragic waste. When the transition involves turmoil and disruption, it becomes a crisis. This may be an opportunity for personal development as the man faces his mortality, mourns his passing youth, and moves on to further personal and social fulfillment.

2. *the sequence of generations*
    With the passage of time, a young adult has the sense of moving from one generation to another as he undertakes the task of getting in touch with both the "child" and the "elder" in himself and his peers. Levinson referred to Erikson's seventh stage, generativity versus stagnation, as a concern of middle adulthood, coinciding with the start of the midlife transition (forty to forty-five). The man moves from being a father of young children in early adulthood to, at forty, assuming responsibility and leadership for new generations of younger adults. In order to become generative, a man must experience, endure, and fight against stagnation. Vulnerability is a source of wisdom, empathy, and compassion.

3. *evolving careers and enterprises*
    Each era reflects evolution in a man's goals, life plan, work, and personal

life. By age forty, he has had a chance to build a life and will examine his progress. For some this is satisfying; for others there is disparity between reality and dreams. For all there is a reevaluation, a consideration of limitations and planning for the next steps.

Some who have been successful may feel trapped and that success is meaningless. Some may see their lives as successful in some areas and lacking in others. Most experience a *culminating event* representing success or failure that indicates what they have accomplished and how far they can go. This event may trigger the midlife transition.

Most men find this a crisis period, a struggle within the self and with the external world. They must deal with questions involving the meaning, value, and direction of life. They question every aspect of life, and many feel they cannot go on as before. It may take years to modify the old life path or establish a new one. Choices must be made, priorities set, and some possibilities rejected. Specific tasks are reviewing and appraising one's life in early adulthood; modifying negative elements of existing structures and testing new choices prior to building a new life structure in middle adulthood; and dealing with polarities that create division.

For some, this is a stable, untroubled period. Levinson felt if this is to be a positive transition, the person must be working on questions about his life unconsciously, or he will pay a price in a later developmental crisis or have a life structure minimally connected to the self. Others consciously try to come to grips with changes, losses, and possibilities for a better life; for them, this phase is manageable and not a crisis. Levinson felt that for the majority, there is a "tumultuous" struggle internally and externally and thus a moderate or severe crisis. They question all aspects of their lives, are full of recriminations against the self and others, and feel the need to modify their life path or choose another route. Levinson believed that recognition of the need to make changes is healthy but also painful, as the person may meet opposition from family, colleagues, and employers. He also felt that during this transition the negative parts of the self seek expression and stimulate modification of existing structures.

As noted above, this phase was of particular personal interest for Levinson. He believed that the most important task is dealing with the polarities present for all, although some may be more problematic or more conspicuous than others. This involves confronting and reintegrating a polarity. Levinson identified four polarities:

1. young/old
   a. alternation between feeling young, old, and in between
   b. consideration of what will be his realistic legacy—the ultimate value of his life—in terms of family, work, and other contributions
   c. images of death and rebirth, mortality and immortality describe the existential issues
2. destruction/creation
   a. experience of his own mortality and the actual or impending death of others
   b. awareness of how others have been destructive to him
   c. recognition of hurting others
   d. strong desire to be creative
   e. eagerness to advance human welfare, especially contributing to coming generations
3. masculine/feminine—the *meaning* of gender
   a. coming to terms with coexisting parts of the self—the basic meanings of masculinity and femininity
   b. working out division of labor with partner that complements weakness in other
   c. modifying life structure so that the feminine will have a larger and freer part
   d. becoming a mentor to both men and women with less fear of sexual involvement
4. attachment/separation—connecting the self and the environment
   a. reducing involvement with the outside world and turning more inward
   b. becoming more critical of his social matrix
   c. integrating need for attachment with need for separateness by creating a better balance between needs of the self and needs of society
   d. greater concern for self-development and integrity

Levinson recognized that the polarities exist throughout the life cycle and are never fully resolved. However, they are of greatest concern in the midlife transition. If the earlier phases have not been successfully completed, the person may lack the inner and outer resources for a minimally adequate middle adulthood life structure and will feel constricted and lacking in inner excitement.

Middle Adulthood spans ages forty-five to sixty and culminates in the end of adulthood. Like early adulthood, it is made up of three phases:

1. *building a new life structure*

   As the man emerges from the midlife transition, he feels a need, between ages forty-five and fifty, for a new life structure based on his commitment to choices that may have involved minimal or dramatic changes in occupation and relationships. Deaths, divorce, moves to new locales, and illness may have also influenced choices. Levinson believed that the degree of satisfaction with the new life structure varies according to its suitability for the self and its workability in the world. If the man has had problems in earlier phases of adulthood, he has limited inner and outer resources for creating a new structure and will experience middle adulthood as constricting and a decline. Some will feel poorly connected to the self but better connected to the world, and thus lack inner excitement and meaning. Others will experience middle adulthood as satisfying and fulfilling. They are less concerned with earlier pressures, ambitions, and passions and are attached to others, yet also centered in the self.

   Although Levinson did not study men over the age of fifty, he proposed the following additional phases:

2. *age fifty transition*

   This phase lasts from fifty to fifty-five and is similar to the age thirty transition. Work is done on the tasks of midlife and the resulting structures can be modified. A crisis will occur if there were too few changes made to unsatisfying life structures during the midlife transition. Levinson believed that at least a moderate crisis is inevitable, either at midlife or at this stage.

3. *building a second middle adulthood structure*

   This phase lasts roughly from fifty-five to sixty and is similar to the settling down phase of early adulthood. It represents the end of middle adulthood. For those who can rejuvenate themselves and enrich their lives, it is a fulfilling time.

4. *late adult transition*

   This period, sixty to sixty-five, ends middle adulthood and begins late adulthood. It is a time of significant development and a major turning point. The tasks are to conclude the efforts of middle adulthood and prepare for the next phase of life.

Like Erikson, Levinson believed that each period affects subsequent ones. He was, however, more optimistic, feeling that each offers the opportunity for further development and the chance to create a more satisfying and suitable life.

FINDINGS

Levinson, like Erikson, saw development as a steady, continuous, but not hierarchical process, although accomplishment of the tasks usually is uneven. He recognized that the process of choice and of exploration is highly influenced by family, class, culture, and social institutions as well as individual motives, values, talents, competencies, anxieties, and life goals. While Erikson proposed a series of stages in ego development, Levinson proposed a model of building, modifying, and rebuilding life structures. Erikson focused on changes within the person, while Levinson went further, looking at the boundary between the self and the world.

As his study progressed, Levinson conceptualized development as a sequence of eras, unfolding in an orderly, fixed progression, that all of the subjects *must* pass through from the end of adolescence to the middle forties. Each era involves biological, psychological, and social factors and is tied to past and future eras, though intrinsically independent. Between eras are cross-era periods that last four or five years. Developmental impairments and past defeats may stop the progression; then the man is "stuck" and in a decline. Tasks reasonably well accomplished in earlier eras provide the foundation for new tasks.

Although Levinson studied men in the contemporary United States, he believed that eras and transitional periods exist in all societies, representing the life cycle.

THE SEASONS OF A WOMAN'S LIFE

In 1979, following the publication of *The Seasons of a Man's Life*, Levinson began his study of women. He had been approached by the Financial Women's Association of New York, which was interested in sponsoring a study of career development in the context of individual life development. They agreed that the study would compare businesswomen with other populations. In 1981 the Teachers Insurance and Annuity Association (TIAA) became a co-sponsor. Judy Levinson, his wife, became his main collaborator in the study and was very involved in data analysis and in writing their book, *The Seasons of a Woman's Life*. The focus of Levinson's work on women was not to develop a theoretical model, but rather to compare the adult development of different groups of women.

From his studies of both men and women, Levinson developed a central, universal concept that he termed *gender splitting*, the rigid division between male and female. It operates on many levels—culture, social institutions, everyday social life, and the individual psyche—creating antithetical divisions and inequalities. The four basic forms of gender splitting are:

1. the domestic sphere and the public sphere as social domains for women and for men, respectively
2. the "traditional marriage enterprise," defined as the split between female homemaker and male provider
3. the distinction between "women's work" and "men's work"
4. the splitting of feminine and masculine in the individual psyche (Levinson and Levinson 1996:38)

Levinson found that over the years of his study, there had been a reduction in gender splitting and modification in the traditional marriage, with women no longer counting on a permanent marriage and a life devoted to domesticity and men somewhat more involved in family life. He attributed this to an increase in longevity, resulting in the need for a larger labor force and increased pressure for women to be employed outside of the home; fewer children, with women having their last child by their early thirties and then being available to work outside the home; the increase in divorce, which has made it essential for many women to be in the labor force; and the entry of women into elite occupations once thought of as the domain of men.

GOALS OF THE STUDY

Levinson made an in-depth exploration of women's lives from the late teens to the mid-forties. He sought answers to four key questions:

1. Is there a human life cycle? Is it fundamentally different for men and women?
2. Is there a process of adult development analogous to the process of child development?
3. What is the significance of gender in women's lives?

4. How are the conceptions of development and gender reflected in the lives of individual women?

Sample and Methodology

Prior to selecting the sample, Levinson obtained questionnaire data from several hundred women; from these, he selected forty-five women, fifteen in each of three groups: traditional homemakers in family-centered lives, although most had worked out of the home at some point; women employed in major corporate-financial organizations, half unmarried and more than half childless; and women on the faculties of colleges and universities, trying to combine family and career.

The homemaker sample was made up of thirteen white and two African American women. Six were Catholic, six Protestant, two Jewish, and one Catholic-Protestant. One had completed eleventh grade, four had completed high school, five had vocational training, and five had completed college. Three came from middle-class, college-educated families; six came from stable working- or lower-class families; and six had grown up in poverty. The latter subgroup had an average of four children, while the other subgroups had three or less, and also had a higher divorce rate. Only a few of the homemaker sample reported a positive family life in childhood and adolescence.

The sample employed in corporate-financial organizations (part of the career sample) was made up of fourteen white women and one African American woman. Two were Catholic, ten were Protestants, and three were Jewish. All of the women in the faculty sample were white. Most of the women in both the corporate and the academic sample grew up in relatively well-educated, middle- or upper middle-class homes. Their mothers lived as homemakers in a traditional marriage enterprise, but were regarded by the women as unsatisfied. Eighty percent of the career women had gone to elite colleges away from home, institutions that traditionally had prepared men for careers and women for marriage to a man with a career.

The method of study was intensive biographical interviewing (Levinson and Levinson 1996:4): major events, relationships, goals, and dreams were elicited within the context of external realities and subjective meaning. Participants and interviewers met weekly for eight to ten sessions, each lasting an hour and a half to two hours, over a two- to three-month period. Participants told their "life stories" from childhood to the present. The researchers then did biographical reconstruction, condensing and ordering the two to three hundred pages of transcribed material from each interview while maintaining qualitative themes and meanings.

THE LIFE CYCLE

For his work on women Levinson used the same transitions and life structures that he had used in his study of men.

EARLY ADULT TRANSITION. For the homemakers studied, this period began a year before or after graduation from high school. Each woman experienced both continuity and change in components of the life structure including family of origin, home base, education or vocation, love/marriage/family, other relationships, and the community. Relationships with parents were a major factor as the woman faced becoming an adult. Most of the sample saw themselves as leading lives very similar to their mothers', but somewhat happier. Remaining close to parents, especially mothers, limited possibilities for exploration and individuation but promised stability and continuity, while moving away led to greater independence and involvement in occupations and to starting a family later. Only four of this group had not married by the end of this transition period, due to failed relationships rather than a decision to postpone marriage. Most of the sample suffered a moderate to severe crisis in this period, feeling overwhelmed with no way to form a "minimally good enough life" as an adult. At the end, three patterns were observed:

1. Seven women had a provisional structure as a homemaker in a traditional marriage enterprise with one to four children. All had major problems stemming from early marriage and motherhood.
2. Three women marked the end of the period by marrying and having a first child (ages twenty-two or twenty-three).
3. Four were single and one divorced, all without children. These women viewed occupations as major but not a central component and saw family as central but an unfulfilled component.

For the career samples, the beginning of the transitional period was related to the move to college; some had begun the transition while in high school as they planned to leave the parental home. Others with strong dependent ties to parents really did not begin the period until they were at least partway through their freshman year. All experienced some difficulty in disengaging from family, high school, peer group, and community and had a sense of being in limbo between college and parental home.

Gender meaning was also an issue for these career women. While the traditional homemaker component was predominant in their thinking, the antitraditional figure influenced plans and choices. Many felt that they knew what they did not want but were unsure how to define goals and relationships for the "new woman." Choosing a major was the first time these women were confronted with an important decision that would be tied to future occupations. The choice was strongly influenced by the masculine/feminine split. Choosing a "male field" would put the women in direct competition with men and in danger of being seen as unfeminine, of being rejected as a woman and thus hurt in a competitive struggle. They would feel resentment if not taken seriously, yet feared being seen as too smart or too accomplished. Most selected a major in the social sciences, arts, or humanities that was neutral ground between the traditional male and female extremes, while 25 percent chose "masculine" fields such as economics or business administration (Levinson and Levinson 1996:231–34). As each woman began to crystallize a dream, she found faculty mentoring very important.

For the career women the end of the early adult transition at age twenty-two was usually concurrent with graduation from college. The women felt external pressure to begin an independent life and internal pressure to "grow up" and decide how to live their lives even if the path was not clear. These women were pioneers, the first generation attempting to move beyond the traditional marriage enterprise, so they had to find their own paths.

Graduate school followed for most of those wanting to enter academia, somewhat extending this period of transition. Mentoring was very important. By the end of this phase, eleven of the academic women were married, but only two had children. They married men who assumed that the woman would be responsible for the home and would work out of the home, but did not think of her as having a "career." Ten of these marriages ended in divorce.

MBA programs were only beginning to admit women when the business-women sample graduated from college. Most of these women did not want to be "tokens" and chose not to go to graduate or professional school, although some did so later. The majority took entry-level jobs in business, mostly in New York, the center of the corporate-financial world. Starting at the bottom, most did not know what a career was or how to get it, and they had few immediate satisfactions. A "career path" was to develop later. Many remained in the transitional phase for up to two years following graduation.

EARLY ADULTHOOD. Entry life structure is the period from ages twenty-two to twenty-eight. Levinson divided this period into three segments (1996:97–99):

1. time of building (twenty-two to twenty-five)—tasks are forming key relationships, strengthening commitment, and getting an early life structure in place
2. age twenty-five shift—with awareness that life has some problems, there is a decision to make changes, often highly specific, re: marriage, children, school/vocation, resulting in a firmer decision about the kind of life she wants and what component(s) are central, peripheral, or excluded in order to make life more integrated and satisfying. The early life structure is crystallized.
3. second phase (twenty-six to twenty-eight)—some women have a relatively satisfying life structure at twenty-six; others need these years to further implement their choice(s)

For all in the homemaker subgroup, marriage/family was the central component. Although some held outside jobs at times, they did not invest in an occupation. For a few, family of origin or religion was also an important component.

Career women entered early adulthood six months to two years after graduation from college. As this period began, fourteen of the thirty women were married, and two had children. Those who did not have children were more concerned with the work component than with the love/marriage/family component. While the single women wanted to marry, they wanted to wait and also did not want a "too-traditional" man. Their dream was of being independent, competent women who would have a reasonable balance between work and love/marriage/family. The women felt pulled between their inner goals and external social pressures (Levinson and Levinson 1996:264–65). By the end of early adulthood, the second phase, the career women had gained a sense of competence and independence as they went through a period of personal development and growing career commitment. All but seven (all businesswomen) had been married and fourteen had children, as they had begun to question whether too great a career focus might destroy the possibility of having a family. The phase ended with many wondering how they would combine career with marriage/family.

THE AGE THIRTY TRANSITION leads to a *culminating life structure* in which women realize to a greater or lesser extent the aspirations of early adulthood.

Tasks of this period are: terminating the early life structure; exploring new possibilities in the self and the world; becoming more individuated; and moving toward formation of the central components of a new life structure (Levinson and Levinson 1996:117–18). In addition, it is important to resolve problems from earlier phases of development that have created anxieties and conflicts that continue into adulthood.

Of the homemakers, three became more involved with their occupations, although they continued to view family as the central component. They saw themselves more as "women" than as "girls." The antitraditional figure was seeking parity with the internal traditional homemaker. Four, while continuing to be primarily homemakers, held either part-time or volunteer jobs but made little attempt to make this a central component, although they were aware of their aversion to domesticity. Eight of the sample felt that their marriages had failed and three of these sought a legal divorce. Five more began a "psychological divorce," greater involvement in outside work with the goal of financial independence. The main reason for leaving the marriage was disappointment in the husband, whom they had expected to be the fulcrum of their adult lives (Levinson and Levinson 1996:117–41).

All thirty of the career women had a life plan for early adulthood after college. By the age thirty transition, they were diverse in their occupational status and in their prospects for the future. Eight of the businesswomen and thirteen of those in academia were married; seven had never married and two were divorced. Five businesswomen and nine faculty women had children at the start of the transition; all together, eighteen were mothers by the end. Three of the women did not want children and the other nine, though disappointed to be childless, came to terms with the fact that motherhood would be an unfulfilled component. Marriage and motherhood, together with a stronger involvement with work and career goals, resulted in a need to establish a reasonably satisfactory balance between these two central components.

Ninety percent of the career women had a moderate to severe crisis in life structure development during the age thirty transition. The focus of the crisis was usually on a specific problem: career, relationship, marital conflict, decisions about becoming a parent, or problems in combining home and job responsibilities. The crisis revolved around the feeling that something had gone wrong in life, either at work or at home. Half of the sample sought psychotherapy during this transitional period.

For all the women, homemakers or career, the age thirty transition was a critical developmental period. All experienced much personal growth as they made changes, but for many there was considerable turmoil and questioning. For many of the career women, the earlier antitraditional dream evolved into a dual antitraditional dream of having a successful career within a nontraditional marriage enterprise. Most who were mothers made a firm decision at the end of this phase that career and family would be co-central components (Levinson and Levinson 1996:296–333).

CULMINATING LIFE STRUCTURE is the period analogous to what Levinson called "settling down" in *The Seasons of a Man's Life.* Although the demarcation is not clear, Levinson saw this period as divided between two phases. In phase 1 (thirty-three to thirty-five or thirty-six), the task is to establish a new life structure, which may involve internal and/or external changes. This may be a period of stress or even of crisis, or may proceed relatively smoothly. In phase 2 (thirty-five or thirty-six to forty), the task is to form an "enterprise" in which to realize major goals of early adulthood, built within the central component of the life structure but including other components as well.

Analogous to becoming one's own man, Levinson believed that between thirty-five and forty, women deal with *becoming one's own woman.* The tasks involves moving from being perceived by the world and the self as a little girl to being perceived as a woman, both externally and internally; and affirming qualities associated with femininity while developing "masculine" qualities such as independence and competence, without jeopardizing identity as a woman (Levinson and Levinson 1996:143–48).

Levinson felt that how a woman deals with these tasks is influenced by personal characteristics as well as external circumstances within the context of the life structure. As the woman fulfills the tasks, she gains a greater sense of meaning and fulfillment and a sounder basis on which to enter middle adulthood. She then affirms what is most important to her. If she does not successfully complete this period, the woman has a sense of failure about her whole life; this may result in a developmental crisis. At about age forty, Levinson believed there is a *culminating event of early adulthood* representing the outcome of that era. The most significant events and messages are those that bear most directly on the central components of the culminating life structure, and the woman, if she is satisfied, will look toward other possibilities in her future.

For the homemaker sample, Levinson identified three patterns. For those who had become more involved in outside work during the age thirty transition, the marital relationship became increasingly egalitarian, with the woman still having primary responsibility for home and children but needing more help from the husband. Outside work resulted primarily in a greater sense of independence and identity, and occupation took on greater meaning. For the four who were in traditional marriages but were considerably disappointed in their domestic life, involvement increased in paid or volunteer work, although this was not a primary component. They continued to see their identity and public image as homemaker but spent considerably less time on home and family chores. Relationships with husbands and sons became less gratifying; however, the women evaluated their lives as satisfactory and comfortable. Five were legally or psychologically divorced. For them this was a difficult period; with little education or occupational training and with a traditional background, they needed to find a way to enter the public world, to find an occupation, and to develop and expand an identity beyond homemaker. At forty, all five were primarily homemakers with jobs that could provide for them, but were not a central or particularly satisfying component (Levinson and Levinson 1996:142–71).

For the career women, this phase had a difficult, unstable, and uncertain beginning. Career and marriage/family decisions were still in flux. The primary task of becoming one's own woman is to maintain the life structure, and changing it or pursuing goals outside of its boundaries is difficult. The second task thus becomes enhancing one's life within the structure. Many of the women at the end of this period found their lives too hard; they worked at demanding jobs and also had almost total responsibility for child and home care, although they envisioned an egalitarian marriage enterprise. Half of the faculty women and some of the businesswomen were able to transform their marriage or to find an egalitarian structure in a remarriage. In the work world, the career women found they must be competent but also "feminine"; reasonably assertive yet not too demanding or ambitious; caring but not maternal; and businesslike but not cold.

Six of the career women were very successful; seven were making significant progress, but with less bright prospects; and seventeen had made only limited career progress. Twelve of the career women were in their first marriage, five in their second, nine divorced, and four never married. Twenty had children. For the seventeen who were married, their culminating life structure had both occupation and family as central components. They had the dual antitraditional dreams of the successful career woman and the neotraditional marriage enterprise, but found it impossible to give both components equal priority. Occupation often came first, especially if they were high achievers. By the end of the culminating life structure, although it had been difficult, the career women had achieved great personal growth and development. They were about to enter a time of inner questioning about choices that would continue in the midlife transition (Levinson and Levinson 1996:334–68).

MIDLIFE TRANSITION. This period represents a shift from early to middle adulthood. During this time, the homemaker sample whose lives were based on the traditional marriage enterprise began to question it and their lives as homemakers. Significant changes were occurring in relationships, occupation, and sense of self, as caregiving no longer was the woman's chief function in life. Levinson believed that the process of change continues through middle adulthood. The women surveyed had two prominent themes: they wanted to be carefree, which included being less obliged to provide limitless care, to be perpetually responsible for others, to be self-sacrificing, and to ignore their own needs; and they wanted the right to be themselves, to make their own choices, and to pursue their own interests. The women saw that these goals would be difficult to attain and would involve establishing a place in the public world. A major cost of the traditional life thus far had been a significant failure to develop the self. Many found it painful not to know what they wanted or how to attain it while also being unhappy with their life (Levinson and Levinson 1996:172–98).

Levinson had a sample of thirteen career women when considering the midlife transition, due to the timing of the interviews. These women felt that their husbands "permitted" or encouraged their careers, but with the expectation that the husbands would only help while the wives had primary responsibility for the children and home. The women saw themselves "on a treadmill," hoping that as their children got older, life would be more stable and satisfying. Like the homemakers, the career women felt that their life choices had not given them the satisfaction they had hoped for and that they must find a new basis for living in middle adulthood. The central question for all was "What do I want for myself?" Almost all went through a moderate or severe developmental crisis. With respect to career, the question was not simply one of changing jobs but rather of changing their relationship to their occupation. The women studied went through a major reappraisal of their careers and made significant changes in all components of their life structures. Marriages also came under scrutiny. The career women looked at the nature of their marriages and considered what they would like to modify or eliminate. Most sought to develop an egalitarian relationship or marriage in which the partners would engage with each other while also being separate and independent. The women questioned whether they had been sufficiently maternal and whether they had used work to escape some of the demands of home and children, but in reappraising relationships with their children, they concluded that they had done the best they could, given their own needs. The career women had more differentiated relationships to their children than the homemakers and were less "resentful" as they left home. In this transitional phase, the women looked for more reciprocity in the mother-child relationship and considered what new kind of connection might evolve.

Levinson felt that for both homemakers and career women the midlife transition, with its shift in era and life structure, was wrenching. The major difference was in priorities. The homemakers had, in early adulthood, made family the central component within the traditional marriage enterprise; in midlife, they saw this as a partial or massive failure and wanted a different kind of marriage, family, and life structure. The career women had pursued the antitraditional dream and added a second one, wanting career success and a neotraditional marriage enterprise. While they wanted balance, in fact they gave more time to work, although career, family, and marriage were all central components. Recognition of sexism in the work world made many of the career women rethink their occupations and look for avenues to greater creativity, satisfaction, and social contribution rather than striving to prove themselves in a highly competitive area (Levinson and Levinson 1996:369–409).

Levinson believed that all the women in the study went through the same sequence of periods in life structure development, although in individual ways. They all dealt with the same basic issues of gender: maintaining or modifying the gender splitting in society and self; maintaining or modifying the traditional marriage enterprise; forming and dealing with the conflict between the internal homemaker figure and the internal antitraditional figure.

The women with careers, corporate or academic, had much in common that differentiated them from the homemakers. Both homemakers and career women made a strong effort to overcome the splitting of masculine and feminine and to develop alternatives to the traditional marriage enterprise. They created an important internal antitraditional figure and strove to establish a balance between family and career. The businesswomen provided a greater contrast to the homemakers than did the academics. It must be noted that the career women studied belonged to the first generation of American women in which a sizable minority opted for a nontraditional path. This made the struggle to find themselves even harder.

Levinson believed that the most significant finding was the *diversity of individual lives*, remarkable variations within the sample and across the study along with common themes (Levinson and Levinson 1996:201–202). With respect to his four previously described questions, Levinson felt that men and women follow the same sequences in a common life cycle at about the same ages, although in some cases women complete them at a slightly older age. He felt that there is an identifiable process of adult development, as has been shown for child development. From the histories given by the women, clearly gender and gender splitting are important factors in adult development.

Levinson made an important contribution in studying both men and women within his conception of the life cycle as overlapping sequences of eras. He presented data supporting his belief that men and women go through the same sequence of periods in adult life structure development and at the same ages; however, he thought the process is more difficult for women than for men. Although his samples were small, without much diversity, he concluded that what he observed could be applied to a much broader population. He noted that the role of women in society is in transition, which further complicates the available alternatives and the decisions they can make. In the twenty-first century, women are still struggling with priorities involving relationships/marriage/family and career, and many do not yet have truly egalitarian marriages.

GEORGE E. VAILLANT

In 1937, the Grant Study of Adult Development, which became part of a larger study known as The Study of Adult Development, was conceived of by a philanthropist, William Grant, and the Director of the Harvard Health Service, Arlie Bock, who believed that medical research was too concerned with disease and ought to take a look at people who are well and continue to do well. A cohort of 268 men was chosen and followed for 35 years. When the study began, all of the men were sophomores in good academic standing at Harvard University, chosen in part by their capacity for self-reliance. Most of the men went on to have distinguished war records; 90 went on to have stable families; and all had occupational success. When the data were reviewed, however, it was clear that none of the men had had "clear sailing." The focus of the study became how men adapt to life.

In 1967, George E. Vaillant, a psychiatrist influenced by Erikson and Neugarten, joined the staff of the study, which had been funded by the Grant

Foundation and the National Institute of Mental Health. In 1977, he published a book, *Adaptation to Life*, which reviewed the findings of the Grant Study. A major criticism was that it dealt with a very elite sample of men. Vaillant was later to look at data from the other two projects included in The Study of Adult Development, the Core City Study and the Terman Study. This section will focus primarily on the Grant Study.

Vaillant is concerned with how *mental health* is defined in contrast to *pathology*. In his work, he chose to define health in terms of objective clinical evidence, with the men considered to be "well" according to the number of areas in which they functioned well, rather than performance in a special area. What a man did was viewed as more important than how he said he felt (Vaillant 1998:6–7). Emphasizing adaptation to life, Vaillant gave much attention to the ego mechanisms of defense as observed in actual behavior, affects, and ideas. He felt that health involves subjectivity and value judgments. Vaillant identified five theoretical concepts that influenced his review of the study data (Vaillant 1998:29–30):

1. Not isolated traumas of childhood but rather the *quality* of sustained relationships with important people shape one's future.
2. Lives change and are filled with discontinuities: what may appear to be mental illness, at another time may be adaptive.
3. Adaptive mechanisms can be differentiated from one another and arranged along a continuum correlated with health and maturity. Personality is dynamic, and no one life follows an entirely predictable trajectory; one defensive style can evolve into another.
4. Human development continues throughout adult life; thus, truth about lives is relative and needs to be studied longitudinally. Retrospective explanations are full of distortions.
5. Positive mental health exists and can be operationally discussed in terms that are at least somewhat free from moral and cultural biases.

Sample

The Grant Study sample was made up of 268 men attending Harvard between 1939 and 1945. Although members of all the classes were considered, reasons for rejecting some were concerns about whether they would meet requirements for graduation, appeared to have physical or emotional problems, or lacked motivation to participate. Sixty-six men were chosen from the 1939 to 1941 classes and 202 from the 1942 to 1945 classes. The study was never considered to be representative, but followed men who had the likelihood of leading successful lives. They were expected to equal or exceed their natural intellectual abilities. Those who felt less need to excel were probably underrepresented. Capacity for intimacy was valued less than capacity for success (Vaillant 1998:30–32).

Vaillant's work dealt with a subsample of 95 men who had graduated between 1942 and 1944, for whom the data had been highly standardized. Socioeconomically, most of the men came from an economically privileged group, although half of their parents had not attended college. Half of the sample had attended some private school and half were on scholarship at Harvard. Their families were relatively stable: only 14 percent had a parent who had died and 7 percent had divorced parents. Forty-one percent were the oldest child, 11 percent were the only child, and 21 percent were the youngest child. Eighty percent were Protestant, 10 percent were Catholic, and 10 percent were Jewish. The participants were all white.

Vaillant defended using this very selective sample who had not experienced prejudice and childhood deprivation and were primed for occupational success. He believed that they had grown up under optimal conditions and that their relative privilege made them most suitable for a study of human adaptation.

METHOD

Participation in the Grant Study was a commitment: it took a minimum of twenty hours that included eight interviews with a study psychiatrist. The psychiatric interviews were not designed to be therapeutic, but to help the researcher get to know the subject by focusing on families, career plans, and value systems. A "social investigator" took a social history from the subjects and also traveled to their homes to meet and interview their families in order to get an extended family history. Development histories were obtained from the mothers.

Each of the participants was given a very thorough physical examination, which included taking an extensive medical history and a battery of physical tests. Physical responses to stress were noted, and each participant had to run on a treadmill for five minutes or until exhausted. The men were also seen by a psychologist, who gave them an intelligence test, a vocabulary test, a version of the Rorschach test, and a block assembly test. For some, SAT and MAT scores were also made available.

From graduation until 1955, study subjects were sent questionnaires annually. After 1955, the questionnaires were sent out every two years. Questions focused on family, employment, leisure activities, and political views. In 1950–1952, the study subjects were interviewed in their homes by a social anthropologist. The interviews focused on lifestyles and also on obtaining a developmental history of the subjects' children. In some instances, the Thematic Apperception Test (TAT) was administered.

In 1967, Vaillant interviewed the surviving study subjects in his subsample. He had reviewed all the records prior to administering a semistructured interview with open-ended questions covering work, family, physical health, and psychological health. Vaillant next developed the thirty-two-item Adult Adjustment Scale to be used by raters who reviewed the entire twenty-five-year period with respect to career, social health, psychological health, and physical health, rating the respondents to determine "best" or "worst" outcomes. Defensive patterns were also examined. From analyzing these data, Vaillant, who was concerned with what underlies successful adjustment (good mental health), concluded that the "inner man" made up of defenses, subjective happiness, and physical health, must conform to the "outer man" represented by his capacity to work, to love, and to play (Vaillant 1998:281–82).

Vaillant felt that these data supported Erikson's formulation of adult development, with intimacy followed by career consolidation followed by generativity (Vaillant and McArthur 1972:419). However, for many, the identity crisis was not resolved in adolescence. Furthermore, in reviewing the men's adjustment, it became apparent that those who negotiated adolescence best were not always the men with best midlife adjustment. Personality traits recognized in adolescence and associated with good midlife adjustment were "well-integrated" and "practical organizing," while those with a poorer prognosis were "asocial," "incompletely integrated," and "cultural interests" (Vaillant and McArthur 1972:419–21).

FINDINGS

In analyzing the data, Vaillant sought to evaluate three areas: the relationship of childhood environment to adaptation; the importance of social relationships to mental health; and the relationship of one's position in the adult life cycle to how one adapts to life.

Vaillant felt that the longitudinal nature of the study allowed him to draw general conclusions about these areas. He acknowledged that the sample was not representative, but believed it would yield important information.

CHILDHOOD ENVIRONMENT. Vaillant reached the following conclusions:

1. Those who were unloved in childhood were less likely to play competitive games, to play games with friends, or to take full and enjoyable vacations.
2. Those who were unloved as adults tended to be distrustful, pessimistic, passive, dependent, and self-doubting.
3. Overall, childhood environment predicts mental illness in adult life: 50 percent of the men with the best childhoods were scored as having the best adult adjustments, while 50 percent of the unloved had been diagnosed as mentally ill at some time.
4. Those who were unloved had significantly poorer physical health.
5. Bleak childhoods were correlated with friendlessness in midlife.
6. Men who in college perceived their fathers as dominant had the best marriages, but those who perceived their mothers as dominating almost invariably were divorced.

SOCIAL RELATIONSHIPS. Vaillant looked at the data assuming that mental health and the capacity to love are linked. He concluded that the capacity to love falls on a continuum and that at times everyone feels lonely while at other times feeling loved and loving. The data on childhood environments showed that childhood affects the person's ability to love in the future. Vaillant identified six tasks for loving):

1. getting married without later getting divorced
2. achieving at least ten years of marriage that neither partner saw as painful
3. fathering or adopting children
4. believing one had one or more close friends
5. appearing to others as having one or more close friends
6. enjoying regular recreation with nonfamily members (1989:60, 1998:305)

Vaillant found twenty-seven men whom he described as "friendly" who had carried out all six tasks, and thirteen whom he called "lonely" who had carried out no more than two tasks. The remainder of the sample fell in between.

When Vaillant looked at these data together with data on defense mechanisms, he found a powerful association between a man's capacity to love and the maturational level of his defenses. Mature defenses such as altruism, suppression, humor, anticipation, and sublimation were strongly correlated with good marriages, overall social adjustment, closeness to children, and raters' assessment of capacity for human relationships. In contrast to the "friendly," the "lonely" used primarily immature defenses such as projection and fantasy (Vaillant 1998:309).

Adjustment of the men's offspring was also studied through each man's biennial descriptions of his children in terms of academic, social, and emotional adjustment. Two thirds of the children whose fathers had had "best outcomes" were emotionally and socially successful and half went to "top-flight" colleges, while only one third of the children whose fathers had "worst outcomes" were emotionally and socially successful and only one sixth went to top colleges. Vaillant believed that the least successful men used projection (an immature defense), imposing their own sense of failure and paranoia onto their children.

Vaillant found that there is no single longitudinal variable that predicts mental health as clearly as a man's capacity to remain happily married. How a man described his marriage predicted his career success, the relative maturity of his defenses, and his own perception of his happiness (Vaillant 1998:320). Further, Vaillant found that men who throughout life have found satisfaction in their marital sexual adjustment are also more likely to have made a good overall adjustment, to enjoy their jobs, and to be successful in their careers. Those whose sexual adjustment was poor were likely to be depressed, passive, and lacking job success, and to abuse alcohol and sedatives (Vaillant 1998:326). However, some who found their sexual relations less than ideal after fifty still had good marriages.

Vaillant concluded that whether a man can love friends, his wife, his parents, and his children is a better predictor of mental health and generativity than later sexual functioning.

ADAPTATION TO LIFE. Vaillant's major contribution to the understanding of personality culled from data from the Grant Study was his identification of a hierarchy of eighteen unconscious adaptive ego mechanisms, defenses. His work built upon that of Sigmund and Anna Freud; however, while S. Freud saw repression as underlying all defense mechanisms, Vaillant viewed it as just one of many defenses. Vaillant believes that the process of adaptation to life results in continued growth and that healthy styles of coping contribute to continuing development of the individual. With time, an individual's defenses should evolve into more mature styles, for immature defenses are maladaptive and mature defenses are generally adaptive. He groups the defenses in terms of their relative theoretical maturity and pathological import, while stressing that although the *phenomenon* of defensive behavior exists, the reification is metaphorical (Vaillant 1998:80). The four levels are:

1. psychotic mechanisms (common in psychosis, dreams, childhood)
   a. psychotic denial
   b. distortion
   c. delusional projection
2. immature mechanisms (common in severe depression, personality disorders, and adolescence)
   a. fantasy (schizoid withdrawal, form of denial)
   b. projection
   c. hypochondriasis
   d. passive-aggressive behavior (masochism, turning against the self)
   e. acting out (compulsive delinquency, perversion)
3. neurotic mechanisms (common to all)
   a. intellectualization (isolation, obsessive behavior, undoing, rationalization)
   b. repression
   c. reaction formation
   d. displacement (conversion, phobias)
   e. dissociation (neurotic denial)
4. mature mechanisms (healthy adults)
   a. sublimation
   b. altruism
   c. suppression
   d. anticipation
   e. humor

Vaillant, like the Freuds, believes that it is not the defenses that are pathological but rather the conflicts to which they respond. Thus, the task of a successful defense is to resolve conflict. He feels that in evaluating defenses, both the context and the degree of flexibility must be considered. Rigidity implies a greater relationship to the past than to the present. The Grant Study, Vaillant believes, illustrates a positive association between using mature adaptive mechanisms and success in most aspects of life.

   A major interest of Vaillant's is the individual's ability to master conflict and harness instinctual strivings. To do this successfully, he agrees with A. Freud, adaptive styles can and must mature. Data from the Grant Study show that in the middle years of adult development there is increased career commitment, greater responsibility for others, and more frequent use of mature defenses. In adolescence, the study men were twice as likely to use immature defenses such as projection, hypochondriasis, and masochism than mature defenses. As young adults they were twice as likely to use mature as immature defenses. In middle life they were four times as likely to use mature as immature defenses, with increased use of dissociation, repression, sublimation, and altruism (Vaillant 1998:330). Acting out and fantasy as defenses decline with maturity, and with this comes an increase in sublimation as a defense. Referring to the Eriksonian model of the life cycle, Vaillant believes that there needs to be a maturation shift in adaptive styles for men to become generative rather than perpetual boys.

Vaillant struggled with where defenses "come from." He concluded that the maturing patterns of adaptation are influenced by biological (physical maturation) and psychosocial factors. In organizing defenses along a developmental hierarchy, he implied moral as well as adaptive implications to human growth and development. Influenced by the work of Piaget and Kohlberg, Vaillant believes that the maturation of defenses, like morality, is linked to cognitive maturity and the evolution of impulse control. However, he believes that ego development is far more reversible than did Kohlberg (Vaillant 1998:340–42).

THE CORE CITY STUDY AND THE TERMAN WOMEN STUDY

Both of these studies were part of The Study of Adult Development. It is important to note that none of the three studies could be viewed as representative of the general population. The data gathered is important, however, as the three samples were very different and were from cohorts up to twenty years apart in age. Vaillant believed that the similarities between groups and the differences within the groups would allow the findings to be generalized to other American Caucasian samples. That all three studies were conducted prospectively from adolescence allowed him to use his experimental methodology to analyze the data (Vaillant 1993:128).

THE CORE CITY STUDY. Data came from a study conducted by Eleanor and Sheldon Glueck at the Harvard Law School between 1940 and 1944 in order to contrast young juvenile delinquents with their socioeconomically matched nondeliquent peers. Their results were published in the book *Unraveling Juvenile Delinquency.* The 456 "nondeliquent" men who were interviewed over a 35-year period came originally from Boston inner-city schools. The boys, all white, had an average IQ of 95; 25 percent had had to repeat two or more grades at school; more than half lived in slum neighborhoods; two thirds of the families were on welfare at some time and known to many agencies; and the fathers had a median educational level of eight years. In spite of low average intelligence, 10 percent of the men graduated from college, and as the men matured they showed marked social mobility, with 51 percent at age 47 belonging to the middle class (Vaillant 1993:122–24).

THE TERMAN WOMEN STUDY. These data came from 90 women who were a subsample of a study of gifted California public school children conducted by Lewis Terman at Stanford University between 1920 and 1922. The subjects' mean IQ was 151 and they were popular with their peers, showing humor, perseverance, and leadership. Sixty-seven percent of the women graduated from college and 24 percent attended graduate school; however, their job opportunities were limited. The sample came from middle-class families where the father's median educational level was 12 years and 15 percent of the mothers had gone to college.

The ninety women in the subsample were followed for fifty years by Terman and his successors. In 1987, twenty-nine of these subjects had died and twenty-one were either not interested in being interviewed or were too ill. Vaillant was able to interview the remaining forty women, whose average age was seventy-eight (Vaillant 1993:124–27). Data from the women not interviewed were extensive enough to be included in the data analysis.

CONCLUSIONS

From his involvement in the Grant Study, Vaillant concluded that there are "patterns and rhythms to the life cycle" (Vaillant 1998:199) that differ from one individual to another. Factors that influence individual development include opportunities or obstacles influenced by class, age, sex, ethnicity, and social change; efforts the individual makes on his own behalf; support and guidance necessary to cope; and personal resources.

Vaillant believes that the study confirms Erikson's life patterns as well as Levinson's midlife transition. Vaillant identified a stage between Erikson's intimacy and generativity that he called *career consolidation versus self-absorption* (Vaillant 1993:149–50; 1998:202, 215–19), in which the task is to establish a specific career identification characterized by commitment, compensation, contentment, and competence. Between twenty and thirty, the young adult, having established independence from his family and some adolescent friendships, acquires a mate and establishes friendships that will deepen. The individual must satisfactorily accomplish intimacy in order to go on to the next stage. He must achieve intimacy, which requires trust, maturity, and a capacity to love, in order to be able to accept a mentor, necessary for career consolidation.

From twenty-five to thirty-five, the men in the Grant Study worked hard, consolidated their careers, and devoted themselves to wives and children. With a focus on tasks and rules, and anxiety about being promoted and accepted, Vaillant felt they lacked self-reflection and resembled latency-age children. Problems may have occurred between thirty-five and forty, as both the men and their wives had conflicts as they became aware of the sacrifices that might be involved in moving up the career ladder.

When career consolidation is achieved, Vaillant feels there is an important inner change involving the acquisition, assimilation, and ultimate casting aside of nonparental role models or mentors. Successful study subjects assumed the role of mentors to younger men, while those who were less successful either did not have mentors after adolescence or only found them in their early forties. A successful resolution of this phase would be acceptance of the level of achievement and becoming less materialistic.

Vaillant sees the beginning of the fifth decade as a *second adolescence* (Vaillant 1998:219–26), a period of reassessing and reordering one's experiences in adolescence and young adulthood. There is also less concern with occupational success and the external world, and more concern with inner life. With the deaths of family members and friends, there is greater awareness of one's vulnerability. Also at forty there is an increase in extramarital affairs. The decade may be a period of dissatisfaction with career and/or marriage. The men may feel uncertain as they did in adolescence; however, this transitional period, if successful, should result in new solutions to old instinctual or interpersonal needs. Vaillant believes that a midlife crisis is seen more in clinical than in community samples and feels, like Neugarten, that development within the life cycle involves growth and change but as a rule is not a crisis. The study showed that although there is agonizing self-appraisal and instinctual reawakening in the forties that may result in depression and turmoil, it does not necessarily mean pathology, but rather a prelude to entering a new life stage (Vaillant and McArthur 1972:427).

After fifty, Vaillant found that for the most part, the study subjects had attained a sense of tranquility, but with an undercurrent of mild regret. They saw their fifties as much "quieter" than their forties. A new generation was taking over, and some felt a sense of alienation and a lessening of personal control. Others had a sense of having crystallized into a final identity. Men in their fifties struggled with reality as they viewed the promises and dreams of their thirties with nostalgia. They were more concerned with the possibility of death of a spouse. Vaillant found, as had Neugarten, that their own physical deterioration, especially decline in sexual powers, was of more concern than their death.

Vaillant feels that his analysis of "best and worst outcomes" supports Erikson's tasks of the life cycle. The thirty "worst outcome" men were three times as likely to have childhoods that did not support the development of basic trust. Raters found that in adolescence the "worst outcome" participants were less integrated and their identities as adults were less secure. In young adulthood they were less likely to master intimacy and in middle adulthood they were much less likely to assume responsibility for other adults, to give to their children, to give of themselves to the world, to meet the tasks of generativity.

Personality, Vaillant concluded, evolves from biological and inner (ego) development. Adaptation to life involves continuous growth and implies success. He disputed many prevalent definitions of mental illness, feeling that neuroses, depression, and personality disorders are outward manifestations of inner struggles to adapt to life. Vaillant identified eighteen basic adaptive mechanisms, defenses, which he believes can predict adult growth and define adult mental health. Poor adaptation leads to depression and anxiety, which lower the ability to tolerate stress, while successful suppression increases tolerance.

Finally, Vaillant felt that the Grant Study revealed that the life cycle is more than an invariant sequence of stages with single predictable outcomes. Adults evolve over time, often with startling changes and surprises. A study of the life cycle cannot predict where we should go; rather, it determines where we are (Vaillant 1998:373). Effective adaptation to stress determines success.

In comparing the three studies that made up The Study of Adult Development, Vaillant concluded that the three most important tasks of adult ego development, which must be mastered in sequence in order for the ego to achieve increasingly complex integration, are intimacy, career consolidation, and generativity. He felt that the biggest challenge he faced was to illustrate that the developmental tasks were as applicable to the Terman women as to the men in the Grant and Core studies. He believes that the occupational roles that result in a sense of competence differ for men and women. The Terman women lived at a time when they may have been excluded from careers of their choice and had to settle for less satisfying occupations. Some saw their careers as homemakers allowing them to experience career consolidation; this made it very difficult to compare the studies. The Terman women, due to the time in which they lived, did not achieve psychosocial maturity as early as did the men, but they were found to adapt well to old age.

In conclusion, Vaillant sees his model as glossing over developmental transitions and feels that the concept of crisis is overemphasized. When there is a crisis, Vaillant believes it is a result of nondevelopmental factors such as psychopathology, role changes that are poorly mediated by the culture, or life transitions that occur out of the normal developmental sequence (Vaillant 1993:163–64). His model, based on the data from the three studies, is of development as a *psychobiological process* that must conform to biology, not social mores or chronological age. Vaillant believes that the model is the same for men and for women and independent of class, educational opportunity, and intellectual capacity. All the tasks must be mastered in sequence. The stereotypical view that the search for intimacy is a female quest, the search for career consolidation is a male quest, and the search for generativity is a quest only for the educated and privileged is invalid (Vaillant 1993:175); both sexes have the same goals. Concerned with empirical research, Vaillant feels that any acceptable model must achieve a reasonable degree of rater reliability and predictive validity (Vaillant 1993:166–71).

NANCY CHODOROW

Nancy Chodorow is a sociologist whose first book, *The Reproduction of Mothering*, was written during the height of the women's movement. It resulted from discussions among a group of women who met to explore "what it meant that women parented women" (Chodorow 1978:vii). Her writing is heavily influenced by psychoanalytic thinking.

Chodorow believes that mothering is one of the main universal and enduring elements of the sexual division of labor, as women, whether they work or not, have primary responsibility for child care. It is taken for granted that this is a woman's role. This role affects family structure, ideology about women, division of labor, and relations between the sexes; it is reproduced through the generations. While feminism has made women look more critically at their personal lives, control of their sexuality and bodies, family relations, and discrimination, it has had less effect on their thinking about reproduction. Chodorow regards the reproduction of mothering as central to social organization. Mothers produce daughters who have a desire and capacity to be mothers, while women as mothers and men as "nonmothers" produce sons with repressed capacity, and need, to nurture. A mother is not only a woman who has given birth but also the person who will socialize and nurture the child, the primary parent or caretaker. Chodorow is concerned that though many theories regarded women's role as mother as central, few have inquired how women have been placed in this particular social and economic position. While biology and role expectations play a part, Chodorow argues that they do not result in *adequate* mothering unless the woman has, on a conscious or unconscious level, the *capacity* to be meternal and the *sense of self* as mother.

Chodorow relies on psychoanalytic theory to analyze family structure and social reproduction. The sexual division of labor produces definitions of gender differences and also reproduces them. Men distance themselves from the family and move into the public sphere, while women have greater interrelational abilities and needs; together, men and women form interpersonal relationships in which women occupy the domestic sphere of reproduction and nurturing the next generation. Women's capacity for mothering, which is gratifying to them, is strongly internalized and acquired developmentally through the family structure and process.

Chodorow believes that the reproduction of mothering has its beginnings in the earliest mother-infant relationship, because the basic psychological stance is founded, people emerge with a memory of a unique intimacy that they wish to re-create, and the experience of the early relationship with the mother provides a foundation for expectations of women as mothers (Chodorow 1978:57). Thus, the most important aspect of early infant development is that it occurs in relation to another person—in Chodorow's view, the mother. The mother is the child's primary caretaker, socializer, and inner object, while the father is a secondary object for both girls and boys (Chodorow 1978:92). The preoedipal experiences of girls and boys differ, however. Girls' mother-love and preoccupation with preoedipal issues are prolonged in a way that is not the same for boys. Because mothers and daughters are the same sex, mothers tend not to see the daughters as separate from themselves, as they do their sons. Some women who have undergone a prolonged preoedipal phase may have problems with primary identification, separateness or differentiation, and ego boundaries (Chodorow 1978:108–10).

The intensity, length, and ambivalence that characterize the mother-daughter preoedipal phase make the daughter in the oedipal stage turn to the father to help her get away from her dependency and merging with the mother. The girl then splits the internal mother image into "good" and "bad," projecting the good traits onto the father and keeping the bad with the mother. This is a much harder period for girls than for boys; they retain much of their dependence, attachment, and symbiosis with the mother, the caregiving parent, and so do not have the exclusivity in the relationship with their fathers that boys have with their mothers. With resolution of the Oedipus complex, girls do not need to repress oedipal attachments to the same degree as boys and are able to transfer their feelings to less emotional and conflicted relationships within the family. Like Freud, Chodorow believes that features of gender *personality* emerge in the oedipal period, but that establishment of an unambiguous and unquestioned gender *identity* occurs in the preoedipal period (Chodorow 1978:158).

In adolescence, girls have a more difficult time than boys, for they have remained more tied to the family and must disentangle themselves before being able to move into extrafamilial relationships and commitments. Breaking from the mother becomes the major task of this period (Chodorow 1978:135), which can be very painful. Mothers and daughter feel ambivalent about each other. Girls, as they move from preoccupation with the mother-daughter relationship to concern, again, with the father and later with other males, may go through a phase of bisexuality, for they are indecisive about the relative importance of females and males; most resolve this dilemma by entering heterosexual relationships (Chodorow 1978:138). In spite of conflict, attachment to the mother, the primary caregiver, remains.

Chodorow believes that the different relational capacities and sense of self experienced by men and women can be traced to growing up in families in which women mother. Both sexes are prepared for adult gender roles in a sexually unequal society where women are primarily within the *sphere of reproduction* (Chodorow 1978:173). A structural split exists between the private, domestic world of women and the public, nonfamilial world of men. Even if women work outside of the home, they remain in charge of home and children, and if men do household chores, these are often determined by women. Men's chief responsibility is to provide for the family, and the husband's occupation determine its class position and status. Chodorow cites studies indicating that since women were economically dependent on men, men tended to love romantically while women loved "sensibly and rationally" (Chodorow 1978:197). Women often seek out other women to meet their relational needs, much as they did with their mothers in childhood, and while lesbian relationships best mirror the mother-daughter relationship, societal taboos and heterosexual preferences make this an unlikely option. The exclusive symbiotic mother-child relationship is then, for many, re-created when they become mothers. They their identification with a mother who parents and train for a woman's role. Women want and need intense primary relationships and find these with their children, since men's fear of intimacy often makes them unavailable. Mothering involves double identification, both as mother and as child. Women have the capacity for primary identification with their child through regression to primary love and empathy associated with the mother (Chodorow 1978:204). The early experience of being cared for by a woman leads to expectations of mothers' lack of interest in or concern with anything other than the infant. Daughters grow up identifying with these expectations and believing that mothers will continue to care for children even after infancy. Women become mothers because they have been mothered by women.

Chodorow in critiquing her own work is very careful to note that her thinking is firmly rooted in psychoanalytic theory. It does not consider children raised without a mother, children with single mothers, families where women have become part of the work world, or families where the father may be the more nurturing parent. She suggests that all of these areas would lend themselves to further research.

Expanding on her first book, Chodorow in 1989 published *Feminism and Psychoanalytic Theory*, the premise of which is that men and women are "constructed" differently and that the experiences of both come from deep within, in our pasts, within our unconscious, and in the emotional relationships in our current life. Women's sense of self is linked to relationships and concerned with boundaries, separation, and connection. Men's sense of self is more distanced, has firmer boundaries, and is based on denial of self-other connections (Chodorow 1989:2). In this later work, Chodorow, while still very influenced by psychoanalytic thinking, is also concerned with object relations theory.

Chodorow believes that sex-role ideology and socialization is damaging to both men and women. Women are ascribed an identity that is devalued in society and results in a sense of inferiority. Men's identity depends on their proving themselves by "doing" in order to feel secure. As long as women must live through their children and men do not contribute to socialization and as role models, sons will be brought up with identities that involve devaluing femininity internally and externally and daughters will have to accept a devalued position and a role that perpetuates the system by producing sons who will later devalue women (Chodorow 1989:44). Since society gives priority to doing, Chodorow concludes that women's mothering role is what contributes most to their universal secondary status.

Heterosexual object choice and the meaning of adult heterosexual experience differs for men and women, and this, Chodorow believes, is because women mother. As girls emerge from the oedipal crisis, they are oriented to their father and men as primarily erotic and secondarily emotional objects. Girls never really give up the tie to the mother, although they use their attachment to the father as a way to achieve greater separation and independence. The intensity of the boy's oedipal relationship with the mother and the threat it represents leads the son to repress affect and deny relational needs and connection to the mother in resolving this crisis. The ultimate result is development of a personality seeking the affect-free public world with contractual and universally constructed relationships (Chodorow 1989:73). However, as adults parented by women, both sexes seek to return to an emotional and physical union with the mother. Men wish to replicate the early mother-child exclusivity but with some fear and ambivalence. Women do not seek exclusivity but wish to have primary relationships with women as well as men in order to meet the emotional needs that they anticipate men will not fulfill.

Chodorow believes that the differences between men and women establish each gender as a unique and absolute category. Gender differences are socially and psychologically created and situated, and are not absolute, abstract, or irreducible (Chodorow 1989:100). They exist within relationships, emerge developmentally, and have their roots in the child's relationship to the mother. Because females mother, the sense of maleness in men differs from and is more conflictual and problematic than the sense of femaleness in women. Men, early in life, have a primary oneness with the mother, resulting in an underlying sense of femaleness that continues, usually unnoticed, and undermines maleness. Learning to be masculine means learning to be not-feminine, or not-womanly (Chodorow 1989:109). Because of this conflicted core gender identity, it becomes more important for men than for women to maintain rigid boundaries between the sexes and emphasize differences. Men deny the feminine identification within themselves as well as feelings that they associate with women: dependency, relational needs, and emotions. They come to believe that individualism, separateness, and distance from others are necessary for autonomy and fulfillment.

For women, establishing a core identity is not as problematic as it is for men. That the experience of oneness with the mother is female is not a problem, for women do not have as great a psychological investment in difference as men do. However, later conflicts may arise from identification with a gender that is devalued, from questions of relative power and social and cultural value (Chodorow 1989:111) in a male-dominated society. Women's lives and self-definition have been oriented to men, but Chodorow postulates that as women become more oriented toward women, the differences between genders will become less salient.

Chodorow's central thesis is that sex-linked personality differences are the unintentional consequences of women's responsibility for mothering. The mother responds differently to a son than to a daughter. The boy, who may have limited contact with the father, achieves his "maleness" by emotionally rejecting the mother and the world of women, and denying feelings of relatedness and dependence. The girl identifies with the mother and develops a personality based on relationships and connections with others. Chodorow proposes that greater equality would exist if boys were more involved with men who took on a major role in child care, while girls were raised by women who in addition to mothering responsibilities had additional valued roles. What would result would be a strong sense of self with a valuable and secure gender identity not encumbered by ego boundary confusion, low self-esteem, and either overwhelming relatedness to others (female) or compulsive denial of connection to or dependency on others (men) (Chodorow 1974:66).

JEAN BAKER MILLER

In 1976, Jean Baker Miller, a psychoanalyst and current director of the Stone Center, published a book, *Toward a New Psychology of Women*, that provided a framework for understanding the psychology of women through understanding "the forces acting on and in women" (Miller 1976:ix). She saw this as an attempt to understand women through looking at their life experience rather than as they have been perceived by those who do not have this experience (men). Thus, she made the focus a study of women, unlike the majority of theorists, who had focused on men and then tried to extrapolate from that work an explanation of women. Miller acknowledged that she did not deal with class and racial differences that strongly affect women's lives, but chose to focus on forces that affect all women because of their gender.

Miller believes that there are many differences between people, with the differences between adult and child being most significant. However, the most basic difference is between men and women, and it leads to inequality in status and power resulting in *dominant* (superior) and *subordinate* (lesser) roles. The subordinate is not viewed as a "person of as much intrinsic worth as the superior" (Miller 1976:5), and the dominant tends to define a less val-

ued role for her. Subordinates are encouraged to develop psychological characteristics such as submissiveness, passivity, dependency, indecisiveness, and
dependency, which are pleasing to dominants. When subordinates show
signs of intelligence, assertiveness, and initiative, they are likely to be viewed
as abnormal. In terms of men and women, despite overwhelming evidence to
the contrary, Miller recognized that the persistent view of women is as passive, docile, submissive, and secondary to men. Dominants believe that what
is good for them is also good for the subordinates: men "know" that women
need and want men to organize their lives. Women (subordinates) become
very attuned to the possible reactions of men (dominants) and are forced to
act and react in disguised and indirect ways. The result can be a lack of self-
knowledge as the subordinate focuses on knowing the dominant better than
the self, which can be very destructive. When women grow and move toward
freer action and expression, they question the "accepted" inequality, and conflict results. The danger for women who try to enrich their lives is that they
may be viewed as attempting to diminish or imitate men. Women are not encouraged to develop as far as they can and are taught that through self-development they will forfeit the possibility of close relationships. A woman is encouraged to seek fulfillment of her needs within the family, through primary
interaction with the children delegated to her. Her role is to serve the needs of
others: first men, and later children. Problems arise because society forces
men to center around themselves and women to center around "the other."
Both suffer, for both sexes need themselves and each other. If men allow
themselves to care for others, they will be thinking and acting in a way that
seems "unmanly" (Miller 1976:69–70). Clearly the structuring of the relationship to others differs greatly for men and women. Miller believes that growth
can only proceed through affiliation, a fact known to women but not to men.

Miller felt that psychoanalysis had moved in the direction of emphasizing
basic feelings of vulnerability, weakness, helplessness, dependency, and neediness, which were kept from conscious awareness in the past because they
were so identified with women and unacknowledged and unexplored by, and
denied to, men by men (Miller 1976:22). Men see emotional attachments and
intense involvement with other people of both sexes as a threat that might result in weakness and passion, feelings they dread and think contrary to their
masculine status. Miller viewed women's ability to tolerate these feelings as a
strength; it makes them more in touch with reality as they learn to work pro-
ductively with weakness to find a way out of it, rather than defending or
denying it (Miller 1976:32).

In her work with patients, Miller found that women are very concerned with giving. They worry if they do not see themselves as women or if they consider not giving. In contrast, men do not see giving as important in their struggle for identity. Their concern is with doing, and they see giving as a detraction. Miller believed that women must learn to take as well as give, and that the women's movement helped bring this into consciousness. Men need to learn that giving is not weakness, but can enhance their personal development.

When Miller wrote *Toward a New Psychology of Women*, the women's movement was well launched. She listed as its main concerns (1976:24–25):

1. *physical frankness*—being in touch with one's own body and not allowing external controls
2. *sexual frankness*—knowledge about women's sexuality in women's terms
3. *emotional frankness*—open expression of feelings not encouraged by men, such as vulnerability and weakness, as well as expression of a sense of power
4. *human development*—for all people, not just children
5. *service functions*—redistribution of responsibility for providing services in basic and psychological ways
6. *objectification*—women no longer will accept being treated as "things" in every aspect of life
7. *humanizing society*—seeing and expressing emotional and personal qualities inherent in all experience
8. *private and public equality*—replacing dominance-oriented, competitive styles with equal, mutual, and cooperative living
9. *personal creativity*—the right to participate in creating one's own self

To achieve personal integrity, Miller stated, women must openly demand these changes. They have a problem admitting their strengths as well as their resources. They need to view strengths in terms of their own life experiences and recognize that they do not need the qualities they have attributed to men. Another task would be to examine and express their own emotions for greater self-knowledge. Women have traditionally been encouraged to concentrate on the emotions and reactions of others.

Miller recognized that changes in women's perceptions of themselves necessitate changes in men's perceptions of themselves—"the very essence of all life is growth, which means change" (Miller 1976:54). She felt that women needto allow themselves to enlarge their emotional experiences and to discover their potential for cooperativeness and creativity (Miller 1976:46). She cautioned that women's psychological strengths are not perceived, for the most part, by the dominant group (men), whose constricted views deny vast aspects of life in a way that is ultimately narrow and self-destructive. As women question the dominant perception of their psychology and focus on their own development and definition, major changes will be needed in how both men and women define themselves and in society. If men become angry or unhappy when confronted and challenged, women must guard against the familiar pattern of blaming themselves.

Miller believed that the roles assigned to women result in their being devalued and treated as if they do not exist except to care for others and have little effect on the direction of society. "Reality" as defined by society implies that women do not "matter" as much as men (Miller 1976:75). As women attempt to use themselves for themselves instead of for others, there will be a transformation of what are viewed as women's *valued* qualities. Women's tendency toward affiliation can be a strength, for only by joining with others in cooperative action will they be able to advance their cause. Women also need to move from subordination to greater authenticity. This will involve experiencing thoughts and feelings that they may have previously felt to be unacceptable, including focusing on their own needs and desires even if they displease others (men). Miller concluded that as women begin to change their situation, there will come a new understanding of women no longer accepting a subservient role. Self-determined goals for women was in 1976 a new phenomenon that Miller saw as leading to a new quality of life. She emphasized that men and women are different and need to be defined, explored, and described in different terms. A male perspective and a male-biased vocabulary do not suffice.

Miller and her colleagues at the Stone Center, from 1977, have conducted an ongoing study of women's development, which they refer to as "a work in progress." They have concluded that models of women's development "inspired" by the male culture have seen women as deficient, too emotional, too dependent, and lacking in clear boundaries. Male health and maturity has been defined as increasing capacity for separation, autonomy, mastery, independence, and self-sufficiency. Miller et al. have termed their work a "relational approach to psychological understanding" whose concepts are women's relational sense of self, the relational path of development, and the importance of empathy or responsiveness in relationships (Jordan et al. 1991:v–vi). The organizing factor in women's lives is *relational growth*.

Miller believes that all growth occurs within emotional connections, not apart from them, and attending to and responding to others, i.e., caretaking, is the basis of emotional growth. Relating to others enhances rather than threatens one's sense of self and self-esteem. While men's goal has traditionally been to develop an independent identity, the developing woman wishes to be a "being in relationships" (Miller 1991:21), to participate in increasingly complex relationships, which is difficult in our culture. Miller believes that it is not because of relationships that women are suppressed or oppressed, but rather because of the nature of the relationships. It is a mistake to encourage and extol independence and separation when what women want and need is to be in relationships that involve engaging with others through understanding and contributing to them.

Miller believes that we live in an "androcentric" society, organized in terms of men's experiences as they have defined them. This society is primarily patriarchal, with men holding leadership, power, and authority. They have been viewed as dominant and women as submissive. While subordination often results in feelings of anger, women have been socialized to believe that they should not, or should not need to, be angry unless in response to a threat to someone else. Anger is perceived as a threat to identity and, if shown, can disrupt a relationship: the person responsible for care cannot also experience anger. Not expressing anger, however, can be destructive, resulting in feelings of weakness and lack of self-esteem and thus increasing a woman's sense of unworthiness and inferiority. This dilemma frequently results in anger not being directly conveyed but showing in symptoms such as depression, lack of direction, and confusion. The only legitimate anger is that experienced by men, who from an early age are encouraged to be aggressive.

Miller defines *power* as the capacity to produce a change (Miller 1991:198). She has concluded that in our culture the myth has been maintained that women do not, and should not, have power, for they do not need it. They are afraid to admit a desire or a need for it. If they do have or use power, it is in the service of others. Women are socialized not to act on their own motivation and self-determination, for this may be viewed as selfish and destructive, leading to abandonment. As the women's movement led to questioning of the status quo, women developed greater acceptance of their need and desire for power and sought out creative ways to negotiate with others personally and professionally. They need to recognize and appreciate that their sense of self is organized around making and maintaining affiliations and relationships, recognizing the need for connections.

With the late Irene Stiver, a psychologist, Miller studied how women form relationships. Their premise is that connections, the experience of mutual engagement and empathy, are the initial and continuing sources of psychological growth. In contrast, disconnections, what one feels when cut off from or overpowered in a relationship, restrict people and block growth, resulting in depression, isolation, and anxiety. Connections, not separations, lead to health.

Looking at differences between men and women, Miller and Stiver believe that men, trained to value action, "take action" in order to override feelings of doubt, confusion, and uncertainty. Women, in turn, are encouraged to provide support and empathy for men's actions in subtle ways. Women do not receive the same kind of support from men in return. Thus, since there is not mutual empathy, there is not mutual empowerment, both of which are necessary for psychological growth. This is a problem for our entire society: it is not based on mutuality and the dominant group is not likely to create a mutually empowering atmosphere, for then it could no longer remain dominant.

In conclusion, Miller made a major contribution in documenting the real experience of women as it differs from what it was said to be. She emphasized that it is not the same as men's experience and cannot be assumed to operate on the same motivations or the same organization of personality. The work of Miller and her colleagues has resulted in recognition of potential for women's development that thus far has not flourished or been recognized or valued. Miller concluded that not only women but society as a whole will benefit from these emerging concepts As she, with Stiver, wrote in 1997, a full-fledged theory of women's psychological development does not yet exist—it is "a work in progress."

CAROL GILLIGAN

Carol Gilligan and Jean Baker Miller each acknowledge the influence of the other on their writings. Both wrote seminal books on women's development in the 1970s. Gilligan would go on to do much research with adolescents, covered in the previous chapter.

In a "letter to readers" in the 1993 edition of her book, *In a Different Voice*, first published in 1983, Gilligan states that in 1973, when the Supreme Court legalized abortion with the *Roe v. Wade* decision, "the underpinnings of relationships between women and men and children were . . . exposed" (Gilligan 1993:ix). Given the right to speak for themselves and to have the final say about ending a pregnancy, many women became aware of an "internalized voice" that had interfered with their ability to speak. It had told them that bringing their voice into a relationship would be selfish, and besides, they did not know what they wanted to do or should do. To speak might upset others and lead to lack of understanding, confusion, retaliation, or abandonment. By remaining silent, women had perpetuated a male-dominated society with a disconnection from women. Gilligan points out that men were leaving women out, but women, by not speaking, were leaving themselves out. Men go through psychological separation based on the male respect for autonomy, selfhood, and freedom, while women go through dissociation that necessitates an inner division or psychic split (Gilligan 1993:xiii). The problem is that men do not recognize their disconnection from women and women fail to recognize their dissociation from themselves. Gilligan sees *Roe v. Wade* as linking voice and choice, initiating a process of psychological and political growth for both sexes.

Gilligan equates voice with "the core of the self," which is powerful, connecting a person's inner and outer world, and is influenced by language, culture, and diversity. She calls voice "a new key for understanding the psychological, social and cultural order—a litmus test of relationships and a measure of psychological health" (Gilligan 1993:xvi). Relationships involve connection, a capacity for empathy, and an ability to listen.

Gilligan's purpose in writing *In a Different Voice* was not to generalize about either sex, but rather to point out the distinction between two modes of thought, as well as a problem with interpretation. She is concerned with the interaction of experience and thought, for she believes that how people talk about their lives is significant and that the language used as well as the connection made shapes their world. She is also concerned with the differences between men's and women's moral development. Men, and society, place the greatest value on personal autonomy and individual achievement; this causes women to make the central issue in their moral development reconciliation of these values with their own, based on responsible, caring relationships.

Gilligan conducted three studies involving interviews focused on conceptions of self and morality and experiences of conflict and choice. These studies expanded on the usual design for research on moral judgment, which focused on subjects' possible resolution of presented oral problems by asking them to define moral problems as well as what experiences they saw as moral conflicts in their lives.

The College Student Study was made up of a sample of 25 students interviewed as sophomores, as seniors, and 5 years after graduation. It explored identity and moral development by relating view of self and thoughts about morality to moral conflict and life choices. The sample was selected from students in a course on moral and political choice. In their senior year, 16 female students who had dropped the course were added to the sample. The Abortion Decision Study was concerned with the relation between experience and thought and the role of conflict in moral development. The sample included 29 pregnant women, ages 15 to 33, from diverse backgrounds, interviewed in the first trimester when considering abortion. Twenty-one agreed to be interviewed again at the end of a year. The Rights and Responsibilities Study involved 8 males and 8 females interviewed once at each of 9 points in the life cycle from ages 6 to 60 (a total of 144 participants). Data were collected on conceptions of self and morality, experiences of moral conflict and choice, and judgments of hypothetical moral dilemmas. The aim of this research was to provide a clearer representation of women's development, especially with respect to identity formation and moral development.

THE COLLEGE STUDENT STUDY (GILLIGAN 1993:64–71). In responses to the questions, a major theme was concern about hurting others and the belief that with a sense of morality, conflicts can be resolved so that no one is hurt. Morality was defined as helping and meeting responsibilities to others while not sacrificing oneself. However, this presented a dilemma for some of the women, who saw themselves as vulnerable and afraid to judge others due to a lack of power. Their reluctance stemmed from uncertainty about their right to make moral statements or a fear of what the statements might elicit. Feeling excluded from full participation in society, the women thought they would be subject to judgments made and enforced by men, on whom they depended for protection and support. Since moral decision involves exercising choice and assuming responsibility for it, the women perceived themselves as having no choice and thus as excused from responsibility. Clearly, there are two different constructions of the moral domain, one associated with masculinity and social power and the other with femininity and privacy in the domestic sphere.

A variety of methods of birth control and legal abortion made choice more central to women's lives. This right to choose, however, placed women in conflict with their traditional view of femininity, which included the moral equation of goodness with self-sacrifice. Ideal adult characteristics for men have been defined as independent judgment and action, while for women the ideals are care and concern for others. Thus a further dilemma is reconciling femininity with adulthood: resolving the conflict between compassion and autonomy and between virtue and power. The task for the wo-man's voice is to resolve the dilemma in order to reclaim the self and solve the problem so that no one is hurt.

THE ABORTION DECISION STUDY (GILLIGAN 1993:71–98). The choice of whether or not to have an abortion raises the question of judgment, which has been considered problematic for women. The decision affects the woman and others, and evokes the moral issue of "hurting." The study focused on the relationship of judgment and action and sought to determine how women think about dilemmas in their lives.

Findings showed that what shapes women's moral judgment and defini-tion of the moral domain differs from what studies have found affects these traits in men. Women saw the moral problem as a problem of care and re-sponsibility in relationships, an *ethic of care*, while men focused on responsi-bility with a formal logic of "fairness" that informs justice. The women had a "moral language" in which inflicting hurt was viewed negatively as selfish and immoral. The study revealed three steps in the development of the ethic of care, with two transitional steps:

Step 1—focus on caring for the self in order to ensure her survival, followed by transitional phase in which step 1 is viewed as selfish, followed by reconsideration of the inequality of self and other and an effort to re-consider relationships and sort out confusion between self-sacrifice and care

Step 2—the well-being of others becomes important; "goodness" is equated with self-sacrifice; conflict between taking responsibility and pressure from others, followed by transition phase of greater objectivity about situ-ation; concern for the well-being of self and others

Step 3—focus on the dynamics of relationships with the tension between selfishness and responsibility lessened through a new understanding of the interconnection and equality between self and other; consequences of actions are recognized and responsibility for decisions is accepted

As the women progressively gained knowledge of human relationships, in-cluding greater differentiation of self and other and a growing understanding of the dynamics of social interaction, they developed the ethic of care. This evolved around the central fact that self and other are interdependent and that care enhances both the self and the other. Abortion focuses on caring for the self, alone.

At the time of the one-year follow-up, eight of the women felt their lives had improved, nine felt they had remained the same, and four felt their lives had worsened. This subsample had viewed the decision about abortion as a crisis and an "encounter with defeat" (Gilligan 1993:108). At the time of the abortion, the women had reiterated a common theme of abandonment by others and then by themselves. Morality for women centers on care; in the absence of care from others, these women felt unable to care for a child or for themselves. Results showed that a crisis has the potential to break a cycle of repetition and can result in a return to a previously missed opportunity for growth. The women's thinking changed with the realization that the self and the other are interdependent and that life is sustained by care in relationships (Gilligan 1993:127).

THE RIGHTS AND RESPONSIBILITIES STUDY (GILLIGAN 1993:98–105). Study results repeatedly showed that the moral imperative for women is an injunction to care and to discern and alleviate the troubles of the world. For men, the moral imperative is an injunction to respect the rights of others and to protect the rights of life and self-fulfillment from interference. Moral development results from discovery of the complementarity of these disparate views.

WOMEN'S RIGHTS

As women have claimed their rights, they have assumed responsibility for themselves, thus addressing issues of responsibility in social relationships. The ethic of self-sacrifice is in direct conflict with the concept of women's rights. Women's development has been further complicated as the moral issue of goodness has been viewed as opposing the adult questions of responsibility and choice (Gilligan 1993:132). Thus the moral ideal has moved from interdependence to the fulfillment of an obligation by giving to others without taking anything for oneself. Changes in perceptions of women's rights changed women's moral judgment, allowing them to consider it moral to care not only for others but for themselves. Care, defined as not hurting others, became an ideal of responsibility in social relationships, with women valuing their understanding of relationships as a source of moral strength.

Gilligan believes that the view of women's development extrapolated from the study of men saw women as moving out of adolescence confusing identity with intimacy, defining themselves through relationships, and subordinating achievement to caring, thus rendering themselves vulnerable to issues of

separation and competitive success that occur in midlife. Her studies point
out the difficulty of using men to define women and suggest that while it is
true that women's sense of integrity is entwined with the ethic of care, the
major transitions in women's lives must involve changes in their understanding and activities of care (Gilligan 1993:171). She concludes that women reach
midlife with a different psychological history and a different perspective on
human relationships than men and thus face a different social reality with
different possibilities for love and work. Women's development has shown
them the limits of autonomy and control, and they are aware of reaching a
sense of maturity through interdependence and caretaking. Given the evidence of differences in men's and women's adulthood, Gilligan saw the need
for more research to delineate in "women's own terms" their experiences and
the effects of these differences on marital, familial, and work relationships.
Men and women "may speak different languages that they assume are the
same," leading to misunderstandings impeding communication and potential for cooperation and care in relationships. Greater acceptance of equality
has led to replacing the hierarchical order of relationships and supported the
need for women to care not only for others but also for themselves. Men,
concerned with independence and autonomy, use their voices to show their
independence and their mastery and control. Women, concerned with relationships and social welfare, use their voices to enhance cooperation and intimacy. Understanding both will lead to a more generative view of human
development (Gilligan 1993:173–74).

Gilligan and Miller, working quite differently, arrived at the same insights
into the psychology of women. Both concluded that when women are seen
and heard, it will represent a challenge to the patriarchal order, which did not
give women a voice. Women bringing their experience to the fore and maintaining connection can be viewed as revolutionary.

MARY BELENKY

Mary Belenky and her colleagues, who are psychologists with a special interest in human development, were influenced by the work of Carol Gilligan.
Their project, in collaboration with Wellesley College and its Stone Center,
began in the late 1970s and led to the publication of *Women's Ways of Knowing*. The goals were to explore women's experiences as "learners" and "knowers." Five perspectives were described relating to how women view reality and
draw conclusions about truth, knowledge, and authority. In addition, the re-

searchers looked at how schools and family promote and hinder women's development (Belenky et al. 1986:1). A major contribution of Belenky's work was the selection of a sample of women from diverse backgrounds. The researchers sought to identify specific aspects of intelligence and ways of thinking that are common and highly developed in women, dispelling the long-held belief that "thinking," considering the abstract and impersonal, defines men while "emotions," focusing on the personal and interpersonal, defines women.

THE STUDY SAMPLE

The number of women interviewed was 135. The initial and any subsequent interviews were 2 to 5 hours in length and were tape recorded. Questions related to the women's experiences with self-image, relationships, education and learning, decision making, moral development, personal changes and growth, catalysts for change, and impediments to growth, as well as their views of the future (Belenky et al. 1986:11). Ninety of the women were recent alumnae or current students at 6 academic institutions with different educational philosophies and diverse student bodies. Forty-five women were selected from 3 family agencies that dealt with parenting issues, which they referred to as "invisible colleges." These agencies were chosen because, unlike most institutions shaped and directed by men, they were almost always shaped and staffed by women. One of the agencies, working with needy teenage mothers, was in an isolated, impoverished rural area; a second was a network of self-help groups for parents who had a history of child abuse and family violence; and the third was a rural children's health program geared toward prevention.

The women in the study differed widely in age, life circumstances, and backgrounds. Their perspectives on knowing were grouped into five epistemological categories:

1. silence—The women saw themselves as mindless, voiceless, and subject to external authority. They were extreme in denial of the self.
2. received knowledge—The women saw themselves as capable or receiving and reproducing knowledge from external authorities but not creating knowledge of their own.
3. subjective knowledge—Truth and knowledge were seen as personal, private, and subjectively known or intuited.
4. procedural knowledge—The women were invested in learning and ap-

plying objective procedures for obtaining and communicating knowledge.

5. constructed knowledge—The women viewed all knowledge as contextual, saw themselves as creators of knowledge, and valued subjective and objective strategies for knowing (Belenky et al. 1986:15).

The researchers recognized that these categories were not fixed or universal, that they could not capture the complexities of an individual woman's thoughts, and that some could be found in men's thinking. In addition, ways of thinking would vary in different social and cultural contexts.

Findings

SILENCE (BELENKY ET AL. 1986:23–34). Only three women, all from the agency sample, viewed the world from this perspective; they were among the youngest and most deprived educationally, socially, and economically. They had not cultivated their capacities for representational thought. Feeling dependent, passive, incompetent, and reactive, they viewed external authorities as all-powerful and unpredictable. They saw obeying authorities as necessary for survival. For these women, describing the self was virtually impossible, as they felt others defined them. They could not consider changes in their lives that could or should occur in the future. Their history showed that they had grown up in isolation, with few friends and at least one parent prone to violence. Silent women had little awareness of their intellectual capabilities and found it difficult to acquire new understanding through listening to others. They lived selfless and voiceless lives. External authorities were seen as all powerful and knowing the truth.

RECEIVED KNOWLEDGE (BELENKY ET AL. 1986:35–51). Most of the women who fell into this category came from agencies or were very young college students. For them, words were central to the process of knowing. They believed that there was only one right answer to a question and were concrete and literal in their thinking, accepting no gray areas. They did not experience ambivalence and could not tolerate ambiguity. They focused on listening to others but lacked confidence in their own ability to speak, except with friends. They believed that women should be listeners, subordinate and unassertive, and that self-advancement was only acceptable when helping or empowering others. They looked to others for definition of the self as well as of their social and occupational roles.

Authorities, not friends, were viewed as the sources of truth and themselves as recipients, not sources, of knowledge. Those in college had difficulty when original work was required. They were most comfortable collecting facts and avoided developing opinions. Interviews in one to four years showed that with exposure to an intellectually challenging environment, they were able to advance beyond this way of knowing. Authorities could be very instrumental in helping these women recognize that they, as well as others, had power. However, most in this category were unable to see themselves as growing, evolving, and changing.

For these women, the sense of self was defined externally and was subjected to sex-role stereotyping and second-rung status. Even if successful, they regarded themselves as having achieved in "a man's world." There was little sense of an authentic voice or a centered self.

SUBJECTIVE KNOWLEDGE (BELENKY ET AL. 1986:52–75). This stage, achieved by half of the sample, represented a significant shift from passivity to action and seeing the self as not static but "becoming," with a protesting inner voice. Truth then became personal, private, and subjective, residing in the self. The researchers found that the move toward greater autonomy was not tied to a specific age, class, ethnicity, or educational level.

Many women in this category came from families that were less advantaged, more permissive, and more chaotic than average. Many had had experimental or community educations; some were identified in the "invisible colleges." Often, an influence was "failed male authority." While many women perceive men as having the power and being the ultimate authority, these were disappointed and outraged by having had no stable male authority in their lives. Many had been victims of sexual harassment and abuse. As the women made the transition to this level of "knowing," they turned to women close to them, mothers and grandmothers, who they perceived understood and knew their experiences, for affirmation that they could think, know, *and* be a woman. When families were unavailable, some turned to agencies and therapists.

Other women in this category came from middle- and upper middle-class families who believed that a good liberal arts education was appropriate for both male and female children. Some felt overwhelmed by options and were fearful of being alone in their choices. They also feared antagonizing others when expressing their opinions and thus jeopardizing relationships. They were reluctant to share their private worlds except with close friends. Like the less advantaged women, they valued others who had had similar life experiences and from whom they got affirmation.

The women at this stage of knowing moved from listening to an external voice to paying greater attention to an inner voice. Authority shifted from external to internal. This inner voice marked the women's emergent sense of self and sense of agency and control. Also at this period, they began to differentiate between *truth* as unique feelings from within based on personal history and experience and *ideas* as something from without. They saw truth as subjective and personal.

These women distrusted logic, analysis, and abstraction, which they associated with male thinking. They placed greater value on intuition. Many rejected science and scientists. Others distrusted books and theories, viewing the written word as "an instrument of oppression." Many preferred to express themselves nonverbally or artistically in order not to categorize or label through language.

At this stage, the women made growth of self their primary quest. While they felt that they "knew," they did not have the ability to express themselves and have others listen.

PROCEDURAL KNOWLEDGE (BELENKY ET AL. 1986:87–130). The women in this category were more homogeneous than those in the previous categories. They were white, privileged, young, and bright, and had attended prestigious colleges. Their voice, the *voice of reason,* was humbler but ultimately more powerful.

The women had moved through the previous ways of knowing before arriving at this stage of "reasoned reflection." Their knowledge was more objective than subjective. This stage was significantly different from the previous stages of knowing. The women became aware that intuitions may be incorrect and irresponsible, that some truths are truer than others, that truths can be shared, and that expertise can be respected. They learned that knowing involves careful observation and analysis and that they had to think before they spoke. They were in the process of acquiring and applying procedures for obtaining and communicating knowledge, and with increasing success they felt an increased sense of control.

Belenky et al. identified two voices, the voice of *separate knowing* and the voice of *connected knowing,* both of which the women used to some extent. The first was often used by women attending or recently graduated from traditional, elite, liberal arts colleges. Critical thinking was fundamental to separate knowing, the opposite of subjectivity. However, they were not comfortable voicing disagreement and avoided reasoned critical discourse, fearing that someone would be hurt. By accepting the standards of those they viewed as authorities who "allowed" independent thought, the separate knowers were vulnerable to criticisms that they had to accept with equanimity. Yet with new powers of reasoning, they were also able to criticize the reasoning of these authorities.

Separate knowers rigidly excluded their own and their adversaries' feelings and beliefs. They strove for objectivity, which meant excluding their own concerns and adopting the perspective of their adversaries. Separate knowers appreciated "disinterested reasoning." For some, however, this could lead to lack of interest, anomie, and monotony with little personal involvement in the pursuit of knowledge.

Connected knowing, used by a similar population as the separate knowers, was based on the conviction that the most trustworthy knowledge comes from personal experience. Thus connected knowers must find ways to gain access to other people's knowledge through the capacity for empathy. The first step is to learn about others' lives and how others think. Emphasis was placed on the *form* rather than the *content* of knowing. Conversation grew out of connectedness and trust. Authority was not based on power or status but on commonality of experience. The goal for these knowers was to understand other people's ideas in their terms.

Belenky et al. saw *procedural knowledge* as objective because it is oriented away from the self and toward the object the knower wishes to understand or analyze. Women using this mode of knowing were *systematic thinkers*, whose knowledge was encapsulated within systems. They were able to criticize a system only in the system's terms and according to its standards. They did well in highly structured colleges and were very successful. Some found this form of knowing lacking and saw a need to integrate feeling and thinking.

CONSTRUCTED KNOWLEDGE (BELENKY ET AL. 1986:131–52). The quest for self and voice, Belenky et al. believed, is central to transformations in women's ways of knowing. Women in this most advanced stage of knowing showed a high tolerance for internal contradiction and ambiguity. They had given up either/or thinking, seen in preceding stages, and no longer suppressed or denied aspects of the self in order to avoid inevitable conflict and stress. They viewed conflict in the context of each person's perspective, needs, and goals. These women chose not to compartmentalize their lives as they perceived men did, and wanted to deal with the external and internal together. They desired a voice that would communicate to others an understanding of life's complexity. They saw all knowledge as *constructed* and the knower as an intimate part of the known. Knowledge must therefore be viewed within situation and context.

Becoming aware of the working of their minds helped these women to establish rules for interactions with others and for self-definition. They become able to care for and relate to others in spite of what appeared to be major differences. They turned from didactic talk to "real talk," which involves listening, sharing, exploring, questioning, and creating an atmosphere so that new ideas can emerge. It is based on individual experience as well as analytical abilities. Real talk was a way to communicate and acquire new knowledge in both their personal and their professional lives. Dominance and authority were replaced with reciprocity and cooperation. The moral response was one of caring for the world and for others. This group, more than those preceding, wished to translate their moral commitments into action.

Finding their own voice did not eliminate problems for these women. Many reported anger and frustration when they felt unheard at home and at work in what remained a male-dominated world. Overwhelmed by wanting to "do it all," these women learned to compromise in a society that urges women to achieve but also assigns to them primary domestic responsibilities. These women were expected to accept the status quo, and many reported acknowledging that change would not come easily.

Belenky and her colleagues, Lynne Bond and Jacqueline Weinstock, followed up her earlier work and in 1997 published *A Tradition That Has No Name*, which examines how women help each other move out of silence, claim the power of their minds, exercise leadership, and ultimately have a real say in how their lives, families, and communities re run. They believe that while many women are stigmatized as different, deficient, and unworthy of participating fully in society and their interests are subordinated to those of the powerful, this is especially true of poor women, immigrant women, and women of color, all of whom face more extreme forms of prejudice (Belenky, Bond, and Weinstock 1997:3–4). Some women are stronger, became community leaders, and try to draw out the silent ones; their stories became the focus of the study. The researchers also looked at several culturally and socially diverse projects with the long-term goal of bringing missing voices into a dialogue with the community.

The Listening Partners Project, a time-limited demonstration project, studied 60 very isolated mothers of preschool children, aged 17 to 34, living in poverty in northern Vermont to learn whether being in a group where the women listened to each other would help them to gain a voice, claim the power of their minds, and break out of their seclusion. The goals were to promote development of voice and mind so that the women could name, question, and overcome stereotypes that had diminished them (Belenky, Bond, and Weinstock 1997:69) and learn problem-solving techniques within and outside of the group. It proved extremely difficult for most of these women initially to conceptualize their intellectual strengths. They did not see themselves as active knowers or thinkers. Seventeen percent were silent knowers, 67 percent were receiving knowers, and 16 percent were subjective knowers. They turned to others for knowledge and direction.

A major finding was that, especially for the most silent and excluded, it was growth producing to speak in settings where others listened and worked collaboratively to solve problems. As the women became more aware of the power of their minds and voices, more self-directed and more empowered, they became more likely to draw out and develop others through dialogue. The participants at the end of the project were aware of how much they valued each other and themselves, and that they had created a caring community in which they could develop knowledge and direction.

Following the end of the Listening Partners project, satisfied that it had led to young mothers gaining a voice and claiming the power of their minds, the researchers decided to look at successful ongoing projects that had given women voices and encouraged fuller participation in community life. The organizations had to be founded and led by women who had reflected on women's experience and role in society, and had to have the primary mission of bringing a "marginalized group into voice." These organizations, described below, appeared to have developed people and communities so well that the researchers thought of them as "public homeplaces" (Belenky, Bond, and Weinstock 1997:155–56).

The Mothers' Centers Movement in the United States and in Germany developed national networks of Mothers' Centers where women met on a regular basis, supported each other, and worked to make public spaces more responsive to the needs of women, children, and families. Data from The Mothers' Centers Movement showed that in our society, women who do not work outside of the home feel left out and deficient, and those who leave work to raise their children sense a drop in their social status. In the United States, the centers studied were located in middle-class suburbs and served a homogeneous population. The goal was to provide public space to support values and knowledge cultivated in the home and to reduce the stigmatization and marginalization of the role of mother. Women who attended these sessions felt that the experience changed their way of relating to their fami-

lies, as they began to teach family members skills of dialogue and collaborative problem solving. They noted that initially spouses fought the changes,
but later they appreciated being in a more equal relationship with a strong,
resourceful, engaged woman. The founding members felt that they had
raised their children to be more engaged, self-directed, and inquisitive, with
the result that many of the daughters were equal partners with their husbands and the sons were involved in daily nurturing of their children (Belenky, Bond, and Weinstock 1997:198).

The National Congress of Neighborhood Women is a national, inter-
racial, intercultural network that supports the development of women's
leadership in grassroots communities, to make those communities more
responsive to the needs of women and children. Individual groups teamed
up with other groups nationwide and have now expanded to include women leaders in developing countries. Data from The National Congress
of Neighborhood Women showed that while there were women leaders
in communities, they were isolated, often worked alone for the community,
did not see themselves as political, and had no official standing, no institutional support, and no public recognition for their efforts. Aware that
they were being rejected by traditional (male) leaders, the women saw
that they would make headway only if they worked together and created a
challenging and supportive place in which to develop leadership (Belenky,
Bond, and Weinstock 1997:208). Beginning locally, the grassroots organizations learned of each other's activities, organized conferences throughout the country, and, in 1975, formed the national organization. In local
"Leadership Support Groups," the women could think out loud about
themselves, the society they lived in, and new possibilities. The Congress has
now become international through GROOTS (Grassroots Organizations
Operating Together in Sisterhood), which was instrumental in bringing the
voices of grassroots women to the 1995 World Conference on Women in
China.

The Center for Cultural and Community Development supports leaders
in oppressed communities who wish to reclaim cultural traditions that enhance the development of individuals, families, and communities. It origi-
nated in the Deep South, based on the efforts of African American women
who called themselves "cultural workers." Its leaders, later working with a variety of different marginalized and silenced cultural groups, saw that like
blacks, these groups became empowered as they recognized and built on
their own cultural heritage. The leaders recognized the importance of cross-
cultural collaboration; they emphasized the art and music of a culture and

used it in the schools to draw out invisible and silent children who might become leaders of their generation.

Belenky, concurring with Gilligan's ethic of care and Miller's work on self-in-relationships, recognized that there is a universal division of labor based on gender, which results in women creating "cultures" that focus on promoting the development of people and communities. Belenky et al. found that black women were able to think of themselves in ways that white women might see as opposing and contradictory. The "ideal" was to be "powerfully voiced," strong-willed, and even cantankerous while also being caring, warm, and nurturing (Belenky, Bond, and Weinstock 1997:26). This was in contrast to the white women, who accepted a dualistic perspective whereby women feel and procreate while men think and create.

The founders of all the public homeplaces studied by Belenky et al. were women with strong convictions who were also open-minded. They questioned, reevaluated, listened, and learned. They established vital, stimulating settings where reflective dialogues were eye-opening and promoted growth. The dialogues would result in action and projects that developed individuals, families, and communities and identified new roles for women. The homeplace women had hands-on practical experience but also gained a larger world perspective and felt less isolated. Discussions developed individual members and the group as a whole. Public homeplaces became the ideal setting for silenced women to acquire skills of separate knowing and take a stand against an unjust society (Belenky, Bond, and Weinstock 1997:282).

Women have always worked to make their communities more nurturing and caring for themselves, their children, their families, and their neighbors; that is the "tradition that has no name," a tradition rooted in maternal practice and maternal thinking.

DEVELOPMENTAL THEORIES OF DIFFERENT POPULATIONS

As noted above, much of the work on adult development has been done with white, middle- or upper-class, heterosexual, primarily male subjects. More recently attention has been given to other populations.

WOMEN OF COLOR

Black women's connections to family and ethnic identity have been sources of love, strength, self-esteem, and stability in their attempts to negotiate be-

tween two cultural worlds, minority and majority, that may deliver conflicting messages. Black mothers have the task of teaching and reinforcing values
in their daughters in a society where their development will be affected by
racism, sexism, and, in many cases, classism. These girls learn early to rely on
themselves while also caring for others and to be cautious in a way that white
women are not, out of fear of not being "acceptable" (Turner 1997a:76). Unlike white women, black women are socialized to integrate the traditional
male focus on achievement, autonomy, and independence with the traditional female role as caretaker and nurturer. Self-reliance while remaining connected with family, ethnicity, and culture is highly valued in black families.

Tatum (1997:93–95) presents a five-step model of the development of
black racial identity:

1. preencounter—by accepting the beliefs and values of the white culture,
   the person forms an internalized negative stereotype as he or she seeks to
   assimilate and be accepted by whites and distances him- or herself from
   blacks
2. encounter—precipitated by an event that forces the person to acknowledge the impact of racism and recognize that her or his identity cannot
   be white and must be that of a person targeted by racism
3. immersion/emersion—begins with avoidance of symbols of whiteness,
   denigration of white people, and glorification of black people, leading to
   own cultural and self-exploration with greater security and a newly defined and affirmed sense of self
4. internalization—while maintaining connections with black peers, the
   person can form meaningful relationships with whites who respect newly established black self-definition
5. internalization-commitment—commitment to concerns of blacks as a
   group will be sustained over time

Tatum added that this process can only occur in emotional connection with
others. It is particularly important in the immersion phase that the person's
experiences be validated by others who have had similar experiences; this is
empowering and helps the individual define racial identity positively.

Tatum (1997) studied the career and relationship issues of black college
women, postulating that being black and female (dual minority status) poses
unique issues when planning for and working toward a career. The four primary barriers to success, racism, sexism, classism, and ageism, are closely in-
terwoven. Tatum noted that different circumstances alter individual think-

ing, but there are certain norms black women share more with each other than with other women:

1. history of combining roles of worker and wife/mother
2. mutual interdependence with men to achieve some semblance of financial stability and security through work outside the home as well as to preserve family and community solidarity
3. denial of meaningful employment to many black men has led to women sharing or taking over the role of breadwinner and to damaged male/female relationships and lack of solidarity of the intact black family
4. black mothers have a heavy sense of responsibility to instill feelings of self-esteem and confidence in their children when dealing with racism and sexism
5. in spite of a history as workers, black women have lower-paying, lower-status jobs than do white females or black and white males (1997b:164–66)

Studying black women trying to achieve career aspirations, Tatum found that trying to fit in with the majority culture caused much anxiety, which interfered with the individual's abilities and resulted in the formation of a negative self-perception and fears of failing or of succeeding, as well as anger at society. She identified the need for black women, especially single black working women with or without children, to develop an *entitled* awareness of the need for a strong personal support system at home and at work.

Sexual Identity

Homosexuals must make a choice between authenticity and conformity. They act on their authentic sexual attraction and thus do not conform to powerful social injunctions against sexual intimacy with others of the same sex. By "coming out" about their sexual orientation, they may risk losing traditional social, and often professional, approval.

Wendy Rosen, influenced by the work of the Stone Center at Wellesley College, conducted a study on the normal developmental experiences of lesbians for her doctoral dissertation. She identified three central aspects of relational development resulting from the mother-daughter relationship: mutual empathy, relationship authenticity, and relationship differentiation (Rosen 1997:247). Prior to their daughters' disclosure of their sexual identity,

mothers, recognizing that their child is not moving in the direction of heterosexuality, experience a sense of failure in not having met the societal expectations of raising a heterosexual daughter who will marry and have children. Thus both parent and child feel a lack of empathy for each other and a
sense of isolation and shame. The mother finds it difficult to accept and authenticate other than heterosexual relationships, and a disconnection results.
The young lesbian will turn to other women for empathy, authenticity, and
emotional connectedness, and her shame and isolation will be diminished
through mutuality in relationships leading to personal integration.

Disclosure results, in part, from the lesbian wanting a connection with
the mother. Often the daughter hopes to clarify the relationship with her
mother and what can be expected in the future. Disclosure represents unfinished business. It is not easy and a risk, for the mother and daughter may
become closer and more empathic or may be permanently estranged. It
is a hard relationship to work out in a culture that rests on sexism and
heterosexism.

Parks (1999), viewing lesbian identity as a development process, conducted a qualitative study of thirty-one Caucasian women using a life history interview that examined social, historical, and cultural aspects of their lives.
Eleven women were ages forty-five to seventy-nine (pre-Stonewall era),
twelve were thirty-three to forty-two (gay liberation era), and eight were
twenty-three to twenty-nine (gay rights era). A majority had college or graduate degrees; only two had not completed college. All but five were employed
full time. A majority owned their own homes. Fourteen lived alone. Seventeen were in an exclusive relationship with a woman. Six had been married
and five had children.

Respondents across generations indicated an internal progression from
self-awareness to self-definition linked to social awareness of, and access to,
other lesbians. The process involved four steps: internal recognition of feelings; beginning and undefined sexual and social contact; high exposure and
involvement in lesbian events; and defined identity and greater selectivity in
contact with lesbian groups and activities.

Data showed the importance of the historical context. Women who had
grown up in the pre-Stonewall era endured a pervasive silence about homosexuality, a sense of isolation, and an ongoing fear of openness. Women maturing in the liberation era experienced tensions and disillusionments during
that transitional period and remained cautious. The younger women, maturing in the gay rights era, were more open, content with their lives, and opti-

mistic about the future. The five stages of lesbian identity development were reached at the following average ages:

AGE	45–79	33–42	23–29
SELF-AWARENESS	18.8	17.0	14.6
FIRST SOCIAL ENCOUNTER	23.9	21.7	19.3
FIRST SEXUAL INVOLVEMENT	22.8	21.1	20.5
FIRST DISCLOSURE	24.9	22.6	21.0
FIRST SELF-LABELING	31.9	25.5	20.3

Clearly the historical context and the experiences of the older women were important factors in earlier identity formation by the younger women.

ATTACHMENT CHANGE

Research has shown that attachment styles are a product of early and current interpersonal circumstances. Some people retain their original style while others change. Davila, Karney, and Bradbury (1999) examined attachment style change in a context that maximizes opportunities for change, the early marital relationship, looking at marital satisfaction. They studied 172 newlyweds. Wives averaged 26 years of age, had 16.2 years of education, and earned $11,000 to $20,000 a year. Sixty-one percent were Caucasian, 15 percent Asian American, 16 percent Latina, and 5 percent African American. Husbands averaged 27.6 years of age, had 15.6 years of education, and earned $21,000 to $30,000 a year. Sixty-seven percent were Caucasian, 13 percent Asian, 15 percent Latino, and 4 percent African American. Spouses completed questionnaires at Time One and in four follow-ups, each six months apart.

Data showed: (1) spouses tend over time to be more secure with each other, more comfortable depending on each other, and less anxious about abandonment; (2) vulnerability created a strong link between marital satisfaction and attachment security in husbands, while wives' anxiety about abandonment fluctuated in relation to their partners' and their own marital satisfaction and their own level of vulnerability; (3) changes in spouses' attachment security may be related to changes in their partners' attachment security through its effect on changes in marital satisfaction; (4) more vulnerable husbands showed stronger associations between their own marital satisfaction and their comfort in depending on others than did less vulnerable husbands, while wives' marital satisfaction changed in relation to their husbands' attachment security, with women becoming less satisfied and secure when their husbands became more secure they felt they might no longer be needed; (5) wives became more satisfied when their husbands became more

comfortable with closeness; and (6) emotional and supportive aspects of relationships matter more to wives' marital satisfaction and psychological
health than to husbands'; therefore, vulnerable women may be especially
sensitive. Thus the process of attachment is influenced by intra- and interpersonal experiences and vulnerabilities. In general, the study revealed that
on average there are positive changes in attachment beliefs in the early years
of marriage.

WOMEN AT MIDLIFE

Sharon McQuaide (1998a, 1998b) noted that there was very limited research
on women in midlife except in terms of menopause and empty nest syndrome, and that what research existed was of limited value, as women's experiences at midlife have been rapidly changing. This scarcity of research has
led to negative stereotyping of women in this life stage.

McQuaide undertook a study to identify factors associated with successful
negotiation of midlife. One hundred and three women, ages 40 to 59, completed a questionnaire on attitudes, beliefs, feelings about midlife, and their
current well-being. All were white and lived in the New York City area. Ninety-one percent had completed at least two years of college, 74 percent were
married or living with a "significant other," 72 percent had incomes over
$50,000 (31 percent were over $100,000), 80 percent worked at least part
time, 35 percent had children at home, and 97 percent were heterosexual.

Findings showed that for most, menopausal symptoms and the "empty
nest" were irrelevant to well-being and midlife was not a "time of torment."
Most of the women were satisfied with their lives and with themselves, but
saw this stage as "challenging." What they did, rather than what they had,
made the biggest difference in their sense of well-being. Three quarters of the
women described themselves as "happy" or "very happy." The most satisfied
women unanimously saw midlife as the best or happiest time of their lives,
because they were actively participating in life and looking forward to new
opportunities in the future. The least satisfied women looked back to earlier
years when they felt there had been greater *possibility* for personal and professional happiness. Both the high and low scorers reported that what they
liked best about midlife was increased freedom and independence. The high
scorers felt that they had freedom to do something new professionally and
personally, and the low scorers reported freedom from menstruation, pregnancy, and worries about appearance. The high scorers felt that in general
they were understood by others, while some of the low scorers felt under-

stood. High scorers were more task oriented and saw their weaknesses as procrastination, disorganization, and overextending themselves. Low scorers were concerned with issues of self-esteem and fear of being controlled by the wishes of others. A strong social network correlated with high scores on satisfaction. Women who did well were aware of dissonance between the increased freedom and power they felt and negative cultural stereotypes, while women who scored low on satisfaction reported less dissonance and greater compliance with cultural messages about obsolescence.

McQuaide concluded that women need decent jobs with a decent income as well as a supportive social environment and must guard against denigrating themselves. Data from the study showed that the predictors of well-being are having an adequate income, having a confidante or groups of friends, good health, high self-esteem, lack of self-denigration, goals for the future, positive midlife role models, high self-effectance, positive feelings about one's appearance, and a benign superego.

"If I Had It to Do Over"

Stewart and Vandewater (1999) noted that many, but not all, of the current middle-aged women were the first generation to benefit from the educational and work opportunities resulting from the women's movement. These women, however, had been socialized in childhood and early adulthood to a traditional female role. Stewart and Vandewater studied two samples of women who at midlife had regrets about choices they had made, and examined how acting on regrets would enhance well-being. Both samples were made up of college-educated women.

The first sample of 83 women was drawn from the class of 1967 at the University of Michigan and was studied in 1967 and followed up in 1970, 1981, and 1992. Data for this study were collected in 1981 and 1992, when the women were ages 36 and 47. At the time of the second follow-up, 86 percent were married or living with a partner, 89 percent had children, 72 percent had had graduate school education, and 90 percent were employed with a median income of $30,000 to $40,000. A goal of the study was to look at regrets about having pursued traditionally feminine roles. Sixty of the women indicated that they would have "done things differently," expressing regrets about their traditional role involvement in terms of education and career, while 15 percent regretted limited traditional role involvement centered around family rather than work or education. The largest percentage of women who made career-relevant changes were those with traditional role regrets. The findings indicated that while regrets might motivate change, the change was not always successful, and for those with traditional role regrets the changes were not always related to these regrets. Those who did make changes were better off in terms of physical and emotional well-being as well as life satisfaction and adult adjustment. They also scored high on the personality characteristic of effective instrumentality and low on rumination.

The second sample was drawn from a longitudinal study of the Radcliffe College class of 1964. Data were collected in 1979 (n = 133), 1986 (n = 193), and 1991 (n = 149), when the respondents were 37, 43, and 48, respectively, with data analysis limited to 76 women who had participated in all three samplings. At age 48, 74 percent were married and 21 percent divorced, 87 percent had children, 71 percent had graduate education, and 86 percent were employed in the upper end of a work status scale; median income was $30,000 to $49,000. Asked if they would choose the same lifestyle pattern if they had it "to do over again," 26 said yes and 50 said no. The majority (85 percent) expressed one regret, while 15 percent expressed two. Traditional role regrets focused on career (65 percent) rather than education (19 percent), marriage (8 percent), and parenting (27 percent).

Reviewing the data from the two samples, the researchers found that early midlife regret motivated goal setting but was not always associated with actual life changes by age 43. Barriers to change were identified as responsibility for children under five; single parenthood; an unemployed spouse; and a spouse with a high-level, demanding job. However, they concluded that regrets alone do not bring about change, just as external barriers are insufficient to prevent it. Those who experienced changes felt a greater sense of well-being, while those women who did not change seemed quite discontent in later middle age.

CONCLUSION

Although adulthood is, for most people, the longest stage of the life cycle, it has not received enough attention from scholars. This is the life stage in which the individual undergoes major physical and cognitive changes. It begins with personal and professional changes that may remain stable or may change over time. It ends with the individual having to accept the choices made and moving into the final life stage, old age. For the majority, passage through adulthood is not smooth. There are "peaks and valleys," and individual experiences may be very varied.

Since optimal physical and psychological development in later life depends on the individual's experience in middle age, more research is needed to identify lifestyle patterns, personality styles, and cognitive perspectives that lead to optimal functioning. While the theorists reviewed have made significant contributions, societal changes such as greater longevity, more opportunities for women, a variety of diverse family compositions, and later parenting result in greater variability and will modify their conclusions. Much more research is needed on the impact of gender, sexual orientation, socioeconomic status, race, and physical and emotional disabilities on the individual in adulthood. Patterns of adult life in the twenty-first century are in a state of flux. Certainly how the individual perceives their self in relation to the environment is influenced by cultural, social, economic, political, and historical factors.

Theories have been seriously limited by being based on study samples of advantaged adultsrather than broader, more integrated groups. As our population is aging, we can hope that some researchers, like Erikson, will look at the their experiences and those of their peers and attempt some retrospective work. Adulthood is a complex, highly individualized experience that deserves more attention.

BIBLIOGRAPHY

Belenky, M. F., L. A. Bond, and J. S. Weinstock. 1997. *A Tradition That Has No Name*. New York: Basic.

Belenky, M. F., B. M. Clinchy, N. R. Goldberger, and J. M. Tarule. 1986. *Women's Ways of Knowing*. New York: Basic.

Chodorow, N. 1974. "Family Structure and Feminine Personality." In M. Z. Rosaldo and L. Lamphere, eds., *Woman, Culture and Society*. Stanford: Stanford University Press.

——. 1978. *The Reproduction of Mothering*. Berkeley: University of California Press.

——. 1989. *Feminism and Psychoanalytic Theory*. New Haven: Yale University Press.

Davila, J., B. R. Karney, and T. N. Bradbury. 1999. "Attachment and Change Process in the Early Years of Marriage." *Journal of Personality and Social Psychology* 76 (5): 783–802.

Erikson, E. 1950. *Childhood and Society*. New York: Norton.

———. 1968. *Identity, Youth and Crisis.* New York: Norton.

———. 1977. *Toys and Reason.* New York: Norton.

———. 1982. *The Life Cycle Completed.* New York: Norton.

Gilligan, C. 1993. *In a Different Voice.* Cambridge: Harvard University Press.

Jordan, J. V., A. G. Kaplan, J. B. Miller, I. P. Stiver, and J. L. Surrey. 1991. *Women's Growth in Connection.* New York: Guilford.

Jung, C. G. 1917. "Two Essays on Analytical Psychology." In *The Collected Works of C. G. Jung,* vol. 7. Princeton: Princeton University Press, 1966.

———. 1933. *Psychological Types.* New York: Harcourt, Brace.

———. 1968. *Analytical Psychology: Its Theory and Practice (The Tavistock Lectures).* New York: Pantheon.

———. 1982. *Aspects of the Feminine.* Princeton: Princeton University Press.

Levinson, D. J. 1986. "A Conception of Adult Development." *American Psychologist* 41 (1): 3–13.

Levinson, D. J., C. M. Darrow, E. B. Klein, M. H. Levinson, and B. McKee. 1974. "The Psychosocial Development of Men in Early Adulthood and the Mid-Life Transition." In D. F. Ricks, A. Thomas, and M. Roff, eds., *Life History Research in Psychopathology,* 3:243–58. Minneapolis: University of Minnesota Press.

———. 1978. *The Seasons of a Man's Life.* New York: Knopf.

Levinson, D. J. and W. E. Gooden. 1985. "The Life Cycle." In H. I. Kaplan and B. J. Sadock, eds., *Comprehensive Textbook of Psychiatry/IV,* 1:1–13. Baltimore: Williams and Wilkins.

Levinson, D. J. with J. D. Levinson. 1996. *The Seasons of a Woman's Life.* New York: Ballantine.

McQuaide, S. 1998a. "Women at Midlife." *Social Work* 43 (1): 21–31.

———. 1998b. "Opening Space for Alternative Images and Narratives of Midlife Women." *Clinical Social Work Journal* 26 (1): 39–53.

Miller, J. B. 1976. *Toward a New Psychology of Women.* Boston: Beacon Press.

———. 1991. "The Construction of Anger in Women and Men." In J. V. Jordan, A. G. Kaplan, J. B. Miller, I. P. Stiver, and J. L. Surrey, eds., *Women's Growth in Connection,* 181–96. New York: Guilford.

———. 1991. "The Development of Women's Sense of Self." In J. V. Jordan, A. G. Kaplan, J. B. Miller, I. P. Stiver, and J. L. Surrey, eds., *Women's Growth in Connection,* 11–26. New York: Guilford.

———. 1991. "Women and Power." In J. V. Jordan, A. G. Kaplan, J. B. Miller, I. P. Stiver, and J. L. Surrey, eds., *Women's Growth in Connection,* 197–205. New York: Guilford.

Miller, J. B. and I. P. Stiver. 1997. *The Healing Connection.* Boston: Beacon.

Monte, C. F. 1980. *Beneath the Mask.* New York: Holt, Rinehart and Winston.

Neugarten, B. L. 1968. "Adult Personality: Toward a Psychology of the Life Cycle." In B. L. Neugarten, ed., *Middle Age and Aging,* 137–47. Chicago: University of Chicago Press.

———. 1968. "The Awareness of Middle Age." In B. L. Neugarten, ed., *Middle Age and Aging,* 93–98. Chicago: University of Chicago Press.

Neugarten, B. L. and D. L. Gutmann. 1968. "Age-Sex Roles and Personality in Middle Age: A Thematic Apperception Study." In B. L. Neugarten, ed., *Middle Age and Aging,* 58–71. Chicago: University of Chicago Press.

Neugarten, B. L. and J. W. Moore. 1968. "The Changing Age-Status System." In B. L. Neugarten, ed., *Middle Age and Aging,* 5–21. Chicago: University of Chicago Press.

Neugarten, B. L., V. Wood, R. J. Kraines, and B. Loomis. 1968. "Women's Attitudes Toward Menopause." In B. L. Neugarten, ed., *Middle Age and Aging,* 195–200. Chicago: University of Chicago Press.

Peck, R. C. 1968. "Psychological Developments in the Second Half of Life." In B. L. Neugarten, ed., *Middle Age and Aging,* 88–92. Chicago: University of Chicago Press.

Parks, C. A. 1999. "Lesbian Identity Development." *American Journal of Orthopsychiatry* 69 (3): 347–61.

Rosen, W. 1997. "The Integration of Sexuality: Lesbians and Their Mothers." In J. V. Jordan, ed., *Women's Growth in Diversity.* New York: Guilford.

Stewart, A. J. and E. A. Vandewater. 1999. " 'If I Had It to Do Over Again . . .': Midlife Review, Midcourse Corrections, and Women's Well-Being in Midlife." *Journal of Personality and Social Psychology* 76 (2): 270–83.

Storr, A. 1991. *Jung.* New York: Routledge.

Tatum, B. D. 1997. "Racial Identity Development and Relational Theory: The Case of Black Women in White Communities." In J. V. Jordan, ed., *Women's Growth in Diversity,* 91–106. New York: Guilford.

Turner, C. W. 1997a. "Clinical Applications of the Stone Center Theoretical Approach to Minority Women." In J. V. Jordan, ed., *Women's Growth in Diversity,* 74–90. New York: Guilford.

———. 1997b. "Psychosocial Barriers to Black Women's Career Development." In J. V. Jordan, ed., *Women's Growth in Diversity,* 162–75. New York: Guilford.

Vaillant, G. 1976. "Natural History of Male Psychological Health." *Archives of General Psychiatry* 33 (May): 535–45.

———. 1989. "The Evolution of Defense Mechanisms During the Middle Years." In J. M. Oldham and R. S. Liebert, eds., *The Middle Years,* 58–72. New Haven: Yale University Press.

———. 1993. *The Wisdom of the Ego*. Cambridge: Harvard University Press.

———. 1998. *Adaptation to Life*. Cambridge: Harvard University Press.

Vaillant, G. and C. C. McArthur. 1972. "Natural History of Male Psychologic Health. I. The Adult Life Cycle from 18–50." *Seminars in Psychiatry* IV (4): 415–27.

Willis, S. L. and J. D. Reid. 1999. *Life in the Middle*. San Diego: Academic Press.

PATRICIA J. KOLB

one two three four five **six**

DEVELOPMENTAL THEORIES OF AGING

INTRODUCTION

As individuals go through their lives, their functioning in each stage of development is influenced by interrelated biological, psychological, and social factors, which contribute to experiences in older adulthood. Atchley has suggested that aging includes many processes and possible outcomes, and the reality is that it may be either positive or negative. Older persons may engage in activities requiring experience, wisdom, and skill, and may serve as advisors and keepers of tradition. Aging may bring personal peace, freedom, and opportunity. It may also bring losses of physical or mental capacities, employment and income opportunities, appearance, positions in organizations, friends, and partner. From the perspective of the individual, the most realistic view may be that aging will include positive and negative changes and that "positive outcomes outnumber the negative by at least 2 to 1." From the perspective of society, "aging is both a social problem *and* a great achievement," which involves problems of reduced income, age discrimination in work and social programs, inadequate health care, and inadequate housing and transportation for a sizable minority of older people. Society's view can also reflect the two-sided nature of aging, since the advantages of age may be stressed in areas such as politics, disadvantages emphasized in areas such as employment, and both advantages and disadvantages incorporated in areas such as the family (Atchley 2000).

Aging encompasses physical, psychological, and social changes, but as Atchley has noted, its significance is largely social even though its primary basis is biological. Defining people as "aged" or "elderly" at an arbitrary age such as sixty-five misclassifies some people, and Atchley suggests that the significance of physical changes associated with aging is related primarily to cultural expectations (Atchley 1994:10). It is therefore necessary to consider what people do with aging, as well as what aging does to us. The former varies in groups diversified by socioeconomic status, race and ethnicity, sexual orientation, gender, ability and disability, and other characteristics. Atchley points out that aging affects how a society or group is viewed as well as how individuals are viewed. Everyone is affected by aging because most people have the potential to reach old age and because we live in groups with older members.

Neugarten (1996a:63) proposed an "age-irrelevant" view in which government programs would be age neutral rather than age categorical, targeting efforts specifically toward individuals in need rather than older adults as a group. This would be a way to adequately address the disparate realities and images of older people. Another alternative is to redefine old age, considering a person to have reached it at seventy-five and synchronizing laws with this age. A third alternative is suggested by Neugarten is "veteranship," in which old age would be viewed as a time for repayment by the community and older people would be positively regarded as elders. Special benefit programs for them would be established by law.

In order to utilize age as a social attribute, we assign it specific indicators, including chronological age, functional capacity, and life stage (Atchley 2000:5, 6). *Chronological age* is used in two ways, to arbitrarily identify the time at which older adulthood begins and to divide older adults into "young old" and "old old" categories (Fisher 1993:78). Some gerontologists divide the older adult population into the young old, under age seventy-five; middle old, seventy-five to eighty-four; and old old or oldest old, eighty-five and over (Atchley 2000:6). Chronological age is also an easily verifiable indicator to use in applying bureaucratic rules and policies and determining eligibility for benefits. The age of eligibility for full Social Security and Medicare benefits is sixty-five, although those who wait until seventy to collect them receive somewhat more income. As of 2000, there were no restrictions on earned income for people over sixty-five collecting Social Security. The age of eligibility for many other programs varies. Widows can receive Social Security survivor benefits at sixty; older adults are eligible for public housing at sixty-two, for most senior centers at sixty, and for membership in the American Association of Retired Persons at fifty. However, for describing differences among older adults, chronological age does not seem adequate.

Functional age, or functional capacity, is defined through observable individual attributes, including physical appearance, mobility, strength, coordination, and mental capacity, which are used to assign people to age categories (Atchley 2000:7). Functional age, though popularly used, is difficult to assess and not generally utilized in research, legislation, or social programs. Neugarten, however, has noted that all societies have age-status systems "in which rights, rewards, and responsibilities are differentially distributed to socially defined age groups. Life periods in the lives of individuals become parallel with age grades in the society; and age grades in turn constitute an age-stratification structure" (1996a:59). She suggested that age-status systems are built upon functional age and develop because they are inherently usable to society, even though social institutions use chronological age as an index. She adds that age-status systems create age distinctions and patterns of norms and expectations regarding age-appropriate behavior. Age norms, which are mechanisms of social control, vary according to the degree to which they are formalized and the strength of the sanctions attached to them.

Broad *life stage* definitions for older adults may include later adulthood and old age. Later adulthood is generally considered to begin in the sixties. Social changes are often the major shifts that individuals experience; these may include retirement, widowhood, deaths of friends and relatives, and caregiving for parents. Changes in physical functioning include greater prevalence of chronic illness, activity limitations, and mortality among family and friends, primarily due to acute episodes of cardiovascular disease. However, for many people, continued physical vigor and freedom from responsibilities make this period relatively open (Atchley 2000:8).

The "old" life stage, as described by Atchley (2000:8), is characterized by extreme physical frailty and typically occurs in the late seventies, although some people in their eighties and nineties do not show many signs of it. This stage is defined more by physical or mental frailty than by the social factors that are the primary characteristics of later adulthood. People have attributes of old age at different chronological ages, and individuals do not generally show all of the signs typical of later adulthood or old age.

A major problem for the elderly is often housing, as they may no longer be able to afford or want to maintain their existing home. This was particularly true for thousands of older low-income tenants who were forced to move in the late 1990s when housing projects opted out of the federal Section 8 rental assistance programs as federal subsidy contracts expired. Two thirds of all

Section 8 contracts will expire between 1999 and 2004, and the federal Department of Housing and Urban Development estimates that 47 percent of these units are occupied by people age 62 and over without children. By summer 1999, owners had opted out of the program in 47 states and were opting out of more than 1,000 Section 8 units monthly (Shashaty 1999:1).

GERONTOLOGY

In 1903, Elie Metchnikoff was the first person to use the term *gerontology*. He believed that aging was the result of "gastrointestinal putrefaction" (Birren 1999:460). Contemporary gerontology has been defined as "the use of reason to understand aging," and it employs the methods found in many academic and practice disciplines. The interrelated aspects of this field of study are physical, psychological, social psychological, and social; they are described by Atchley (2000:3) as:

1. *physical aging*, which examines the causes and consequences of the body's declining capacity to renew itself; the physical effects of bodily aging; and the means for preventing, treating, or compensating for illness or disability caused by or related to physical aging
2. *psychological aging*, which focuses on sensory processes, perception, coordination, mental capacity, human development, personality, and coping ability as they are affected by aging
3. *social psychological aging*, which focuses on the interaction of the individual with his or her environment and includes such topics as attitudes, values, beliefs, social roles, self-image, and adjustment to aging
4. *social aging*, which refers to the nature of the society in which individual aging occurs, the influence that society has on its aging individuals, and their impact on society; also includes interactions among various social institutions, such as the economy or health care, as they apply to the needs of an older population

The field of social gerontology is a subfield of gerontology dealing with the nonphysical side of aging. It involves the study of individual aging as well as aging and society. Physical aging interests social gerontologists only as it influences the ways individuals and societies adapt to one another (Atchley 2000). Social gerontology was conceptualized as a field of study in the 1950s. Prior to the 1940s, older people were primarily the concern of physicians who cared for the ill and disabled and social workers who assisted the poor and isolated. Mental health professionals were seeing almost no older people at all because the problems of old age were regarded as untreatable. Research was based on hospitalized or institutionalized elderly and the prevailing stereotype of old people was as people who were sick, needy, and desolate. Physical and mental decline were considered "inevitable" beginning at age sixty-five (Neugarten 1996b). In the 1940s, a small group of social scientists began to study groups of older people leading normal, healthy lives.

Research and education about the social aspects of aging have developed rapidly in gerontology and other disciplines, including anthropology, economics, social history, and sociology, since 1960. Behavioral sciences, particularly cognitive and developmental psychologies, had long studied infancy and childhood, but now they began to focus on adulthood and aging. Campbell and O'Rand (1988) point out that as the field of gerontology has developed, it has become a highly specialized, multifield discipline, with separate journals, research programs, and societies. Social science traditions have expanded gerontological study to look at old age as part of the life course (or life span) to be studied within historical and cultural contexts, basing research on the process of aging rather than the "aged."

Increased interest in issues pertaining to older adults became apparent in the development of professional organizations, research, professional literature, and federal legislation and funding for service programs and research beginning in the 1940s. The Gerontological Society of America, an interdisciplinary organization of researchers, practitioners, and educators, was founded in 1945. The American Society on Aging held its first annual meeting in 1954. By the end of the 1950s, three handbooks summarizing research on the biomedical, behavioral, and social aspects of aging resulted from the relationship between scientists and federal agencies, and in 1961 the first White House Conference on Aging took place. Medicare and the Older Americans Act were enacted by Congress by the end of 1965. In 1975, Robert Butler, M.D., who had coined the term *ageism* in 1968, became the founding director of the National Institute on Aging, authorized by Congress as part of the National Institutes of Health. A special center focusing on the mental health of older persons was established in the National Institute of Mental Health.

The Age Discrimination Act of 1975 barred discrimination based on age in any program receiving federal support if the program was not explicitly aimed at a particular age group. The ADA applies across the age spectrum, to both the "young" and the "old." In 1978 an amendment to the Age Discrimination in Employment Act of 1967 was passed. The 1967 act barred workplace discrimination against people ages forty to sixty-five; the 1978 amendment raised the protections to age seventy, prohibited mandatory retirement in the privated sector before age seventy, and prohibited mandatory retirement altogether for most federal employees.

In her book, *The Fountain of Age* (1993), Betty Friedan suggests that only within the past few years have gerontologists admitted that previous assumptions about age as genetically programmed catastrophic decline were based on pathological aging.

DEMOGRAPHIC CHANGES

The dramatic increase in the population age sixty-five and over in the United States during the twentieth century has been a prelude to an "agequake." The term was coined by Julia Tavares Alvarez, Ambassador, Alternate Permanent Representative of the Dominican Republic to the UN since 1978 and champion of older persons' issues, to refer to the global population explosion of older adults projected for the twenty-first century. This phenomenon compels us to focus on the realities of the lives of a large and ever-increasing older adult population throughout the United States and the rest of the world.

The median age of the global population increased from 23.5 years in 1950 to 26.1 years in 1998 and is projected to increase to 37.8 years by 2050 (UN 1999:1–2). The total number of older people throughout the world is projected to increase from 580 million in 1998 to almost 2 billion in 2050; the number 80 and over is expected to be 311 million in 2050, 5.3 times the number in 1998; and centenarians are expected to increase to 2.2 million in 2050, which is 16 times the number in 1998 (UN 1999:2–3). Because women live longer than men, the feminization of older population groups is occurring throughout the world; among persons 80 and over, there were 190 females for every 100 males in 1998, most of whom were widows (UN 1999:3–4). By the end of the twentieth century, the population of older persons was increasing at a more rapid rate in developing countries than in the United States (U.S. Bureau of the Census 1996:v). Demographers project that almost two thirds of the world's population of older adults will live in developing countries by 2020, compared to over half in 1994 (U.S. Bureau of the Census 1996:v).

During the twentieth century, the population age sixty-five and over in the United States increased because of gains in life expectancy resulting from lower death rates among younger people, increases in the total number of live births, and the large number of immigrants. Life expectancy was forty-seven in 1900 and is now approximately seventy-six (Rowe and Kahn 1998:3). The relative size of the older population has increased, due primarily to the decline in birth rates, which has been consistent in the United States with few exceptions since 1790; the most notable exception has been the post–World War II "baby boom." Throughout the nineteenth century, the net decline in fertility affected the growth of the older population as a proportion of the entire population less than in the twentieth century because of the influence of other demographic factors, including increased life expectancy experienced primarily by the youngest age groups. Immigration patterns also differed in the nineteenth and twentieth centuries because twentieth-century legislation significantly limited legal immigration of middle-aged and younger people, resulting in a proportionally larger older immigrant population (Achenbaum 1978:90).

The progressive aging of the population in the United States is reflected in the fact that half was over age 20 in 1860, half was age 34 and older in 1994, and at least half of the population may be 39 or older by 2030. The population under age 65 increased threefold from 1900 to 1994 while the population 65 and over increased elevenfold. The number of people age 100 and over has more than doubled since 1980. The ratio of those 65 and over to those under 65 will almost double from 1990 to 2050, and the proportion who are 65 and over for all races is projected to increase from 12.5 percent to 20.4 percent of the total population in the United States (U.S. Bureau of the Census 1996:v, 2–18).

Bureau of the Census projections indicate that racial and ethnic diversity within the older population in the United States will continue to increase. Although women live an average of about seven years longer than men, white women live an average of six years longer than black women, and on the average, black men live about eight years less than white men (Rowe and Kahn 1998:4). Demographic projections indicate that there will be increases in the proportion of the population that is 65 and over in all racial groups. Between 1990 and 2050, the proportion age 65 and over who are American Indian, Eskimo, and Aleut is projected to increase from 5.6 percent to 12.6 percent; Asian and Pacific Islander from 6.0 percent to 15.3 percent; black from 8.2 percent to 13.6 percent; Hispanic from 5.1 percent to 14.1 percent; and white from 13.4 percent to 22.8 percent. It is predicted that in 2050, 10 percent of the older population will be black, non-Hispanic; 7 percent will be Asian and Pacific Islander; less than 1 percent will be American Indian, Eskimo, and Aleut; and 16 percent will be Hispanic, while white non-Hispanics will decline from 87 percent of the older adult population in 1990 to 67 percent. The reality of a higher proportion of older people among whites compared to other racial groups has been attributed to whites' better chance of survival to age 65 and lower fertility in recent years. The decline in non-Hispanic white immigration since the 1960s may also be a contributing factor, since immigrants are generally much younger than 65. Other groups in the United States, especially people of Asian and Hispanic ancestry, have generally younger populations because they include larger proportions of immigrants (U.S. Bureau of the Census 1996:v, 2–18).

Variations over time in the fertility, mortality, and migration rates of different groups have influenced the racial composition of the elderly population. Black fertility rates have declined more slowly than white rates since Reconstruction, and black mortality rates have continued to be higher. Immigration has increased the proportion of the white population that is older but does not appear to have affected the age structure of the black population. Laws passed since the 1920s contributed to a dramatic increase in the proportion of older immigrants; 9.7 percent of foreign-born white Americans were over age 65 in 1920, and this increased to 33.5 percent over the next 40 years. Because of these factors, the proportion of African Americans past the age of 65 has always been smaller than the proportion of the white population past age 65, with the disparity increasing since 1920 (Achenbaum 1978:92–93).

Differences in the relative numbers of older women and older men increased during the twentieth century. From 1900 to 1930, only a slightly greater proportion of all women were over age 65, compared to all men. Numerically, there were slightly more men than women over age 65 until 1930, but by 1940 there were more women than men in this age group. By 1970, 11.2 percent of all women and 8.5 percent of all men were at least age 65. The disparity in the proportional representation of men and women has also been influenced by the higher death rates for men compared to women at each stage of life (Achenbaum 1978:91–92).

There have continued to be significant income and poverty differences among older adults in different racial and ethnic groups in the United States. In 1992, older white men had a higher median income than other groups of older people. The poverty rate for older blacks was 33 percent, for Hispanics 22 percent, and for whites 11 percent. There are still gaps in life expectancy at birth among gender and racial groups. In 1991, life expectancy at birth was about 80 years for white females, 74 for black females, 73 for white males, and 65 for black males. In 1994, there were three elderly women for every two older men and five oldest old women for every two oldest old men. Globally, there were four older women for every three older men (U.S. Bureau of the Census 1996:v, vi).

The population age 80 and over is projected to increase substantially as a proportion of the population 65 and over. The oldest subgroup of the older black population is projected to increase from 20.5 percent in 1990 to 29.5 percent in 2050. The oldest subgroup among older adults of Hispanic origin is projected to increase from 19.2 percent to 36 percent, and the proportion of white older adults in the oldest subgroup is projected to increase from 22.6 percent in 1990 to 40.2 percent in 2050 (U.S. Bureau of the Census 1996:2–18).

ATTITUDES ABOUT AGING IN THE UNITED STATES

HISTORICAL PERSPECTIVE

Although the context in which people experience aging has changed since the founding of the United States, the historian Andrew Achenbaum has noted that there are many important meanings and realities of old age that have remained the same. While many of the features of growing old are universal phenomena, Achenbaum has also described old age as having a "dynamic history" (1978:4).

While the way that older Americans have lived and have been described has changed since the late eighteenth century, it has been difficult to reconstruct the history of attitudes toward old age because the necessary material is biased, incomplete, or missing; scholars have handled data and interpreted trends in different ways and reached different conclusions. Achenbaum (1978:5) disagrees with the evolutionary perspective of some who have studied the history of older persons' experiences in the United States, suggesting that the historical record is complex and that the fundamental problem with many existing analyses is that they are based on scant, undigested evidence taken out of its temporal context. He believes that there have been neither "sudden nor radical transformations in conceptions of old age or the elderly's condition during any specific decade(s) or period(s)" (Achenbaum 1978:4, 5).

There does not appear to have been a "golden epoch" in the history of old age, although over time modernization has affected the perceived and actual status of older Americans. Perceptions of their positions and functions since 1790 appear to have been related to definitions of the inherent assets and liabilities of old age and conditions and values prevalent at specific times. In the

United States, old age has always been considered a distinctive phase of the life cycle, and biogerontologists suggest that the human life span has remained the same. However, variations in estimates of the age at which this phase begins existed prior to 1790. Some earlier writers suggested that old age began with a "grand climacteric" at sixty-three (Achenbaum 1978:1, 2, 4, 5).

The contemporary definition of older people's place in society is a striking contrast to the early American definition. Between the Revolutionary and Civil Wars, people in the United States believed that creation of the new society depended upon the commitment and ability of men and women of all ages. Older people were regarded with respect because living a "long and fruitful life" was considered a worthwhile achievement. However, people in the United States did not necessarily prefer old age to other stages, and life was not rewarding for all older people. Nevertheless, exceptin a few state judgeships, there were no structural obstacles such as mandatory retirement impeding the participation of older people in society or social prejudices related to age interfering with the right to employment. It was considered foolish to stop working only because of age, for deterioration in later years was attributed primarily to disuse (Achenbaum 1978).

Achenbaum has identified differences in emphasis before and after the 1830s in views of old age. He suggests that prior to the Civil War, older people were regarded favorably because they were sources of inspiration and consolation; their experiences provided them with insights into the human condition. However, there were changes related to "republican" and "romantic" modes of thought. The former prevailed before the 1830s and recognized disparities among individuals but regarded shared characteristics most highly. Achenbaum has said,

> Believing that certain characteristics of old age made the elderly special, such writers emphasized the ways in which the old contrasted with other people and idealized them because of their distinctiveness. The shift from republican to romantic justifications for the elderly's physical and economic woes ultimately had a profound impact on perceptions of the aged's worth because it made the liabilities of age subject to a less rosy interpretation later in the century. (1978:27, 28)

Achenbaum suggests that there was an important transition in ideas about old age from 1865 to 1914. Increasingly, writers began to describe older people as ugly and disease-ridden rather than stately and healthy. Popular and scientific commentators described them as incapable of contributing anything to society instead of extolling their "moral wisdom and practical sagacity." Achenbaum believes that the increasingly negative attitude "reflected and resulted from the impact of new scientific, bureaucratic, and popular ideas converging with innovations in medical practice, the economic structure, and American society itself" (1978:39, 40).

After World War I, demographic and socioeconomic concerns in the United States were making old age a national problem as well as a personal misfortune. Believing that the plight of older men and women was rapidly becoming more visible and acute and attributing this to contemporary conditions, the government expanded existing means of helping them. The Depression was particularly devastating for the elderly. As a result, there was public and government support for federal legislation to protect people from hardships related to unemployment and growing old. In 1935, the Social Security Act was passed, and federal funds were allocated to enable states to provide assistance for "aged needy individuals" through mandatory programs. The SSA guaranteed income for retired, formerly employed people, their spouses, and the widowed.

Some observers have suggested that the older population has become a much greater burden on society since World War II. Achenbaum has pointed out that this belief rests upon the assumption that when most people reach old age they cannot and/or do not support themselves. In reality, some older persons remain economically independent because they continue to work or have corporate retirement pensions and/or savings. However, since World War II there has been a substantial decline in the proportion of men and women over age 60 who are gainfully employed, and this is true across occupational categories and classifications of race, place of birth, and region. In 1900, about two thirds of all men over age 65 were working, compared to 23.9 percent in 1970. Until 1970, no more than 10 percent of females over 65 were employed outside of the home at any given time. Agriculture provided the greatest employment for men over age 65 and a livelihood for many older women, but these opportunities have declined. While the proportion of all older workers who are professionals has increased, rapid expansion in other areas of the economy has not resulted in a significant concurrent increase in the number of older workers in manufacturing, transportation, communication, trade, and service industries to offset the loss of employment in agriculture. Furthermore, while the employment of women in clerical positions increased during the 1900s, there were few opportunities for older women in this area. The withdrawal of older Americans from the labor force accelerated throughout the century (Achenbaum 1978).

Achenbaum suggests that the major economic factor contributing to the decline in labor force participation has been the development of alternative sources of support for older people, not industry's preference for younger, better-educated workers. "The upsurge in the number of people eligible for Social Security insurance benefits, the rising payment level of these benefits, and the remarkable growth of pension plans and disbursements in both the public and private sectors of the economy have made it financially possible for many older people to afford leisure" (1978:105).

DEVELOPMENT OF CONTEMPORARY ATTITUDES

Reflecting upon metaphors of aging, sociologist Dale Dannefer (1991) has considered the significance of the collective aging of an entire birth cohort. According to Dannefer, both popular and scientific cultural metaphors of collective aging reflect and shape the way that individuals define themselves and think about their own lives. Dannefer suggested that the metaphors currently dominant in Western culture often influence people's lives negatively. Because aging is a complex and multifaceted phenomenon, it is always depicted metaphorically; even when information regarding aging is presented as fact, it is naming nature from the perspective of the scientist's preexisting stock of knowledge (1991).

In addressing metaphors of aging in contemporary Western discourse, Dannefer (1991:156, 157) saw aging in an individualistic cultural context, as something that begins and ends with the individual and is governed by the independent variable, time. The process of aging can also be collective, intergenerational, and intragenerational. Birth cohorts provide a dimension for research on behavioral and social aging. In contrast to the preindustrial orientation toward vertical relations within the family, sustained by the economic importance of inheritance, the concept of collective aging in modern industrialized societies is oriented toward age-grading because of the opportunities for work and mobility. An individual's life chances are tied to those of peers, and peer group relationships remain important throughout much of adulthood.

As modernization occurred in the United States, there was a dramatic decrease in the age differences between spouses. Time spent by men socially began to be organized to a greater extent along age lines, and recent research suggests that employees consider age-grading in organizations to be a very serious matter. Progress in comparison with age peers is a primary axis in evaluation of one's own progress within an organization.

Equally important in consideration of age-peer awareness is the fact that there are a relatively fixed number of age-graded roles in society. For example, there are a limited number of positions available at each level in the corporate hierarchy, a limited number of pension dollars in retirement systems, and a disproportionately small number of widowers among older people. Dannefer (1991:163) stated that "virtually all of our culturally available images of collective aging involve a sense of life as a contest among age peers."

Dannefer (1991) suggested that terms generally related to aging as a collective process are *convoy, contest,* and *tournament. Contest* and *tournament,* terms drawn from sociology of education, imply competition and conflict. *Convoy* suggests noncompetitive relationships and is conceptualized as a remedy against the dominant forces of society. Kahn, Antonucci, and their associates have used this term to describe the dynamic concept of social networks over the life course (Antonucci 1985); a convoy may involve age peers and also people such as one's parents who are not age peers (Dannefer 1991:163, 164).

Dannefer (1991) noted that there are some individuals, including many women, whose life experiences have provided critical distance from the idea of life as a race. Women have had diverse responses to employment opportunities, but their increased participation in the labor force has brought changes in the workplace and in the meaning of job and career. The competitive "dominant cultural metaphors of collective aging" can be contrasted with the metaphors of traditional cultures and also with trends in modern societies. Finally, "culture is not nature, and cultural metaphors are the humanely constructed interpretations of a specific set of sociohistorically specific arrangements" (Dannefer 1991:170).

Barbara Frey Waxman (1999) has described the work of literary gerontologists and novelists, autobiographers, and biographers who have placed dynamic older characters, including themselves, at the center of their works as creators of a "quiet revolution" in the last quarter of the 1900s. These writers have not minimized the difficulties of aging, but in their work old age is portrayed as transforming, passionate, and rooted in the present.

CONCEPTUAL ISSUES IN THEORY DEVELOPMENT ON AGING

Theories of aging have developed within the field of gerontology and in diverse social science disciplines and reflect the interests of these fields. The diversity of aging studies and perspectives has variously been described as a strength and a weakness. Kenyon has called it a major problem in the field, with the result that "far less attention has been paid to the ongoing process of interpreting and integrating these diverse findings in order to arrive at a more comprehensive and systematic understanding of both the processes of aging and the older person" (1988:3).

In contrast, Moody has written that it is impossible to develop an overarching "theory of aging" because aging is inherently multidimensional. Observing that people are multifaceted biological, psychological, social, and spiritual beings, he said that a single theory of aging is unlikely to include all of these areas. Moody (1988:20) considered one of the most serious problems in gerontology to be the question of the relationship between different levels or domains of theory, but has suggested that it is incorrect to assume that the problem of theory construction can be adequately addressed by "a positivist presumption of a 'unified science.'" A more humanistic and self-reflexive approach to social gerontology is necessary in order to address the fragmentation of empirical work, the lack of self-criticism, and the need for a broader historical understanding of social theory and political advocacy. He supported the use of the humanities and social sciences as resources for constructing theories of aging that correspond to fundamental ideas of time, narrative, and development over the life course. Moody recommended that critical theory, as developed by Jurgen Habermas and other sociologists of the Frankfurt School, be used in the development of a more humanistic and self-reflexive approach to social gerontology (Moody 1988:19–20).

Neugarten has suggested that for "the anthropologist and the sociologist, age is a major dimension of social organization. To the psychologist, it is a major dimension by which the individual organizes his life course and interprets his life experience" (1996a:58–59). Birren and Lanum suggested that the psychology of aging "must describe how behavior comes to be organized, how it changes over the adult years, and the conditions under which it becomes disorganized" (1991:113). The compartmentalization of subspecialties within psychology has contributed to the diverse perspectives on aging, and "on one extreme, aging is viewed as the unfolding of a predetermined pattern of changes dictated by the genome that is universal and characteristic of the species. At the other extreme, the adult organism is seen as a product of random events which retains plasticity and potential" (1991:115, 126). Components or contributions from biology, psychology, and the social sciences are necessary in the psychology of aging, but "the past metaphors of psychology do not readily promote an ecological point of view of an evolved species interacting with a social and physical environment to result in different pathways characteristic of old age" (Birren and Lanum 1991:126).

Although gerontology has often been described as atheoretical, Atchley has pointed out that in reality it contains many theories, including many regarding individual aging, that focus on diverse areas including the stages of adult development, stress and coping in later life, caregiving stresses, social isolation, adaptation to role loss, and other areas. Nevertheless, he has said, none of the many existing theories has become an organizing framework of a recognized general theory of individual development and adaptation to aging.

Reflecting upon models and explanations in gerontology existing at the end of the twentieth century, Bengtson, Rice, and Johnson (1999) addressed the questions of what constitutes theory and its importance in developing knowledge about aging, the state of theory in gerontology, the reasons for its devaluation during the late twentieth century, and reasons why researchers and practitioners in gerontology in the twenty-first century should pay more attention to theory development and how they should accomplish this. They defined theory as "*the construction of explicit explanations in accounting for empirical findings,*" emphasizing that the key process is explanation, and added that "the principal use of theory is *to build knowledge and understanding,* in a systematic and cumulative way, so that our empirical efforts will lead to integration of what is already known as well as a guide to what is yet to be learned" (Bengtson, Rice, and Johnson 1999:5). Theoretically based research provides depth of understanding, and theory is useful in integrating and explaining knowledge, making predictions about what is not yet known or observed, and applying and advancing existing knowledge in order to develop interventions to improve human conditions. Nevertheless, Bengtson, Rice, and Johnson believed that many researchers and practitioners in the field of aging seem unconcerned about theories of aging. Bengtson and his colleagues (1991:9) suggested that we have developed many empirical generalizations *describing* aging, but relatively few have been employed in the more fundamental tasks of *understanding* and *explaining* aging.

Addressing the question of why theory development in gerontology had been devalued in the late twentieth century, Bengtson, Rice, and Johnson suggested that this stems from four trends: the failed quest for a "grand theory"; the drive for applications and solutions in gerontology; postmodernist epistemological critiques; and resistance to cross-disciplinary and interdisciplinary investigations in gerontology (1999:10). They believed that contributions of individual studies in gerontology are likely to have little impact without theory.

ASSUMPTIONS IN THEORIES OF AGING

Several psychologists, sociologists, and philosophers have suggested that it is important to examine the assumptions made in aging research (Birren and Schroots 1984; Cole 1983; Eisdorfer 1983; Kenyon 1988; Maddox and Campbell 1985; Marshall 1986; McKee 1982; Philibert 1982). Kenyon (1988:5) suggested that diverse perspectives in the field of aging can lead to different interpretations of phenomena and conclusions about human nature as people become older. Assumptions explicitly or implicitly guide research and therefore should be identified and explicated.

In response to these concerns, Kenyon proposed an interpretation of human nature he called "personal existence," which he believed contains assumptions about human nature that can serve as useful guidelines for synthesizing knowledge and developing theories (1988:3, 6). Not enough attention has been paid to interpreting and integrating diverse research findings on aging; rather, the focus has been on narrowly defined variables such as depression and intelligence. Kenyon's interpretation supports inclusion of the "self-creating aspects of human nature" in theories of aging (Kenyon 1988:13).

Four basic principles of his view are that human beings: are embodied and self-aware; exist in situations and therefore are "fundamentally relational entities who are necessarily involved with other persons and have a physical and social environment"; are intentional creatures who place meaning on things and therefore see their body, the world, and others as "structures of significance"; and "actively constitute their worlds, even as they are constituted *by* that world . . . there is a self-determining, self-creative aspect of human nature" (Kenyon 1988:6–7).

Kenyon's "personal existence" perspective was influenced by Riegel's (1973, 1976) view of adult intellectual competence, based on a changing person in a changing environment and emphasizing more context-specific claims about concrete actions of individuals in a concrete social world. Riegel saw person and environment as changeable through physical, psychological, and social interventions and believed that development occurs through the *asynchronies*, which create crises and catastrophes for individuals and society among four *progressive* life events: an inner, biological progression in which individuals gain significance in society's normative, age-graded system, including maturation and sensorimotor deficiencies in later life; an outer, physical progression involving such events as accidents and death of a spouse; dimensions of individual psychological and sociocultural progressions that affect an individual's *readiness* to interact in society; and different societal expectations at different points in the life cycle and at different historical periods. Riegel, concerned with social competence and human development, believed that there is no smooth transition from one stage to the next in the interaction between the person and the social context, and no single prescribed route.

Kenyon identified an additional idea of psychosocial competence that is compatible with the assumptions of "personal existence." Thomae's (1980) perspective emphasized process-centered approaches to the understanding of competence. This view is compatible with Riegel's through Thomae's argument that "the emphasis on the notion of equilibrium or homeostasis may be useful as a guideline in certain situations, but it leads to the danger of assuming that there is a *modal adjustment pattern* that one must live up to in order to be considered competent." Older people may mistakenly be seen as deficient or incompetent if they do not function in a manner consistent with this pattern. According to Thomae (1980), people are capable of "*cognitive restructuri*ngs that are related to adaptation to situations but do not reflect achievement activity, external adaptation to institutions, and/or aggression," and they develop competency strategies that reflect genuine choices (Kenyon 1988:12).

Kenyon believed that there is a contradiction between the linear and unidirectional way that the life span is divided into "boxes" of education, work, and retirement, and the reality of many people's experiences "outside of the box," such as early retirement. His perspective has two major implications for intervention in policy, research, treatment, and education in the field of aging: it is important to be cautious in making generalizations about older people, and therefore greater emphasis should be placed on critical thinking and the personal existence perspective in training researchers and practitioners; and besides accommodating needs for services such as medical care and pensions, which are associated with losses related to age, policies need to be developed that will "facilitate the expression of the self-creating aspects of human nature throughout the life span," possibly preventing some of the losses (Kenyon 1988:14, 15).

Birren and Lanum (1991) have suggested that psychology's exploration of aging was delayed because many questions that did not have clearly quantifiable external referents were avoided in the field's attempt to be a science under the influence of logical positivism. Personal and cultural factors also contribute to avoidance of the study of aging, as researchers and providers may see aging as something to be feared. Birren and Lanum pointed out that in our future-oriented society, it is easier to identify with earlier developmental stages than with later periods when the probability of dying increases and individuals are reminded of their own mortality. The unknown is threatening, and denial of and misperceptions about aging are relatively common.

GERONTOLOGICAL THEORIES OF OLDER ADULT DEVELOPMENT

During the 1900s, numerous theories regarding physical, psychological, and social changes in middle and late adulthood were developed by gerontologists, sociologists, psychologists, and scholars in the field of education, as well as by anthropologists and historians. Some of the earliest studies, including the psychologist G. Stanley Hall's *Senescence*, published in 1922, examined premodern models of aging. Psychological perspectives included Jung's idea that there is increased introversion during the later life stages as well as the reorganization of value systems, and Erik Erikson's theory that the psychosocial crisis of integrity versus despair occurs in later adulthood. Neugarten and her colleagues' work, beginning in the 1950s, suggested that there is a shift from an outer-world orientation in middle age to an inner-world orientation, or increased "interiority," in old age (1985:365, 366). In their "grand" theory, grounded in biology and Erikson's epigenetic principle and derived from data from one of several longitudinal studies, Cumming and Henry (1961) argued that inevitable waning of physical and psychic energy initiates individual withdrawal from relationships and that this is reinforced by societal recognition that roles and resources need to be distributed to younger members. Successful disengagement is perceived as resulting in mutual satisfaction because this mutual withdrawal is personally and socially desirable. In response to "disengagement theory," other researchers adopted the perspective of "activity theory," and some responded that "the fact of disengagement and its outcomes varied within and between societies; maintaining continuity of lifestyles, whether engaged or disengaged over the adult years, was more likely to be the fact and more likely to produce a tolerable outcome" (Busse and Maddox 1985:121). Contrasting with disengagement theory but also offering broad generalizations about the functioning of older adults, activity theory assumed that older persons' sense of life satisfaction will be greater if individuals' activity level is greater.

Lieberman and Falk (1971), Tobin and Etigson (1968), and others built upon Butler's (1963) concepts of life review to study reminiscence, and have said that middle-aged people consciously select from past experiences in order to solve problems in the present; older people, in contrast, "put their store of memories in order, as it were, dramatizing some and striving for consistency in others, perhaps as a way of preparing an ending for the life history" (Neugarten 1985:366).

The following sections provide an overview of theories of aging developed through the work of interdisciplinary research teams involved in longitudinal studies and by individual psychologists, sociologists, and scholars in the field of education, based upon research and/or practice.

DISENGAGEMENT THEORY AND LIFE SPAN DEVELOPMENTAL THEORY: KANSAS CITY STUDIES

Disengagement theory, developed by Elaine Cumming and William Henry as a universal theory of human aging, proved highly controversial. Cumming and Henry belonged to a group of social scientists who began their work at the University of Chicago in the 1940s and participated in the interdisciplinary Committee on Human Development, which conducted the Kansas City Studies of Adult Life, longitudinal studies of older adults. One of the Kansas City studies included a cross-section of more than 700 women and men in the community who were between the ages of 40 and 70 and were from all socioeconomic levels, and a second included another group of about 300 people between the ages of 50 and 90 who were interviewed over a 6-year period. At various times, the Chicago group of researchers included Bernice Neugarten, Robert Havighurst, William Henry, Ernest Burgess, Everett Hughes, Martin Loeb, Robert Peck, Warren Peterson, David Riesman, Ethel Shanas, Sheldon Tobin, W. Lloyd Warner, Elaine Cumming, Richard Williams, and David Gutmann. Their studies included social and psychological research issues related to successful aging, personality patterns, adaptational patterns, the meaning of work and retirement in various occupational groups, intergenerational families, disengagement, and engagement.

In *Growing Old: The Process of Disengagement* (1961), Cumming and Henry presented a formal statement of disengagement theory that they described as provisional. They examined ideas about "successful aging," suggesting that a person is a "successful ager" if "she has competently disengaged from the bonds of earlier relations and has done so in good spirits" (1961:184). Their definition of *disengagement* was "an inevitable process in which many of the relationships between a person and other members of society are severed, and those remaining are altered in quality" (1961:211). Cumming and Henry's disengagement theory was based on nine postulates:

Postulate 1: Although individuals differ, the expectation of death is universal, and decrement of ability is probable. Therefore, a mutual severing of ties will take place between a person and others in his society. . . .

Postulate 2: Because interactions create and reaffirm norms, a reduction in the number or variety of interactions leads to an increased freedom from the control of the norms governing everyday behavior. Consequently, once begun, disengagement becomes a circular, or self-perpetuating process. . . .

Postulate 3: Because the central role of men in American society is instrumental, and the central role of women is socio-emotional, the process of disengagement will differ between men and women. . . .

Postulate 4: The life cycle of the individual is punctuated by ego changes—for example, aging is usually accompanied by decrements in knowledge and skill. At the same time, success in an industrialized society is based on knowledge and skill, and age-grading is a mechanism used to ensure that the young are sufficiently well trained to assume authority and the old are retired before they lose skill. Disengagement in America may be initiated by either the individual because of ego changes or by the society because of organizational imperatives, or by both simultaneously. . . .

Postulate 5: When both the individual and society are ready for disengagement, completed disengagement results. When neither is ready, continuing engagement results. When the individual is ready and society is not, a disjunction between the expectations of the individual and the members of his social system results, but usually engagement continues. When society is ready and the individual is not, the result of the disjunction is usually disengagement. . . .

Postulate 6: Because the abandonment of life's central roles—work for men, marriage and family for women—results in a dramatically reduced social life space, it will result in crisis and loss of morale unless different roles, appropriate to the disengaged state, are available. . . .

Postulate 7: (a) If the individual becomes sharply aware of the shortness of life and the scarcity of time remaining to him . . . and if he perceives his life space as decreasing . . . and if his available ego energy is lessened . . . then readiness for disengagement has begun. . . .

Postulate 8: The reductions in interaction and the loss of central roles result in a shift in the quality of relationship in the remaining roles. . . . There is a wider choice of relational rewards, and a shift from vertical solidarities to horizontal ones. . . .

Postulate 9: Disengagement is a culture-free concept, but the form it takes will always be culture-bound. (1961:211–18)

The original presentation of disengagement theory was based on findings in the Kansas City studies regarding intrapsychic psychological changes, and it was postulated that decrease in social interaction is characterized by mutuality between society and individuals as they became older. People were believed to withdraw from earlier activities because of decreased emotional involvement in the activities. People who have disengaged were considered to psychologically have a sense of well-being and high life satisfaction (Cumming and Henry 1961).

Bernice Neugarten and some of the other researchers in the Chicago group were uncomfortable with the idea that in old age the disengaged person has a sense of psychological well-being and high life satisfaction. They devised new measures of social interaction and psychological well-being and found that people who were socially active and involved were more often those experiencing high life satisfaction. Additionally, there was diversity in the responses that could not be accounted for by disengagement theory. A set of empirically derived personality types was worked out to account for the diversity (Neugarten 1996a:274). Neugarten and Havighurst (1996:293) suggested that part of the difference between Cumming and Henry's findings and their own in interpretation of the Kansas City data resulted from the fact that Cumming and Henry based their analysis on interviews conducted over a period of four years, while Neugarten, Havighurst, and Tobin based theirs on data gathered over six years. Additionally, Cumming and Henry based their interpretation on three social roles used to measure social interaction and on a Morale Index as a measure of psychological well-being; in contrast, the Havighurst, Neugarten, and Tobin analysis utilized ratings of performance in twelve social roles as a measure of social interaction and a set of ratings on life satisfaction as the measure of psychological well-being (Neugarten and Havighurst 1996:293).

Neugarten and her colleagues who questioned disengagement theory believed that the data revealed consistent age-related differences in the ways people see themselves in relation to their environment, an intrapsychic change that reflects consistent age differences in the movement from active to passive mastery. They also described a process of increased "interiority," a greater preoccupation with the inner life rather than the environment. In contrast, however, age was not significant in relation to socio-adaptational variables, such as those in Erikson's concepts of ego development or variables related to adaptive, goal-directed, and purposive behavior.

Activity theory was another general point of view in social psychology regarding optimum patterns of aging that did not reflect the diversity of successful aging experiences. According to Havighurst, Neugarten, and Tobin (1996:281), activity theory implied that older people are the same as middle-aged people except for changes in biology and health, and assumed that they have basically the same psychological and social needs. Furthermore, aging men and women were assumed to desire the same amount of social interaction as in middle age, and decreased interaction was assumed to result from society's withdrawal from older people. People were believed to age optimally when they remain active, maintaining activities pursued in middle age for as long as possible and finding substitutes for activities unavoidably given up (Havighurst, Neugarten, and Tobin 1996:281). Psychological well-being was not related to age (Neugarten 1996a:272).

In terms of interaction with others, there did seem to be a long-term decrease with age in the amount of daily interaction, performance in various life roles, and ego investment in present social roles, but there did not seem to be dramatic discontinuities before the late sixties. Neugarten believed that intrapsychic changes in middle and later life were not necessarily synchronous with changes in social interaction or psychological well-being. She and her colleagues demonstrated that people have different patterns of growing old and "age in ways that are consistent with their earlier life histories." In a relatively supportive social environment, people of all ages will choose combinations of activities, compatible with established value patterns and self-concept, that offer the most ego involvement. In adapting to biological and social changes, the elderly person will draw upon the past as well as the present (Neugarten 1996a).

Focusing on the second half of life, Neugarten (1996a:272) and her colleagues studied, over a 6-year period, personality changes associated with age in two groups: one of more than 700 relatively healthy men and women, ages 40 to 70, from all social status levels, who were leading normal lives in the community; and about 300 people ages 50 to 90. Successive samples were selected from this pool. The researchers found age differences in covert or intrapsychic areas, supporting the idea of movement from active to passive mastery as aging occurs. Their findings also indicated that people move toward increased interiority, greater preoccupation with inner rather than external events. In contrast, when Neugarten and colleagues considered socio-adaptational variables, including Erikson's concepts related to ego development, as well as psychological well-being, age was not significant and older people demonstrated "different capacities to cope with life stresses and to come to terms with their life situations" (Neugarten 1996a:272).

Neugarten and her colleagues also studied age status, age norms, and age expectations, since they believed that these provide the cultural context for a person's evaluation of his or her lifetime. In a sample of 600 middle-aged and older people, they found that in spite of the fact that changes in age roles are not synchronous in social institutions in modern industrial society, there was widespread agreement in perceptions of role changes occupationally, in the family life cycle, in health, in psychological attributes, and in social responsibilities in young adulthood, maturity, middle age, and old age. In several studies in which participants were asked about their actual experiences in the timing of major life events, there were striking similarities between the experiences and the norms, and the researchers suggested that the norms seemed to function as a system of social control (Neugarten 1996a:276–78). The same general patterns were found in studies with other groups of respondents, including men and women in their twenties living in a small city in the Midwest, middle-class African Americans in a medium-sized city in the Midwest, and people in their 70s in a small New England town (Neugarten 1996a:276–78).

Findings in a six-year study indicated that neither disengagement theory nor activity theory adequately described the experiences of the participants. Havighurst, Neugarten, and Tobin (1996:264) found a positive correlation between the extent of social interaction and psychological well-being, greatest for persons seventy and over. The relationship between life satisfaction and activity level was not consistent, however, as there were older persons with a low level of activity who had high life satisfaction and some with high levels of activity but low satisfaction.

Neugarten, Havighurst, and Tobin decided to study differences in personality when it appeared that there were people with certain personality types who were able to "disengage with relative comfort and who remain highly contented with life." Some of the other participants experienced a great deal of discomfort in disengaging, and their life satisfaction diminished. Other participants had experienced low levels of role activity for a long time but had been satisfied, and there was not very much change as they became older. The researchers concluded that "In this view, then, personality becomes the important variable—the fulcrum around which the other variables are organized" (Havighurst, Neugarten, and Tobin 1996:264, 266).

After 6 years, about 60 percent of the original study participants remained. These included 59 who were between ages 70 and 79, 50 of whom fell into one of the 8 patterns of aging identified by the researchers. The patterns were based on an ego psychology model and included "integrated," "armored or defended," "passive-dependent," and "unintegrated" personality types. The researchers further divided these groups according to role activity score and life satisfaction ratings, resulting in 8 patterns (Havighurst, Neugarten, and Tobin 1996:264–65).

People with *integrated* personalities were described as "well-functioning persons who have a complex inner life and at the same time, intact cognitive abilities and competent egos. These persons are accepting of impulse life, over which they maintain a comfortable degree of control; they are flexible; open to new stimuli; mellow, mature. All these individuals, it appears, were high in life satisfaction. At the same time, they were divided with regard to amount of role activity" (Havighurst, Neugarten, and Tobin 1996:264–65).

The researchers identified three subgroups with integrated personalities. One group, "reorganizers," were described as "the competent people engaged in a wide variety of activities. They are the optimum agers in some respects—at least in the American culture, where there is high value placed on 'staying young, staying active, and refusing to grow old.' These are persons who substitute new activities for lost ones; who, when they retire from work, give time to community affairs or to church or to other associations. They reorganize their patterns of activity" (Havighurst, Neugarten, and Tobin 1996:266).

A second subgroup was referred to as "focused." These were people with medium levels of activity and high satisfaction. "They have become selective in their activities, with time, and they now devote energy to, and gain their major satisfaction from, one or two role areas" (Havighurst, Neugarten, and Tobin 1996:267).

The third subgroup was referred to as "disengaged," with low activity and high satisfaction; "persons who have voluntarily moved away from role commitments, not in response to external losses or physical deficits, but because of preference. These are self-directed persons, not shallow, with an interest in the world, but an interest that is not embedded in a network of social interactions. They have high feelings of self-regard, just as do the first two groups mentioned, but they have chosen what might be called a 'rocking-chair' approach to old age—a calm, withdrawn, but contented pattern" (Havighurst, Neugarten, and Tobin 1996:267).

The second personality type was described as *armored* or *defended*. They were "the striving, ambitious, achievement-oriented personalities, with high defenses against anxiety and with the need to maintain tight controls over impulse life." The two subgroups of aging within this personality type were "holding-on" and "constricted." The first was "the group to whom aging constitutes a threat and who respond by holding on, as long as possible, to the patterns of their middle age. They are quite successful in their attempts, and thus maintain high life satisfaction with medium or high activity levels." The other group, with the constricted pattern, were described as "busily defending themselves against aging; preoccupied with losses and deficits; dealing with these threats by constricting their social interactions and their energies and by closing themselves off from experience. They seem to structure their worlds to keep off what they regard as imminent collapse; and while this constriction results in low role activity, it works fairly well, given their personality pattern, to keep them high or medium in life satisfaction" (Havighurst, Neugarten, and Tobin 1996:267).

The third personality type was described as *passive-dependent.* One of its subgroups was "succorance-seeking," people with strong dependence needs who seek others to meet their emotional needs. They maintained medium activity levels and life satisfaction. "These are also 'rocking-chair' people, but with very different personality structures from those called 'the disengaged.' The second subgroup is apathetic, seen in persons in whom aging has probably reinforced long-standing patterns of passivity and apathy" (Havighurst, Neugarten, and Tobin 1996:267).

The fourth personality type was referred to as *unintegrated.* These were "persons who had gross defects in psychological functions, loss of control over emotions and deterioration in thought processes." These individuals were low in role activity and life satisfaction. Their pattern of aging is disorganized (Havighurst, Neugarten, and Tobin 1996:268).

Neugarten and colleagues' empirical research supported the idea of a personality-continuity or developmental theory of aging rather than the activity and disengagement theories. They concluded that people are not at the mercy of either the social environment or intrinsic processes as they age; rather, "the individual seems to continue to make his own 'impress' upon the wide range of social and physical changes. He continues to exercise choice and to select from the environment in accordance with his own long-established needs. He ages according to a pattern that has a long history and that maintains itself, with adaptation, to the end of life. . . . Those characteristics that have been central to the personality seem to become even more clearly delineated, and those values the individual has been cherishing become even more salient" (Havighurst, Neugarten, and Tobin 1996:267–68).

NORMAL AGING: DUKE LONGITUDINAL STUDIES

The Duke Longitudinal Studies also addressed issues raised by Cumming and Henry's disengagement theory, but focused on the differences in the social characteristics of adults of the same chronological age and the continuation of these differences. A University Council on Aging was founded in 1955 at Duke University, and by 1957, Duke was chosen by the National Institutes of Health as a regional center for the study of aging. Four distinctive ideas were important components of studies there: a multidisciplinary perspective, distinguishing primary from secondary processes of aging, longitudinal observation of individuals in order to study aging as a process, and a firm institutional commitment to the systematic study of aging (Busse and Maddox 1985:3, 4).

In 1955, the Duke Longitudinal Studies began "to explore and illustrate the potential and limits of the contribution of multidisciplinary, longitudinal research to the scientific understanding of human aging," with specific objectives "for the development of a theoretical perspective, methodology, and the organization of multidisciplinary, longitudinal research." The idea was to design research in which the interaction over time of biomedical, behavioral, and social factors in aging processes in natural settings could be studied. The primary initial interest of the Duke Longitudinal Studies was a systematic description of aging processes, with particular attention to the identification and interaction of a broad range of individual and social variables that could influence them. The proposed longitudinal research design was to permit description of individual change over time and interpersonal differences and differential patterns of change (Busse and Maddox 1985:4–8).

While a "master theory" of human aging has not been developed, investigators attracted to the Duke Longitudinal Studies tended to share a theoretical perspective on aging as a process of interaction between person and environment, not explainable by biological theory alone. The Duke researchers suggested that because of this interaction, it was necessary to differentiate *primary aging*, described as developmental changes in the later years that are universal in a benign environment, and *secondary aging*, the response of older persons to environmental influences. They noted that the quality of the environment must be considered because poverty, ignorance, isolation, or the standard of living in an underdeveloped country could adversely affect the experience of being old.

Because the Duke researchers perceived aging experiences to be diverse, they focused on aging within the broader community, rather than within institutions. This was also consistent with their interest in *normal* aging, as opposed to experiences in older age likely to be caused by disease. Primary and secondary aging processes observed in the longitudinal study may also be time-bound and culture-specific. Busse and Maddox (1985:5) suggested retrospectively that *normative* may be a preferable term to *normal*.

The sample of the first Duke Longitudinal Study was made up of noninstitutionalized persons aged 60 to 94, with a mean age of 70.8 for those in the initial phase and a mean age of 85.2 at the time of the last observation. Eleven observations of surviving panelists were completed over the next 21 years, gathering data from physical, psychological, and social examinations. The study began with 270 people; 260 in the first round of observations and 10 more who were added in the second round. The time between examinations diminished as the research continued, and in 1976 the final round of observations of 44 subjects was made. Fifty-two percent of the participants in the final observation were female, and 63.8 percent were white.

A second longitudinal study was begun in 1968 after the first study had established the significance of a range of variables and their dynamic interaction over time. It included an age- and sex-stratified sample of 502 persons whose age range was 45 to 69 and included panelists drawn from the membership list of the major health insurance association in the area and a subsample aged 65 to 69 from the record files of the Duke Medical Center. People who were illiterate, institutionalized, or homebound were excluded because it was believed that they would not be able to participate in all of the exams, and African Americans were excluded because "their inclusion in a relatively small total sample would have made adequate statistical analysis by race impossible" (Busse and Maddox 1985:20).

The second study took into consideration the methodological implications of the age/period/cohort problem (APC), which emerged in research in the field of aging in the mid-1960s. According to Busse and Maddox, "The heart of the APC problem is the recognition that in research on aging processes, chronological age, the time of measurement (i.e., the exogenous environmental variables impinging on individuals), and the location in a cohort (i.e., individuals with potentially different historical experience related to the environments in which they were born and reared) are typically confounded" (1985:7). This study was designed to cover six years so that subjects in a number of five-year age cohorts would move from one age category to another.

The second study had two distinctive characteristics, according to Busse and Maddox (1985:7, 8). First, it focused on adaptation to major life events such as retirement, illness, and widowhood that challenge individuals. People adapt differentially depending on availability of physiological, psychological, and social supports. Second, it included several ancillary studies, involving examination of the central nervous system through the psychophysiological aspects of cognition, cerebral lateralization, cerebral blood flow, and brain morphology at autopsy; exploration of the personal meaning of life events; and studying and refining methodology of studies on the complex interaction of variables in the aging process. Physical, social, and psychological data were collected 4 times through 1976. The major reason for attrition in the second study was refusal to continue (15 percent) rather than death (10 percent), a difference from the first study, in which 79 percent of the subjects were dead by round 11—a reflection of the older ages of the participants.

In both studies, about a thousand variables and indices were coded for each person, and a cross-sequential design was utilized to separate out the effects of age, period, and cohort. The studies provided substantial information that contributed to the understanding of social factors in aging. Social history was an integral component of the research, and data gathered included information on social and demographic characteristics, interpersonal relationships, kinship, work, and perceived well-being. The Duke studies focused on person-environment interaction in order to understand human aging processes. The studies also responded to major issues in the sociology of aging as well as the broad field of social gerontology, focusing on disengagement in later life as an adaptive process; age stratification; the succession of age cohorts; potentially stressful effects of normative role transitions and of social change in later life; and the factors that predict successful adaptation to these changes (Busse and Maddox 1985:120). The research problems as well as the research design were influenced by these theoretical issues.

For most of the participants in both of the Duke studies, levels of social interaction tended to decrease in many, but not all, activities. However, many subjects maintained, redirected, or increased their social activity as they aged. The total number of people in social networks tended to remain constant. Disengagement, defined as the sense of substantial or total social isolation and inactivity, was rare. For example, church attendance tended to increase through the sixties and level off in the seventies, only afterward appearing to decline. In addition, although the majority of the participants decreased their sexual activity, generally because of widowhood or declining health, over the years that they participated in the study, a substantial minority maintained or increased their sexual activity.

The decision to stop working generally did not have negative effects on health, adjustment, and life satisfaction. Involuntary retirement, however, did tend to affect life satisfaction negatively, while return to work tended to affect participants positively. The findings suggested that a person's attitude toward work and ways of compensating for the loss of full-time employment are more important than the fact of retirement (Busse and Maddox 1985:125).

Busse and Maddox summarized additional findings as follows:

1. There was clear evidence that various forms of activity tend to contribute to, and predict, better health, happiness, and longevity.
2. The strongest social activity predictors of health and happiness were (a) continuation of leisure activities; (b) secondary group activities; (c) interactions with people; and (d) total quantity of social activity.
3. Greater longevity among men was predicted by work satisfaction and group activity.
4. Changes in family composition and relationships (often widowhood) was associated with poorer health and unhappiness for middle-aged adults, but not for the older adults.
5. Maintenance of sexual activity was associated with better health and happiness and related to longevity for both men and women in their 50s and 60s.
6. Children leaving home did not typically produce long-term negative effects, and the last child leaving resulted in increased life satisfaction and happiness for both parents.
7. Children and friends living nearby is associated for women with maintaining life satisfaction.
8. Number of friends is associated with better health, but not longevity. (1985:125, 126)

These data showed that the second basic hypothesis of disengagement is not true. Activity, not disengagement, predicts better life satisfaction, health, and longevity. It was also postulated that those least integrated in social networks have been relatively isolated over a period of years. Maintaining a preferred lifestyle, whether disengaged or active, was believed to be the crucial issue.

Data from the Duke studies suggested that negative stereotypes of older persons should be viewed with caution and are probably more wrong than right, at least in the United States. In these studies the characteristics of the participants were quite varied, and the variations continued as they aged. Furthermore, the studies presented a relatively positive image of the lives of working-class and middle-class adults, and the researchers anticipated that the physical, behavioral, and social profile of adult cohorts age sixty-five and over in the future would be better due to higher educational levels; a decrease in poverty; declining smoking and consumption of high-cholesterol diets and salt; increased physical activity; and increased availability of medical care (Busse and Maddox 1985:128, 129).

SUCCESSFUL AGING: THE MACARTHUR FOUNDATION STUDY

The MacArthur Foundation Study focused on the issues of what it means to age successfully, what each person can do to achieve this, and what changes in the United States will enable more people to age successfully. According to Rowe and Kahn (1998:xi), prior to this study, researchers in the field had become preoccupied with disease, disability, and chronological age, and also seriously underestimated the influence of lifestyle and other psychosocial factors on the well-being of older people. They suggest that in the mid-1980s progress in the field of gerontology began to stall because it lacked the broad conceptual background necessary to understand the biological, psychological, and social aspects of aging.

The goal of the MacArthur Foundation Study was to conduct a long-term research project to gather knowledge needed to improve the physical and mental abilities of older adults in the United States. The study was rooted in the researchers' idea of "successful aging," conceptualized as the factors permitting individuals to function effectively physically and mentally in old age. They emphasized positive aspects of aging and wanted to move beyond a limited chronological perspective to clarify genetic, biomedical, behavioral, and social factors responsible for retaining and enhancing functioning in later life. Their definition of successful aging was "the ability to maintain the key behaviors or characteristics of low risk of disease and disease-related disability; high mental and physical function; and active engagement with life" (Rowe and Kahn 1998:xii, 38).

The projects conducted by a research network of sixteen biological and social scientists included a major study of more than a thousand high-functioning older people that continued for eight years. In addition, there were studies focused on hundreds of pairs of Swedish twins in order to identify the contributions of genetics and lifestyle, laboratory-based studies of stress, studies of the aging of the brain in humans and animals, and dozens of individual research projects. Rowe and Kahn believe that the MacArthur Foundation Study contributed strongly to a rapid reorientation toward "successful aging" as a major theme of the "new gerontology" (1998:xiii). The findings of these projects, supported by data from other research, refute the following six myths about the elderly that are familiar in the United States (1998:11).

MYTH #1: TO BE OLD IS TO BE SICK. In the contemporary United States, chronic illnesses are much more prevalent than acute, infectious illnesses. In *Successful Aging* (1998), Rowe and Kahn write that in this country the most common illnesses experienced by older people now include arthritis (about half of older persons), hypertension and heart disease (one third), diabetes (11 percent), hearing disorders and other disorders affecting communication (32 percent), cataracts (17 percent), and other vision impairment (9 percent). Furthermore, from 1982 to 1989, the prevalence of arthritis, arteriosclerosis, dementia, hypertension, stroke, and emphysema, as well as the average number of diseases an older person has, decreased significantly. They add that there has been a dramatic reduction in high blood pressure, high cholesterol levels, and smoking, which are all precursors of chronic disease, when data for sixty-five- to seventy-four-year-old individuals are compared for 1960 and 1990.

Rowe and Kahn (1998) point out, furthermore, that what is most important is how diseases affect a person's ability to function, not the number and type of diseases they have. Individuals' ability to remain independent is generally assessed by their ability to manage their own personal and nonpersonal care. According to Rowe and Kahn, sixty-five-year-old men have a life expectancy of fifteen more years, twelve of which will probably be spent with fully independent functioning; at age eighty-five they are likely to be inactive or dependent about half of their remaining years. Women age sixty-five are likely to live almost nineteen more years and be active and independent almost fourteen of those years.

MYTH #2: YOU CAN'T TEACH AN OLD DOG NEW TRICKS. Encouraging research in the MacArthur Study has refuted this myth by demonstrating that older people can and do learn new things.

MYTH #3: THE HORSE IS OUT OF THE BARN. Rowe and Kahn (1998:22, 23) assert that it is possible to reduce risk and promote health in old age and even sometimes to increase functioning beyond a person's prior level.

MYTH #4: THE SECRET TO SUCCESSFUL AGING IS TO CHOOSE YOUR PARENTS WISELY. This myth assumes that the rate at which bodily functions decline with age is the result of heredity, but the MacArthur twin studies indicated that while genes and aging are connected in a meaningful way, the role of genetics is tremendously overstated. Rowe and Kahn suggest that similarities within families may be related more to shared conditions such as diet than to genes and that heredity influences aging the most through genetic diseases that can shorten life. The MacArthur projects showed that environment and lifestyle had a powerful impact on the likelihood of developing a mental or physical disorder in all but the diseases that are most strongly determined genetically.

MYTH #5: THE LIGHTS MAY BE ON, BUT THE VOLTAGE IS LOW. The data reflected tremendous individual differences, although they indicated that sexual activity tends to decrease with age. Chronological age was not demonstrated to be the critical factor. Researchers found that cultural norms, health or illness, and availability of a partner were more significant variables.

MYTH #6: THE ELDERLY DON'T PULL THEIR OWN WEIGHT. It is now illegal to "force people to retire solely because of their age, and millions of older men and women are ready, willing, and able to work." Older workers often "meet or surpass expectations, and may bring increased insight and experience to the workplace" (Rowe and Kahn 1998:34–35).

Rowe and Kahn state that the MacArthur Studies and others demonstrate that "older people are much more likely to age well than to become decrepit and dependent" and that an optimistic "vision of aging" holds true (1998:14, 17). They suggest that because of information from these studies and other research it is possible to identify lifestyle and personality factors that increase the chance of successful aging. Rowe and Kahn describe their main message as the belief that we "can have a dramatic impact on our own success or failure in aging" (1998:18), but they add that what people can do for themselves depends to some extent on opportunities and constraints in the form of attitudes and expectations regarding older adults, as well as on social policies.

CONTINUITY THEORY: OHIO LONGITUDINAL STUDY OF AGING

In *Continuity and Adaptation in Aging: Creating Positive Experiences* (1999), Robert Atchley describes the findings and implications of the Ohio Longitudinal Study of Aging and Adaptation (OLSAA), which was conducted in an Ohio town from 1975 to 1995 to study people as they went through the retirement transition. The project began with more than 1,000 people who were age 50 or over, and more than 300 were still participating at its conclusion.

The subjects were surveyed in 1975, 1977, 1979, and 1981 through a grant from the National Institute of Mental Health and in 1991 and 1995 with funding from the Ohio Long-Term Care Research Project and the Scripps Gerontology Center of Miami University in Oxford, Ohio. At these intervals, the participants were interviewed and given questionnaires to gather the following information:

1. inner psychological framework of beliefs, attitudes, values, goals, motives, emotions, and temperament
2. external social frameworks that made up their lifestyle
3. household composition
4. marital status
5. number of children
6. occupation
7. employment status
8. leisure activities
9. community involvement
10. involvement with family and friends
11. race
12. gender
13. religious affiliation
14. education
15. health and disability
16. financial resources
17. retirement
18. widowhood (Atchley 1999:viii)

There were positive and negative changes over time in adult development, aging, and adaptation, and the findings indicated that the overwhelming majority adapted well to changes. The longitudinal data were used to identify areas of continuity and stability as well as ways in which the study participants experienced discontinuity. They were also used to look at adaptation to change ranging from gradual and minor physical changes to profound disability; minor swings in morale and motivation to a sharp downturn in mood; minor shifts in social roles to complete disengagement; and minor changes in social support networks to sharp reductions in the size of social networks (Atchley 1999:ix).

In *Continuity and Adaptation in Aging*, Atchley describes continuity theory, examines its major tenets through consideration of data from the OLSAA, and shows how it can be used. He developed continuity theory to meet the need for an organizing framework within gerontology, believing that the theory, based on empirical findings, would show that the majority of aging adults maintain physical, psychological, and social well-being as well as satisfying relationships and lifestyles in a often antagonistic, youth-oriented society. Atchley (2000:vii) believes that people learn continuously from life experiences and evolve in ways of their own choosing. *Continuity theory* explains the importance of continuity of ideas and lifestyle to adult development in midlife and later. He saw continuity as a common coping strategy of people faced with changes in middle and later life. Older adults show consistent patterns over time in cognition, activity, lifestyles, and social relationships.

Acknowledging that aging undeniably brings change, Atchley sees continuity as the most prevalent form of adaptation and believes that continuity and change exist simultaneously. The task then becomes achieving balance between them at various points over time and life transitions. Both continuity and change are matters of degree. Atchley further believes that it is important to assess the degree to which people are motivated by the desire for continuity in making life, especially age-related, changes. He identifies two patterns of continuity: lack of change and minor changes within general patterns. In contrast, in patterns of discontinuity, there are dramatic shifts such as cessation of an activity, which involves significant departures from, not minor fluctuations within, past patterns (Atchley 2000:1–4).

Atchley describes continuity as feedback systems theory, a theory of continuous evolution. It posits that an initial pattern influences behavioral choices or decisions, and these in turn influence the nature of life experience. Through life experience, people evaluate, refine, or revise their initial pattern, their orientation, and also evaluate, refine, or revise their process of making choices regarding behavior. Continuity theory focuses on global internal mental frameworks including the self, personal goals, or belief systems, and external frameworks including lifestyles, networks of social relationships, and activity profiles. Adults make effective decisions based on their lifetime of experience involving their concept of the world and how it works, their own strengths and weaknesses, their capabilities, and their likes and dislikes.

Continuity theory, Atchley believes, is constructivist in its assumption that people develop individualized personal constructs in response to life experiences; it assumes that social constructions of reality from others, including the media, influence our personal constructs but are not determined by them. People are free to make their own decisions about their personal reality. An important implication of this theory is that subjective perceptions of continuity are as theoretically relevant as researchers' perceptions of objective continuity. Continuity theory also includes the development and maintenance of adaptive capacity as a result of long-term evolution and the construction and use of enduring patterns to enhance life satisfaction and adaptation to change. Atchley adds that most people, with diverse personality types and lifestyle patterns, adapt successfully (Atchley 1999:7).

Continuity theory provides a conceptual way of organizing the search for coherence in life stories and of understanding the dynamics that produce basic story lines, but it has no ideology concerning which stories are right or successful (Atchley 2000:7). Atchley believes that internal continuity represents the maintenace of consistent frameworks of ideas about the self and the world. External continuity represents consistency over time of social roles, activities, living arrangements, and relationships. Personal goals defined an ideal self and lifestyle based on individual values. Adaptive capacity can be assessed by the degree to which morale is maintained in the face of discontinuity (Atchley 1999:154–55).

Atchley did not develop continuity theory as a theory of successful aging or as a deterministic theory predicting specific outcomes. It does not predict that successful adaptation will result from using a continuity strategy but assumes that continuity is the first adaptive strategy of most people. The results may not be positive; evidence indicates that even those with low self-esteem, abusive relationships, and poor social adaptation resist the idea of abandoning their internal and external frameworks. Apparently, the familiar is preferable to the unknown future. Thus, although positive feedback loops may produce positive change, negative feedback loops can produce disorder.

The basic ideas of continuity theory are supported by data from the study, which provide evidence that continuity strategies are generally effective. Atchley (2000:158) suggests that continuity theory has promise as a framework useful in explaining how a majority of people experience aging positively and as a gentle slope, in spite of the modestly negative effects of aging on physical and mental functioning, the widespread erroneous beliefs in our culture about the extent and degree of the negative effects, and the high prevalence of age discrimination in our social institutions. A major contribution of data from the project has been to address topics including the process of retirement, gender differences in the retirement experience, adjustment to widowhood, the impact of retirement on couples, and attitudes toward retirement.

PSYCHOLOGICAL THEORIES OF OLDER ADULT DEVELOPMENT

ERIK ERIKSON'S SINGLE-STAGE THEORY OF OLDER ADULTHOOD

Old age, Erik Erikson believed, is a time for caring for oneself after a lifetime of being cared for or caring for others. If the earlier stages have been successfully completed, the person will be satisfied with life as it has been; however, if earlier crises have not been resolved, the person may not be able to accept the end of the life cycle and will fear death.

Erikson defined the psychosocial crisis of later adulthood as ego integrity versus despair. The virtue, or ego strength, is *wisdom* for those successfully coping with this stage. Wisdom involves synthesizing and consolidating the past seven stages and becoming aware of the ideas, meanings, and people that the individual has helped to create. It is an affirmation of his or her life and acceptance of people who have been significant, and that life can be defended against all physical and emotional threats. The ritualization is called *the integral*, an ability to positively integrate the past phases.

Individuals who are unsuccessful at this stage experience despair and disgust. The ritualism is a distortion of wisdom, *sapientism*, the pretense of being wise (Erikson 1977:112). These people see time as short, leaving no chance to pursue alternate routes to integrity. They may appear to be disgusted, misanthropic, or chronically contemptuous and displeased (Erikson 1980:104–105).

Erikson and his wife, Joan, in their eighties, developed a more detailed description of the lessons contributed in each stage of life to wisdom in old age. They suggested that trust, which begins to be developed in infancy, contributes in old age to appreciation of human interdependence; learning in early childhood to control one's own body is reflected in acceptance in old age of bodily deterioration; preschool development of initiative and purpose, as well as playfulness and creativity, is reflected in old age as empathy and resilience, and also a sense of humor about life. Commitment and fidelity result from the adolescent struggle to overcome confusion and to achieve lifelong identity; the young adult conflict focused on balancing lasting intimacy and the need for isolation takes the form in later adulthood of "coming to terms with love expressed and unexpressed during one's entire life; the understanding of the complexity of relationships is a facet of wisdom." Finally, the tension between generativity and stagnation in the adult years is expressed in old age in passing on one's contributions to life to the next generation, a generativity that could save the human species by promoting positive values. They considered wisdom in old age to include two aspects—*caritas*, caring for others, and empathy, in the sense of *agape*—and believed that the final stage of life "culminates in a full wisdom to the degree each earlier phase of life has had a positive resolution." According to the Eriksons, "If everything has gone well, one achieves a sense of integrity, a sense of completeness, of personal wholeness, that is strong enough to offset the downward psychological pull of the inevitable physical disintegration" (Goleman 1988:C1, C14).

THEORIES OF MULTIPLE STAGES OF OLDER ADULTHOOD

Further differentiating psychological development in old age, Robert Peck (1968:88) proposed that Erikson's eighth stage should be divided into two periods, each containing a series of "psychological learnings and adjustments." According to Peck, middle age learning involves the ability to value wisdom versus valuing physical powers; to socialize versus sexualize in human relationships; to develop cathectic flexibility versus cathectic impoverishment; and to develop mental flexibility versus mental rigidity. Old age learning and adjustments, Peck believed, were ego differentiation versus work-role preoccupation; body transcendence versus body preoccupation; and ego transcendence versus ego preoccupation. Like many theorists, Peck focused on men, but his framework has also been used to explain women's development.

In Peck's stages, there is the expectation that adjustments will occur in specific periods but that the time sequences will vary for individuals. Peck suggested that stages in later adulthood "may have to be much more divorced from chronological age than is true of the childhood stages" (Peck 1968:92). He accepted the fact that while there are delimitable periods such as middle or old age that may describe the "average person," some people do not fit the definitions and may behave older or younger than expected. Thus he concluded that the best way to obtain research samples with homogeneity in relation to life stage wold be to use "stage" criteria such as imminent retirement rather than chronological age.

Levinson et al. (1978:38), also studying men, suggested that older adulthood can be divided into the sequential stages of late adulthood and late late adulthood. In contrast to Peck, Levinson and his colleagues (1978:34, 38) differentiated the stages on the basis of chronological age, stating that late adulthood extends from about sixty to eighty-five and that around eighty the era of late late adulthood begins. Late adulthood is described as including bodily decline, frequent deaths and serious illnesses among friends, reduction in heavy responsibilities, changed relationships between oneself and society, and living in phase with one's own generation. Late late adulthood is marked by infirmity, coming to terms with death, and engaging in an ultimate involvement with oneself. Levinson's model proposes that periods of stability alternate with periods of transition in an orderly manner, so late adulthood appears to emphasize change while late late adulthood appears to reflect final stability (Fisher 1993:78). Fisher has suggested that the tasks in the earlier stage appear to emphasize those identified by Havighurst, and Levinson's concept of late late adulthood appears to emphasize the tension described by Erikson. However, Levinson and his colleagues' theory of older adulthood does not have the same empirical foundation that supported their study of early and middle adulthood, as it lacks adequate specificity and comprehensiveness (Fisher 1993:78).

In classifying unique and recurring tasks, Havighurst identified developmental tasks that occur at older ages within the biological, psychological, and cultural or social domains. Havighurst and Albrecht (1953:10) suggested that older people have special problems but also share some of the problems normally experienced by adults of all ages. Special problems of older people include physical helplessness, poverty, the feeling of rejection, loss of husband or wife, loss of work, and "the insults of aging," which include loss of physical attractiveness, lessening of physical health and vigor, and loss of status. They also suggested that in some ways old age is familiar territory, that experiences of earlier years reappear in slightly altered forms. These include making satisfactory living arrangements, making new friends, finding more leisure-time activities, and treating grown children as adults. Havighurst and Albrecht (1953:223, 224) identified advantages of old age, which include enjoying the results of one's labors, being independent, and being altruistic.

Havighurst's (1952) classification of developmental tasks and crises in the stage of later maturity identified some of the experiences as special problems and some as familiar problems. Tasks include adjustment to decreasing physical strength and health; adjustment to death of a spouse; establishing an explicit affiliation with one's age group; adjustment to retirement and reduced income; meeting social and civic obligations; and establishing satisfactory physical living arrangements.

FISHER'S AGE-INDEPENDENT PERIODS OF OLDER ADULTHOOD

In contrast to the more limited number of developmental periods in later life included in earlier theories, James Fisher (1993) developed a framework of five age-independent periods of developmental changes occurring during older adulthood after retirement. It is based on results of a research study prompted by the absence of a systematic way of identifying and describing periods of retirement with different goals and levels of autonomy, as well as the lack of a systematic framework incorporating the richness and hetero-geneity of the older adult experience (Fisher 1993:78). He presented his framework as an alternative to models intended to describe successful aging, which are therefore prescriptive rather than descriptive. The participants in his study included 74 people ages 61 to 94, 45 percent of whom were 75 or younger. Ninety-five percent were Caucasian and 5 percent African Ameri-can. Seventy percent were female. Fisher recruited the participants from a nursing home and 4 senior citizens' centers.

Fisher theorized that developmental change occurs during older adult-hood in a pattern of three periods of stability alternating with two major transitional periods. His research showed that each individual experiences each period for a different length of time. The periods are (1) continuity with middle age; (2) an early transition; (3) a revised lifestyle; (4) a later transition; and (5) a final period. He believed that this framework could identify the needs of older adults in relation to particular periods of development and thus assist in targeting appropriate educational and other programs (Fisher 1993:76).

Stage 1, *continuity with middle age*, was described by some people as simi-lar to middle age but without employment. Working was replaced by relax-ation, sleeping late, travel, hobbies, and volunteering. For others, continuity with middle age meant ongoing responsibility as well as continuing hobbies or activities related to their work prior to retirement. Many said that this time was carefree but also expressed concern about their finances, their own health, or the health of relatives or friends.

Stage 2, *an early transition*, was often initiated by the death of a spouse, onset of poor health, or the need to relocate. Sometimes it was the result of accumulated losses related to death of a spouse or the need to care for rela-tives. Some of the events experienced were involuntary and others, such as seeking part-time paid employment, volunteer work, or relationships, were personal decisions. Fisher suggested that the events and choices made during early transition move older adulthood in a new direction. The process resembles the five tasks identified by Clark and Anderson (1967) as necessary for adaptation in later adulthood and old age: "(a) recognition of aging and definition of instrumental limitations; (b) redefinition of physical and social life space; (c) substitution of alternative sources of need satisfaction; (d) reassessment of criteria for evaluation of the self; and (e) reintegration of values and life goals." This early transition appeared to be the introduction to older adulthood for the participants in Fisher's study.

Stage 3, *a revised lifestyle,* was adapting to the choices made in the previous stage. The participants generally adapted and maintained their independence and control over their lives. Many continued with the same kinds of activities. Some affiliated with other older adults for socialization, and for some, organizational membership was a way to achieve their goals. Lifestyle changes were highly individualized, and some adapted to changes very positively. Fisher suggested that during the preceding transition and this period, many tasks identified by Havighurst (1952) are completed: adjusting to reduced income, adjusting to the death of one's spouse, affiliating with one's own age group, and establishing satisfactory living arrangements.

Stage 4, *a later transition,* resulted primarily from loss of health and mobility and the necessity of establishing new goals and activities. Some participants made the transition from greater independence to dependence voluntarily through actions such as application to a retirement community while they were still active, but most made the transition as a result of disabling events. Disabilities, illnesses, and accidents, as well as the death of a spouse, a relative's relocation, or the loss of a caregiver precipitated the loss of independent living.

Stage 5, a *final* period, was stable and included revised goals and activities implemented within a context of limited mobility. Some of the participants enjoyed positive new activities and growth in settings including nursing homes, although they also experienced resignation and loneliness.

The participants generally described their movement as sequential through the periods, although there were exceptions when a spouse had died before completing all periods or a participant had experienced a disabling illness before or during the first period and gone directly into the later transition period. The experience of returning to earlier stages occurred among subjects who remarried. For those who experienced Fisher's framework sequentially, the periods, beginning with retirement and ending with death, differed in length. For women who had experienced little or no employment outside of their home, retirement was more of an elusive concept.

SOCIOLOGICAL THEORIES: AGING, SOCIAL STRUCTURE, AND SOCIAL CHANGE

Theories of aging developed by sociologists in the United States during the last half of the twentieth century attempted to explain the experiences of older adults within the context of industrialization and modernization. In their application of role and exchange theories to older adults, Irving Rosow (1976) and James Dowd (1975) attributed marginalization of older persons to changes associated with a developing capitalistic economy and generally presented the negative results as irremediable. In contrast, Matilda White Riley and her colleagues (1994) have focused on the differential effects of social changes on the lives of cohorts of older adults, describing a more optimistic view of their future as well as for people of all ages, as they propose remedies to alleviate what they conceptualized as "structural lag." Kuypers and Bengtson (1973), using social breakdown theory, analyzed social breakdown and competence in older adults and proposed specific approaches for social reconstruction.

ROSOW'S CONCEPTUALIZATION OF ROLE THEORY

Rosow, using role theory, suggested that it would be impossible to develop a comprehensive theory of status and role change throughout the lifespan without clarifying the concepts of status and role. Since age is a major status variable and because age-grading involves roles, discussion of life course changes tends to reflect the ambiguities he believed are associated with these concepts, particularly in discussion of old age (Rosow 1976:458, 462). Rosow challenged the assumption that status and role are always complementary, and developed a typology of status-role permutations that treated them as independent:

1. institutional, representing statuses with roles, with institutional roles linked directly to definite social statuses
2. tenuous, representing statuses without or with insubstantial roles
3. informal, representing roles without statuses
4. nonrole, a combination in which there are neither roles nor statuses (Rosow 1976:462–63)

Rosow described older adults as the prototypes of persons with tenuous role types. He believed that with rapidly changing technology, the older worker becomes obsolete. Vacuous roles are not simply a function of personal incompetence, obsolescence, or worthlessness, but result from judgments about an individual's social utility. Loss of roles results in a lessening of major responsibilities and may affect others. As long as older people remain relatively independent, their behavior has little effect on others and they are socially inconsequential, with little impact on the system. Although the elders have age status, loss of responsibility and functions is the basis of their role limitation. There are few normative expectations or social guidelines (Rosow 1976:465, 466).

Rosow believed that older people are devalued and excluded from significant social participation because of their loss of roles. When they reach old age, systematic status loss occurs for the first time in their life stages for an entire cohort. Because our society does not socialize its members "to the fate of aging," the lives of older persons are socially unstructured, with no specific age role. Older adults are judged invidiously because of social pressures they lack power to dispel. Their social position is determined by the loss of major responsibility and authority (1976:466–67).

Rosow's (1976:474) diagrammatic curves of institutional, tenuous, and informal role types suggest that in late life, institutional roles become least important, informal roles of intermediate importance, and tenuous roles of greatest importance. Informal roles appear to have relatively greater stability than the other two types over the life course, and they assume greater importance during old age. Informal roles exist in both institutional and informal contexts, involve lower social responsibility and fewer people, and vary with personal styles.

Rosow considered the gap between informal and tenuous profiles after age seventy-five to be an effective role "deficit." If a social policy objective is maintenance of roles for older people, then a goal would be to minimize this deficit. He believed that in another social system, less imperfect or more idealistic and sentimental, the tenuous position of older adults might be reduced by maintaining their institutional roles, although he felt that this is unlikely in modern advanced societies (Rosow 1976:479).

Finally, Rosow suggested that greater flexibility exists in informal roles and that a more viable policy alternative would be to enlarge the area of these roles. This would require attention to the informal social system, particularly friendship networks and similar linkages with spontaneous associations and voluntary activities. Social policy needs to support and strengthen conditions that stimulate social ties and natural opportunities for informal roles. From a strategic standpoint, efforts that address the social context of lives, environment, and the world in which the elderly live and move would be more effective than direct service programs. They would optimize normal social forces congenial to spontaneous relationships, voluntary groups, and informal roles (Rosow 1976:479).

Dowd and Social Exchange Theory

A basic assumption of *exchange theory* is that all behavior has costs, if only the probability that there are rewards associated with an alternative activity not being pursued. Homans established that the profit from social exchange, as well as from economic exchange, equals rewards minus costs. Exchange theory proposes that interaction is most likely to continue if the people involved profit from it; they will terminate their exchange if they do not perceive it as more rewarding than it is costly. The variable of power is involved when the rewards gained in the relationship are valued more by one person than the other.

According to Dowd (1975:586), the basic assumption underlying exchange theory is that interactions between individuals are characterized as attempts to maximize material and nonmaterial rewards. Interaction is maintained over time because it is rewarding, not because of normative expectations that it be maintained or because it fulfills a social need. However, in addition to rewards, costs are inevitable; they may be unpleasant or positive. Dowd suggested that the inability of a partner in the social exchange to reciprocate rewarding behavior provides the basis of power and can be used to secure the compliance of the person with less power.

Dowd believed that impaired health, depleted income, and loss of spouse partly explain decreased social interaction of older persons in the United States. He proposed that exchange analysis could reveal additional sources of variation. From the exchange perspective, the decreased social interaction of older persons results from a series of exchange relationships in which their relative power is decreased until all that remains is compliance through mandatory retirement in exchange for entitlements such as Social Security and Medicare (1975:587). Dowd believed continued engagement in social relationships is a function of the existing power relationships between the aging individual and the society, in which society has the advantage (1975:588).

According to Dowd (1975:588), older people have had less to offer since the Industrial Revolution and the associated specialization of knowledge. Also, the difference between younger and older age cohorts is not related as much to differential patterns of attitude constellations, cognitive functioning, task efficiency, and other factors resulting from the debilitation of aging as to differences in the cohort-defining levels of education, socioeconomic status of the family of origin, and occupational aspirations (Dowd 1975:588). The problems of older workers thus include diminished skills and lack of earlier training in skills that would be marketable later in life. Dowd believed that the institutionalization of mandatory retirement was an inevitable outcome of social change and involved society's exchange of leisure time for older persons for the availability of additional positions in the work force for younger persons.

Social Change and the Life Course

A theoretical perspective that provides a more optimistic view of future relationships between older adults and the structural changes in society that affect their lives has been presented by Matilda White Riley and her colleagues. The idea of age stratification in society was first formally expressed in the work of Riley and Foner in the 1970s. Riley and her colleagues have suggested that while in modern industrial societies increasing numbers of people live longer and remain capable, the opportunity structures have remained static or more constrained (Riley, Kahn, and Foner 1994:1). They refer to this phenomenon as "structural lag"; during the twentieth century there has been a mismatch between people and social structures, institutions, and norms. This has created a poor fit between social institutions and people's capabilities and responsibilities at every age (Riley, Kahn, and Foner 1994:2). Riley and her colleagues propose that a challenge for the twenty-first century is to bring about social change to overcome the structural lag that occurred in the twentieth century.

In an earlier essay, Riley (1982:11) proposed that a dynamic interplay exists between society, which is experiencing change, and the people in society as they grow older. There are two interdependent yet distinct processes, which she and her colleagues refer to as "dynamisms":

1. People in successive cohorts (or generations) grow up and grow old in different ways because the surrounding social structures are changing. That is, the process of aging from birth to death is not entirely fixed by biology, but is influenced by the changing social structures and roles in which people lead their lives.
2. Alterations in the ways people grow up and grow old, in turn, press on the surrounding social structures to change them. That is, the roles

available to individuals at particular ages are not fixed or immutable but are reshaped by the collective actions and attitudes of the people, who are continually aging, moving through the roles, and being replaced by their successors from more recent cohorts. (Riley, Kahn, and Foner 1994:4)

Riley, Foner, and Riley have described the aging and society (A&S) paradigm as a conceptual framework developed to design and interpret studies of age and the place of age in lives and the surrounding social structures. The central theme is that against the backdrop of history, changes in people's lives influence and are influenced by changes in social structures and institutions (1999:327).

Riley and Riley (1994:19) pointed out that while changes in human lives have been occurring with dramatic rapidity over the past century, social structures, norms, and institutions have failed to adapt. They proposed that structural lag develops through a process they described in three general principles and a corollary:

1. Each dynamism is a distinct and separate process that responds in its own way to broad social, economic, scientific, and other historical trends and events.
2. Though distinct, the two dynamisms are interdependent: that is, each influences the other.
3. The two dynamisms differ in timing: that is, they tend to be asynchronous.
4. Today, as a corollary, their interdependence and lack of synchrony produce a structural lag that creates pressure for new structural changes.

Riley and Riley (1994:26, 27) suggested that there are pressures toward structural change from legislators, public officials, employers, educators, practitioners, and men and women in general as they are living their lives. Structural changes of the future may be shifts from the current age-differentiated structures in leisure, work, and education, bolstered by ageism, to new age-integrated structures in which role opportunities in all of these areas are available to people of all ages. The Rileys and their colleagues hope that in the future, retirement, as we know it, will be replaced by periods of leisure interspersed throughout the life course with periods of education and work. Opportunities for paid work would be spread more evenly across all ages, and older people would be seen as productive assets, not burdens. Work would be valued as much for its intrinsic satisfactions as for economic returns (Riley and Riley 1994:33).

Riley and Riley (1994:22, 23) noted that the potential for change in the lives of individuals through alteration of the social environment has been documented as follows, in research on interventions affecting the lives of very old people:

1. Among elderly patients in nursing homes, social activity, immune functioning, and perhaps even survival can be enhanced—provided that the social environment is altered to increase the sense of personal control and independence.
2. Among older workers, intellectual functioning improves with age, provided the work situation is challenging and calls for self-direction.
3. Very old people whose performance on intelligence tests has deteriorated can be brought back to their performance levels of twenty years earlier, provided that the social environment affords incentives and opportunities for practicing and learning new strategies.
4. Memory can be improved, provided that the impoverished context often characterizing retirement is altered to include the stimulation of a rich and complex environment.
5. Among very old nursing home residents (average age ninety), speed and distance of walking ability can be improved, leg muscle strength doubled, and muscle size increased, provided that length-strength training is included in the regimen.

Riley, Foner, and Riley (1999:330) have proposed that the aging and society paradigm should be used in the following manner:

Multilevel. People can be viewed either as individuals or as populations, just as structures can be viewed singly (as in a case study of the family) or as aggregates (as in comparing families with work organizations).

Age-inclusive. Old age relates to all ages; aging takes place from conception to death, and changes at one age affect all ages.

Dynamic. While people are growing older, society is changing around them.

Includes subjective attitudes and feelings, as well as overt actions, in the lives and structures involved.

Multidisciplinary, following the model of James Birren's lifetime contributions. Sociologists recognize that social aspects of aging cannot be understood without reference to biology or psychology, nor can structures be understood without reference to history, anthropology, and all the social sciences.

Collaborative. To cover this broad ground, research has been aided by a wide array of colleagues here and abroad, including social, behavioral, biological, medical, and mathematical scholars.

The aging and society paradigm formulated a web of concepts that they hoped would be helpful in the future for researchers searching for new interpretations, broad agendas, and innovative methods in the study of aging.

Consistent with Riley, Foner, and Riley's theoretical perspectives and observations, O'Rand and Campbell (1999) have suggested that during the last two decades of the twentieth century empirical observations and the methodological innovations that have enabled them have reestablished the phenomenon of aging in social theory. The observations are still not explained very well by the available theories, but the prevailing view of how the life course is organized has been changed. O'Rand and Campbell (1999:61) suggested that the study of aging has been influenced by the following major sets of findings:

1. Life course transitions are decreasingly tied to age; events in family, education, work, health, and leisure domains occur across the life span at different (and many at increasingly later) ages than previously expected. Life transitions are less age-segregated and more age-integrated.
2. Life transitions are less disjunctive and more continuous: transitions are not necessarily abrupt nor irreversible events, but often gradual and reversible processes. Such transitions as family formation, education completion, career entry and exit, divorce, and retirement are often more protracted and multidirectional than previously recognized.
3. Specific life pathways in education, family, work, health, and leisure are interdependent within and across lives. Trajectories within these domains develop simultaneously and reciprocally within and across individual lives.

SOCIAL RECONSTRUCTION THEORY

Drawing upon the original formulation of social breakdown syndrome by Gruenberg (1964) and Zusman (1966) to explain the development of negative psychological functioning in the general population, Kuypers and Bengtson

(1973:182) described *social breakdown syndrome* (SBS) as a systems perspective in which "an individual's sense of self, his ability to mediate between self and society, and his orientations to personal mastery are functions of the kinds of *social labeling* and valuing that he experiences in aging." They argue that because of the nature of *social reorganization* in later life, older adults are likely to be susceptible to and dependent on social labeling.

Kuypers and Bengtson (1973:182) believed that in later life social reorganization occurs because in the normal process of aging certain social conditions such as role loss, vague or inappropriate normative information, and lack of reference groups deprive the person of feedback concerning identification, appropriate roles and behavior, and individual value in their social world. The lack of feedback creates a vulnerability to, and dependence on, external sources of labeling, some of which give the negative message that the individual is useless and obsolete, leading to social breakdown.

Kuypers and Bengtson (1973:183–84, 186–87) identified three aspects of social systems changes that increase the vulnerability of older adults: loss of normative guidance, shrinking of roles, and lack of appropriate reference groups. These changes create a general susceptibility to the syndrome, and "the dominant societal view of assigning worth, *personal worth through social utility*, is a fulcrum in creating a negative spiral of breakdown." Any theory of normal aging must consider these experiences as a backdrop. Kuypers and Bengtson focused on "expectable psychological consequences to certain noxious social reorganizations in late life," rather than defining successful aging "*within* the range of adaptation to environmental change" (1973:182). They listed seven steps of social breakdown constituting a circular process:

1. precondition of susceptibility
2. dependence on external labeling
3. social labeling as incompetent
4. induction into a sick, dependent role
5. learning of "skills" appropriate to the new dependent role
6. atrophy of previous skills
7. identification and self-labeling as "sick" or inadequate (1973:187)

Kuypers and Bengtson believed that the theory offered insight into the dynamic among the person's sense of self, the development of skills for dealing with self and environment, and the feedback given by the outside world.

Kuypers and Bengston identified three types of competence that suffer in the cycle of breakdown: successful social role performance, adaptive capacity, and personal feelings of mastery and inner control. They believed that efforts should be made to liberate the elderly person from the view that worth is contingent on economic or "productive" social roles, and they proposed interventions to enhance adaptive capacity by lessening debilitating environmental factors such as poor health, poverty, and substandard housing while facilitating personal strengths by enabling an internal locus of control (1973:199). They saw self-determination and control of policy and administration as the foundation for competent aging.

THEORETICAL PERSPECTIVES ON THE EFFECTS OF INEQUALITY ON AGING

The different effects of experiences related to gender, race, ethnicity, socioeconomic status, and sexual orientation have been addressed only minimally in developmental theories of aging. Dannefer and Uhlenberg (1999:311) have suggested that in life course work the intercohort focus has been emphasized, and therefore heterogeneity within cohorts and the forces accounting for it have been given little sustained attention until recently. Eleanor Palo Stoller and Rose Gibson (1997, 2000) have, however, incorporated attention to intracohort diversity into their conceptualization of life course theory. They have identified earlier life experiences related to gender, race and ethnicity, and social class that result in inequalities in experiences in later adulthood and the "different worlds in aging" that result. In addition, Richard Friend (1991) has developed a theory of successful aging addressing the diversity of experiences of older lesbian women and gay men.

Different Worlds of Aging: Gender, Race, and Class

Eleanor Palo Stoller and Rose Campbell Gibson (2000:1) have proposed that gender, race or ethnicity, and social class are factors that structure "different worlds in aging." There are discernible patterns in the experiences of different segments of the older population, reflecting social structural arrangements and cultural blueprints within society. Stoller and Gibson have suggested that although gender, race or ethnicity, and social class are often regarded as "attributes" of individuals, these characteristics are social constructs, classifications based on social values. They have explored these constructs from the perspective of sociologist Beth Hess's (1990) conceptualization of gender, race, and class as labels attached to individuals and as properties of hierarchical social structures within which people form identities and realize their life chances (Stoller and Gibson 2000:4). They also investigated the ways in which diverse views of social reality are determined by peoples' positions along these multiple hierarchies. This was done by listening to descriptions of aging and of old age from many perspectives in order to give "voice" to those whose perspective had been overlooked.

Stoller and Gibson (2000:4) have pointed out that focusing on hierarchies of gender, race or ethnicity, and social class makes it possible to recognize elements of discrimination influencing the lives of older adults. Discrimination throughout the life span results in an accumulation of disadvantage in old age. For example, a lifetime of poverty may result in poor health in later life. Occupying several disadvantaged positions, such as being a black female, results in multiple jeopardy, greater risk for negative outcomes in old age.

In addition, systems of privilege are created through these same hierarchies, providing unearned advantages to individuals because they are white, male, and middle- or upper-class, although the emphasis on disadvantage sometimes masks this reality (Stoller and Gibson 2000:4). These privileges are unearned because they are ascribed rather than achieved. Stoller and Gibson (2000:6, 7) believe that the difference between *privileged* and *disadvantaged* is complex because a person may be disadvantaged in some areas and privileged in others. Lifetime experiences along the hierarchies contribute to diversity in old age with respect to quantity of accumulated resources, relationships, meaning attached to aging, and definitions of social reality.

Stoller and Gibson (2000:7) have also emphasized strengths as well as deficits, pointing out that the multiple jeopardy approach to studying inequality in old age emphasizes negative outcomes of living in disadvantaged positions. However, it is also important to learn how older persons experiencing multiple jeopardy create meaning in their lives despite barriers resulting from these hierarchies.

Similarly, Deborah Padgett's (1999) exploration of the economic, psychosocial, and cultural dimensions of the aging process among minority women in the United States suggested that although women belonging to minority groups experience more poverty than white women at similar ages, minority women have adaptive advantages in growing older. Addressing the concept of quadruple jeopardy, a term coined by Jacqueline Jackson in 1971 to refer to the experiences of black women, Padgett (1999:175) said that research on individuals who are old, poor, female, and of minority status has resulted in mixed messages in support of the quadruple jeopardy perspective. Low income and self-reported health status are not necessarily linked to lower levels of social support, family interaction, self-reported life satisfaction, or higher mortality rates after age eighty-five.

Nevertheless, there is evidence that the health and mental health status of aging minority women is related to marked disparities in income, including higher morbidity rates for diabetes, hypertension, and kidney disease. Studies suggest a higher degree of risk for mental disorders for people with lower incomes regardless of race or ethnicity, but decreasing prevalence of all psychiatric disorders except organic brain syndromes with increased age (Myers et al. 1984; Padgett 1999). Padgett advises caution, however, in relating data regarding lower rates of psychopathology to aging minority women because epidemiological studies tend to be limited to measurement of disorders meeting strict *DSM-III* (*Diagnostic and Statistical Manual of Mental Disorders, Third Edition* 1987) criteria and utilize instruments or scales that have not been validated for use in different minority groups and with older adults (1999:176). In addition, members of some ethnic groups tend to somatize symptoms of distress.

In support of "an adaptive perspective on successful aging among minority women," research has suggested that sharing limited economic and social resources among Hispanic and black elderly is a positive adaptation to poverty. Older minority women assist their families as "kintenders," and traditional cultural values can reduce feelings of alienation among older Mexican Americans (Padgett 1999:177). Padgett concludes that reliance on kinship and ethnicity is not a static carryover of traditional ways, but rather a dynamic response to a changing and possibly threatening environment (1999:178).

Stoller and Gibson have also introduced the life course perspective as a framework providing an inclusive approach to the study of aging. Their perspective has four main premises:

1. The aging process is affected by individuals' personal attributes, their particular life events, and how they adapt to these events.
2. Sociohistorical times shape opportunity structures differently for individuals with specific personal characteristics, such as being in a subordinate position in a social hierarchy. Thus, people's life events, adaptive resources, and aging experiences differ.
3. Membership in a specific birth cohort (i.e., being born in a particular time period) shapes the aging experience. Within cohorts, however, the experience of aging differs depending on one's position in systems of inequality based on gender, race or ethnicity, or class.
4. Sociohistorical periods shape the aging experiences of cohorts. These

historical times, however, have different impacts on the experiences of disadvantaged and privileged members of the same cohort. (Stoller and Gibson 2000a:19)

This life course perspective introduces the elements of personal biography, sociocultural factors, and sociohistorical periods, which have been neglected by earlier theories of aging, providing a broader approach to understanding the aging process. The life course framework focuses on how that process is affected by the interrelatedness of individual attributes, social roles, unique life experiences, and adaptive resources within a sociohistorical context. Different sociohistorial periods provide different opportunities and different roles that affect experiences and adaptive resources. Ways in which people adapt to life stressors also shape the aging experience (Stoller and Gibson 1997:3, 4).

DIVERSITY OF EXPERIENCES: SEXUAL ORIENTATION

Sexual orientation is another factor affecting aging. Kochman (1997:2) believed that the helping professions have neglected older gay men and lesbians. Richard Friend (1991:99) developed a theory of successful aging relating to the diverse experiences of older lesbians and gay men. His findings disagreed with the common negative stereotypes of older gay men as lonely, depressed, oversexed, and lacking support from family and friends, and stereotypes of older lesbian women as unattractive, unemotional, and lonely. His review of earlier studies (Kelly [1977], Berger [1982a, 1982b], Friend [1980], Kimmel [1978], Francher and Henkin [1973], and Weinberg [1970]) identified older gay men who are well adjusted, self-accepting, and adapting well to the aging process. He cited research findings by Almvig (1982) and Raphael and Robinson (1980) in which over half of the older lesbian women subjects were happy and well adjusted. Kehoe (1988:41) also found that most of the women in her study of lesbians over the age of sixty sustained relatively high morale and life satisfaction.

Friend (1991:100) believed that these disparate views of older gay and lesbian people reflect the social construction of homosexuality as a negative identity. Some people internalize the negative view, while others see homosexuality in positive and affirmative ways. In presenting his theory of successful aging, Friend (1991:100) proposed that with a positive lesbian or gay identity, certain skills, feelings, and attitudes are also acquired that facilitate adjustment to aging. Applying social construction theory, Friend developed a model to describe the diverse ways in which sexual identity is formed by older lesbian women and gay men. A theory of successful aging emerges through recognition of the relationship between the social construction of gay and lesbian identities and the individual psychology of the men and women who have made their lives meaningful in a particular sociohistorial period.

Friend drew upon the aspect of social construction theory that regards sexual functions and feelings as having no intrinsic or essential meaning of their own; they are given meaning by the ideological system developed for their explanation. He believed that in developing an identity as gay or lesbian, a person must make meaning out of messages about homosexuality (1991:100–103). The process reflects a relationship between the individual's psychology and social construction and can be accomplished along a set of two associated continua. One end of the cognitive/behavioral continuum is the pervasive heterosexual belief that homosexuality is "sick" and negative; the affective response is internalized homophobia with feelings of self-hatred, low self-esteem, and minimal or conditioned self-acceptance. The other end is the response that challenges or questions the validity of these negative messages. The result is a positive and affirmative reconstruction of what it means to be gay or lesbian. At this end of the affective response continuum are feelings of greater self-acceptance, high self-esteem, empowerment, and self-affirmation.

Friend believed that the idea of two continua, cognitive/behavioral and affective, is consistent with other developmental models of lesbian, gay, and bisexual identity formation and that his model highlights the significance of and relationship between these processes. Contemporary gay and lesbian older adults share a sociohistorical context, having lived a major part of their lives in historical periods of active hostility and oppression toward homosexuality. Friend proposed that there are at least three different groups of older lesbians and gay men, characterized by different cognitive-behavioral and emotional responses to their experiences that represent three styles of identity formation:

1. *stereotypic older lesbian and gay people* whose cognitive/behavioral responses to heterosexism reflect extreme internalized homophobia and who are lonely, depressed, and alienated
2. *affirmative older lesbian and gay people* whose response to heterosexism has been to reconstruct a positive and affirmative sense of self and who are psychologically well-adjusted, vibrant, and adapting well to the aging process

3. *passing older lesbian and gay people* who, as persons in the mid-range of the continua, believe that heterosexuality is inherently better but marginally accept some aspects of homosexuality, and who are strongly invested in passing as persons who are not gay or lesbian, or not stereotypically lesbian or gay (Friend 1991:103–104)

According to Friend's theory, the second group, affirmative older lesbians and gay people, would be the one whose members will age successfully. Friend suggested that when older lesbian women and gay men have achieved high levels of adjustment it is as a partial response to the negative messages about homosexuality they experienced growing up. His theory examines successful aging as a result of reconstruction of homosexuality as a positive attribute within the contexts of individual psychology. This occurs through the development of crisis competence, flexibility in gender role, and reconstruction of personal meanings of homosexuality and aging; social and interpersonal dimensions that include planning for one's own future security, redefinition of family, and reinforcing family supports with those of friends and community; and the development of legal and political advocacy skills to directly manage heterosexism and ageism.

Friend (1991:104) pointed out that because this is a linear model, it is limited—human beings are flexible, creative, and unique in their developmental patterns. However, he offered the model to facilitate conceptualization of a complex process and assist in forming a theory of successful aging.

CONCLUSION

This chapter has reviewed approaches to the conceptualization of age in terms of chronological age, functional capacity, and life stage; development of gerontology as an academic discipline; past and present attitudes in the United States toward aging and older adults; demographic trends; conceptual issues and assumptions in theories of aging; and developmental theories of aging. Lack of attention to the effects of a lifetime of experiences of inequality related to ethnicity, gender, race, sexual orientation, and socioeconomic status, as well as disability, has prevailed in much of the theoretical work, and recent theories that endeavor to address this neglect have been included. During the twentieth century in the United States, research on aging and older adulthood was influenced by prevalent popular and academic views that have changed over time; increasing awareness of the diversity of experiences in older adulthood should result in future theories that reflect and foster increased understanding of the variety of experiences in aging.

The search for a very broad, general, "grand" theory of aging has reflected the lack of specificity of other grand theories and is unlikely to deepen understanding of the diversity of individual experiences in older adulthood, which is essential for the desires and needs of older adults to be addressed adequately. Attempts to identify "normal" or "successful" aging must evaluate the experiences of individuals from a biopsychosocial perspective, with the understanding that perceptions of older adults, their families, and their communities of what is normal or successful varies because of diverse cultural values and norms. The history of the theoretical developments described in this chapter demonstrates that in practice, research, and theorizing regarding older adults and their families, it is critical to acknowledge and understand one's own subjective attitudes about aging and older adults to achieve professional objectivity and understand differences.

There are infinite variations in the process of aging resulting from biological, psychological, and social factors. When older adults require assistance, professionals must assess and address their needs and experiences with a knowledge base adequate for understanding the complexities of their lives. In addition to the theories described in this chapter, minitheories, or "local knowledge" (Bengtson, Rice, and Johnson 1999:18) have begun the work of explaining diversity in experiences such as intergenerational relationships.

It is essential to remain mindful of the strengths of older adults and their power to contribute to their individual and collective welfare and the general welfare of society in spite of continued ageism. In the United States, their strengths have been evident in ongoing individual and collective accomplishments, including the abolition of mandatory retirement, a policy assumed to be necessary and inevitable by some of the earlier theorists. Older adults' strengths must be respected and utilized in micro-, mezzo-, and macro-level interventions by professionals.

BIBLIOGRAPHY

Achenbaum, W. A. 1978. *Old Age in the New Land: The American Experience Since 1790*. Baltimore: The Johns Hopkins University Press.

Almvig, C. 1982. *The Invisible Minority: Aging and Lesbianism*. New York: Utica College of Syracuse University.

Alvarez, J. 1999. *Reflections on an Agequake*. New York: United National NGO Committee on Aging.

Antonucci, T. 1985. "Personal Characteristics, Social Support, and Social Behavior." In R. Binstock and E. Shanas, eds., *Handbook of Aging and the Social Sciences*, 94–129. New York: Van Nostrand Reinhold.

Atchley, R. 1972. *Social Forces in Later Life*. Belmont, Ca.: Wadsworth.

———. 1994. *Social Forces and Aging*. Belmont, Ca.: Wadsworth.

———. 1999. *Continuity and Adaptation in Aging: Creating Positive Experiences*. Baltimore: The Johns Hopkins University Press.

———. 2000. *Social Forces and Aging: An Introduction to Social Gerontology*. Belmont, Ca.: Wadsworth.

Bengtson, V., C. Rice, and M. Johnson. 1999. "Are Theories of Aging Important? Models and Explanations in Gerontology at the Turn of the Century." In V. Bengtson and K. W. Schaie, eds., *Handbook of Theories of Aging*, 3–20. New York: Springer.

Bengtson, V. and K. Schaie, eds. 1999. *Handbook of Theories of Aging*. New York: Springer.

Berger, R. 1982a. "The Unseen Minority: Older Gays and Lesbians." *Social Work* 27:236–42.

———. 1982b. *Gay and Gray*. Urbana: University of Illinois Press.

Birren, J. 1999. "Theories of Aging: A Personal Perspective." In V. Bengtson and K. W. Schaie, eds., *Handbook of Theories of Aging*, 459–71. New York: Springer.

Birren, J. and J. Lanum. 1991. "Metaphors of Psychology and Aging." In G. Kenyon, J. Birren, and J. Schroots, eds., *Metaphors of Aging in Science and the Humanities*, 103–29. New York: Springer.

Birren, J. and J. Schroots. 1984. "Steps to an Ontogenetic Psychology." *Academic Psychology Bulletin* 6:177–90.

Buckley, W. 1967. *Sociology and Modern Systems Theory*. Englewood Cliffs, NJ: Prentice Hall.

Busse, E. and G. Maddox. 1985. *The Duke Longitudinal Studies of Normal Aging 1955–1980: Overview of History, Design, and Findings*. New York: Springer.

Butler, R. 1963. "The Life Review: An Interpretation of Reminiscence in the Aged." *Psychiatry* 26:65–76.

———. 1975. *Why Survive?: Being Old in America*. New York: Harper and Row.

Campbell, R. and A. O'Rand. 1988. "Settings and Sequences: The Heuristics of Aging Research." In J. Birren and V. Bengtsen, eds. *Emergent Theories of Aging*, 58–79. New York: Springer.

Clark, M. and B. Anderson. 1967. *Culture and Aging*. Springfield, Ill.: Thomas.

Cole, T. 1983. "The 'Enlightened' View of Aging: Victorian Morality in a New Key." *Hastings Centre Report* 13 (3): 34–40.

Coleman, P. and D. Jerome. 1999. "Applying Theories of Aging to Gerontological Practice Through Teaching and Research." In V. Bengtson and K. W. Schaie, eds., *Handbook of Theories of Aging*, 379–58. New York: Springer.

Cumming, E. and W. Henry. 1961. *Growing Old: The Process of Disengagement.* New York: Basic.

Dannefer, D. 1991. "The Race is to the Swift: Images of Collective Aging." In G. Kenyon, J. Birren, and J. Schroots, eds., *Metaphors of Aging in Science and the Humanities*, 155–72. New York: Springer.

Dannefer, D. and P. Uhlenberg. 1999. "Paths of the Life Course: A Typology." In V. Bengtson and K. W. Schaie, eds., *Handbook of Theories of Aging*, 306–26. New York: Springer.

Dowd, J. 1975. "Aging as Exchange: A Preface to Theory." *Journal of Gerontology* 30 (5): 584–94.

Eisdorfer, C. 1983. "Conceptual Models of Aging: The Challenge of a New Frontier." *American Psychologist* 38 (2): 197–202.

Erikson, E. 1977. *Toys and Reasons.* New York: Norton.

——. 1980. *Identity and the Life Cycle.* New York: Norton.

Fisher, J. 1993. "A Framework for Describing Developmental Change Among Older Adults." *Adult Education Quarterly* 43 (2): 76–89.

Francher, S. and J. Henkin. 1973. "The Menopausal Queen." *American Journal of Orthopsychiatry* 43:670–74.

Friedan, B. 1993. *The Fountain of Age.* New York: Simon and Schuster.

Friend, R. 1980. "GAYging: Adjustment and the Older Gay Male." *Alternative Lifestyles* 3:231–48.

——. 1991. "Older Lesbian and Gay People: A Theory of Successful Aging." *Journal of Homosexuality* 20:99–118.

Goleman, Daniel. 1988. "Erikson, in His Own Old Age, Expands His View of Life." *The New York Times*, June 14, C1, C14.

Gruenberg, E. and J. Zusman. 1964. "The Natural History of Schizophrenia." *Int. Psychiat. Clin.* I:699.

Hall, E. 1983. "A Conversation with Erik Erikson." *Psychology Today* 17 (6): 22–30.

Hall, G. S. 1922. *Senescence: The Last Half of Life.* New York: Appelton.

Havighurst, R. 1952. *Developmental Tasks and Education.* New York: David McKay.

——. 1973. "Social Roles, Work, Leisure, and Education." In C. Eisdorfer and M. Lawton, eds., *The Psychology of Adult Development and Aging*. Washington: American Psychological Association.

Havighurst, R. and R. Albrecht. 1953. *Older People*. New York: Longmans, Green.

Havighurst, R., B. Neugarten, and S. Tobin. 1996. "Disengagement, Personality, and Life Satisfaction in the Later Years." In D. Neugarten, ed., *The Meanings of Age: Selected Papers of Bernice L. Neugarten*, 281–87. Chicago: University of Chicago Press.

Hendricks, J. and A. Achenbaum. 1999. "Historical Development of Theories of Aging." In V. Bengtson and K. W. Schaie, eds., *Handbook of Theories of Aging*, 21–39. New York: Springer.

Hess, B. 1990. "Beyond Dichotomy: Drawing Distinctions and Embracing Differences." *Sociological Forum* 5 (1): 75–93.

Kehoe, M. 1988. "Lesbians Over 60 Speak for Themselves." *Journal of Homosexuality* 16 (3/4): 1–111.

Kelly, J. 1977. "The Aging Male Homosexual: Myth and Reality." *The Gerontologist* 17:328–32.

Kenyon, G. 1988. "Basic Assumptions in Theories of Human Aging." In J. Birren and V. Bengtson, eds., *Emergent Theories of Aging*, 3–18. New York: Springer.

Kenyon, G., J. Birren, and J. Schroots, eds. 1991. *Metaphors of Aging in Science and the Humanities*. New York: Springer.

Kimmel, D. 1978. "Adult Development and Aging: A Gay Perspective." *Journal of Social Issues* 34:113–30.

Knipe, E. 1971. "Attraction and Exchange: Some Temporal Considerations." Paper presented at annual meeting of the Southern Sociological Society, Atlanta, Georgia.

Kochman, A. 1997. "Gay and Lesbian Elderly: Historical Overview and Implications for Social Work Practice." In J. Quam, ed., *Social Services for Senior Gay Men and Lesbians*, 1–10. New York: Haworth Press.

Kuypers, J. and V. Bengtson. 1973. "Social Breakdown and Competence." *Human Development* 16 (3): 181–201.

Levinson, D. 1986. "A Conception of Adult Development." *American Psychologist* 41 (1): 3–13.

Levinson, D., C. Darrow, E. Klein, M. Levinson, and B. McKee. 1978. *The Seasons of a Man's Life*. New York: Knopf.

Lieberman, M. and J. Falk. 1971. "The Remembered Past as a Source of Data for Research on the Life Cycle." *Human Development* 14:132–41.

Longres, J. 1995. *Human Behavior in the Social Environment*. Itasca, Ill.: F. E. Peacock.

McKee, P., ed. 1982. *Philosophical Foundations of Gerontology*. New York: Human Sciences Press.

Maddox, G. and R. Campbell. 1985. "Scope, Concepts, and Methods in the Study of Aging." In R. Binstock and E. Shanas, eds., *Handbook of Aging and the Social Sciences*. New York: Van Nostrand Reinhold.

Marshall, V., ed. 1986. *Later Life: The Social Psychology of Aging*. Beverly Hills, Ca.: Sage.

Moody, H. 1988. "Toward a Critical Gerontology: The Contribution of the Humanities to Theories of Aging." In J. Birren and V. Bengtson, eds., *Emergent Theories of Aging*, 19–40. New York: Springer.

Myers, J., M. Weissman, C. Holzer, P. Leas, H. Ovraschel, J. Anthony, J. Boyd, J. Burke, M. Kramer, and R. Stoltzman. 1984. "Six-Month Prevalence of Psychiatric Disorders in Three Communities." *Archives of General Psychiatry* 41:969–70.

Neugarten, B. 1985. "Time, Age, and the Life Cycle." In M. Bloom, ed., *Life Span Development*, 360–69. New York: Macmillan.

——. 1996a. "Personality and Aging Process." In D. Neugarten, ed., *The Meanings of Age: Selected Papers of Bernice L. Neugarten*, 270–80. Chicago: University of Chicago Press.

——. 1996b. "Social and Psychological Characteristics of Older Persons." In D. Neugarten, ed., *The Meanings of Age: Selected Papers of Bernice L. Neugarten*, 176–92. Chicago: University of Chicago Press.

Neugarten, B. and R. Havighurst. 1996. "Disengagement Reconsidered in a Cross-National Context." In D. Neugarten, ed., *The Meanings of Age: Selected Papers of Bernice L. Neugarten*, 288–295. Chicago: University of Chicago Press.

Neugarten, D., ed. 1996. *The Meanings of Age: Selected Papers of Bernice L. Neugarten*. Chicago: University of Chicago Press.

O'Rand, A. and R. Campbell. 1999. "On Reestablishing the Phenomenon and Specifying Ignorance: Theory Development and Research Design in Aging." In V. Bengtson and K. W. Schaie, eds., *Handbook of Theories of Aging*, 59–78. New York: Springer.

Padgett, D. 1999. "Aging Minority Women." In L. Peplau, S. DeBro, R. Veneigas, and P. Taylor, eds., *Gender, Culture, and Ethnicity: Current Research About Women and Men*, 173–81. Mountain View, Ca.: Mayfield.

Peck, R. 1956. "Psychological Developments in the Second Half of Life." In J. Anderson, ed., *Psychological Aspects of Aging*, 42–71. Washington, D.C.: American Psychological Association.

——. 1968. "Psychological Developments in the Second Half of Life." In B. Neugarten, ed., *Middle Age and Aging: A Reader in Social Psychology*, 88–92. Chicago: University of Chicago Press.

Philibert, M. 1982. "The Phenomenological Approach to Images of Aging." In

P. McKee, ed., *Philosophical Foundations of Gerontology*. New York: Human Sciences Press.

Raphael, S. and M. Robinson. 1980. "The Older Lesbian." *Alternative Lifestyles* 3:207–29.

Riegel, K. 1973. "Dialectical Operations: The Final Stage of Cognitive Development." *Human Development* 16:346–70.

———. 1976. "The Dialectics of Human Development." *American Psychologist* 31:689–700.

Riley, M. 1982. "Aging and Social Change." In M. Riley, R. Abeles, and M. Teitelbaum, eds., *Aging from Birth to Death: Vol. II. Sociotemporal Perspectives*, 11–26. AAAS Symposium, 79. Boulder, Colo.: Westview Press.

Riley, M., A. Foner, and J. Riley. 1999. "The Aging and Society Paradigm." In V. Bengtson and K. W. Schaie, eds., *Handbook of Theories of Aging*, 327–43. New York: Springer.

Riley, M., R. Kahn, and A. Foner. 1994. "Introduction: The Mismatch Between People and Structures." In M. Riley, R. Kahn, and A. Foner, eds., *Age and Structural Lag: Society's Failure to Provide Meaningful Opportunities in Work, Family, and Leisure*, 1–12. New York: Wiley.

Riley, M. and J. Riley. 1994. Structural Lag: Past and Future. In M. Riley, R. Kahn, and A. Foner, eds., *Age and Structural Lag: Society's Failure to Provide Meaningful Opportunities for Work, Family, and Leisure*, 15–36. New York: Wiley.

Rosow, I. 1976. "Status and Role Change Through the Lifespan." In R. Binstock and E. Shanas, eds., *Handbook of Aging and the Social Sciences*, 457–82. New York: Van Nostrand Reinhold.

Rowe, J., and R. Kahn. 1998. *Successful Aging*. New York: Pantheon.

Shashaty, A. 1999. "Major Section 8 Housing Losses Force Out Elders Nationwide." *Aging Today* 20 (4): 1, 6.

Stoller, E. and R. Gibson, eds. 1997. *Worlds of Difference: Inequality in the Aging Experience*. Thousand Oaks, Ca.: Pine Forge Press.

———. 2000. *Worlds of Difference: Inequality in the Aging Experience*. Thousand Oaks, Ca.: Pine Forge Press.

Thomae, H. 1980. "Personality and Adjustment to Old Age." In J. Birren and R. Sloane, eds., *Handbook of Mental Health and Aging*. Englewood Cliffs, N.J.: Prentice Hall.

Tobin, S. and E. Etigson. 1968. "Effects of Stress on Earliest Memory." *Archives of General Psychiatry* 19:435–44.

United Nations Department of Public Information 1999. *Towards a Society for All Ages, International Year of Older Persons 1999: Demographics of Older Persons*. New York: United Nations.

U.S. Bureau of the Census 1996. *65+ in the United States.* Current Population Reports, Special Studies, P23–190. Washington, D.C.: U.S. Government Printing Office.

Waxman, B. 1999. "Got books?" *Aging Today* 20 (4): 9–10.

Weinberg, M. 1970. "The Male Homosexual: Age-Related Variations in Social and Psychological Characteristics." *Social Problems* 17:527–37.

Zusman, J. 1966. "Some Explanations of the Changing Appearance of Psychotic Patients: Antecedents of the Social Breakdown Syndrome Concept." *Millbank Memorial Fund Quarterly* 64.

EPILOGUE

Developmental theories were devised to serve as guidelines for determining "normal" behaviors, skills, and parameters for a defined age group. In addition, they were designed to help professionals assess developmental progress and identify variables and deviations. However, no one theory has been created to encompass all aspects of human development, and most theories reflect the culture and life experience of those who developed them.

Although these theories provide a baseline for the study of human development, caution must be used to be sure that what ought to be called "normal" is not too quickly viewed as "abnormal." While normal developmental milestones include significant biological, psychological, emotional, intellectual, and social points of reference that occur in most people's lives, it is essential not to lose sight of the person as an individual, experiencing a unique process of growth and change. Thus the reference points of normal psychological development need to be understood in order to identify possible signs and symptoms of psychopathology.

Most of the theorists whose work has been discussed in this book have focused primarily on white, privileged individuals, often male. While these contributions have been significant and the earlier works provided the foundation for more recent work, not enough attention has been paid to the diversity of socioeconomic and cultural factors impinging on development. Clearly, while some aspects of development are universal, there are cultural differences in thinking and perceptions as well as differences in the ages at which persons are expected to pass through stages of the life cycle. Theorists must now develop new models for research that will take into account cultural and gender influences.

Professor Richard Nisbett, a psychologist at the University of Michigan, recently compared the thinking of North Americans and East Asians (E. Goode, "How Culture Molds Habits of Thought," *The New York Times*, Aug. 8, 2000, F1). He found that, in general, given a situation to consider, Asians were more sensitive to context and quicker than Americans to detect when situational pressures determined a person's behavior. They were also more focused on the individual than on universal thinking. When assessing conflicts, the Asians were better able to see merit to both sides of an argument. Presented with philosophical arguments devoted to resolving contradictions, the Americans favored analytic, logical knowledge while the Asians chose a dialectic, experiential approach. This interesting study clearly points out the importance of culture as a variable.

Society today presents many obstacles to "smooth" development throughout the life cycle. A variety of family arrangements and the need in many cases for two incomes means that the mother as consistent caregiver is a rarity for children passing through infancy and toddlerhood. Divorce, single-parent households, blended families, and same-sex parents are increasingly common. Children may be placed in day care within weeks of birth. Latency-age children may be "latch-key" children, many with some household responsibilities in addition to their homework and activities.

Adolescents are often pushed into activities involving sex and addictive substances by peer pressure before they are comfortable with their own choices. Decisions about their futures and perceived parental expectations may evoke fear of failure and depression. As has been seen in recent years, adolescent rage can lead to violence, with devastating consequences.

The stage of adulthood has also become more complex. Choices about relationships, marriage, and children made in early adulthood, once thought to be "forever," may change, as evidenced by the higher divorce rate and new family forms. Marriage and having children often occur at later ages, as people may elect to establish a vocation or career first. There have been many changes in the world of work. The majority of women work outside of the home at least part-time, and many more have entered professions once viewed as the purview of men. Job stability rarely exists; in the past, a person began with a company and expected to stay until retirement, but this now is less likely to occur. Most people change jobs at least three times during their careers, and advances in technology frequently result in the need for worker retraining. Families relocate more often, thus lessening the availability of support from extended family.

Retirement is not nearly as prevalent at age sixty-five as it was earlier in the twentieth century. Many older adults choose to work well into their seventies or eighties, either at paid employment or as volunteers. Advances in medicine and technology have made it possible for older people to live longer but can result in ethical and financial problems when the quality of life fades.

The challenges that people will face as they move through the life cycle in the twenty-first century will be many. There will be changes within their own culture as well as increased contact with other cultures and lifestyles. Thus it will be important for researchers to build on the foundation earlier developmental theorists laid by looking at a broader range of people and their environments.

INDEX